A HISTORY OF EAST AFRICA

Also by Kenneth Ingham
EUROPE AND AFRICA

A HISTORY OF
EAST AFRICA

Revised Edition

KENNETH INGHAM

FREDERICK A. PRAEGER, *Publishers*
NEW YORK · WASHINGTON

BOOKS THAT MATTER

Published in the United States of America in 1965
by Frederick A. Praeger, Inc., Publishers
111 Fourth Avenue, New York, N. Y. 10003

Third printing, 1967

© Kenneth Ingham 1962, 1963, 1965

Library of Congress Catalog Card Number: 65–17934

Printed in the United States of America

To my wife, Elizabeth

CONTENTS

PLATES

PLATES

x

ACKNOWLEDGMENTS

I am deeply grateful to the East Africa High Commission for sponsoring this book and to the Research Grants Committee of Makerere College for financing research expeditions. To the Governments of the East African territories I am also indebted for permission to use their archives and I should like to thank the Librarian of the Macmillan Library, Nairobi, for allowing me to see back numbers of the *Pioneer of East Africa*. The Editor of the *East African Standard* was kind enough to allow me to see back copies of his newspaper and other publications of the East African Standard Press, and to him also I should like to express my thanks and to the Editor of the *Tanganyika Standard* for permission to see early numbers of that paper and of the *Tanganyika Times* and *Dar es Salaam Times*. I am grateful, too, to Mr. O. T. Hamlyn of Dar es Salaam for allowing me to make use of his unpublished manuscript, *An Historical Sketch of the Tanganyika Constitution*, to Mr. Wilbert A. Klerruu, a graduate of Makerere College, who permitted me to refer to material contained in an unpublished essay and to Mr. A. W. Mayor and his colleagues at Maseno School for letting me see an unpublished summary of the history of the Luo people. Nor could I possibly fail to pay tribute to the assistance given by Mr. H. B. Thomas, O.B.E., who so generously gave up his time to read through my manuscript, and by Mr. J. S. Kirkman who also read the first chapter. To neither of these gentlemen can be attributed any of the errors which may occur in the book and to both I am indebted for greatly reducing the number of those errors.

K. I.

The publishers would like to thank the following for their kind help in obtaining the illustrations:

T. R. ANNAN & SONS LTD.—David Livingstone

LADY ALTRINCHAM—Sir Edward Grigg (later Lord Altrincham)

BARNABY'S PICTURE LIBRARY—Jomo Kenyatta

BASSANO—Lord Delamere

WALTER BIRD, J. RUSSELL & SONS—Sir Donald Cameron

CAMERA PRESS—Sir Edward Twining (now Lord Twining)

CHATTO & WINDUS LTD.—Sir Charles Eliot

EAST AFRICAN RAILWAYS & HARBOURS—Laying the first railway line, Mombasa, 1896; Old trolley lines, Mombasa; First train to leave Kilindini; First coffee crop, St. Austin's Mission, 1902; British Troops embarking for the front, Nairobi; Cartoons depicting the outcome of the East African Campaign during the First World War

ELLIOT & FRY—Sir Apolo Kagwa

EXCLUSIVE NEWS AGENCY—General Paul Von Lettow-Vorbeck

THE GOVERNORS OF BROMSGROVE SCHOOL—George Wilson

F. H. GOLDSMITH—John Ainsworth

HAMISH HAMILTON LTD.—Tippoo Tip, Seyyid Barghash, Mutesa I of Buganda and Lord Cromer (photograph by E. C. Beresford & Emery Walker)

The picture of Mukama Kabarega is reproduced, with permission, from *Abakama Ba Bunyoro Kitara*, by J. W. Nyakatura, W. H. Gagne & Sons, Canada, 1947.

DEPARTMENT OF INFORMATION, KAMPALA—Sir Andrew Cohen and Serwano Kulubya

MACMILLAN & CO. LTD.—C. W. Hobley and Sir Charles Dundas (photograph by Sanderson & Dixon)

SIR PHILIP MITCHELL for his own picture (photograph by J. Russell & Sons)

PAUL POFFER LTD.—Milton Obote

RADIO TIMES HULTON PICTURE LIBRARY—Sir Richard Burton, Emin Pasha, Dr. Carl Peters, Lord Lugard and Sir Evelyn Baring (later Lord Howick)

ROYAL GEOGRAPHICAL SOCIETY—John Hanning Speke and Sir Henry Morton Stanley

FRAU ADA SCHNEE—Dr. Heinrich Schnee

TANGANYIKA INFORMATION SERVICES—Julius Nyerere and Sir Richard Turnbull

MRS. LLEWELLIN-TAYLOUR—Sir Hesketh Bell (photograph by Lafayette)

THE WHITE FATHERS MISSIONARY SOCIETY—Mgr. Hirth

THE CHURCH MISSIONARY SOCIETY—Dr. Ludwig Krapf, Alexander Mackay, Sir Albert Cook and the Mwanga of Buganda

PROLOGUE

The early history of East Africa is still largely a matter of conjecture. A few isolated but important records carry the story of the coastal region back to the first century A.D., but anything approaching continuity in the written sources can only be claimed for the period since the late fifteenth century. Written records concerned with the interior are still more recent, dating back only to the nineteenth century. So it is to the archaeologist, the anthropologist and the linguist that the historian must turn for assistance in filling out his story. Progress in these fields has been not inconsiderable. Dr. L. S. B. Leakey in Kenya and Mr. J. S. Kirkman, Dr. G. S. P. Freeman-Grenville and Mr. N. Chittick on the Kenya and Tanganyika coasts have investigated a number of archaeological sites. Valuable anthropological studies have been made of a number of tribes, and Dr. W. Whiteley has made recordings of coastal legends which may prove to be important sources of information. But much remains to be done in all these fields.

Even in the coastal area where archaeological investigation has provided a fuller guide to chronology there is practically no information about what happened before the thirteenth century. In some parts of the interior, meanwhile, tribal legends have been handed down orally from generation to generation. They embody in uncertain proportions a mixture of genuine history, mythology, dogma and self-justification. To the north and west of Lake Victoria these and other themes are incorporated into genealogies of ruling families which, by cross reference, might provide the rudiments of a continuous story growing ever more slender in content as it delves further back in time. Preliminary investigations by Dr. Roland Oliver have suggested that legend and archaeology might go hand in hand towards the clarification of the historical story. The association of certain personalities and events with known sites offers an opportunity to archaeologists to see if it is possible to confirm or add to the accounts of the lives of the rulers of the north western lake region. The establishment of an accurate chronology of events which took place in the interior of East Africa before the nineteenth century is still, therefore, a task for the future.

A HISTORY OF EAST AFRICA

CHAPTER ONE

EARLY HISTORY

THE title *Ausanitic coast*, which was applied to the east coast of Africa south of the straits of Bab el Mandeb as early as the first century A.D. may indicate a link between East Africa and Southern Arabia already, stretching back for several centuries.[1] The first reliable account of external trade with the East African coast, however, is contained in the *Periplus of the Erythrean Sea*. This guide to the commerce of the Red Sea and Indian Ocean was written in the second half of the first century A.D. and was probably the work of a Greek trader of the Roman Empire living in Egypt. Its importance lies in the fact that it would appear to establish the existence of trading stations along the East African coast as far south, perhaps, as modern Tanganyika, although the town of Rhapta, which marks the furthest bounds of the author's knowledge, has yet to be located.[2] These trading posts were visited by Arab sailors who brought with them iron implements, some of which were specially made for the trade. They also brought gifts of wine to mellow the peoples of the coast. The *Periplus* records a variety of trade goods accepted in return, including ivory, palm oil, rhinoceros horn, tortoise-shell, cinnamon, frankincense and slaves. It is difficult, however, to decide which, if any, of these items were collected from the coast of what are now Kenya and Tanganyika. Some of them were probably exported from districts farther north, Somalia and the Red Sea coast, while the cinnamon may well have been supplied by Indian traders using the East African coast as an exchange market.[3] In these early times

[1] G. A. Wainwright: 'Early Foreign Trade in East Africa.' *Man* Vol. XLVII, November, 1947, p. 143.

[2] G. Mathew: 'The East Coast Cultures.' *Africa South*, Vol. 2, January–March, 1958, p. 60.

[3] Sir Mortimer Wheeler: *Rome beyond the Imperial Frontiers*. G. Bell and Sons Limited, London, 1954, p. 113.

1

it seems likely that slaves already formed one of the chief exports of East Africa, although their importance was to decline some centuries later before being revived in the nineteenth century. Ivory remained one of the main attractions of East Africa's trade through the whole period.

No material relics of this early coastal culture have been discovered. It is only possible to guess at the nature of the people who evolved it. Ptolemy, writing in the second century A.D., had nothing further to add to the account contained in the *Periplus*, although his geographical knowledge of the coast extended farther south than did that of the earlier author. A recent writer has hazarded the suggestion that these early coastal people may have been negroid,[1] although it is more likely that they were Hottentots or Hamites. He has based his thesis on the writings of various Arab geographers of the Middle Ages. Al Masudi, whose book *The Meadows of Gold and the Mines of Gems* was finished in A.D. 947, refers to the same area of trade which was said by the author of the *Periplus* to have been flourishing nine hundred years earlier. The inhabitants of this area, which had become known as the Land of Zinj, were described by Al Masudi as being black men, with hanging lips, who worshipped trees and feared the spirits of the dead. They had a king and a capital city, their armaments were made of iron and they hunted the elephant in order to export the ivory. None of the sites referred to by Al Masudi has yet been located, however. A twelfth-century Arab geographer, Al Idrisi, gave a similar description of the Land of Zinj, and referred more explicitly to the existence of towns, mentioning Malindi, Manrisa (probably Mombasa) and Kilwa by name. Again, at the end of the thirteenth century, yet another geographer, Dimashqui, also remarked that the East African coast was inhabited by a black people who were idolaters.

These isolated references can at best only give rise to surmise about the history of the coast in the first millennium A.D. They do suggest that further inquiries should be made into the truth of the legend of a Shirzai state, stemming from Persia and said to have been founded in the tenth century A.D. with its headquarters at Kilwa. This legend, which has gained wide acceptance, is based upon three abbreviated versions of a much larger work, now lost, the *Sunna al-Kilawia*, or Tradition of Kilwa. Of the three shorter versions one

[1] G. Mathew: op. cit., p. 60.

is in Arabic and was written in 1862, another is written in Swahili, while the third appeared in Barros's *Asia* which was published in 1552.[1] It is possible, however, that the earlier parts of this record were added at a later date to give antiquity, and thereby prestige, to the claims of Kilwa to a place of predominance on the coast. Certainly, many of the remains hitherto ascribed to Persian settlement in the eleventh or twelfth centuries are in fact buildings of the seventeenth and eighteenth centuries, while there is little or nothing of Persian as distinct from Arab influence to be found in the relics of the past or in surviving customs.[2] The earliest historical fact so far confirmed by archaeological investigation is the inscription on the *mihrab* of the *Jamia* of Kizimkazi on Zanzibar Island with its date A.H. 500 (A.D. 1107),[3] but this discovery stands in isolation and there is no archaeological evidence for the existence of an empire of any kind at this early date. It is quite possible, however, that larger settlements such as Kilwa, Lamu or Pate had their origins even earlier than this and it is more than likely that they were able in turn to dominate areas of varying size along the coast.

The towns of Gedi and Kilepwa, some fifty miles north-east of Mombasa, and Ungwana, near the mouth of the Tana River, were certainly founded by the thirteenth century and may have existed in the twelfth century.[4] The majority of the inhabitants of these towns were black men, but the towns themselves were the creation of Arab colonists, some of whom were probably themselves black and some of whom undoubtedly intermarried with the people of the coast. The only architectural relics which could possibly have had an African origin are the pillar tombs which may derive from the phallic pillars of the Galla people of East Africa. Even these are so varied in shape, however, that their phallic origin, if such it was, appears to have been

[1] G. S. O. Freeman-Grenville: 'Some Recent Archaeological Work on the Tanganyika Coast.' *Man*, Vol. LVIII, p. 108.

[2] J. S. Kirkman: 'Prosperity and Plunder.' *Kenya Weekly News Travel and Tourist Supplement*, October 1958. A more sympathetic treatment of the genealogies contained in the Kilwa Chronicle is to be found in G. S. P. Freeman-Grenville: 'Chronology of the Sultans of Kilwa.' *Tanganyika Notes and Records*, No. 50, June 1958.

[3] J. S. Kirkman: 'Historical Archaeology in Kenya.' *The Antiquaries Journal*, Vol. XXXVII, January–April 1957, p. 23.

[4] J. S. Kirkman: 'The Culture of the Kenya Coast in the Later Middle Ages.' *South African Archaeological Bulletin*, Vol. XI, No. 44, December 1956, p. 90.

forgotten by the builders. The tableware in use in these towns was Chinese or Arabo-Persian, the hardware was Indian and the glass Arab. Most of the local earthenware was made in forms of Arab or Semitic origin.[1]

These coastal towns first felt the full impact of Islam in the late thirteenth century. The famous medieval traveller, Ibn Battuta, who visited Mombasa in the early 1330s, wrote of the inhabitants that they were pious, honourable and upright and had well-built mosques made of wood. In fact the buildings were probably of lath and mud. Of Kilwa, too, which he described as being a fine and substantially built town, again with 'wooden' buildings, he stated that the inhabitants were constantly engaged in war because of their contiguity with the heathen Zinj.[2] It is possible, therefore, that the Mongol advance in Asia had diverted the interest and attention of the Arabs more firmly southward while the increasing demand for ivory and gold not unnaturally directed the endeavours of traders towards the East African coast. Certainly, the emergence of Kilwa as an important trading centre at this time was due to its control of the gold supplies which originated in the kingdom of Monomotapa in the interior of what are now Northern Rhodesia and Portuguese East Africa and which came by caravan to the minor town of Sofala.[3]

In the fourteenth century there was a marked expansion in the material culture of the coast, followed in the fifteenth by the full flowering of Islamic influence. The reason for the fourteenth-century development is uncertain. It has been suggested that the unusually heavy equatorial rainfall during this period might have resulted in greater agricultural prosperity. Or, again, it may have been that political and tribal movements in the Amharic and Galla territories to the north led to the abandonment of the Arab settlements along the coast farther north in favour of the rising towns to the south.[4] Whatever may have been the reason, one of the results of the greater activity along the East African coast was a considerable increase in the variety of imports during the latter half of the fourteenth century.

[1] J. S. Kirkman: Letter to the Editor. *Kenya Weekly News*, April 3, 1959.

[2] Ibn Battuta: *Travels in Asia and Africa*. Trans. H. A. R. Gibb. Routledge, London, 1929, p. 12.

[3] G. Mathew: op. cit., pp. 60–61.

[4] J. S. Kirkman: 'The Culture of the Kenya Coast in the Later Middle Ages.' *South African Archaeological Bulletin*. Vol. XI, No. 44, December 1956, p. 91.

Perhaps the most interesting of the new imports was celadon from China. This was mainly Ming, with some Yuan. Most of China's import trade consisted in luxury goods and African ivory had been greatly prized in China for many centuries. But China does not appear to have traded directly with the East African coast before the fifteenth century. Even then Chinese sailors only reached East Africa on two occasions. Between 1417 and 1419 an expedition visited Malindi, and between 1421 and 1422 another expedition reached as far only as Mogadishu. Information concerning these voyages found in the official annals of the Ming dynasty is not always accurate. It has been filled out from an account by a Muslim interpreter, Ma Huan, who accompanied some of the expeditions, and from a further account by Fei Hsin, a scholar who travelled as an intelligence sergeant. In the 1930s more accurate information as to the dates of these voyages was discovered on stone inscriptions found in China in the temples of the Celestial Spouse located in two of the ports from which the fleets set out on their voyages. The stones upon which the inscriptions were written were erected in the year 1431 as a tribute to the goddess who, in the midst of a hurricane, had brought reassurance to the sailors by means of a miracle. In addition to the dates of the expeditions their destinations were also listed and it is clear from the inscriptions that the main object of the voyages was not so much the extension of trade as the expansion of the influence and glory of the Ming dynasty. Indeed, the items brought back from the journeys were mainly such as would appeal to the court and the harem by their unusual character of rarity. On the other hand the amount of celadon which steadily found its way into East Africa for many centuries was considerable. Unfortunately, most of it appears to have been of a normal trade character and is not easily dated with accuracy.[1]

During this period of advance, stone houses, palaces and mosques were replacing the earlier buildings of lath and wood. Fine walled cities were growing up under the control of rulers who exercised great authority. Zanzibar was becoming more important, as is indicated by two attempts made by the inhabitants of that island to encourage usurpers in Kilwa. Barter as the means of exchange was being supplemented though not supplanted by the growth of a money

[1] J. J. L. Duyvendak: *China's Discovery of Africa*. Arthur Probsthain, London, 1949, pp. 27-30.

5

economy. Coins from China have been discovered which belong to this period, while from the late thirteenth century and at intervals through the fourteenth and fifteenth the Sultans of Kilwa and probably Zanzibar issued their own coins which circulated in southern Tanganyika but not in Kenya or Pemba. Nevertheless, this flowering of Islamic culture in the coastal Sultanates immediately preceded disaster. At the very end of the fifteenth century the restless energy of western Europe intruded upon the sun-swept cities and gardens of the East African coast like an unseasonable monsoon for which the inhabitants were wholly unprepared.

The inspiration and dogged determination which together had carried Portuguese explorers farther and farther along the unknown coast of West Africa was rewarded in 1486 when Bartholomew Diaz rounded the Cape of Good Hope. His success stimulated the interest of the nations of western Europe whose overland trade links with the Indies were blocked by the fanatical forces of the Ottoman Empire. But Portugal alone among the western powers possessed navigators capable of exploiting the gains made by Diaz. Barely a decade elapsed before Vasco da Gama was on his way to India by the Cape route. Within little more than another decade the east coast towns of Africa had bowed before the virile energies of the Portuguese conquerors.

These swift developments came as a shock to the peoples of the coast, for da Gama, with his three vessels and apparently friendly mien, could not have seemed a formidable invader in spite of the cannon which his ships mounted. Nevertheless, his arrival aroused serious concern among both the inhabitants of Kilwa, whose buildings impressed the Portuguese as much as they had done Ibn Battuta, and the townsmen of Mombasa, which had risen more recently to a position of importance. Malindi, on the other hand, Mombasa's chief rival, welcomed da Gama, and on his return to Portugal in 1499 the Portuguese commander took with him an ambassador from the ruler of this more northerly town. In this way there began a friendly association which lasted throughout the period of Portuguese control along the coast. But the disquiet felt in Mombasa and Kilwa was soon to be justified. The Portuguese had only one aim, and that was to seize the whole trade of the Indian Ocean and of the distant Spice Islands. There was to be no sharing of the spoils. Swift Portuguese vessels dominated the trade routes. Portuguese soldiers seized strategic points from which to launch attacks upon rival traders or where water and supplies might be taken aboard.[1] The towns of the East African coast were not so vital to the attainment of these objectives as were Aden, Hormuz or Malacca, but they attracted the attention of the Portuguese soldier, Affonso d'Albuquerque, who believed that to maintain any sort of position in the Indian Ocean more military bases would be necessary.

In 1502 Vasco da Gama set out upon his second voyage round the Cape. In Sofala he learned about the gold-mines of the interior and that the trade in gold was largely in the hands of the inhabitants of Kilwa. His interest was immediately aroused and in the middle of the year he sailed into the harbour of Kilwa with nineteen ships. The ruler of the town, Ibraim, was put in irons and ransomed only after he had promised to pay an annual tribute of 1,500 gold meticals and to recognize the supremacy of the King of Portugal. The following year, Ruy Lourenço Ravasco cruised along the coast capturing shipping and levying tribute from a number of towns. The son of the ruler of Mafia Island fell into his hands and was held to ransom. The port of Zanzibar was blockaded and, after a sharp skirmish, submitted and agreed to pay an annual tribute of 100 meticals of gold.

These startling strokes marked only the beginning of Portuguese aggression in East Africa and Kilwa was still strong enough to refuse a demand for tribute by the Portuguese captain, Lopes Suarez, homeward bound from India in 1504. The following year, however, Portugal launched her main attack, excited in part by Vasco da Gama's news about the gold-fields of the interior. The campaign was entrusted to the leadership of Francisco d'Almeida who sailed from Lisbon with more than twenty ships and 1,500 men under orders to seize strategic points along the shores of the Indian Ocean and to plant Portuguese colonies where they might prove necessary. Along the East African coast his objectives were the gold-exporting town of Sofala and the cities of Kilwa and Mombasa. Sofala offered little resistance and was quickly seized by a subsidiary force. When the main Portuguese fleet approached Kilwa the inhabitants followed the

[1] The chief authority for the Portuguese period in East African history is J. Strandes: *Die Portugiesenzeit von Deutsch-und-Englisch Ostafrika* of which an English translation by Jean Wallwork is shortly to be published by the Kenya Historical Society. Sir Reginald Coupland's *East Africa and its Invaders*, O.U.P., 1938, also covers this period and an excellent summary with particular emphasis upon the work of Portuguese missionaries is contained in Sir John Gray's *Early Portuguese Missionaries in East Africa*, Macmillan, London. 1958.

example of their ruler, Ibraim, and fled. The town was sacked and then, in accordance with instructions, a fortress was built and garrisoned with between 80 and 100 men under the command of Pedro Ferreira Forgaça. A new ruler was crowned but his reign was short. He was killed by rivals for the throne and for the next few years various claimants struggled to succeed him until Ibraim was finally restored. After seven years the Portuguese garrison was withdrawn and the fort was destroyed at the end of 1512 or early in 1513.

After his easy successes in Sofala and Kilwa, Almeida had moved on to Mombasa where he met stronger resistance. But the Arab and African inhabitants were no match for the trained forces of Portugal. The invaders advanced street by street until the townsmen were finally driven out. Mombasa, like Kilwa, was looted and when the Portuguese had taken away as much gold, silver, ivory and provisions as they could carry with them the town was burnt and the attackers withdrew to continue their voyage to Malindi. No garrison was left in Mombasa but a column of white marble was erected as an indication that the land now belonged to the King of Portugal.

In 1506 and 1507 Tristão da Cunha sacked and burned the northern towns of Oja and Brava, both of which had tried to resist the extension of Portuguese overlordship. Lamu, on the other hand, quickly submitted and agreed to pay an annual tribute. Pressing on northward with the sailing season almost at an end the Portuguese force next seized the island of Socotra which commanded the entrance to the Red Sea. The defenders were annihilated and their mosque turned into a church for the Portuguese garrison. Two years later, in 1509, the islands of Mafia and Pemba were successfully attacked and Zanzibar was looted. Madagascar and the adjacent groups of islands had been visited by da Cunha and d'Albuquerque in 1506 but no steps were taken to occupy them since they appeared to possess neither commercial nor strategic value.

These swift successes on the part of the Portuguese were greatly assisted by the inability of the coastal towns to compose their rivalries and jealousies even when faced by a greater and more dangerous enemy. The ruler of Mafia, for example, had been responsible for the death of the Portuguese puppet ruler of Kilwa and the dead man's son had then enlisted the support of a local African chief in order to encompass the destruction of Mafia. Yet even when these disagreements are taken into account the extent of the Portuguese success was

remarkable. Their forces were never large, yet by 1509 they dominated the whole East African coast from the settlement at Mozambique in the south to the satellite town of Malindi in the north. The
situation was recognized by the appointment of a Governor-General
for the Portuguese possessions in Africa and Arabia but he died
almost immediately and was not replaced. The Portuguese then
resorted to an arrangement whereby the two senior officials along the
coast, the Captains of Mozambique and Malindi (later Mombasa),
were individually responsible to the Viceroy of Goa.

The resounding success at arms had a disappointing sequel. The
Portuguese do not appear to have attempted, any more than the
Arabs did before them, to establish a systematic form of government
along the coast. Nor was any effort made to administer the hinterland.
The relations of both Portuguese and Arabs with the native population appear to have been simply of a diplomatic character, mainly
friendly, but occasionally resulting in fighting.[1] Whereas, too, it is
probable that Arabs had formerly sent caravans some distance into
the hinterland during the years of their prosperity, the Portuguese
made no attempt to establish active trading relations with the people
of the interior. Even along the coast commercial activity was limited
in scale. There were probably two main reasons for this lack of
enterprise by a people who elsewhere had colonized and traded so
extensively. The first was that before long it was found that the best
route from Mozambique to India was that dictated by the south-
westerly monsoon straight across the Indian Ocean. At the best
sailing season, therefore, it was unnecessary to call at the ports
along the East African coast, so that their original importance
declined. Secondly, having gained control over the gold trade of
Sofala the Portuguese were scarcely attracted by the less accessible
and apparently far less rewarding commerce of the coast farther
north.

Even exploration appears to have been largely ignored by the
normally adventurous Portuguese, although the lack of evidence of
their penetration into the interior may to some extent be due to the
subsequent disappearance of some of the tribes who then inhabited
the more immediate hinterland At all events, in 1506 two Portuguese,
John Gomes and John Sanches, together with a Tunisian Moor

[1] J. S. Kirkman: 'Historical Archaeology in Kenya.' *The Antiquaries
Journal*, Vol. XXXVII, January–April 1957, p. 16.

named Sidi Muhammad, were landed at Malindi with the object of
discovering a route to the land of Prester John, the legendary Christian ruler of Abyssinia. They met with no success owing to the fierce-
ness of the tribes in the neighbourhood of the town. In March 1508,
they tried again from a place farther north near Guardafui. From
there they were able to reach the court of Helena, the Regent of
Abyssinia. For fully a century no further exploration of note took
place. Then, early in the seventeenth century a new attempt was
made to penetrate the interior along the line of the Zambezi. This
isolated endeavour bore little fruit but it deserves mention because
the initiative shown by the individuals concerned was more in keeping with the tradition established by Portuguese pioneers in other
parts of the world. We owe the account of this exploit to a Portuguese nobleman, Caspar Bocarro, who lived for many years in the
vicinity of the Zambezi and who was employed by another Portuguese named Diogo Simoes. Diogo claimed to have discovered silver
on the southern bank of the Zambezi some distance above Tete. As
a reward for the assistance rendered by Diogo and others employed
by him, a chief of that neighbourhood granted the ownership of the
silver-mines to Diogo who in turn transferred them to the King of
Portugal. In 1613 Diogo was ordered to march up the Zambezi and
take possession of the mines, but he met with opposition from the
natives and he suffered from lack of support from the Portuguese
authorities at the coast. In spite of his difficulties he managed to
build a fort in which he successfully withstood the repeated attacks of
hostile tribesmen until shortage of supplies compelled him to abandon his position. Then began a withdrawal of between 700 and 800
miles to the coast at Kilwa which provided the best information
available even now as to the state of the country lying between Lake
Nyasa and the Indian Ocean in the early seventeenth century. The
Portuguese had known nothing of this area before and they learned
little afterwards. Bocarro, however, tells us that at the time of
Diogo's journey the country between the upper Zambezi and the
Rovuma river was both peaceful and prosperous. Immediately
north of the river the Ma-Nyanja people, who were ruled over by a
paramount chief, were less prosperous. Between their country and
the coast the travellers three times passed through areas of desolation
which took them several days to cross. The first of these deserts had
been created by the passage of the warlike Zimba in the course of a

predatory march northward some years earlier.[1] Nearer the coast the
desert country was the work of nature. Yet in spite of the hazards
which separated them from contact with the coast the Ma-Nyanja
appear to have travelled regularly from their homeland into the
neighbourhood of Kilwa. Trade was carried on, though only on a
small scale, for caravans never penetrated to the country of the Ma-
Nyanja. So, while the tribe was able to obtain sufficient cloth to
meet its needs it maintained its immunity from foreign incursions
and from the slave-trade which, two centuries later, was to torment
the peoples round about Lake Nyasa.[2]

Where commerce and curiosity made little headway missionaries,
too, met with only limited success. The Jesuits, Dominicans and
Augustinians who formed the spiritual spearhead of Portuguese
colonization in India and South America had less impact in East
Africa. A Jesuit mission which was founded beyond the gold-fields
of the interior was soon abandoned after its leader had been murdered in 1561. Dominican missionaries along the coast gave themselves unsparingly for their cause but had little effect upon the
Muslim and pagan population. Augustinians in Mombasa and
Zanzibar ministered to the needs of the small groups of Portuguese colonists and made a number of converts among the native
population. But Islam, first of the monotheistic religions in the
East African mission field, had gained a firm hold which Christianity, unsupported by large-scale European settlement or by any
systematic secular administration, could not hope to loosen. When
the Portuguese withdrew, Christian teaching also was withdrawn.
While Islam contrived to leave its imprint upon the coast Christianity
moved over the coastal scene as over the surface of the sea, creating
ripples but leaving no lasting mark.[3]

Although the immediate impact of the arrival of the Portuguese on
the coast had proved shattering to the Arab towns, the tenuous control exercised by the invaders enabled them to make a quick recovery.
The number of new houses and mosques that were built in the sixteenth century suggests that their prosperity continued for some time
at least. Only a few Portuguese traders settled in the towns, but

[1] For an account of the Zimba migration see pp. 13–14.

[2] Sir John Gray: 'A Journey by Land from Tete to Kilwa in 1616.' *Tanganyika Notes and Records*, No. 25, June 1948, pp. 37–47.

[3] Sir John Gray: *Early Portuguese Missionaries in East Africa.* Macmillan,
London, 1958, *passim*.

while Malindi alone remained consistently loyal to the Portuguese only Mombasa was prepared to risk the heavy displeasure of Portugal by raising the standard of revolt. For the next four hundred years the town was to have a tumultuous history. It recovered rapidly from the defeat and disaster of 1505 and soon adopted an overt attitude of defiance towards Portuguese authority. But the armed forces of Portugal proved too strong. A Portuguese expedition with assistance from Zanzibar, Malindi and Pemba once again attacked and burnt the town. The sheikh was forced to recognize the overlordship of the King of Portugal and to pay him tribute, and Mombasa gave little further trouble for half a century. None the less, although Portuguese authority, unsupported by forts or garrisons, remained a thing of little weight, it was still actively resented.

Open resistance did not break out again until 1585. By that date Portugal had been for five years subject to the King of Spain and her overseas activities had been proportionately curtailed. For some time, too, the Portuguese had been harassed in the north-western sect or of the Indian Ocean by the power of Turkey. A Turkish Amir, Ali Bey, sailed down the East African coast in 1585 preaching a *jehad*, or holy war. His single vessel constituted no serious threat to Portuguese control but he promised the coastal towns further help in the near future. One after another the towns welcomed him, Mombasa declaring itself ready at any time to cast aside the dominion of the Portuguese and to declare its loyalty to the Turkish Sultan. Malindi alone remained faithful to Portugal.

The hopes raised by Ali Bey proved to be premature. Retribution not riches was the reward of the East African towns' defection. After looting a number of tiny Portuguese settlements the Bey sailed away northwards, and instead of Turkish seamen it was a flotilla of Portuguese men-of-war that sailed over the horizon from Goa in 1587 in response to a call for help from Malindi. Mombasa was evacuated before the avenging force arrived, while most of the sheikhs in the other towns either made good their escape or pleaded their military weakness as an excuse for their submission to the warlike Turk. After making the town of Faza a scapegoat for the errors of the rest and for the part played by its citizens in the torture and death of a Portuguese subject, the naval squadron withdrew. In 1589 Ali Bey was back again with more ships and more men. The coastal towns greeted him with open arms and once again a *jehad*

12

was proclaimed. The inhabitants of Pemba, whose ruler supported the Portuguese, revolted against him with Ali Bey's encouragement. The Bey himself landed on Mombasa Island and began to prepare a joint attack with Mombasa against Malindi. But the Portuguese, although no longer the ruthless power they had been a century earlier, were still able to rise to the occasion. Reacting quickly to the new threat they dispatched a strong naval and military force from Goa which was reinforced by the ruler of Malindi and by the Portuguese captain. A quick attack upon Mombasa drove the Turks from their entrenchments and from the town. The Turkish ships were burnt in the harbour and the Turks themselves, along with the inhabitants of Mombasa, sought refuge in the interior of the island.

It was at this point that a new element intervened from an unexpected quarter. Soon after the middle of the sixteenth century a horde of Bantu tribesmen, the Zimba, had begun to trek eastward probably from the present region of Angola or the Congo. The party consisted entirely of males except for such women as were taken along as food, for the Zimba were cannibals. Their aim is not clear. They showed no inclination to settle, but instead they raided and pillaged as they pressed onward to the Zambezi. On reaching the river they divided, one group advancing to the sea and following the coastline to reach Kilwa in 1587. The invaders stormed the town and slaughtered the inhabitants before moving on again to appear like a storm cloud before Mombasa at the critical moment before the Portuguese attack. They witnessed the Portuguese success and, attracted by the prospect of loot, offered their co-operation. The Portuguese were at first reluctant to enter into an alliance with this strange horde, but after some delay they allowed the Zimba to intervene. The latter immediately crossed to the island where they massacred all upon whom they could lay hands. Ali Bey himself only escaped their spears by seeking refuge with the Portuguese who carried him off as a prisoner to Lisbon.

Their looting done, the Zimba did not delay in Mombasa. Turning their faces again to the north they launched a threat against Portugal's ally, Malindi, and even succeeded in breaching the walls of the town. But the wave of their advance broke against the resistance of the Wasegeju, a tribe whose friendly relations with Malindi were of long standing. They were defeated even as they swarmed

13

over the walls, and only a hundred were able to withdraw. From that time the Zimba disappeared from the coastal scene and from recorded history. The battle of Malindi has been described as one of the decisive battles of African history.[1] Had the Zimba been victorious they might well have simply abandoned Malindi to continue their wanderings in search of loot farther northward. But the destruction of Malindi would have had a serious effect upon the position of Portugal on the East African coast in the crucial years which were to follow.

While the Zimba were suffering defeat in the north the Portuguese, with a revival of their former vigour, were pressing home their success. The ruler of Pemba was restored and other towns were either forced to pay tribute or were destroyed. The rising had convinced the Portuguese of the need to adopt a more effective policy for controlling the northern towns. In implementing this policy they were helped by events in which they played no direct part. In spite of the terrible defeat which the town had suffered at the hands of the Zimba, the ruler of Mombasa and his people were soon in warlike mood once more and inciting the people of Kilifi to attack Malindi. Again the Wasegeju came to the aid of Malindi and of the Portuguese. They captured and destroyed Kilifi; the forces of Mombasa were defeated, and the Wasegeju, following their retreating enemy, seized the town. Mombasa, however, was of little value to a pastoral people. The Wasegeju therefore offered it to the ruler of Malindi who agreed to move his headquarters.[2] His old protectors, the Portuguese, approved and moved with him. In 1593 they began work on the construction of the almost impregnable Fort Jesus on Mombasa Island. At the same time attempts were made to establish a Portuguese colony in the vicinity. These latter efforts met with only limited success since few Portuguese were interested in making agricultural experiments in this uncertain land. However, a number of Portuguese traders, some of them from Malindi, settled on the island under the protection of a commandant and garrison of 100 men who were also transferred from Malindi. There were further Portuguese trading communities on the islands of Zanzibar and Pate. There is little accurate indication of the extent of the trade which was deve-

[1] Sir John Gray: 'Portuguese Records Related to the Wasegeju.' *Tanganyika Notes and Records*, No. 29, 1950, p. 89.

[2] Sir John Gray: op. cit. pp. 89-90.

loping along this section of the coast, but Portugal's part in it undoubtedly increased at this period. Ivory, slaves and gum copal were regularly exported to India, and Indian manufactured cloth constituted the bulk of the return trade.

Now, for almost a century and a half, Portuguese activities along the east coast were to be based upon the garrison in Fort Jesus. As a result, a marked decline was noticeable in the Arab culture of the towns, a decline which was still further accelerated by the growing threat from the Galla in the interior. These latter people had begun their southward advance from the region of Ethiopia and the hinterland of Somalia some two centuries earlier. In the early seventeenth century they began to press hard upon the Wanyika, the tribal allies of the northern coastal towns. Their migration, which is referred to in both Arab and Bantu coastal traditions, delivered the final blow to an already crumbling society, causing the inhabitants of the coastal towns to evacuate their homes and take refuge on the off-shore islands of Mombasa, Lamu and Pate in the first half of the seventeenth century. Whether or not the Galla defeated the coastal peoples in battle is unknown, but the date of the latter's withdrawal to the islands is fixed by the last broken relics of pottery found among the ruins of their towns.[1] Even the Wasegeju, whose doughty exploits had put to rout the fearsome Zimba, were forced to retreat westward before the Galla advance. Following a well-watered route they marched into Ukamba before turning southward to Vumba which they reached about the middle of the seventeenth century. After this they virtually passed out of history.

Meanwhile, in Mombasa, the Portuguese were still faced with a restless population. In 1614 a dispute broke out between the Portuguese commandant in Fort Jesus and his ally, the former ruler of Malindi, now Sultan of Mombasa. The Sultan fled to the mainland but returned after some sort of reconciliation had taken place. Two years later he fled again having heard rumours that he was to be arrested. He took refuge on the mainland where, at the instigation of the Portuguese, he was murdered by Wanyika tribesmen. In an attempt at restitution the Sultan's young son, Yusuf, was sent to Goa to be trained to succeed his father if he should prove suitable. After his initial education and his Christian baptism as Jeronimo

[1] J. S. Kirkman: 'Historical Archaeology in Kenya.' *The Antiquaries Journal*, Vol. XXXVII, January–April 1957, pp. 16–17.

Chingulia he is reported to have joined the Portuguese fleet. In 1627 he was allowed to return to Mombasa where he began to rule with all the oppressiveness towards his Muslim subjects which might be expected of a recent convert. His position was not an easy one and he resented the ill-manners shown him by successive Portuguese commanders in the fort. His early respect for Christianity gave way to a feeling of intense hatred and in 1631 he led a revolt against the foreigners who had brought him to office. Almost the entire Portuguese population of Mombasa was slaughtered, but the other coastal towns responded only half-heartedly to Yusuf's call for a general rising. Nevertheless, a naval expedition from Goa which arrived in 1632 failed to make any impression on Yusuf's forces in Fort Jesus. The lack of support from the other towns and the fear of stronger Portuguese attacks weakened Yusuf's resolve, however. He abandoned the fort, which fell once again into the hands of his enemies. Until his death in 1637 he continued to plot against the Portuguese but his efforts met with little success. A new garrison was introduced into Mombasa and Portugal could again claim to control the coast.

Yet, if Portugal appeared still to be in a strong position in East Africa, the decline of Portuguese imperial power was already being signalled elsewhere. In the East Indies Dutch and British trading rivals had swept the Portuguese from the seas. Along the northern coast of the Indian Ocean the Persians had begun to challenge Portuguese authority. So, too, had the rising state of Oman, situated in the south-east portion of the Arabian peninsula. It was from this latter barren soil that the next invaders of the East African coast were to come. Mombasa was again to the fore in inviting assistance against its Portuguese overlords although the growing sea-power of the Imams of Oman took some time to reach a point where it could challenge the Portuguese to a large scale battle. In 1652 a raiding party from Oman destroyed the Portuguese settlements in Zanzibar and Pate and although it could attempt no more the Portuguese were themselves too weak to contemplate retaliatory measures. Further raids on Faza and Mombasa in 1660 and an expedition which reached the very walls of Mozambique in 1669 demonstrated the new trend of events. The Portuguese exacted fierce reprisals from the coastal towns in the course of an expedition, led by the Viceroy of Goa himself, in 1678, and again in 1686. But their triumphs faded before the advance of further squadrons from Oman.

During the ten years which followed, the northern raiders concentrated their venom upon the Portuguese positions along the coast of India and in the Persian Gulf. But in March 1696, a fleet from Oman arrived in Kilindini harbour and laid siege to Fort Jesus. The siege lasted thirty-three months and although the fort was never subjected to any serious attack until the final assault was launched the hardships undergone by the Portuguese garrison through lack of supplies and the ravages of sickness were severe in the extreme. At length disease exacted so great a toll that the fortitude of the handful of gallant survivors could no longer sustain it and the last fierce resistance of the defenders was overcome.

The fall of Fort Jesus proclaimed the end of Portuguese rule north of the Rovuma River. In 1699, in 1703 and again in 1710 expeditions were sent from Lisbon or Goa to try to recapture Mombasa, but all failed. Yet the Portuguese did not give up hope. Taking advantage of a dispute between the black slave soldiers comprising the Omani garrison of the Fort and the local inhabitants, led by a member of the old Malindi ruling family, and while the ruler of Oman was taken up with civil disorders and Persian aggression at home the Portuguese stepped ashore once again as conquerors. For nearly two years, from March 1728 to November 1729, the Portuguese flag flew over Fort Jesus. In 1729, however, the inhabitants of Mombasa became incensed by the outrageous conduct of their overlords who ill-treated their leading citizens and threw stones at the people at prayer. They therefore rose and ejected their conquerors with the assistance only of their Wanyika neighbours. By 1740 Oman had shaken herself free of internal dissension and Portugal's claim to control the coast north of the Rovuma River was no more than a shadow.

Although the unfruitful years of Portuguese overlordship, together with the southward advance of the Galla, had destroyed the culture of the coastal towns there still flourished a lively spirit of independence on the offshore islands. This spirit not infrequently manifested itself in war and rivalry between the islands themselves or against Oman. For, although it had been necessary for the islanders to seek the aid of Oman in ridding themselves of Portuguese control, there were some like the inhabitants of Mombasa and more recently of Pate who, having so firmly resisted Portuguese domination, felt no desire to exchange the Portuguese yoke for that of Oman. Nevertheless, when the Portuguese were ejected from Mombasa the townsmen, fearing reprisals, found themselves in a difficult position and so appealed for aid once more to Oman. The ruler of Oman sent a garrison and a new governor, Muhammad Said el-Maamri. The latter appears to have been well-liked in Mombasa, but his successor, an Arab from the Hadramaut, proved to be an oppressive governor who, to counter the anger which his rule aroused, encouraged divisions and strife between rival sections among the inhabitants of the island. Complaints were made to Oman and a new governor, Muhammad bin Athman el Mazrui, was sent to replace him.

With the arrival of Muhammad in Mombasa there began the rule of a family which was to be one of the most severe thorns in the flesh of Oman for a full century. Trouble started in 1744 when the ruling dynasty in Oman was overthrown by Ahmed bin Said el-Busaidi. The Mazrui governor of Mombasa at once seized the opportunity to renounce the overlordship of Oman and there began the struggle between the Mazrui and Busaidi houses which, in part at least, led to the rise to power of Zanzibar in the nineteenth century when the ruler of Oman moved his capital there. The rulers of Oman made repeated attempts to overthrow the Mazrui power but were unsuccessful. Mombasa, meanwhile, had other interests and was growing more ambitious. At the request of the inhabitants of the island of Pemba forces from Mombasa overthrew the governor appointed by the Sultan of Pate, overlord of Pemba, and installed another candidate who was a relative of their own Mazrui ruler. Pate retaliated by attacking Mombasa and a compromise was reached whereby the island of Pemba was shared between the rival towns. This was an important success for Mombasa which was far from being self-supporting, there being little food available on the mainland in the immediate vicinity of the town. The grain from Pemba made good this deficiency as it had done during the Portuguese period.

Kilwa, meanwhile, had also taken the opportunity to revolt against Omani overlordship, but the growing importance of the slave-trade from that town induced the Imam to appoint an Omani governor there in 1780. Mafia, a dependency of Kilwa, simultaneously fell under Omani control. Zanzibar, where members of the El-Harthi family had been appointed to various offices by Oman, remained as loyal to the Busaidi dynasty as it had to its predecessors. It appeared, therefore, to present a constant threat to the security of the rebellious

Mazaria[1] of Mombasa. The latter accordingly launched an attack upon Zanzibar in 1753 but met with only partial success. Still their restless energy drove them on. For twenty years in the latter half of the eighteenth century they were involved in an endemic struggle over the sucession to the sultanate of Pate and finally, in 1807, they seized the opportunity to impose their own candidate and to declare their overlordship over the rival townsmen. Pursuing their defeated opponents the Mazaria went on to attack Lamu but were heavily repulsed.

But signs were not lacking of danger to the Mazrui military power both from within Mombasa itself and from outside. In 1782 the town was divided against itself because of rival claimants to the sultanate, a danger which in Muslim society was likely to arise on the death of each successive ruler. In 1785, too, an expedition from Oman entered Fort Jesus in the absence of the main body of the Mazaria on a raiding expedition. The invaders received the submission of the Governor of Mombasa before withdrawing and, although the ruler of Oman was too involved in quarrels at home to enforce his claim, within half a century Oman was to intervene in the affairs of the East African coast with telling effect. Two reasons, closely knit, lay behind that intervention. First, was the rise to power in Oman of a young and vigorous ruler, Seyyid Said, who, in 1806, dispelled with a knife thrust the rival claims to the throne of his cousin. Second, was Britain's concern at the rapid expansion of the slave-trade from the East African coast in the latter half of the eighteenth century. It was the interplay of these two factors rather than the individual significance of either which was to mould the future history of East Africa. For, on his accession, Seyyid Said was no more able to concentrate his energies upon East African affairs than his predecessors had been, since he was forced to struggle hard to maintain his position in Oman. Meanwhile, the Sultan of Mombasa returned defiant answers to Seyyid Said's demand for tribute. At the same time Britain had shown little interest in East Africa in spite of her expansionist programme in India and the Far East. It was the slave-trade which proved to be the catalyst and it was the French who were largely responsible for the revival of that trade and for its being brought to the attention of the British.

Two requests from the French East India Company for permission

[1] Singular, Mazrui; plural, Mazaria.

to trade at Mombasa and Pate had been brusquely rejected by the Portuguese. In fact, although Portugal still claimed a monopoly of the trade along the East African coast she was quite unable to enforce it. The French East India Company did not pursue its inquiries but a number of private French traders began to take an active interest in East Africa in the latter part of the eighteenth century. The main stimulus for this interest came from the Île de France which La Bourdonnais, who became governor in 1735, had hoped to develop as a naval base. Although the French Government abandoned the scheme after giving it only brief support, the Governor himself continued to use every available resource to promote his ambitions. He extended the sugar planting which had been started by the Dutch. He established cotton and indigo factories. He started on a programme of road construction and bridge building and he tried to encourage European settlers to make their homes on the island. These development projects resulted in the revival of the slave-trade. At first the majority of the slaves came from Madagascar, but the hostility of the natives soon encouraged the French to look elsewhere. The coast of Mozambique was not entirely closed by the Portuguese but their attempt to enforce an embargo upon trade with other European powers created difficulties for the French. Not surprisingly, therefore, the latter turned their attention to Zanzibar, only 1,700 miles away across the ocean. Kilwa, too, offered opportunities of trade although Mombasa and the towns farther north were too involved in their mutual struggles to take advantage of any commercial link with the outside world. A French sailor, Morice by name, made several voyages along the East African coast after 1770. From the Sultan of Kilwa, who at that time was still independent, and from the Arab governor in Zanzibar he obtained the sole right to trade in slaves. These he shipped to the Île de France and also round the Cape to the West Indies. The trade appeared so profitable that Morice submitted a scheme to the Governor of the Île de France in 1777 to exploit the whole coastal area commercially. Since the French East India Company had been closed down in 1769 Morice proposed the creation of a new company to undertake the development of the East African trade and he further suggested the establishment of a colony in Kilwa which would act as headquarters for the whole scheme. The Arabs of Kilwa knew little about France although they were vaguely aware of the strength of the French nation. They were, however, most ready to benefit from the trading opportunities which Morice had to offer. In addition to this favourable situation Morice also argued that if the French were inactive the Dutch would be almost certain to intervene before long. As an earnest to his own good faith he went on to state that he was prepared to surrender to the French Government the right granted to him by the Sultan of Kilwa in 1776 to purchase 1,000 slaves annually before the traders of any other nation would be allowed to enter the field. Given adequate encouragement and backed by French settlements in Kilwa and on the mainland he saw no reason why there should not develop the same sort of profitable triangular trade as already existed between Europe, the West African coast and the West Indies. French goods, particularly fire-arms and brandy, would be shipped to Surat, in India, where a proportion would be exchanged for trade goods which would attract the Africans along the east coast. At Kilwa the contents of the ships would then be exchanged for slaves and ivory and probably for foodstuffs and livestock also. But the slaves would form the main item of trade. They could be bought cheaply and Morice estimated that for the first four or five years it would be possible to obtain over 3,000 slaves annually from Kilwa and a further 2,000 from the coast farther south. After that he hoped to see the number rise to 10,000 a year.

Morice's scheme was not accepted by the French Government. They did, however, take advantage of his agreement with the Sultan of Kilwa over the purchase of slaves by making a treaty of commerce with the Sultan, fixing the price of slaves at a sum similar to that arranged by Morice. Several French ships called at Kilwa and slaves were transported to the French and Spanish West Indies and also to Java and the East Indies. The French did not occupy the town, however, and the fort was never rebuilt.

The revival of the slave-trade on the East African coast dates from the period of French intervention in the latter part of the eighteenth century. As has been shown, it was the rapid rise to prosperity of Kilwa resulting from its trade with France which attracted the attention of the ruler of Oman and induced him to reassert his authority there in 1780. The French Revolution resulted in a sharp reaction against the slave-trade in France but there was no similar response in the French dependencies in the Indian Ocean. The Île de France and Bourbon were coming to depend increasingly upon slave labour for their agricultural development and it was British men-of-war rather than revolutionary legislation which imposed a check upon the islands' participation in the slave-trade. Indeed, Napoleon once again legalized the trade as far as the French colonies were concerned in 1802.

While the French trade was rapidly expanding, the Arab slave-trade which had been in progress for several centuries also prospered and may well have been increasing. Few of the coastal towns, however, gained greatly from this trade owing to the endemic warfare which was being carried on. European observers commented upon the depressed condition of the coastal towns, Zanzibar alone among the more northern centres showing any signs of real prosperity. Zanzibar, owing to its close association with Oman, rapidly increased in importance through the export of slaves to Arabia, the Persian Gulf and India. Each year fleets of dhows were swept by the north-easterly monsoon from Oman to Zanzibar, returning with their cargoes of slaves when the monsoon changed. Annually *banyans*, or merchants, journeyed to Zanzibar from India to take part in the commercial activities of the island and in particular to help in financing the slave-trade.

The prosperity of Zanzibar was not shared by all its inhabitants. Perhaps three-quarters of the population of the island were slaves. Upon the rest the Sultan of Oman made heavy financial demands to help to maintain his constant struggle against warring elements in the Arabian peninsula. An English naval visitor in 1812 said that £12,000 was raised annually in Zanzibar as tribute to Oman. This sum was the product of a customs duty of 5 per cent imposed by orders from Oman, but only the Arabs paid such a low percentage, the Indian *banyans* sometimes being required to contribute as much as 20 per cent. The *banyans* also paid a high proportion of the irregular levies made at the command of the Sultan of Oman when he had particular need for money to finance his wars against the puritan Wahabi or other opponents of his authority.

Until the nineteenth century the greatest naval power in the Indian Ocean, Britain, paid little attention to East Africa. Even during the Napoleonic Wars which made the Indian Ocean an important battlefield Britain's main interest had been to protect the direct route from the Cape to India and to block French attempts to advance overland to India through the Middle East. It was in pursuance of this latter object that Britain entered into a treaty with Oman in 1798 by the terms of which the ruler of Oman agreed to put a stop to trade with the French and the Dutch. It was, too, to maintain the friendly relations so established with this strategically placed sultanate that the British were a little tardy in launching their anti-slave-trade campaign in the western half of the Indian Ocean.

The speed and vigour which marked Britain's attack upon the slave-trade on the west coast of Africa after the passing of the prohibition act of 1807 is one of the striking phenomena of the early nineteenth century. Many years had been spent in debate and discussion, yet once the decision was taken even the country's preoccupation with her struggle against Napoleon did not deter the British Government from prosecuting its anti-slavery campaign. Although the Act itself could only refer to British subjects, Britain's supremacy at sea enabled her to impose some check upon other European powers. With the coming of peace, diplomatic action induced both friends and defeated enemies to give formal support to Britain's aims, but this did not prevent the subjects of these other powers from secretly taking part in this profitable trade. In the Indian Ocean the Portuguese mainly confined their activities to the coast of Mozambique and the main offenders were the French. Britain, also, was faced for a time with a novel problem. The Île de France, captured from the French in 1810 and renamed Mauritius, continued to rely heavily upon the import of slaves for the maintenance of its economy. The Governor, Sir Robert Farquhar, held the view that a law passed in 1807 would not apply to a dependency acquired after that date. He was quickly put right by Lord Liverpool in 1811 and from that time did his utmost to put down the slave-trade in spite of strong opposition from the large French population of the island. This lack of support from his own subjects quickly convinced Sir Robert that if his campaign was to be effective he must attack the slave-trade at its source rather than at its outlet. A large proportion of the slaves still came from Madagascar where Radama, chief of the important Hova tribe, had recently gained ascendancy over most of the island. Radama was a progressive man and was anxious to establish friendly relations with the powers of Europe and particularly with Britain. On October 23, 1817, therefore, a treaty was signed between Radama and the British by which the former agreed, in return for compensation, to do everything in his power to check the export of slaves from the island. Six years later a further treaty was made enabling British cruisers to capture slavers sailing in Madagascar's waters.

Farquhar thus made speedy amends for his earlier error of judgement. Yet the problem of the slave-trade was only half solved. Zanzibar was still carrying on a flourishing trade both with the Muslim north and with any European slavers who cared to take on cargo there. Zanzibar, however, was a loyal dependency of Oman and hitherto the British had been anxious to avoid disturbing their friendship with the Sultan. Now France no longer presented a serious threat to British interests in India and the strategic importance of Oman was proportionately reduced. Farquhar therefore began overtures to Seyyid Said while simultaneously writing to the Governor-General of India asking him to negotiate an agreement with the Sultan similar to that which Farquhar himself had recently made with Madagascar. Lord Hastings, the Governor-General, was anxious to do all he could to assist the campaign against the slave-trade. Owing to Britain's reluctance to interfere too deeply in the customs and traditions of the Indian population the Act of 1807 had not been applied to India. Nevertheless, the Governments of Bombay and Bengal had introduced measures to check the slave-trade hoping that in time the trade would die out in those parts of India which were under British control. These hopes were undermined because the regulations did not apply in adjacent areas still subject to Indian princes. It became clear therefore to Hastings, as it had to Farquhar, that the slave-trade must be tackled at its source. In 1812 the Government of Bombay informed Seyyid Said of the regulations issued to prevent the import of slaves into British India giving as their reason their anxiety to prevent any of the Sultan's subjects offending against the British law. No further action was taken until 1815 when the Bombay Government decided to approach Oman more openly, and even then the language in which their letter was couched was such as to convince Said that no immediate action on his part was called for.

During the next few years the situation changed rapidly. The success of British attacks upon the pirates who infested the Persian Gulf had a twofold effect upon Seyyid Said. The pirates had been a constant source of trouble to Oman and their defeat strengthened

Seyyid Said's position while increasing his friendship for Britain. At the same time Britain's success impressed upon the Sultan the effectiveness of British sea power and suggested to him the benefits which might result from the development of legitimate trade with Britain's overseas possessions. Early in 1820 the Court of Directors of the East India Company, under pressure from the African Institution, precursor of the Anti-Slavery Society, agreed to send instructions to the Bombay Government urging the latter body to get in touch with the Sultan of Oman. With this official stimulus a joint request from Mauritius and Bombay was sent to Seyyid Said in 1821 asking him to put an end to the slave-trade or, failing that, to check the trade between his subjects and the subjects of Christian countries. Seyyid Said was in the mood to recognize the importance of accepting this advance. The tone of it made it clear that the British appreciated the Sultan's dilemma. To abolish slavery completely would almost inevitably bring Seyyid Said into violent conflict with his subjects who already gave him plenty of trouble. To prohibit the slave-trade entirely would also involve heavy financial loss to Seyyid Said's subjects and to the state of Oman itself which derived revenue from the sale of slaves by any subjects of the state. The British proposal, however, implied a readiness to allow the continuation of the slave-trade within the Sultan's Muslim dominions.

Farquhar had already sent a draft agreement to Seyyid Said and in 1822 he dispatched a naval officer, Captain Moresby, to conclude a formal treaty. Happy to participate in the work which the navy had been assisting by means of patrol activity, Moresby brought to his task both energy and enthusiasm. The Moresby Treaty was signed on September 22, 1822. It contained simply a formal statement of the proposals put forward by the Bombay Government. All trading in slaves between the subjects of the ruler of Oman and the subjects of any Christian power was forbidden. British naval vessels were authorized to seize Arab ships violating the terms of the agreement and an area was defined which purported to cover the dominions of the Sultan of Oman within which the slave-trade might be carried on between Muslims. This latter provision was potentially the most important as regards the history of East Africa. The signing of the treaty did not necessarily bring the trade to an end. British vessels were hard pressed to patrol effectively the wide spaces of the Indian Ocean, and in spite of the co-operation of Seyyid Said himself the Sultan's subjects broke the treaty whenever they could safely do so. But by the terms of the treaty Britain had recognized the claims of Seyyid Said over a section of the East African coast stretching northwards continuously from Cape Delgado to the Horn of Africa. The Sultan's control of this coastline with the exception of the island of Zanzibar and, to a lesser extent, of Kilwa, was in fact extremely tenuous. With his own resources it is doubtful whether he would ever have dared to embark upon an attempt to establish his authority over such a wide field. Backed by British friendship, however, he was in a different position. The Moresby Treaty, it might fairly be said, launched Seyyid Said into East Africa.

The first to suffer the impact of Seyyid Said's new-found confidence were the Mazaria of Mombasa. The aggressiveness of these latter had won them many enemies and brought many restless subjects under their authority. The Mazrui empire, if such it can be called, was built on insecure foundations. The Mazrui Governor of Pemba, Rizike, who succeeded his father in 1806, was troubled by endless intrigues which may have been supported by Zanzibar. So concerned did he become at the insecurity of his position that in October 1809 he took the opportunity of a visit by the British ship, H.M.S. *Racehorse*, to offer to place himself and Pemba under the protection of the Bombay Government. Although the information was passed on to the Secretary of the Admiralty no action appears to have been taken and it is uncertain whether Rizike had obtained the approval of the Sultan of Mombasa for his offer. Meanwhile, the dissident groups within the island grew more active and an appeal for aid was made to Oman in return for the offer that Pemba would pay taxes to Seyyid Said and allow him to establish a foothold on the island. Trouble in Pate also brought about a conflict of interests between Mombasa and Oman. In 1819 there was yet another dispute over the succession to the sultanate. One faction sent a request to Seyyid Said for assistance in overthrowing the Mazrui candidate and the Sultan agreed to send a fleet to the East African coast. On its way the Omani force gained the submission of Brava on the Somali coast above Lamu. The defence of Pate was in the hands of Mbarak, brother of the Sultan of Mombasa, a man whose reputation as a military commander is still preserved in the songs of the children of the coast. But Pate was not prepared to withstand a long siege. Although the first attack by the Omani ships was repulsed Mbarak had neither the supplies nor the ammunition to resist a lengthy onslaught. He therefore accepted the offer of the Omani leader to allow him to withdraw in safety.

The fall of Pate marked the beginning of the decline of the Mazaria. It was followed almost immediately by a similar setback in Pemba. The people of Pemba were themselves on the point of revolt and the Governor of Zanzibar took advantage of the approach of the Omani fleet to land a force in Pemba and to seize the Mazrui stronghold. The indomitable Mbarak made two attempts to recapture the island but he was unsuccessful. Almost immediately afterwards, on May 24, 1823, the Sultan of Mombasa died. For a moment the shadow of internal strife hovered over the island. At this crucial time the Mazaria displayed an uncharacteristic solidarity. In spite of the undoubted claims of Mbarak and another brother of the dead Sultan, the Mazaria united to support the candidature of the unfortunately ineffectual Suleiman bin Ali, uncle of the two other claimants. Furthermore, the loss of Pemba was too clear a signal of approaching danger to be ignored. In 1823 the Mazaria sent an appeal to Bombay for British protection against Oman. The Bombay Government, however, was committed to friendship with Seyyid Said and the request was rejected.

The deputation from Mombasa gained a sympathetic hearing in an unexpected quarter. As a result, and because of the personal conviction and determination of one man, the affairs of the East African coast took an entirely new turn for a period of two years.[1] Captain William Fitzwilliam Wentworth Owen, Commander of H.M.S. *Leven*, had been engaged for some time in a survey of the East African coast. In November 1823, Owen arrived in Bombay to revictual his ship and there got in touch with representatives of the Mazaria. Like many other naval officers of his time Owen was violently opposed to the slave-trade and believed that he had a mission to do everything within his power to put an end to it. What he had seen of the activities of Seyyid Said's deputies along the East African coast had convinced him that they had little interest in enforcing the Moresby Treaty. The request of the Mazaria for British protection, therefore, appeared to him to offer an excellent opportunity for carrying the war against the slavers into their own

[1] Sir John Gray: *The British in Mombasa*, 1824–1826. Macmillan, London 1957.

country. He immediately appealed to the Governor of Bombay to reconsider his decision, but the latter refused.

Not long afterwards Owen left Bombay with letters to Seyyid Said requesting assistance and safe conduct in carrying out his further survey along the East African coast. Here was his chance. Arriving in Oman, Owen bluntly informed the Sultan that his representatives had failed to fulfil the terms of the Moresby Treaty. He further announced that he would himself be visiting Mombasa in the near future and if, as he fully expected, the Mazaria asked for British protection he would feel it his duty to agree at least until firm orders were given by the British Government. Seyyid Said was both startled and angered by this outspoken statement. Being anxious to avoid a dispute with a British officer, however, he politely expressed his pleasure at Owen's visit but immediately sent representations against Owen's proposed action to the Bombay Government. Owen, who appears to have formed a surprisingly poor opinion of Seyyid Said's honesty, left Oman on New Year's Day, 1824. Calling *en route* at Socotra, Mogadishu and Lamu, he reached Mombasa on February 8. The following day he went ashore, where he was greeted by the Sultan with a request for British protection. Owen offered to forward this request to the British Government and, provided the Sultan would accept his terms, he agreed to take charge of Mombasa pending a reply from Britain. His main stipulation was that the slave-trade should be abolished in Mombasa, but he kept this clause until the end of his proposals. His other terms were that the sovereignty of the state should continue to be exercised by the Mazrui Sultan and that the title should be hereditary in his family, that there should be an agent of the protecting power residing with the Sultan, that the customs revenues should be equally divided between the British and the Mazaria, that trade with the interior should be restricted to British subjects and that Great Britain should reinstate the Sultan of Mombasa in his former possessions. If the abolition of the slave-trade was Owen's main objective there can be no doubt that it was the last of the conditions listed above which carried most importance in the eyes of the Mazaria. It is surprising that Owen agreed to the inclusion of this item in view of the clearly defined policy of the Bombay Government. Yet, so great was the pressure put upon Owen by the Mazaria that he agreed to take immediate steps for the recovery of Pemba. Together with the Sultan's nephew, Mbarak bin

Ahmed, and fifty of the latter's followers he sailed from Mombasa to Pemba where the Governor had already received instructions from Oman to assist Owen's survey in every way possible. The Governor at once offered to supply Owen with all the provisions he required and in the years which followed proved to be wholly co-operative not only with the survey party but also in his general efforts to enforce the Moresby Treaty. But he was adamant over the question of returning Pemba to Mombasa.

Owen had to admit defeat for the time being. He continued his voyage to Zanzibar where he found the Omani Governor much less co-operative than the Governor of Pemba had been. All that he could offer to the disappointed Mbarak was an onward voyage to Mauritius and the opportunity to state his claims to the British Governor. The ship arrived in Mauritius on May 21, 1824, and Owen began his lengthy campaign to convince higher authority of the need to support his actions in Mombasa. Sir Lowry Cole, who had succeeded Farquhar as Governor, found himself faced with both conflicting and confusing evidence. Contradicting Owen's opinion, Captain Moorsom, who had visited Mombasa even more recently than Owen himself, stated categorically that he did not believe the Mazaria would accept a British garrison. To add to the uncertainty, Mbarak, while affirming that the Mazaria had voluntarily agreed to become British subjects, was vague when questioned on their attitude towards a British garrison. At the same time he was quite firm in pressing for British assistance in the recovery of Pemba, Pate and the other former dependencies of Mombasa in return for putting an end to the slave-trade. Cole was unable to reach any decision over this difficult issue without reference to Britain. Yet he was undoubtedly impressed by Owen's argument that to accept a protectorate would help in the campaign against the slave-trade and in his correspondence with the British Government he suggested that British protection should be offered to Mombasa and that a British commercial agent should be posted there. Pending a reply from Britain Cole asked Commodore Nourse, Commander-in-Chief at the Cape, to continue the protection granted by Captain Owen. Simultaneously he wrote to Seyyid Said informing him of the steps he had taken and asking him to refrain from all hostilities against Mombasa until a reply was received from Britain. Owen had set the wheels turning and could only await the decision of the British Government.

Mbarak, meantime, had received little satisfaction in his main campaign for the recovery of Mombasa's former dependencies.

When he left Mombasa Owen had placed Lieutenant John James Reitz in charge as Governor of the island. Reitz was given no clear definition of his powers and responsibilities but it was clear that the Governor's main duties were to collect the customs revenue to be shared with the Mazaria and to issue passes to ships sailing from Mombasa. Reitz appointed as collector of customs Midshipman George Phillips who, together with a corporal of Marines and three British sailors, had been left in Mombasa with him. The chief items of export were ivory and gum copal. The ivory was obtained either at a large fair held annually a few miles inland from Mombasa or from the Wanyika who carried on a regular trade with Mombasa in ivory, rhinoceros horn, hides and gum copal. The principal items of exchange consisted of beads and brass wire. The trade continued to be on a small scale, however, and few of the Arabs were even moderately wealthy. The most prosperous people in Mombasa were the Indian *banyans* who financed much of the trade, but their position was a precarious one as they were frequently victimized by the more powerful Arab families.

Reitz held his post for only a few months. While attempting to explore the hinterland he contracted fever and died on May 29, 1824. The Governorship then devolved upon Midshipman Phillips who bravely carried out the duties of his office until August 25 when the arrival of three British vessels gave him the opportunity to hand over his responsibilities to Lieutenant James Emery. The closing weeks of Phillips's period of office had been made difficult by the return of Mbarak with the disappointing news that there appeared to be no immediate prospect of British help towards the recovery of Pemba. Emery, too, met with endless frustrations during close on two years of governorship. The climate proved a severe test, more particularly in view of the serious inadequacy of his medical resources. There were liberated slaves to provide for. The Arab population, disappointed at their failure to recapture Pemba, proved increasingly unwilling to recognize Emery's authority. There was growing opposition to the payment of the agreed customs dues. Emery himself was insulted and on occasion his life was threatened. When he appealed to the Sultan the usual reply was that it would not happen again and it was virtually impossible for him to get redress for his grievances. The protection of the *banyans*, who were British subjects, constituted an almost continuous problem since they were frequently imprisoned arbitrarily for refusing to give goods to the Arab rulers without payment. When Emery remonstrated with the Sultan he was told that the latter might do as he wished in his own territory. Indeed, it is surprising that the lure of profit was strong enough to encourage the *banyans* to continue in such insecurity and to submit to such ill-treatment.

Emery's vigil was enlivened by the arrival, towards the end of the year, of Captain Owen. The latter enjoyed to the full this return visit to his own little garrison. He also took the opportunity to offer his protection to Fumoluti, a former Sultan of Pate, who, having been rejected by his own people, had created for himself an independent sultanate on an island in the Tana River. Owen was further prevailed upon to take Mbarak and a group of supporters to Pemba and Zanzibar once more in the hope of inducing those islands to submit to Mombasa. This second appeal to Pemba proved to be as fruitless as the first had been, in spite of Owen's having written to Seyyid Said asking him to surrender the island to the British as soon as an adequate force was available to occupy it. Mbarak, therefore, was still unsatisfied, but Owen did manage to achieve something. Through his negotiations with Pemba and Zanzibar he was able to ensure that adequate supplies of food would always be available for Mombasa and that trade would be carried on freely between Mombasa and the islands. But, important though these gains undoubtedly were, they did not fulfil the ambitions of the Mazaria who showed their disapproval by creating constant difficulties for the Governor.

In September 1825, popular opinion brought about the overthrow of the Sultan Suleiman. Of the two former claimants to the sultanate Mbarak had already surrendered his claims. His brother, Salim Rashid, was appointed to replace Suleiman and since both the brothers were men of energy and intelligence there was hope of an improvement in the administration of Mombasa and in the relations between the Sultan and the British Governor. Unfortunately, this hope was not wholly fulfilled. The inhabitants of Mombasa believed that they were paying too high a price for the nominal protection offered by Owen and consequently complaints against the customs duties became more frequent. Nevertheless, Emery contrived to make the Protectorate pay its way although his relations with the Sultan became steadily more strained.

There was one matter which had attracted Emery's attention and which added interest to the depressing round of his normal duties. The former Sultan of Pate, Fumoluti, told him of a large lake said to be in the interior of the continent, nearly due west of Mombasa, the shores of which were reported to be thickly populated. This information preceded by over twenty years the news acquired by the German missionaries, Krapf, Rebmann and Erhardt, whose famous 'slug' map, showing a large lake shaped like a slug in the centre of Africa, drew so much attention from explorers in the 1850s. It was Emery's hope that if he were replaced as Governor of Mombasa he might follow up this information by penetrating into the interior and perhaps crossing the whole continent. This hope remained unfulfilled and in the light of Reitz's disastrous journey it was perhaps well for Emery that he was unable to carry out his plan.

Meanwhile, the struggle for the retention of the Protectorate was being carried on on a number of fronts. Seyyid Said had made a counter-appeal to Bombay although his claims over Mombasa could not appear very strong even if Mombasa's own claims to Pemba and other areas were equally weak. The Governor of Bombay, Mount-stuart Elphinstone, wrote to the Court of Directors on December 15, 1825, explaining the difficulty in which he found himself. While recognizing the weakness of Seyyid Said's claim to Mombasa he stressed the Sultan's co-operation with the British at all times. On the other hand, if Seyyid Said's claims proved to be as weak as they seemed there might well appear to be a good case for retaining Owen's Protectorate as a check upon the slave-trade. In these circumstances it would seem appropriate to compensate Seyyid Said. Elphinstone's minute was passed on by the Court of Directors to the Secretary of State, Lord Bathurst, but it reached him too late to influence the British Government's action. For it had already been decided to disallow Owen's action on the ground that Mombasa did not appear genuinely to want British protection. Instructions to this effect were accordingly dispatched to the Governor of Mauritius but no indication was given as to the steps by which the Protectorate should be terminated. The Governor, Cole, was none too anxious to carry out his orders, and Owen, who was in Mauritius when the dispatch was received, continued to press his case. Similarly, when

32

the same instructions belatedly reached the Commander-in-Chief at the Cape nine months afterwards, Owen was at the Cape and was just as vocal in his opposition as he had been in Mauritius. The Commander-in-Chief, Commodore Christian, was no more enthusiastic than Cole had been about acting upon his orders. He therefore sheltered behind the excuse that the wording of the dispatch was not very clear. The British Government remained firm and eventually action was taken on the spot by Lieutenant Emery himself. Even as late as July 22, 1826, Emery was still prepared to support the continuance of the Protectorate in spite of the many difficulties which he had to face. He was also afraid that for the British to reject the Protectorate would throw the Mazaria into the arms of the French.

On July 24, however, the situation changed completely. Four days earlier Captain Acland had arrived in Mombasa on board H.M.S. *Helicon* and during the course of his visit affairs reached their climax. At a meeting attended by Acland and Emery the leaders of the Mazaria denied that they had ever ceded their fort to the British and also renounced the authority of the British Government. This turn of events wrought a complete change in Emery's opinions. Concluding that a British Protectorate was now impossible he urged Acland to agree to the withdrawal of the garrison. Acland accepted Emery's advice and immediately set on foot the removal of both personnel and stores. This decision came as a shock to the Mazaria who had hoped, by promises of more friendly behaviour in the future, to retain British support without the onus of British overlordship. But Emery's patience was exhausted and the *Helicon* sailed on July 29, 1826. Owen's Protectorate was at an end.

As soon as he heard this news Seyyid Said demanded the immediate surrender of Fort Jesus. In his greatly weakened circumstances Sultan Salim of Mombasa was prepared to go so far as to recognize Seyyid Said's overlordship but he refused to surrender the fort except to force of arms. Seyyid Said then prepared a fleet for the conquest of Mombasa and the ships set sail with the north-east monsoon in 1827. Arriving off Mombasa on January 4, 1828, Seyyid Said, who was not a great military leader, attempted to achieve his objective by negotiation. When this approach failed he was compelled to resort to arms. The town was bombarded and the Mazrui Sultan agreed to hand over the fort and to allow a garrison

33

of fifty men of Oman to be stationed there. During the next few days further companies of soldiers were infiltrated by stealth into the fort until the garrison numbered over two hundred men. Finding himself now in a dominating position Seyyid Said ordered the Sultan and the remaining Mazaria to evacuate the fort and before quitting the scene of his success Seyyid Said strengthened the garrison still further.

From Mombasa the Omani Sultan sailed on to Zanzibar. The prosperity of the island, together with its attractive climate, cast their spell over him at once and it may well have been on the occasion of this first visit that Seyyid Said determined to transfer his capital from the arid soil of Oman, with its endless disputes, to the more fertile and peaceful setting of Zanzibar. For the time being, however, it was necessary for him to return to Oman.

Events on the east coast soon drew Seyyid Said back again. Nasser bin Suleiman, the Governor of Pemba, who hitherto had been one of Seyyid Said's loyal supporters, paid a visit to Mombasa where he claimed to have been sent on instructions from Oman to replace the Mazrui Governor, Salim. The Mazaria resisted and Nasser took refuge with the Omani garrison in the fort, where he was immediately besieged. The garrison held out for seven months before being compelled to surrender. The Mazaria took command of Fort Jesus and the work of Seyyid Said's first expedition had been completely undone. Once again, therefore, towards the end of 1829 an Omani fleet put to sea to recapture Mombasa. On this occasion Seyyid Said was less successful. Although Salim agreed to make a treaty with him he refused to hand over the fort, and with this compromise Seyyid Said had to rest content. From thence he sailed on to Zanzibar, but a rebellion in Oman summoned him back to his homeland almost immediately. For some time thereafter he was deeply engaged in the affairs of his own country. By 1833, however, he was making preparations for a third campaign against Mombasa. Finding himself seriously limited in manpower he cast around for support and his attention was attracted to Madagascar. The former ruler, Radama, who had entered into a treaty with the Governor of Mauritius to suppress the slave-trade, had died in 1828. He had been succeeded by one of his widows, Ranavolana, a woman of powerful personality and cruel disposition. Ranavolana was as violently opposed to Europeans as her husband had been attracted to them.

34

What appealed to Seyyid Said, however, was neither her personality nor her disposition. It was the large number of well-equipped troops which she had at her disposal. He accordingly sent messages asking for military aid and in return offering himself in marriage. Surprisingly, the Queen replied that, while she could not marry Seyyid Said, he might have as many troops as he wished. Unfortunately for Seyyid Said the troops never materialized. He now found himself committed to an expedition from which his pride would not let him withdraw but for which he lacked the necessary military strength. His attacks upon Mombasa proved abortive and after another brief visit to Zanzibar events in Oman once again called him home.

The next attempt upon Mombasa was made in 1836 and on this occasion Seyyid Said relied upon diplomacy rather than upon military strength. The death of Sultan Salim in 1836 had given him the opportunity for which he was looking. Enlisting the support of some of the disappointed claimants to the sultanate Seyyid Said induced the new Sultan, Rashid, to accept a treaty similar in terms to the earlier agreement of 1828. Under this new arrangement Rashid remained as Governor of Mombasa but the fort was garrisoned by Omani troops. Seyyid Said did not stop here. Only a few months later he contrived by treachery to murder Rashid and his leading supporters. By this step the Mazrui governorship was brought to an end and the Mazaria split into two branches, one ruling in Gazi, a small town to the north of Mombasa, and the other in Takaungu, farther south. From this time onwards Mombasa was directly administered from Zanzibar until a concession was granted by the Sultan of that time to the British East African Association in 1887. In 1840 Seyyid Said took the step which he had contemplated for some years. His headquarters were finally moved to Zanzibar and by this move Seyyid Said inaugurated a new period in the history of East Africa.

CHAPTER TWO

ARAB TRADERS AND
THE TRIBES OF THE INTERIOR

THE Wanyika tribes who provided the immediate background to the coastal struggles of the Mazaria and Oman belonged to a large body of Bantu peoples who inhabited a considerable part of what is now British East Africa. The word Bantu has no racial or physical connotation. It is a purely linguistic description although it is difficult even to define Bantu languages.[1] The Bantu are, however, a basically negro people who have undergone varying degrees of change through many generations as a result of the infusion of Hamitic or Nilotic blood. Their original home was probably in West Africa and they penetrated East Africa from the south and west, encroaching steadily upon the older Hamitic inhabitants. Along the coast their northward advance was swifter until they were checked by the southward pressure of the Hamitic Galla and Somali. As the Bantu then began to penetrate inland into the region of what is now Kenya they came up against a new invasion of Nilo-Hamitic peoples from the north including the Masai, Nandi, Kipsigis, Turkana and Suk who, during the last few centuries, have occupied the grazing lands of the interior. The Nilo-Hamites also spread into northern Uganda, numbering among their tribes the Karamojong, the Iteso and probably the Lango. These people in their turn bordered upon the territories of the Nilotic Acholi and Alur, while another branch of the Nilotic invasion extended as far as the eastern shore of Lake Victoria where the Luo finally made their home in the nineteenth century. South of the Nile and to the west and north-west of Lake Victoria Nilotic and Hamitic influences have also been strong and have succeeded in influencing the organization of Bantu society to a considerable extent. In these areas, however, the in-

[1] C. G. Seligman: *The Races of Africa*. O.U.P., London, 1957, pp. 162 ff.

habitants are still referred to as Bantu because the more recent immigrants have adopted a Bantu form of language.

The types of political or, more correctly, tribal organization to be found in East Africa before the influence of European nations was felt, varied from extreme autocracy and strong central organization to the other extreme of democracy bordering at times almost upon anarchy. The Bantu appear to have had two main variants upon the more democratic type of government. One form consisted of a series of councils with spokesmen acting on behalf of their own local group either as individuals or as members of higher councils. The Kikuyu, Wakamba and Wanyika tribes offered perhaps the best examples of this type of organization. In the area now known as Tanganyika the more typical Bantu pattern would appear to have been that of tribes comprising people who recognized an affinity with each other but who, for the purpose of political organization, united under chiefs or clan heads or even under village headmen each of whom had authority over only a limited number of people. The Wagogo and, until the nineteenth century, the Wahehe, Chagga and Yao were all organized on this basic pattern. Among the more nomadic peoples skill in war often counted for more than wisdom in council. Here, therefore, the age-group system and class system was more pronounced, while in the area to the north-west of Lake Victoria there were hereditary chiefs who exercised unlimited authority.

The economy of all these tribes, agricultural and pastoral alike, was of a subsistence character. The agriculturalists grew foodstuffs, including maize, millet, sweet potatoes, *cassava* and bananas. Some of the pastoral tribes lived entirely upon animal produce while others compelled the agricultural peasantry over whom they ruled to grow some of their food for them. In some areas simple iron working was carried on; by the Banyoro between Lake Albert and Lake Victoria, by the Kikuyu near the foothills of Mount Kenya, by the Wahehe in the plateau country of southern Tanganyika and by the Masai in the highlands of western Kenya. In most of these tribes iron workers were held in great respect. The Masai provided an exception to this rule, however. They, it appears, acquired their knowledge of iron working from the people whom they overran in the course of their southward advance, and they may well have considered that an art acquired from a conquered people was inferior in character.[1] From Lake Albert and Lake Katwe, in the extreme west, salt was collected and there were communities who devoted the greater part of their time to this work. The village of Kibero on Lake Albert has gradually grown to ever higher levels upon the broken remnants of pottery which has been used for the evaporation of the salt water. Villages of fishermen also grew up alongside many of the lakes and some tribes, like the Bavuma on the northern shore of Lake Victoria, acquired considerable prowess in the minor aspects of naval warfare using canoes manned by large numbers of warriors.

These elementary industries gave rise to a limited trade. Samia supplied most of western Kenya with iron hoes; the people of Kamsingiri in South Nyanza sold salt to the people living around Lake Victoria and the Luo of Kenya obtained their sewn canoes from the Sese Islands and Busoga. Within a tribe friends might exchange presents, and tribute would be paid to the chief in the form of foodstuffs or iron implements or weapons. In their turn the chiefs might hand on some of those gifts in return for labour or as presents for their more important subjects. There might, too, be cases where a tribe sent presents to a neighbouring tribe whose friendship was worth cultivating or whose enmity they wished to avert. When the Arabs came in search of ivory and slaves in the nineteenth century the goods they brought with them, beads, copper wire and cloth, were used not so much as items of exchange as in the form of presents to purchase a safe passage or to encourage a chief to permit the traders to stay within his frontiers while they collected the slaves and ivory for which they had come in search. These latter items were frequently given to the traders as presents from the chiefs in whose country they stayed. But there was no suggestion of one item being exchanged for another or of any equivalence in value between the gifts of the chief and the goods of the trader. In general, tribal or even family self-sufficiency was one of the pronounced features of East African society. It undoubtedly restricted the development and spread of new ideas, for it was the product not of maturity but of suspicion and fear. Indeed, inter-tribal contacts were greatest in time of war.

By the time Seyyid Said moved his headquarters to Zanzibar several of the tribes which had dominated the northern sector of East

[1] A. Galloway: 'A Note on the Iron-Smelting Methods of the Elgeyo Masai.' *South African Journal of Science*, Vol. XXXI, November 1934, pp. 500–4.

Africa were already in decline or had reached the limits of their power. The Galla, a handsome, pastoral and nomadic race, who recognized a loose monarchical type of government by hereditary rulers, had made their appearance in history in the sixteenth century when they invaded Ethiopia from the west. Afterwards they had turned southwards, pushing before them the Wanyika of the coastal belt until they had crossed the Tana River. Their destructive effect upon the coastal towns has already been noted, but before the middle of the nineteenth century their advance had been halted and even turned back by the spears of the Masai warriors. Sandwiched between the Masai to the south and the ruthless Somali to the northeast their power began steadily to decline.

The Masai were never a numerous people, yet their influence swept over almost the whole of Kenya and penetrated to the very heart of Tanganyika. Their name became a byword for ferocity, and travellers, entering the land with trepidation, tended to ascribe to them a more widespread authority than their nomadic existence justified. In the early years of the nineteenth century they were still pressing southward and to the east. From time to time their raiding parties reached the coast near Mombasa or, swinging northwards to the Tana River, came into conflict with the Galla. In the south their advance was finally halted about 1830 by the Wahehe. Drawing back from the arid highway which ran through the country of the Wagogo the Masai then established their outposts in the hills to the north. From this secure refuge they launched cattle raids across the no-man's-land which they had created between themselves and the Wahehe. They never again advanced farther southward, but they left their imprint on the Wagogo who adopted the red earth covering of their bodies and the hair style of the Masai without ever being able to assume the careless confidence and insolent grace of their neighbours. Far to the north the Masai were soon to encounter other difficulties. About the middle of the nineteenth century the Turkana drove them from the country to the west of Lake Rudolf leaving them to take refuge father south. Again, to the west, the Nandi now inhabiting the escarpment overlooking Lake Victoria had adopted Masai customs while proving wholly impervious to Masai raids.

These setbacks did not mean that the Masai had lost any of the vigour which had made them the scourge of the country and the terror of the Bantu peoples who inhabited parts of it. It merely made it clear that their limited numbers could not range indefinitely over a vast territory without dissipating their strength. But the whole of the Masai social system was geared for war and conquest. Their age-grade system, which divided the tribe into youths, warriors and elders, gave pride of place to the warrior class. Although the elders were respected and gave their advice about raids, to the warriors was given the glory, and it was they who dominated the situation. For this reason the Masai were not builders of nations and empires. They raided, they took cattle, they captured women, and then they returned to their huts to enjoy the fruits of their victory. The focus of their political life was war, but the unifying influence of the leader in battle was of only a temporary character. The one permanently unifying feature in the tribe was the office of Laibon, or medicine man, which was occupied by a person who was held in great respect for his magical powers but who was in no sense the ruler of the tribe.

The check received by the Masai in their southward advance resulted in one section of the tribe, the Baraguya, abandoning their pastoral pursuits and taking up agriculture. In time they threw in their lot with the Wataveta who inhabited the south-eastern slopes of Mount Kilimanjaro. This was a striking change in the members of a tribe who firmly believed that all cattle were created especially for their use. Another important group turned again northward and struggled through Kikuyuland to the fine pastures of Laikipia, while yet another section crossed the rift valley to the superb grazing grounds of the Uasin Gishu plateau. This latter group found room enough for their herds but their warlike spirit was undimmed. Probably in the late 1850s they launched an attack upon the Masai of the plains around Naivasha. Although taken by surprise the Naivasha Masai responded with equal vigour and several pitched battles were fought, involving fierce hand-to-hand encounters, before the Naivasha Masai were driven back. By this time other Masai from the region of Kilimanjaro had hurried to the sound of conflict and gave their aid to their defeated fellow-tribesmen. With the arrival of these reinforcements the tide of battle turned against the Masai of the Uasin Gishu. The majority of them were killed and their cattle were captured. Famine added to their death roll and many of the survivors were compelled to become agriculturalists in the country south of Lake Baringo. Only a handful of them remained on the Laikipia, while the whole of the Uasin Gishu was swept clear of Masai. Of those who fled to the west only a handful escaped death at the hands of the Nandi to find refuge in the district of Kavirondo beside Lake Victoria.

Towards the end of the nineteenth century, on the death of a famous Laibon, Mbatian, the tribe split into two as a result of a disputed succession between the former Laibon's two sons, Lenana and Sendeyo. Although Lenana had been recognized by his father as the lawful successor, Sendeyo refused to acknowledge his authority and civil war broke out. After a period of unremitting strife Sendeyo took his followers southwards and occupied territory which is now in Tanganyika. Lenana, with his supporters, remained in southern Kenya. Yet even these cruel interecine struggles did not dim the Masai's lust for war. They continued to bar the way to large caravans anxious to pass through their grazing grounds in search of ivory, but they do not seem to have objected to the passage of smaller caravans which could not threaten their arrogant domination of the land between Mount Kenya and Kilimanjaro.

Still farther west, between the great lakes Victoria and Albert, another power was in decline. The Kingdom of Bunyoro-Kitara, the largest of the kingdoms of the lake area, had begun to outgrow its strength even by the end of the eighteenth century. The emergence upon the East African scene of the kingdoms of the great lakes was the result of a process of migration which had begun some centuries earlier. The origins of the earliest invaders are not easy to discover. Evidence of the southward extension of the knowledge of iron-working suggests a possible link with the ancient civilization of Meroe which flourished in the Sudan, about 100 miles to the north of the present site of Khartoum, between the seventh century B.C. and the fourth century A.D.[1] On the downfall of Meroe the royal family moved westward through Kordofan and Darfur, taking with them the knowledge of iron working which had helped to make Meroe famous. This knowledge appears to have spread towards Lake Chad before doubling back in a south-easterly direction to the southern Sudan. It seems possible, therefore, that remnants of this, civilization were among the earliest immigrants into the Bantu

[1] This subject was discussed in a broadcast by Fr. Gervase Mathew, Dr Roland Oliver and Mr. A. Wright in November, 1953.

country of the great lakes. Perhaps some five or six hundred years ago legend indicates a more positive immigration of Bahima from the north. Whether or not these invaders are to be identified with those who brought the iron-working culture into Uganda is not clear. Various indications suggest, however, that the Bahima may have originated somewhere in the Sudan between the Nile and the Red Sea and that they entered Uganda from the north-east, through western Ethiopia. One legend states that some of them at least may have entered south-western Uganda from the Congo area passing between Lake Kivu and Lakes Albert and Edward. It is possible, therefore, that the Bahima formed a second wave of the same immigration which brought the iron culture to East Africa. It is equally possible, however, that they were an entirely different group of people.

Preliminary archaeological investigations have indicated that the Bahima, although a pastoral people, built towns of some considerable size. In Ankole, in western Uganda, a number of sites have been located which show signs of occupation and which are associated in legend with the capitals of the Bahima or, in one case, of a Muchwezi ruler. On some of the sites there is little to be seen on the surface except fragments of pottery which may be either recent or ancient in origin. In one case there are earthworks some four or five feet high, built in a *U* shape and enclosing as much as three quarters of an acre of land. Beyond, the levelling and terracing of the ground suggest a settlement covering an area a quarter of a mile square and surrounded by a very low earthwork.[1] These settlements were ruled over by chiefs, or kings, and the Bahima appear to have gained their first main foothold in Uganda in the territory immediately to the east of Lake Albert. Subsequently they moved farther south into the districts now known as Ankole, Bukoba and Biharamula. The Bantu agriculturalists who already occupied the land were treated as a subordinate race whose duty it was to produce food for their overlords. There appears to have been relatively little inter-mixture of the two peoples, since the Bantu accepted their subservient role.

It is impossible to refer to the Bahima without mentioning one of the perennial problems of East African prehistory, that of the

[1] These investigations were made by Professor Roland Oliver of the London School of Oriental and African Studies and Dr. Merrick Posnansky, formerly Curator of the Uganda Museum.

Bachwezi. Who the Bachwezi were it is as yet impossible to say. One writer has suggested that the name may have been a poetic reference to the early days of Bahima splendour. Others have assumed that the Bachwezi were the ruling caste of the Bahima, while it is possible that they were a final flowering of the Bahima before the days of their disintegration set in, since great feats are attributed to them in legend. The name lingers on in Tanganyika to the present day without any ethnic significance. It refers to a not very secret society among the Baha, in the extreme west of Tanganyika, which appears to have something of the functions of free-masonry in Europe.

Probably contemporary with the later stages of the Hima invasion, that is, some four or five hundred years ago, a new group of immigrants began to pour into northern Uganda. These were the Luo who originated in the Bahr el Ghazal region of the southern Sudan. Because of overcrowding in that area the Luo began to trek in search of new territory. Their southern neighbours, the Azande, were unfriendly, so that their first move was in a northerly direction, passing between the Dinka and the Nuer. They then swung eastward and southward to enter Uganda. Legend suggests that there were not infrequent quarrels between various sections of the migrating horde, so that from time to time groups split off and took different directions. One group, the Alur, crossed the Nile north of Lake Albert and settled in the region beyond. Possibly the main body established itself in what is now Acholi while other groups continued southward to cross the Victoria Nile whence some returned again to swing eastward into the area about Lake Kyoga. Ultimately this latter group was pushed southward by new invaders until they eventually took up their home in the eastern shore of Lake Victoria in what is now the Nyanza Province of Kenya.[1]

It is not unlikely that in the course of their advance the Luo mingled with some of the later Hima emigrants from whom they may have absorbed various ritual features such as that of divine kingship. But they were an aggressive people, and their militant outlook brought them into conflict with the more peaceful Bahima who had occupied the country south of the Nile. Crossing the river the Luo advanced into what is now Bunyoro, driving the Hima

[1] Rev. Fr. J. P. Crazzolara: *The Lwoo: Pt. I, Lwoo Migrations.* Museum Combonianum, Verona, 1950. This is the most authoritative study of the Luo migrations.

southward before them and annexing the land by right of conquest, and establishing the ruling Babitu dynasty of Bunyoro-Kitara. Nor did their restless energy permit them to stay their onward march even now. The Babito pushed the frontiers of their new kingdom ever farther to the east, to the south and to the west. Such is the pride of some present-day Banyoro in these achievements that they claim their kingdom at one time bordered on the lands of the Kikuyu in Kenya and extended far into the Congo. The Bakama,[1] or kings, of Bunyoro-Kitara exercised supreme authority, their position as secular rulers being strengthened by their priestly participation in the ritual of their people's religion.

One offshoot of this lively and aggressive dynasty established the new kingdom of Buganda which replaced an earlier Bantu state in the area immediately to the north of Lake Victoria. For a time Buganda was infinitely weaker than the larger kingdom of Bunyoro-Kitara to the west. Eventually, however, the relative strengths of the two kingdoms began to change. Harassed by war in numerous parts of its far-flung borders. Kitara wasted its resources and energies in trying to maintain a large empire. Buganda, on the other hand, was a small, compact and intensely centralized state which became steadily more aggressive. In earlier times the Bantu inhabitants of Buganda had been organized on a clan basis. All the land had been owned by the clans and the clan heads had been the most important figures in society. Without destroying this older form of organization the Nilotic invaders contrived to superimpose a new hierarchy centring upon the Kabaka, or king. All power and all wealth rested in his hands, to be distributed to lesser chiefs and to others who did him service. Even the distribution of the land became his prerogative. This did not involve a change in the ownership of the land since the Kabaka simply controlled it in the interests of his tribe. When he allocated a district to one of his chiefs it was not a gift but it carried with it the right to collect tribute and taxes from the occupants of the area for as long as the grantee served in his capacity of chief. There might be a sharp struggle over the succession to the throne, but once in office a strong Kabaka was in an almost impregnable position. His whim, not the tradition of the people, was law. His more important chiefs spent much of their time sitting at his feet in sycophantic admiration of his every action.

[1] Singular, Mukama; plural, Bakama.

Meanwhile, the tightly-woven bureaucracy of lesser chiefs ensured that all the people recognized the unassailable authority of their ruler.

In the late eighteenth and early nineteenth centuries a succession of very able Kabakas exalted their kingly office even more highly than before. Simultaneously a series of pacific Bakama destroyed the edge of the military weapon which had forged the kingdom of Kitara. A number of smaller outposts of the Kitara empire sought to throw off the yoke of their overlord by appealing for aid to the rising power of Buganda. In doing so they surrendered a remote and increasingly ineffectual control for a determined and efficient overlordship. The expansion of Buganda began in the 1780s and continued for more than a century. Kitara, meanwhile, suffered a severe blow in the early nineteenth century when the eldest son of Mukama Kyebambe III, tiring of his father's longevity, carved out for himself the independent kingdom of Toro to the east of the Ruwenzori Mountains. The Kitara empire crumbled steadily until the 1870s when there was a brief and bloody resurgence led by the warlike Mukama Kabarega. What might have been the outcome of a conflict between Kitara and Buganda at that stage it is impossible to assess. By that time, however, other forces had entered into Uganda, and while Buganda allied herself with the power of Britain, Kabarega wasted the final resources of his empire by opposing the British advance. Meanwhile, the Bahima chieftains also were beginning to acknowledge the pre-eminence of Buganda without recognizing any formal subordination to the Kabaka. Gifts were exchanged between successive Kabakas and the Bahima chiefs, while the latter trod warily lest they should offend their more powerful neighbour.

In spite of the high degree of organization achieved in Buganda and, in a different form, in Kitara, there are few material relics of these states which can be accurately dated beyond four or five generations back. Many of the burial sites of the Abakama and Kabakas are still preserved. They consist of ceremonial huts of mud and wattle, with thatched roofs, which shelter the remains of the rulers. In the case of the Bakama of Bunyoro-Kitara a shaft was dug, up to thirty feet in depth, and the remains of the dead ruler were left in a chamber leading off the shaft. The shaft itself was then covered with a bull's hide and in some cases the blade of a spear was left projecting above the hide. The spear was the royal standard and had stood on the roof of the Mukama's hut during his lifetime. The Baganda did not bury their Kabakas but, instead, left them covered with bark-cloth in the funeral hut. The huts themselves are in most cases extremely humble in appearance and are only rebuilt when they become very dilapidated. The chief exception is the fine structure, built along traditional lines, which houses the bodies of the most recent Kabakas, Mutesa I, Mwanga and Daudi Chwa. The interior furnishings of the huts consist of the weapons, drums, wooden stools, bead ornaments, eating and drinking utensils and other personal possessions of the dead ruler. They are all simple and crude in character and suggest no development of an aesthetic sense.[1]

Kiziba, in the present Bukoba District, was the southernmost outpost of the Babito dynasty, but the Hima kingdoms, of which Karagwe in the present district of Biharamulo was probably the greatest, extended still farther southwards beyond Lake Victoria. The Bantu inhabitants of Sukumaland, which is situated between the town of Shinyanga and Lake Victoria, appear to have invited the Bahima to take up residence in their country. The Bahima, no doubt, held out a double attraction as hunters of considerable prowess who could supply the meat which the Bantu people wanted for food and as new-comers to the district who, because they had no associations with the existing clans, would be valuable as impartial judges. Although accustomed to relatively large and powerful chiefdoms the Bahima did not introduce a similar structure into Sukumaland. Instead, they contented themselves with establishing a number of smaller chieftainships which were frequently at war with each other but which appear to have suffered little harm in the process. In time, too, all traces of Hima custom were absorbed and little now remains except the legends of the origins of the various chieftainships, each of which endeavours to attribute to its own chiefdom a more important history than that of its neighbours.

The term Sukuma itself has no ethnic or clan significance. In the language of the people of that area it simply means 'north'. The Wasukuma, together with their southern neighbours, the Wanyam, wezi, form part of a common language group and there is virtually no distinction between the two peoples. The Wasukuma, however-

[1] K. Ingham: 'The Amagasani of the Abakama of Bunyoro.' *Uganda Journal*, Vol. 17, 1953.

perform exceptionally elaborate rites in connection with the ancestor worship common to many of the Bantu tribes. Because of their relatively peaceful history they have tended to live in scattered settlements suited to the agricultural pursuits of a people among whom each peasant prefers to have his fields close to his own hut. In the south-east, however, the threat of the Masai made it necessary for the population to live in villages.[1]

To the south of the Wasukuma lived the Wanyamwezi, divided like their northern neighbours into many units of population. Indeed, it is difficult to know whether they can rightly be described as a single tribe or even if they had a common origin. The Wanyamwezi themselves maintain that their name, which means the 'people of the moon', was given to them by coastal people to imply, simply, that they were the inhabitants of the country to the west where the new moon is first seen. The use of the term 'Unyamuezi' by the sixteenth-century writer P. Pigafetta, who referred to the discovery of gold in the interior, probably had the same vague meaning and was, no doubt, picked up from the coastal peoples without having any reference to a clearly defined area. The Wanyamwezi have a variety of traditions which suggest that they originally lived to the north-west or west of their present habitation, but there appears to be no ground for assuming that their name is associated with the Mountains of the Moon. Indeed, the Wanyamwezi give themselves a variety of names, which is not surprising since they are divided into more than a hundred distinct groups consisting of between 2,000 and 100,000 people.[2] Their main importance in history, however, lies not so much in their origins or organization as in the adventurous spirit which caused many of them to travel freely over vast distances and which frequently took them to the coast. Although primarily an agricultural people who kept some cattle they yet provided a large proportion of the porters who manned the caravans of East Africa. It was they, too, who, straddling the main slave route to Lake Tanganyika, supplied a large number of the slaves who found their way to the coast in the latter part of the nineteenth century.

Turning once again to the Nilotic immigrants in the north, legend maintains that when they started their journey they were united

[1] H. Cory: 'The People of the Lake Victoria Region.' *Tanganyika Notes and Records*, No. 33, July 1952, pp. 22–26.

[2] Rev. Fr. P. Bosch: *Les Banyamwezi*. Aschendorffsche Verlagsbuch-handlung, Munster, I.W., 1930, pp. 3–9.

under one chief. The migrations, however, tended to stress the importance of the clans which were, in fact, simply extended family units. The head of the family was the *Rwot* whose office was hereditary although his authority was not great. When the main body of the Luo settled in Acholi the *Rwodi*[1] were regarded as the 'owners' of the land on behalf of their clans. So light was the pressure of population, however, that individuals virtually owned the land they cultivated.[2] In spite of the loosely knit character of this new type of social and political organization, the inhabitants of Acholi were frequently brought together by the threat of attack from their Madi neighbours beyond the Nile. This intermittent struggle between the Acholi and the Madi lasted for some considerable time and the Acholi were often compelled to appeal for aid to their eastern neighbours, the Lango. Even these combined efforts generally met with failure, however, and eventually the Acholi made peace with the Madi.

The inhabitants of southern Acholi had not been so seriously affected by these wars but, probably during the eighteenth century, they began to feel pressure from the advancing Lango. Harassed, too, by drought and famine these Luo of southern Acholi migrated again to the east. Passing through the country to the south of Mount Elgon they eventually made their homes, towards the middle of the nineteenth century, in the region to the north-east of Lake Victoria which some of their forebears had reached more than two hundred years earlier. Their tribal organization closely resembled that of the Acholi, the clans being the most important units. They retained their name, Luo, and continued to take pride in the story of their migrations.

The origins of the Lango are still obscure. One Luo tradition refers to them as Luo,[3] but if this is so they must have undergone a greater admixture of Hamitic blood than did any of the other groups of Luo. Possibly they were of Nilo-Hamitic origin and adopted the Acholi language for convenience.[4] They were primarily a pastoral people until disease destroyed their herds in the late nineteenth

[1] Singular, *Rwot*; plural, *Rwodi*.

[2] R. M. Bere: 'Land and Chieftainship among the Acholi.' *Uganda Journal*, Vol. 19, 1955, pp. 49–53.

[3] A. W. Mayor: *A History of the Luo People*. Unpublished MS.

[4] Rev. Fr. A. Tarantino: 'The Origins of the Lango.' *Uganda Journal*, Vol. 10, 1946.

century and forced them to take up agriculture. Their first appearance on the historical scene occurred about the end of the seventeenth century, when the forward elements of the tribe reached the Tochi River near its junction with the Nile.[1] Simultaneously, another migration was taking place to the east of the Lango. This was the south-westerly advance of the Iteso, another Nilo-Hamitic tribe, who, like the Lango, first set foot in the area which is now their home in the seventeenth century. Both tribes appear to have halted for a period before finally occupying their new territory in the late eighteenth or early nineteenth centuries.[2] The tribal unity of both the Lango and the Iteso dates only from the period of British rule in the twentieth century. The Iteso, however, had a well developed clan system similar to that of the Acholi, but the Lango were loosely organized, their political units rarely extending beyond the village and sometimes being limited to a single family.

A number of other tribes which won prominence either by their spirited opposition or willing response to the first Europeans to enter East Africa were also beginning to make their presence felt for the first time in the early nineteenth century. The Wahehe, who checked the southward advance of the Masai, proved to be an almost equally serious obstacle to European expansion. Yet it was only in the latter half of the nineteenth century that they emerged as a truly united tribe to dominate the hill country about the present site of Iringa. The process of unification was the work of two chiefs Myugumba, and his son, Mkwawa, who welded the Wahehe into a political unit by the strength of their own personalities and through victory in war against the surrounding tribes. Each of these two men combined within himself the functions of lawmaker, guardian of the law and judge. They were the leaders in battle and the repository of the wealth of the tribe. They distributed gifts and offered prayers for rain, performing the latter function because they alone were descended from the ancestral spirits of former chiefs to which the tribe appealed in times of emergency. Upon the powers exercised by these two men the unity of the tribe depended. Because they were an agricultural people growing maize and millet for food the Wahehe did not, like the Masai, range widely over the countryside. Instead

[1] Rev. Fr. A. Tarantino: 'Notes on the Lango.' *Uganda Journal*, Vol. 13, 1949, pp. 146–8.

[2] J. C. D. Lawrance: 'A History of Teso to 1937.' *Uganda Journal*, Vol. 19, 1955, pp. 14–20.

they built up a compact and powerful state, and although they established no lasting empire over the surrounding tribes their regular victories kept alive their aggressive spirit. Before their unification they had withstood the Masai, and in their new-found strength they were to prove worthy opponents even of the modern weapons of the Germans.[1]

The most stubborn opposition encountered by the Wahehe in their rise to power came from their southern neighbours, the Ngoni. As neither tribe was able to conquer the other they agreed to recognize a mutual boundary and to delcare an armistice until their sons should be of an age to resume the struggle. The Ngoni were themselves recent arrivals in the neighbourhood of Songea and came originally from Zululand whence they had fled in the 1820s to escape incorporation in Chaka's empire. In the course of their northern migration their numbers had been greatly increased by the addition of numerous captives. When they reached the southern tip of Lake Tanganyika, about 1845 their leader, Zongendaba, died. The original group then split into several smaller units which scattered to north and south. Some even reached the southern shore of Lake Victoria where they formed a small colony. Others settled in Northern Rhodesia, while one group skirted the northern end of Lake Nyasa to arrive at Upangwa in southern Tanganyika. Here they encountered another group, the Maseko, who had travelled independently of the main body and had reached Upangwa by following the eastern shore of Lake Nyasa. Relations between the two groups fluctuated uncertainly. For a time it appeared that the Maseko Ngoni would dominate the new arrivals, but in the late 1850s they were themselves driven southward and the victors settled in the region of Songea in the early 1860s. There the descendants of two leaders split into separate groups, each of which began independently to raid the surrounding countryside in the hope of extending its authority. It was one of these groups which in 1878 and again in 1881 became involved in war with the Wahehe and found its northward expansion sharply checked. It was able to turn to the east, however, while the other group was extending its power over the peoples to the south and west. Soon the Ngoni allied themselves with the slave-traders from the coast and as a

[1] G. G. Brown and A. McD. B. Hutt: *Anthropology in Action.* O.U.P. London, 1935, pp. 23–37.

Helen M. Dunlap

result of that alliance they reached the peak of their strength about 1890. So active were they in pursuit of slaves that the surrounding country was completely depopulated. Some of their victims, however, instead of being sold as slaves, were absorbed into the tribe, and although they were condemned to a state of serfdom they were looked upon as Ngoni and in time were permitted to set up their own homesteads. Eventually they came to outnumber the true Ngoni and adopted their customs and outlook to such good effect that they became more aggressive than the Ngoni themselves.[1]

Even more actively involved in the slave-trade were the eastern neighbours of the Ngoni, the Yao. They, too, were recent immigrants into the country north of the Rovuma. The first group crossed the river from the south in the 1850s. At that time they had probably been in contact with the Arabs at the coast for some two hundred years and by the end of the eighteenth century they were competing with the Arabs for the inland trade. They were a soldierly people and although they suffered heavily at the hands of Ngoni raiding parties they were never subject to their western neighbours. Like the Wanyamwezi, the Yao were mainly agriculturalists but enjoyed travelling, particularly to the coast, where Arab trade goods, guns, gunpowder, swords, beads, coloured cloth and earthenware proved a great attraction.[2]

Another Bantu people who reached their peak in the nineteenth century were the Sambaa who inhabited the Usambara mountains some fifty miles inland from Tanga.[3] Legend records that at some time in the eighteenth century the Sambaa accepted as their ruler a man named Bega and he it was who began to build up the kingdom with its southern border on the River Pangani. He was succeeded by his son and grandson who extended their authority steadily northwards, but it was the next ruler, Kimweri, who led the kingdom to its highest point of achievement. By a series of conquests Kimweri brought the eastern plain between Usambara and the coast under his control and subjugated the land north-westward towards Mount Kilimanjaro. His ambition to extend his domain southward, beyond the Pangani, was frustrated by the stern resistance of the Wazigua,

[1] P. H. Gulliver: 'A History of the Songea Ngoni. *Tanganyika Notes and Records*, No. 40, September 1955, pp. 1–10.

[2] M. Tew: *Peoples of the Lake Nyasa Region*. O.U.P., London, 1950, pp. 2–8.

[3] Sir Reginald Coupland: *East Africa and its Invaders*. Clarendon Press, Oxford, 1956, pp. 345–52.

a tribe which was among the first to obtain firearms from the merchants at the coast. In spite of this setback Kimweri ruled over a sizeable kingdom and his authority was unchallenged from within and scarcely threatened from without. The kingdom itself was divided into districts administered by governors, many of whom were Kimweri's own sons. His subjects, who numbered half a million, paid tribute on his demand, never daring to amass wealth for themselves lest it should attract the envy of the king. His power over them was no less complete than was that of the Kabakas of Buganda over their subjects, but discretion induced him to handle his eastern subjects more leniently than the rest lest they should seek the aid of the Sultan of Zanzibar. At Kimweri's death, which occurred in about 1860, there was a period of dissension within the tribe, but after a short time one of his sons established himself as ruler. Yet, in spite of the strength of the Sambaa in the mid-nineteenth century and their readiness to accept Christian missionaries, they played a relatively unimportant part in the great changes which swept the country towards the end of the century.

The Chagga, near neighbours of the Sambaa who inhabited the slopes of Mount Kilimanjaro, were far less united than the Sambaa in the nineteenth century, yet emerged in the twentieth to take a leading role in the modern development of Tanganyika. They were a people compounded of elements from many neighbouring tribes, particularly the Wateita and Wakamba, and they probably began to make their home on the slopes of Kilimanjaro in the late sixteenth or early seventeenth centuries. The advance of the Masai may also have encouraged them to rely upon the mountain for security. In earlier times the tribe had consisted of some four hundred clans spread among many tiny chiefdoms. This number was reduced to twenty-two as the result of constant warfare. Gradually, too, there emerged a number of ruling clans from which chiefs were chosen by all the members of a chiefdom. The chiefs then ruled with the advice of a council consisting of both elders and young men.[1] The rivalry between the chiefdoms was emphasized by the existence of three widely differing dialects which continued to complicate communication between different sections of the tribe in spite of close ties of blood and frequent inter-marriage between members of

[1] T. L. M. Marealle: 'The Wachagga of Kilimanjaro.' *Tanganyika Notes and Records*, No. 32, January 1952, pp. 57–60.

different chiefdoms. Such marriages were usually the result of captives being taken in war, but no one chiefdom was ever able to
establish paramountcy over the rest. Indeed, it was only the arrival
of the Germans in the late nineteenth century which drew the Chagga
together in the face of a common danger. Even then, after a brief
resistance they became extremely co-operative with the invaders and
it was only in the twentieth century that they rose to prominence.[1]

The Kikuyu of central Kenya had an even longer record of un-
distinguished development before they came to prominence in the
twentieth century. They emerged as a distinct people in the vicinity
of Fort Hall some centuries ago, although legend traces their origin
to a district much farther east. From being hunters they gradually
became agriculturalists. They cut down the forests which extended
southward towards the Athi plain, westward to the dark brows of
the Aberdares and northward to the slopes of snow-capped Mount
Kenya. In spite of the various forces which are said to hold primitive
populations in a state of numerical equilibrium the Kikuyu population expanded steadily. The growing demand for land could not be
met to the south-east, where the country was open, because of the
resistance of the Wakamba. These latter, although similar in origin
to the Kikuyu, guarded their land with determination against any
encroachment from their neighbours. A strip of land running from
north to south on the eastern side of Fort Hall was maintained as a
no-man's-land or battleground for the two tribes, neither being
able to establish a permanent claim upon it. For some time it remained possible for the Kikuyu to spread northwards, beyond
Nyeri. Then further advance was checked by the fear of the Masai
who roamed that area. The families who migrated westward,
gradually creeping up the slopes of the Aberdares, were also halted
in time by the cold rawness of the climate and the steep mountain
slopes which discouraged further agricultural efforts. It was to the
south, therefore, that the Kikuyu made what was to prove their most
significant advance when, early in the nineteenth century, they
crossed the Chania River into Kiambu. This southward expansion
continued for the rest of the century although as the years went by
it became more difficult for the later arrivals to find gaps in which
to settle. For here, too, the Masai provided an obstacle to expansion

[1] W. Andrew (now Wilbert A. Klerruu): *The Machinery of Chagga Local
Government*. Unpublished MS.

although it is true that the drier plains to the south offered comparatively little attraction to a primarily agricultural people. On those plains the Masai warriors were invincible. To protect themselves the Kikuyu left a belt of forest along the southern edge of Kiambu which separated them from their foes. Amid the trees and undergrowth they laid their traps or, armed with poisoned arrows, waited in ambush for Masai raiders. These precautions did not guarantee complete immunity, but a measure of safety was obtained. It was clear, therefore, that unless some new factor was discovered the Kikuyu had reached the furthest possible limit of territorial expansion by the end of the nineteenth century. A serious epidemic of smallpox brought havoc in the early 1890s and for a time reduced the pressure upon the land. This was only a temporary relief and the question of overcrowding inevitably recurred some years later.

This constant movement in search of new land resulted not so much in the emergence of a variety of new forms of political and social organization as in a reversion to earlier stages of the same basic form in the more recently occupied regions. The Kikuyu had no strong central organization. Even their local associations were mainly the result of a family's need for some apparatus to regulate claims upon land or of the problems arising from the juxtaposition of different families in an agricultural society. Land which had been newly cleared and occupied was, in a sense, the property of the occupier. In fact, he automatically regarded himself as holding it in trust for his descendants. When the first owner died another trustee would then be appointed to act as guardian of the land on behalf of the family. The members of the family could use the land freely to satisfy their needs. In time the land available for any one family or for a clan, which was a family in its widest form, might become inadequate and further expansion in the same region might be impossible. A sub-clan would then move away to establish itself in a virgin area and the process of land occupation would begin over again. But the clan links would still remain. The head of the clan would still act as judge in matters of dispute affecting the rights to clan land even in widely scattered areas. This arrangement was still further complicated by the practice of loaning land to individuals who possessed no claim to it except their need for soil from which to obtain their subsistence. In such cases payment might or might not be asked for. In either event the ownership of the land was never transferred and the clan could redeem it at any time, no matter how great the lapse of years.

While clan and sub-clan leaders continued to exercise authority in family matters an alternative form of organization was necessary, particularly for purposes of defence and to govern relations between different clans living in close contact with each other. The terrain determined the nature of this additional form of organization. Kikuyuland consists of a series of ridges divided by valleys and streams which run in a south-easterly direction. On topographical grounds each ridge became a natural unit of defence and each ridge consequently developed a council representing the clans or sub-clans which occupied it. These councils were essentially democratic and acted only on the joint advice of the members. The latter regarded themselves not as the rulers of the sub-clans they represented but simply as the spokesmen. In times of emergency a leader might come to the fore who later, in more peaceful circumstances, might continue to wield considerable authority in council. But that authority was simply due to the recognition of his personal ability and was in no case transferable to his son or heir.

In Kiambu, the most recently cocupied area, neither the system of land tenure nor the form of political organization had reached this advanced state by the end of the nineteenth century. In many cases the land was in the possession of its original occupier, while no complicated political organization had as yet emerged. Furthermore, the Kiambu area suffered particularly heavily from the small-pox epidemic, which retarded development still further. It was, then, the least stable section of Kikuyu society with which the first Europeans made contact, a factor which undoubtedly contributed to the difficulties in the way of establishing a satisfactory relationship between the two peoples.

Two unifying forces existed among the Kikuyu to counteract the many divisions which circumstances had forced upon them. The first of these was the age-set system. Boys and girls belonging to similar age-sets, even though widely separated geographically, still regarded themselves as possessing some special relationship or affinity with each other. This feeling imposed upon them a responsibility for showing friendship and offering assistance to each other when they met. More important even than the age-set, perhaps, was the unifying force of religion. Like many other Bantu tribes the

Kikuyu recognized one god, the Creator. They did not use the more common Bantu name of *Mulungu*, but adopted the Masai name of *Ngai*. *Ngai* was thought by the Kikuyu to inhabit Mount Kenya which for that reason had attributed to it a number of religious or holy characteristics. Faced, then, by the powerful new forces of the twentieth century the Kikuyu, although lacking a strong central administrative organization, nevertheless acted with a degree of unity which enabled them to exercise the greatest influence upon events.

Although the tribes of East Africa with their low standards of material civilization were largely self-contained, east coast influences began to penetrate into the interior at least by the closing years of the eighteenth century. The slave-trade in the extreme south-east, with its outlet in Kilwa, provided a lively attraction for the coastal Arabs. They in their turn produced the goods with which they hoped to encourage the tribesmen to deliver up their slaves, and as a result the south-eastern region became increasingly receptive to Arab influences. Yet, important though Kilwa undoubtedly became as the chief market for slaves in the late eighteenth century, Arab caravans can only have begun to penetrate into the interior with any degree of frequency in the second quarter of the nineteenth century. *Banyans* who had lived in Zanzibar for many years told Colonel Rigby, Political Agent and Consul there from 1858 to 1861, that when they first came to the coast the whole country behind Kilwa was densely populated. In Rigby's time it was necessary to travel into the interior for eighteen days before coming upon a village. This desolation of the immediate hinterland was confirmed by the German explorers, Roscher and von der Decken, and it was clear that the depopulation was due to the activities of the slavers who were gradually pushing further inland. By the late 1850s the slave-trade had reached the western shore of Lake Nyasa and Arabs were building dhows on the lake to transport the slaves across. David Livingstone also noted that districts in the vicinity of the lake, which in 1859 were occupied by flourishing agricultural communities, were found some two or three years later to contain not a single human being for distances of as much as a hundred miles. Rigby himself, while registering emancipated slaves, found that the tribes nearer the coast which had supplied most of the slaves in the past were no longer represented in his lists, while others in the interior, quite unknown in Zanzibar only a short time previously, now provided the vast majority. Natives of Kilwa also confirmed that it was only in the late 1840s and 1850s that Arabs, accompanied by large numbers of followers, had gone into the interior to hunt systematically for slaves.[1]

Farther north another route into the interior appears to have been developed at a rather earlier stage and in this case Africans rather than Arabs were the pioneers. Something has already been said of the Wanyamwezi and of their willingness to travel widely over the country. By the mid 1770s small quantities of ivory were finding their way to the coast opposite Zanzibar, and about the same time the Kabaka of Buganda is reported by Sir Apolo Kagwa to have obtained cups and plates which must have reached his kingdom from the coast.[2] A later Kabaka, Semakokiro, who ruled in the closing years of the eighteenth and early part of the nineteenth centuries, maintained a steady if not entirely regular trade, obtaining cloth, copper bracelets and cowrie shells in return for presents of ivory. This trade was carried on through the kingdom of Karagwe and it seems probable that it was the Wanyamwezi who were responsible for bringing the coastal goods into the interior. By the end of the first quarter of the nineteenth century large caravans consisting of hundreds of porters were making their way at intervals to the coast with ivory to satisfy the demands of the Arabs. These caravans appear to have met with very little opposition from the tribes through which they passed. Yet such large numbers of porters demanding food and water must have placed a very heavy strain upon the limited resources of the peoples along the caravan route. The demands for tribute, about which there were so many complaints in later years, can be readily sympathized with when one recognizes the threat which such large bodies of men in transit would create not only to the security but also to the means of livelihood of the villages through which they passed.

The first non-Africans to penetrate as far as Unyamwezi appear to have been two Khojas from Surat, in India, in 1825. Before that time Arabs had reached the fringes of Unyamwezi but had never advanced beyond. The Busaidi Governor of Zanzibar was anxious, therefore, to support this new venture and he it was who equipped

[1] Mrs. C. E. B. Russell, ed.: *General Rigby, Zanzibar and the Slave Trade.* Allen and Unwin, London, 1935, pp. 128–9.

[2] Sir Apolo Kagwa: *Ekitabo Kya Basekabaka.* Sheldon Press, London, 1927, p. 88.

the expedition of the two Khoja brothers, Sayyam and Musa Muzuri. The venture was most successful in that a large quantity of ivory was collected. Sayyam, however, died while returning to the coast and Musa arrived alone. In the years which followed Musa led a number of caravans into the interior and became one of the most successful pioneer traders in the region south of Lake Victoria.

These early pioneer efforts received an important stimulus from the Sultan, Seyyid Said. When Seyyid Said transferred his headquarters to Zanzibar in 1840 he was attracted as much by the prospects of trade as by the peacefulness and fertility of Zanzibar. The export trade from East Africa consisted mainly of slaves and ivory, gum copal and the products of the palm tree, but in spite of the efforts of individuals the amounts involved remained small and certainly did not approach the level of the great days of Arab supremacy before the coming of the Portuguese. Nevertheless, Seyyid Said believed that an opportunity was open to men prepared to devote their energy and skill to fostering the commerce of the East African coast and to developing the port of Zanzibar. It was, in any case, vital to Seyyid Said that trade should prosper since in the absence of direct taxation export and import duties were the main source of revenue for his government. To finance the trade the assistance of Indian *banyans* was essential and Seyyid Said, who had welcomed them in Oman, also encouraged their settlement in Zanzibar. Their numbers increased rapidly both on the island of Zanzibar and in the Arab towns on the mainland, and although many of the Arabs treated them harshly Seyyid Said invariably showed them every consideration. They were among his leading advisers in financial matters and the chief collector of customs in Seyyid Said's reign was an Indian *banyan*. Not only Hindus but Muslims also responded to the Sultan's friendship and the Muslims became permanent residents in Zanzibar or along the coast, unlike the Hindus who tended to return to India at regular intervals with their profits.

Seyyid Said did not content himself with simply providing a good commercial base in Zanzibar. He was himself a trader and he took an active interest in promoting caravan expeditions on the mainland. It was during his reign that the caravans began to penetrate deep into the interior. Each cool season expeditions were set in train, and in spite of the heavy casualties which they seem so frequently to have suffered there was no lack of enthusiasm. The climate took its toll of the porters, and the tribes through whose country the caravans passed grew increasingly fearful of these recurrent invasions so that they took to ambushing the travellers either in self-defence or in the hope of seizing the goods which the caravans carried. Gradually the country nearer the coast became sated with the beads and cloth which the Arabs had to offer and more reluctant to meet the demands which the traders made for slaves. The caravans travelled ever farther inland. In 1841 and 1842 Arabs made their first attempt to investigate the shores of Lake Tanganyika. The expedition ended in disaster but later travellers were not deterred from their attempt to extend still farther the bounds of their trading territory. In the late 1840s the first Arab to reach Buganda, Ahmed bin Ibrahim, had the courage to rebuke the Kabaka, Suna, for ill-treating his own subjects. Suna was so impressed by this bold action that he began to develop an interest in the Islamic faith, but it was an interest which declined rapidly after Ahmed's departure. Subsequently other caravans occasionally reached Buganda but in the middle 1850s Suna closed his borders on hearing reports of the ill-treatment of his subjects by the leaders of the caravans.[1] Direct communication with Buganda then ceased for several years until the trade route was opened again in 1860.

Early in the 1850s a still more spectacular advance was made. In 1852 a caravan led by three Arabs and carrying ivory and slaves reached Benguela on the west coast of the continent. The caravan had set out from Bagamoyo the previous year and, having disposed of all their trade goods before they reached the heart of the continent, the leaders decided to continue westward across Lake Tanganyika in the hope of exchanging ivory and slaves for other goods which they had heard were available to the west. In the course of their lengthy journey they suffered severe hardships but only three members of the caravan died. There is no further record of the travels of these adventurous men, but another Arab traveller, Said bin Habib el-Afifi, who first started out from Zanzibar in 1844 to trade in the interior, claimed to have made at least three journeys across the continent to Loanda from about 1855 onwards. It was a meeting with David Livingstone in September 1855, while the

[1] Sir John Gray: 'Ahmed bin Ibrahim, the first Arab to reach Buganda.' *Uganda Journal*, Vol. 11, 1947, p. 88.

latter was returning from Loanda, which encouraged Said to make his first journey to the west coast. He took with him ivory from Sekeletu, chief of Linyanti on the banks of the Zambezi, which he hoped to exchange for trade goods. He returned to the east coast via Lake Nyasa and reached Zanzibar in 1860. There he informed the British Consul, Rigby, that he had suffered very little inconvenience in the course of his travels through ignorance of the languages of the countries through which he passed since his porters rapidly picked up the various languages and dialects which they encountered.[1]

Ivory was the main attraction which drew the Arab traders ever farther into the interior. Slaves were important, however, more particularly in view of the shortage of porters due to the increasing number of large caravans. Slaves served a dual purpose, since they transported the ivory to the coast and could then be sold themselves. Nevertheless, along the route to Tabora if not in the region of Lake Nyasa, slaves appear to have been a secondary consideration, since the harsh treatment they received on their way to the coast frequently resulted in their death, and it seems as if the Arabs cared little so long as the ivory reached its destination safely. At the same time, slaves were so cheap in the interior that a handsome profit could be made at the coast even on the sale of a handful of survivors. It has been remarked that in the interior a cannibal might have lived more cheaply on human flesh than on the meat of cattle or goats.

In order to encourage chiefs to disgorge their supplies of ivory and also to assist in capturing slaves the Arabs were ever ready to take part in raids between one village and its neighbour. Their firearms made them almost invincible allies. Rumanika, ruler of Karagwe, owed his succession to the assistance given him by the Khoja, Musa Muzuri, who intervened in the struggle between the rival claimants to power in about 1854 and even enlisted the support of Kabaka Suna of Buganda on the side of Rumanika by giving him a large bribe of ivory. Yet, although they were able to play an important part in the political affairs of the tribes with whom they came in contact, the traders did not wish to set up any political dominion. Several established homes in Tabora or Ujiji whence

[1] Sir John Gray: 'Trading Expeditions from the Coast to Lakes Tanganyika and Victoria before 1857.' *Tanganyika Notes and Records*, No. 49, December 1957, pp. 226–46.

some of them never returned to the coast. Of these a number were men who had failed to make good with their caravans and dared not face their creditors while others, captains of the trade, preferred to have their homes in the very centre of the web of caravan routes. While the merchant princes of Tabora exercised considerable influence over the local chief, they took little part in the administration of his people as long as he remained friendly and allowed them to live in peace. They were dangerous only if interfered with. The Munyamwezi chief, Mnywa Sere,[1] who succeeded his father as ruler of Tabora in about 1859, had come to power mainly through the assistance of the Arabs. Once in office, however, he attempted to impose a tax upon the Arab trade. The Arabs threatened to dethrone him and to replace him by his half-brother. Encouraged by the sympathy if not the active support of Musa Muzuri, Mynwa Sere was bold enough to accept the challenge. For some five years he waged a desultory war against the Arabs and for considerable periods he was able to block the trade routes and to inflict several serious blows upon his opponents. But from the outset he was a king without a kingdom, for the Arabs drove him from Tabora and he quickly became little more than fugitive brigand. Eventually in 1865, he was captured and beheaded. The Arabs, meanwhile, were content to leave the administration of the country to his more amenable brother, Mkasiwa. Their object was profit and profit could not accrue from long-drawn-out struggles for power nor yet from a country depopulated by constant warfare. They were ready enough to strike a sudden blow which would terrorise some chief into accepting trading relations with them or in order to obtain a satisfactory bag of slaves. But, as slave-raiding took them further into the country, they became less prodigal in their terrorist methods. They had no desire to colonise in any elaborate sense, and although even those Arabs who settled in the interior continued to acknowledge the overlordship of the Sultan of Zanzibar, neither he nor the Arabs themselves were ever in a position to assert any continuing authority over the interior.

The Arabs' ruthless methods of trade brought their own retribution however anxious the traders might be to maintain peaceful relations with the people of the interior. Tribes who had been pillaged in the past strove to exact revenge from the travellers who

[1] Known to Speke, Stanley and other travellers as Manwa Sera.

passed through their country. This, in turn, made it necessary to increase the size of the caravans for the sake of their own protection, and the larger caravans made still greater demands upon the food supplies of the country, thus arousing still further the animosity of the tribesmen. The behaviour of the Arabs in Buganda had always been reasonable and honest, with the exception of the brief disturbance in Suna's reign, because the powerful Kabakas were able to maintain control over traders so far removed from their base. Similarly one learns from Livingstone about Nsama of Itahua, in Tanganyika, who was able to assist the Arabs because he was confident of his own ability to keep them under control.

One further man also merits attention because he was at once unique in the degree of his success against the Arabs and was at the same time the archetype of what many other African chiefs would have liked to be. This was Mirambo. Mirambo's career probably began in the early 1860s, for the explorer Captain Speke made no mention of him in 1861 when he passed through his country. Yet by 1871 Mirambo's name was uttered with hatred by Arabs travelling between Tabora and the coast and with the deepest fear by Arabs and Africans alike who found themselves west of Tabora. Mirambo's origins were obscure but he appears to have been a petty chief before he launched out as a small-scale freebooter offering the assistance of his armed band to other chiefs in search of aid in the prosecution of their local rivalries. Soon he began to build up an empire of his own to the west and north-west of Tabora. This automatically brought him into conflict with the Arabs. Westward from Tabora ran the all-important caravan route to Ujiji and to the wealth of Manyema beyond Lake Tanganyika. North-westward lay the main routes to Karagwe and Buganda. By his own standards Mirambo was only making a reasonable demand for tribute from caravans passing through his territory. He was not fundamentally hostile to the Arabs although he could muster 7,000 warriors if need be to enforce his will and had 500 professional fighting men almost permanently engaged in raiding other chiefs. He genuinely wanted the caravans to pass through his country but he wanted to benefit from their passage. The Arabs must pay for the protection he could offer and they must be prepared to give him due deference as an important chief. The Arabs did not see the situation in the same light. To pay transit dues would have seriously reduced their profits. Mnywa Sere had tried the same trick upon them, and in spite of the inconvenience he had caused they had finally triumphed. The Arabs therefore decided to resist, and from 1871 to 1875 a sporadic struggle brought trade to a standstill west of Tabora. As soldiers the Arabs were not as effective as their success in slave-raiding might suggest. Mirambo's forces, many of them armed with muzzle-loading weapons and a few with breach-loaders, were no helpless villagers to be taken by surprise and easily terrorized. Nor were their well-stockaded habitations to be attacked with impunity. So the struggle was a hard one, and although Mirambo was not always victorious either in the numerous skirmishes or in the pitched battles he was successful in his main object of blocking the arteries along which the wealth of Arab commerce had to flow. Even far to the south-west of Tabora his armies made their mark, and eventually the Arabs were compelled to sue for peace. Mirambo was ready enough to agree, but although peace of a sort then came to the trade routes the Arabs never forgave and never trusted Mirambo, and ever afterwards they went in fear of him.

For Mirambo peace with the Arabs was only a prelude to more widespread raiding expeditions against other African tribes. He was himself a born fighting man, nearly six feet tall, wiry and possessing boundless energy. He often led the vanguard of his troops into action and when the fighting was at an end he firmly controlled the sharing of the spoils. Northward and southward he ranged although he never wholly overcame the Wasukuma nor reached the town of Ujiji. He was unsuccessful, too, in an attempt to secure friendship with Kabaka Mutesa of Buganda in 1876 because one of Mutesa's caravans had been attacked by a band of raiders professing allegiance to Mirambo. Yet, although he became a byword for rapacity and for his skill in springing military surprises upon his unsuspecting victims, such Europeans as actually met Mirambo grew to like and respect him. Since these Europeans included among their number such widely differing characters as the explorer, Henry Stanley, Captain Hore and Dr. Ebenezer Southon of the London Missionary Society and the Irish trader and former missionary, Charles Stokes, Mirambo was clearly a man of some distinction. He was always friendly towards Europeans and was disappointed when the first members of the Church Missionary Society refused to turn aside from their projected mission to Buganda in order to settle in his territory. He readily offered a place to the representatives of the London Missionary Society who followed some time later. The motives behind his friendly attitude were mixed. On the negative side he feared and respected British influence with the Sultan in distant Zanzibar. Although it is clear that the Sultan could not hope to challenge the military supremacy of a chief in the heart of Africa, Mirambo could not fully appreciate this fact. In any case, if the Sultan had wished he could have cut off the supplies of gunpowder and probably of arms to the interior and that would have weakened Mirambo considerably. From a more positive standpoint Mirambo readily acknowledged that he could benefit greatly from the knowledge and skill of European visitors. Like many other African chiefs, he believed that the presence of Europeans in his country gave him added prestige. He also hoped that the knowledge that missionaries were allowed to move freely through his territory might act as an encouragement to would-be traders.

Mirambo's behaviour created a favourable impression upon the British Consul-General in Zanzibar, Sir John Kirk. The latter never met Mirambo, but the universal praise bestowed upon him by the Europeans who travelled through his country interested the Consul-General greatly. This friendly disposition was shattered by unforeseen circumstances. Two Englishmen belonging to the King of the Belgians' elephant expedition were slain by the vanguard of one of Mirambo's armies in 1880. The army had camped outside a village which was to be attacked the following day and Mirambo himself was in command. The headman of the village, seeing his plight, urged the two Englishmen who were passing near by to camp inside the village, hoping to enlist their support against the besieging horde. It is unlikely that Mirambo knew of the Europeans' existence and his leading troops overran the village stockade before dawn. They came to a halt before the Englishmen's camp, but after some parley they opened fire and the Englishmen were killed. Dr. Southon was able to prove some time later that Mirambo himself took no part in the slaughter. The whole occurrence was contrary to Mirambo's consistent aim to avoid any charge of molesting Europeans. Nevertheless, Sir John Kirk could never again be induced to give him his friendship.[1]

[1] R. J. Harvey: 'Mirambo.' *Tanganyika Notes and Records*, No. 28, January 1950, pp. 10–28.

The empire which Mirambo built was a purely personal one and had none of the lasting qualities of the kingdoms to the north. In victory he was no more cruel than any other chief of his time. Conquered villages were looted because victorious armies expected booty. Defeated peoples who submitted were quick to recognize the advantages of living in friendship under Mirambo's overlordship rather than continuing in danger as his opponents. Captured youths of good physique were readily permitted to serve as soldiers and most of Mirambo's army consisted of Wanyamwezi with a stiffening of Wataturu. On his death in 1884 the whole of Mirambo's creation collapsed, for he had roots neither in a unified people nor in traditional lands. He created no constitution and he did not live long enough to display his administrative talents under a constitution imposed by the Germans. Unlike Mkwawa of the Wahehe, he had no scattered elements of a tribe to weld together. In spite of his personal qualities Mirambo left behind him the memory of a successful adventurer rather than of an able ruler. He was a typical, if a rather outstanding example, of the East African chiefs of the eighteenth and nineteenth centuries.

The Arabs, too, had their able leaders, and although many of them were ruthless in their pursuit of wealth many were men of refinement, and European explorers frequently found it necessary to rely upon their hospitality. Outstanding among the Arabs was Hamed bin Muhammad, better known as Tippoo Tip. Tippoo was of mixed Arab and African descent, and through the marriages of his father, Muhammad, was closely linked to the ruling African family in Tabora. Muhammad himself lived most of his life in Tabora and it was there that he married Karunde, the daughter of Fundi Kira, chief of Unyanyembe, as Tabora was called, and on her death married her younger sister, Nyaso. By means of these marriages Muhammad greatly increased the already important commercial interests which he had inherited from his father, Juma bin Rajab. Tippoo himself was born in the early 1840s, the son of Muhammad's first wife, Bint Habib bin Bushir, who was the daughter of another wealthy commercial family. With these auspicious origins Tippoo began his career as a trader at the age of eighteen and soon distinguished himself, not only as the able son of a wealthy father, but also by his bold participation in the early overthrow of Mnywa Sere and by his courage in a skirmish with the

65

redoubtable Nsama of Itahua in 1867 during which, although wounded, he more than held his own. On July 29, 1867, Tippoo met David Livingstone in a village some three days' journey from Lake Mweru. This was the first of many encounters with the great European explorers of the nineteenth century towards whom Tippoo invariably showed great courtesy and to several of whom he rendered vital assistance.

Then came a period of particular importance in Tippoo's life. After making a number of journeys to the coast he skirted the southern shores of Lake Tanganyika in the early 1870s and entered Utetera, between the Lomami and Lualaba Rivers, where he occupied himself in building a great commercial empire founded upon the trade in ivory and slaves, moving subsequently a little farther east into Manyema. Lieutenant Cameron, sent by the Royal Geographical Society in search of Livingstone, passed through Tippoo's domain in 1874, while Stanley, in the course of his first expedition across the African continent, enlisted Tippoo's support in promoting his onward march. In 1879 messengers from Zanzibar brought to Tippoo a summons to return and answer his creditors since the repayment of the advances made to him for two years was ten years overdue. So great was Tippoo's empire that he needed a further year to settle his affairs before he could start on his return journey with his caravans of ivory. During his absence in Manyema the struggle between the Arabs and Mirambo had reached its height and it was uncertain whether Tippoo's large caravans could traverse with safety the country between Lake Tanganyika and Tabora. Mirambo, however, was predisposed in Tippoo's favour. The latter had never been personally involved in the long-drawn-out struggle and perhaps more important, Tippoo's grandfather, Juma, had assisted Mirambo's own grandfather, Mwura, to become chief of the tiny state of Ujoa which Mirambo had inherited. Mirambo may also have been shrewd enough to surmise that by showing friendship to Tippoo he might be able to separate one influential family from the already disunited Arab party. Whatever may have been the reason, Tippoo was able to pass through Mirambo's territory in safety. Subsequently both he and his son, Sef, were cordially received by Mirambo at his headquarters and in spite of Arab attempts to poison them against the African chief they succeeded in trading amicably in his territory.

Arriving in Zanzibar in November 1882, Tippoo found the Sultan, Barghash, anxious about European interest in East Africa and hoping to find Tippoo willing to act as his Wali in Tabora. Although Tippoo could be a loyal subject of the Sultan when it suited his ends, his own power in Manyema was far greater and far more tangible than any which Barghash himself could ever hope to exercise on the East African mainland. A Belgian was already urging Tippoo to enter into a partnership to control the trade of the Upper Congo so that, learning this news and recognizing the value of Tippoo's position in Manyema as a counter-balance to European activities in Africa, Barghash did not press his original plan. Instead he urged Tippoo to return quickly to Manyema, and by the middle of 1883 the merchant was back in his own domain His power, however, was already threatened by the advance of the Belgian forces of King Leopold, ruler of the Congo Free State. Recognizing the inevitability of a European triumph Tippoo reluctantly accepted the governorship of the Stanley Falls district on behalf of the Congo State in 1887. But in 1890 he set out for the last time for the coast to answer charges brought against him by Henry Stanley who claimed that he had gravely endangered the success of Stanley's latest expedition into the interior by failing to fulfil a contract to supply porters. In any case, the days of the Arabs in Manyema were numbered. Driven by the twin fires of humanitarianism and imperial ambition Leopold launched an attack upon the slavers of the Upper Congo in the early 1890s. Challenged thus from the west and with their eastern trade routes dominated by the Germans the Arabs might resist but they had no hope of success.[1] Tippoo spent his closing years in Zanzibar where a young military officer who saw him in 1903 said of him that although he was extremely wealthy and still as hospitable as ever he was not very talkative and seemed reluctant to recall his slave-trading days.[2]

Like Mirambo, Tippoo founded no permanent kingdom, but whereas the former was simply a freebooter translated briefly by the strength of his own personality to a position of local eminence like other chiefs before him, Tippoo was peculiarly the product of his own age. In Tippoo's day the interior of East Africa was being

[1] H. Brode: *Tippoo Tib*. Edward Arnold, London, 1907.

[2] R. Meinertzhagen: *Kenya Diary*, 1902–1906. Oliver and Boyd, Edinburgh and London, 1957, p. 79.

suddenly subjected to the influences of more developed and more versatile people. Any man possessing knowledge outside the limited field of local warfare and supersition might attain to a position of note, and genuine ability could raise a man to pre-eminence in a region as wide as some of the greatest countries of Europe. Tippoo was a pioneer of trade in a pioneering and commercial age and, unlike the other Arabs, he did establish something of a political as well as a commercial empire. When more settled administration followed, however, the rough justice and ruthless business methods of the pioneers were out of place. Tippoo had blazed trails through savage country which others had thought to be a pathless wilderness. Yet Sir Charles Eliot, Commissioner of the British East Africa Protectorate, was not far from the mark when he wrote 'Tippoo Tib's commercial journeys were, in the main, plundering expeditions. Anything else, any introduction of law and order, any spread of civilization, was merely subsidiary and incidental'.[1] Tippoo, it is true, was virtually king of an enormous country, but his authority was never recognized by the great nations of the world nor even, until it was too late, by the Sultan of Zanzibar. Had the Sultan, at an earlier stage, formally recognized Tippoo's status while yet claiming him as one of his own subjects, subsequent events might well have been different; for one of the main arguments put forward by Germany to justify her claims on the East African mainland was that Arab sovereignty did not extend beyond a ten-mile-wide coastal belt.

Although the routes into the interior from Bagamoyo and Kilwa were the most heavily used there was yet a further road which caravans were known to follow. Starting either from Mombasa or from the mouth of the Pangani River travellers aimed their footsteps towards the southern slopes of Kilimanjaro. From thence they crossed Masai country and continued onward to the Kavirondo Gulf of Lake Victoria or even beyond. The Masai, as has already been shown, were unpredictable, and consequently the northern route was not so extensively used. There is on record a journey made to Masailand in 1852 by Juma bin Mbwana, a Swahili with, possibly, some Indian extraction. Juma suffered heavily from Masai persecution and would never make the journey again. Nevertheless, there is interesting evidence of the use of this route and also of a more

[1] H. Brode: op. cit., Introduction, p. viii.

northerly extension of it in the 1860s in Christie's map of the spread of the cholera epidemic which raged through East Africa between 1864 and 1871.[1] Originating in Arabia the epidemic crossed the Red Sea and Indian Ocean by two channels. One passed through Ethiopia and into northern Kenya and thence southward, keeping to the east of Lake Baringo after which it forked, one branch turning westward from the Naivasha area to Lake Victoria, the other running southward to Kilimanjaro. From Kilimanjaro it continued down the Pangani River to the coast and Zanzibar before crossing again to the mainland and following the trade route from Bagamoyo to Lake Tanganyika. The other channel was through Somalia and southward to the mouth of the Juba River. The manner in which the disease spread along the main trade routes gives strength to the argument in favour of the existence and use of the less well-known routes.

This evidence is further supported by an article, accompanied by a map, which appeared in the Journal of the Royal Geographical Society in 1870. The article, describing the trade routes in the region north of Kilimanjaro, was written by T. Wakefield, a missionary in Mombasa, and was based upon information given him by an Arab named Sadi bin Ahedi.[2] General Lloyd Mathews, writing in 1885, also referred to native traders, old friends of his, who accompanied caravans trading for ivory into the Masai country.[3] The meaning of the term 'native' employed by Mathews is not clear, but he was probably referring to the Swahili of the coast. Moreover, the casual nature of his reference to these traders suggests that commercial contacts with the Masai for their ivory were not uncommon by the mid 1880s. Even as early as the mid-nineteenth century Wakamba caravans were bringing ivory to the coast at Mombasa, while at a rather later date Arab traders were lured by accounts of rich stores of ivory to travel these northern routes beyond Lake Baringo to Mount Elgon and even farther north to the land of the Suk and Turkana.[4]

[1] J. Christie: *Cholera Epidemics in East Africa.* Macmillan, London, 1876.

[2] T. Wakefield: 'Routes of Native Caravans from the Coast to the Interior of East Africa.' *Journal of the Royal Geographical Society*, Vol. XL, 1870, pp. 303 ff.

[3] R. M. Lyne: *An Apostle of Empire.* George Allen and Unwin, London, 1936, p. 73.

[4] A. T. Matson: 'The Founding of Kericho.' *Kenya Weekly News*, October 31, 1958.

Thus the earliest travellers along the East African trade routes appear in most cases to have been the Africans themselves although perhaps only a few tribes took part in this adventure. It was the Arabs, however, who transformed these meagre pathways into broad highways of commerce and pillage in the course of the later nineteenth century. But their days of profit were short and a new and greater power, that of the countries of western Europe, trod hard on the heels of Arab exploitation.

CHAPTER THREE

THE AWAKENING OF
EUROPEAN INTEREST

THE conflict which developed between Europeans and Arabs in East Africa in the late nineteenth century was scarcely presaged by the activities of the Europeans in the earlier years of the century. The first Europeans to make trading contacts with the coast after Seyyid Said's migration to Zanzibar received a friendly welcome from the Sultan. Seyyid Said was anxious to develop the wealth of Zanzibar by every means at his disposal. When he first settled on the island there was little cultivation but, as the largest landowner, he showed considerable foresight in developing the cultivation of cloves for which the climate and soil of the island were particularly suitable. A steady income resulted from this enterprise. Meanwhile, Arab sailors were voyaging as far afield as the Indian coast and even to China and the East Indies, bringing still further wealth to Zanzibar by their trading efforts. But Seyyid Said was alert to the advantages of a diversified economy and the growing interest shown by western powers in the trading possibilities of the East African coast attracted from him a ready response.

In the early years of the nineteenth century the most important foreign traders were Americans. Until the War of Independence these latter, as British subjects, had been excluded from trade in the Indian Ocean by the East India Company's monopoly. When the restriction was removed American vessels, particularly ships from Boston and Salem, began to trade in eastern waters. The Salem men concentrated for the most part on the shores of India while the Boston traders ranged more widely. During the Anglo-American War of 1812–15 these activities were checked and Salem declined in importance. A few Salem ships persisted in the old trade with India but the majority began to turn elsewhere for their commerce. In this casual fashion the East African coast came within the orbit of American trade. American attention had also been drawn to the coast for different reasons. Whaling ships from the United States were beginning to operate more extensively in the southern waters of the Indian Ocean in the early nineteenth century and frequently they sailed to East Africa in search of water and supplies. Even before Seyyid Said's transfer to Zanzibar, therefore, American vessels were a common sight in the harbour and in other ports along the coast. Seyyid Said himself had also made contact with the Americans. Early in 1832 an American officer, Captain Edmund Roberts, was instructed to sail round Cape Horn and across the Pacific to the Far East in order to make trading treaties with the rulers of Cochin China, Siam and Oman. In Oman he was welcomed by Seyyid Said who was delighted by the prospect of extending his political friendships and widening his trading contacts. In September 1833, Seyyid Said and Roberts signed a treaty of commerce and friendship. By the terms of the treaty American citizens were entitled to trade freely in any of the ports in Seyyid Said's dependencies while an all-inclusive duty of 5 per cent was charged on cargo landed from American ships. The President of the United States was also entitled to appoint consuls to reside in any of the ports where trade would be carried on. The American government was highly satisfied with this arrangement. It meant a considerable reduction in trading expenses since hitherto the duties on both imports and exports had amounted to as much as 7 per cent and there had been numerous incidental payments to be made to avaricious port officials. Seyyid Said, for his part, was content with the agreement since it helped to strengthen his economic position while the Americans showed no disposition to interfere in the political affairs of his dominions.

The number of Americans engaged in the East African trade was never large. The trade itself was far from easy and adequate cargoes could only be collected by perseverance. The Salem merchants were persistent, however, and contrived to make a steady profit from their activities. It was they who brought to East Africa the white cotton cloth woven in the mills of Massachusetts which not only ousted Indian and British manufactured cloth but even became in due course, under its title of *merikani*, a form of currency along the trade routes into the interior. The value of American cotton cloth imported into East Africa mounted steadily and in its turn the

72

American export trade from East Africa also increased. The merchants did not carry on their trade directly but acted through middle men, in which capacity the Indian *banyans* made ample profits for themselves. Seyyid Said benefited too, since the customs duties of the country also increased.

Some time after the Americans, came German merchants from Hamburg who began to trade in Zanzibar in 1847. They, too, exported ivory, gum copal, cloves and hides from East Africa while their imports were varied in character and consisted of minor items such as hardware, mirrors, beads, soap and other items of haberdashery. Like the Americans the Germans were welcomed by Seyyid Said. They, too, appeared to have no ambition to interfere in the administration of his territories and he welcomed the extension of the Zanzibar trade which their presence encouraged. In 1859 a trading agreement, similar in terms to the American treaty, was signed between the representatives of the Hanseatic Republics of Lübeck, Bremen and Hamburg and the Sultan of Zanzibar, Majid, who had succeeded Seyyid Said three years earlier.

The result of these commercial activities was reflected not only in the wealth of the Sultan but also in the rapid growth of Zanzibar itself. From being in the early years of the nineteenth century a small and relatively unimportant village it became in little more than a generation the most important trading centre along the East African coast, taking precedence over Kilwa. This success was almost entirely due to the initiative and powers of organization of Seyyid Said.

French interest in the East Coast was of longer standing than that of either the Germans or the Americans. It differed, however, in that the French, in addition to the pursuit of legitimate trade, were also interested in the slave-trade. After the breakdown in relations between the French and Oman which had occurred during the Napoleonic wars the French were anxious to renew their trading association with Seyyid Said's dominions the moment a new opportunity arose. As early as 1822 they entered into an agreement with Seyyid Said to regulate contacts with his dependencies and when news of the American treaty with the Sultan reached them, the French at once became anxious to obtain similar privileges themselves. Seyyid Said, however, was disturbed by the aggressive attitude which the French adopted in their haste to gain their objectives.

Nevertheless, in November 1844, he consented to a trading agreement being made, and later in the same month he confirmed the appointment of a French Consul in Zanzibar. So far, in spite of misgivings, his relations with the French differed little from those he had established with other powers. In the background, however, lurked the constant desire of the French to carry on the slave-trade. Slave-trading had been prohibited by French law in 1818 and the penalties for breaking the law were increased in 1827. But the enforcement of these rules was lax until after the overthrow of the Bourbon dynasty in 1830. In the following year a new law was passed which granted British ships a reciprocal right of search, and this strengthened the hand of the British naval patrol along the East African coast.

The French planters on the island of Bourbon, formerly in a favourable position compared with their fellow countrymen in Mauritius, which had been annexed by the British, found that the situation had been reversed. They, who hitherto had met their urgent labour requirements through the slave-trade, saw with envy the arrangements made by the British Government for the inhabitants of Mauritius. For, anxious to encourage sugar production in the former Île de France, the British Government agreed in the 1830s to the introduction of coolies from India. This arrangement was suspended in 1839 after investigations had revealed a number of abuses, but it was reinstituted in 1842 under stricter supervision which did not seriously affect the inflow of labourers. Excluded from the benefits of this arrangement the planters of Bourbon looked to the shores of Africa for an alternative labour supply. The Moresby Treaty and the watchful British naval patrols restricted the slave-trade between East Africa and countries outside Seyyid Said's dominions, but there was no reason, the French argued, why free labourers should not be made available to them. The British were reluctant to admit this, being fully aware of the difficulty of drawing a clear distinction between free labour and slavery in the circumstances pertaining in East Africa. British resistance was rendered difficult in 1845, however, when, by the terms of a new agreement, France agreed to maintain a naval patrol on the west coast and Britain surrendered her right of search. This opened the way to considerable activity by the French on the east coast and it was difficult for the British to investigate closely the nature of French negotiations with those who supplied them with labourers in Zanzibar or elsewhere. Frequently, too, the French ships collecting labourers were escorted by men-of-war which still further inhibited British intervention. Faced with this problem the British Government agreed in 1859 to open negotiations for the importation of coolies from British India into the French dependencies under strict safeguard. In return the French declared themselves ready to put an end to the transport of labourers from East Africa. Although attempts were still made to smuggle labourers to Bourbon the British campaign against the East African off-shore slave-trade was now made easier.

Their activities in connection with the slave-trade were not the only grounds for Seyyid Said's suspicion of the French. More dangerous in his eyes was their patent desire to establish a foothold on the East African mainland or at least on one of the off-shore islands. Left with only the wreckage of their former empire in the Indian Ocean the French could not hope to make much impression upon the overwhelming preponderance in both trade and dependencies which had been acquired by the British. The isolated towns which the French still held in India were surrounded by vast tracts of territory subordinate to British rule. Developments on the island of Bourbon had been eclipsed by the progress of Mauritius. Madagascar continued to resist French attempts to extend their influence there. The first step taken by the French to remedy this adverse situation, therefore, was heralded by the arrival in Zanzibar of a French corvette in the middle of 1840. The commander of the vessel asked permission to establish an agent in Zanzibar and to build a fort and other buildings in Mogadishu and Brava. Seyyid Said was absent in Oman and the Frenchman, receiving an unsatisfactory answer from his son, sailed after the Sultan to repeat the request. Seyyid Said evaded a definite answer. He was alarmed by the French interest in the East African coast and he became more gravely concerned when he learned later in the year that the French had occupied the island of Nossi-bé near the northern tip of Madagascar. Seyyid Said himself had formerly laid claim to the island although he had done nothing to justify his action beyond the gift of a flag to the inhabitants. Nevertheless, on learning of the French occupation he protested at once to Lord Palmerston. It was an auspicious moment for Seyyid Said since Palmerston was in the midst of a dispute with France over her support of Muhammad Ali's aggression against his overlord, the Sultan of Turkey. Palmerston therefore wrote to Seyyid Said urging him to resist any pressure from the French. His support was short-lived, for only a few days later the threat of war with France was averted and Palmerston began to retreat from his former position. When he was replaced by the more pacific Lord Aberdeen Seyyid Said's chances of obtaining British assistance over Nossi-bé faded completely.

None the less, Britain was not wholly indifferent to French activities along the East African coast. The anti-slavery motive which was primarily responsible for British interest in the area ensured that suspicions of French participation in the slave-trade did not pass unnoticed. Simultaneously, the development by Muhammad Ali of the overland route through Egypt to India brought to the fore once again the strategic importance of Seyyid Said's estate in Oman. It was, in fact, with a view to strengthening relations between Britain and Seyyid Said, rather than due to any particular attraction towards East Africa, that a British Agent and Consul-General was appointed to Zanzibar in 1841. British trade with East Africa was virtually non-existent and it was the activities of Indian *banyans* which resulted in the creation of the combined post of Political Agent on behalf of the Government of India and consular representative of the British Government. The *banyans* at that time handled the greater part of Zanzibar's trade and Britain benefited indirectly in that, with the exception of the *merikani* cloth imported from the United States, most of the goods brought to East Africa by traders of all nations were made in Britain. Nevertheless, the commercial treaty signed by Britain and Zanzibar in 1839 was mainly intended to foster the goodwill already existing between Seyyid Said and the British and did not indicate any desire on the part of the latter to divert their attention from the far more wealthy centres of trade in India and the Far East.

Captain Hamerton was the first British Agent to hold office in Zanzibar and he was immediately instructed to warn Seyyid Said of the danger which might arise from the interest shown by other powers in his East African dominions. Yet Seyyid Said remained reluctant to accept the idea of asserting greater political authority over the coast. Perhaps he was held back by memories of his lack of success in his military exploits against the Mazaria. If this was so his opinion could only have been confirmed by the failure of two expeditions which he undertook against Pate in the early 1840s. Indeed, along the mainland his influence was strictly limited to the coastline. In Mombasa he maintained a fairly strong garrison and the Governor, Seyyid Said's representative, exercised a steady rule from the security of Fort Jesus. Although caravans travelled into the interior from Mombasa Seyyid Said's authority did not go with them. His influence ended on the eastern edge of the dry hinterland. Another garrison was stationed in Tanga, but there the authority of the Governor was restricted by the neighbouring power of the ruler of Usambara with whom Seyyid Said wisely maintained a friendly relationship. Southward from the mouth of the Pangani River to beyond Cape Delgado the coastal peoples recognized Seyyid Said's authority to a greater or less degree. Seyyid Said, however, had no ambition to extend the narrow confines of his power. He was chiefly anxious to hold what he had and to prevent others from interfering and thereby damaging his trading relations with the interior. Yet, although he was no imperialist his word carried weight along the slave routes even as far to the west as Lake Tanganyika and to Lake Nyasa in the south. Travellers carrying his message of introduction received the help and assistance of Arabs far in the interior.

Although the British were unlikely to permit any blatantly political activities by the French, Seyyid Said was conscious of potential weakness within his own dominions and feared that the French might try to exploit it. British insistence upon the observation of the Moresby Treaty caused discontent among most of Seyyid Said's subjects and if the French, whose interest in the slave-trade was well known, were to ally themselves with the disgruntled Arabs Seyyid Said's position would be in grave danger. He was still further weakened by his signature of the Hamerton Treaty in 1845. This treaty was the next stage in Britain's campaign against the East African slave-trade. Thanks to Seyyid Said's co-operation the Moresby Treaty had undoubtedly reduced the trade in slaves to Christian countries although the British naval patrol, consisting of three or four cruisers, could not hope to be uniformly effective. It was clear, however, that ships apparently sailing with slaves from one part of Seyyid Said's dominions to another might easily slip away to regions where the demand for slaves still remained heavy. Palmerston had been the instigator of further steps to counter such activities when he was at the Foreign Office in 1841. It was then that he suggested that the Bombay Government should call upon Seyyid Said to forbid all slave-trading by sea and to permit British naval vessels to search and seize all Arab ships with slaves on board wherever they might be encountered. The payment of £2,000 a year was offered to offset the loss in customs dues until some alternative form of trade had been found to restore Seyyid Said's profits. Seyyid Said resented this approach by the Bombay Government which he still tended to look upon as the agent of a trading company. But his injured pride was as nothing compared with the fears to which the proposals gave rise. To accept them would be to deprive his Arab subjects of the main source of their livelihood, while his apparent approval of foreign intervention threatened to arouse the hatred of all his subjects. At the same time he did not wish to antagonize the British who, apart from their strange aberration concerning slavery, were much less dangerous allies than the French and were potentially far more dangerous enemies.

Seyyid Said did not surrender without a struggle and, having been assured by Hamerton that the Bombay Government had the support of the Foreign Office, he sent his emissary, Ali bin Nasir, to England to present his case. He could have had little hope that the mission would be successful and, in fact, Ali returned to Zanzibar in February 1843, empty-handed. The Sultan, therefore, pleaded that the transport of slaves along the East African coast between Lamu and Kilwa should still be permitted in order to avoid interfering with the practice of domestic slavery. After lengthy discussion this proposal was embodied in a treaty signed by Hamerton and Said on October 2, 1845, which took effect on January 1, 1847. The main theme of the treaty differed little from Palmerston's earlier proposals. Seyyid Said agreed to prohibit the export of slaves from his African dominions to his possessions in Asia while British naval vessels and ships of the East India Company were empowered to confiscate vessels belonging to Seyyid Said or his subjects which were found to be transporting slaves outside the permitted limits. That the publication of the treaty did not result in Seyyid Said's downfall may well have been mainly due to the fact that it was patent to all that it could not be rigidly enforced. The demand for slaves was great and the profits of the slave-trade remained tempting. Although Seyyid Said himself was sincere in his attempt to meet his obligations he could not hope to control his subjects completely. The enforcement of the treaty mainly rested with the overworked vessels of the British coastal patrol.

If Seyyid Said's loyalty to the British in their anti-slavery campaign was a constant source of danger to the peace of his country another source sprang from the rivalry of his sons over the succession. Seyyid Said's eldest son, Hilal, differed temperamentally from his father, being aggressive and warlike instead of being inclined towards diplomacy and trade. Inevitably he attracted to himself a faction which challenged Seyyid Said's authority. It is by no means certain that Hilal had any dealings with the French, but had they wished to promote their interests in that way the French might easily have made him the centre of intrigue. In any case, Seyyid Said decided in 1844 that he must take action to curb Hilal's influence. He therefore wrote to Lord Aberdeen, informing him that his trader son, Khalid, was to inherit the Sultanate of Zanzibar and his African possessions while his third son, Thwain, would succeed him as ruler of Oman. Hilal hastened to England to appeal against his disinheritance, but although he was treated with respect he was unable to win support. On his return to Zanzibar there was a temporary reconciliation with his father, but in 1849 he was banished to Lamu and died two years later in Aden while on a pilgrimage to Mecca.

There was a lull in French activities along the coast about this time but the eclipse and death of Hilal did not mean that the Arab critics of Seyyid Said lacked a focus for their discontent. Khalid, the careful man of commerce, had few friends, but another, younger son, Barghash, possessed all the fiery qualities necessary to endear him to the Arabs. When, therefore, the flagship of the French Admiral La Guène, sailed into Zanzibar harbour on December 4, 1853, Seyyid Said at once cast a watchful eye upon his son. The Sultan himself was on the point of sailing to Oman on one of his periodical visits during which he was usually accompanied by Hamerton. The arrival of the French ship on this occasion threw everything into confusion and Seyyid Said, together with his leading supporters, appealed to the British Agent to stay in Zanzibar and watch over affairs in the Sultan's absence. Hamerton agreed and Seyyid Said took the wise precaution of requiring Barghash to accompany him on his journey. The importance of this action was greatly increased when Seyyid Said's designated successor, Khalid, died during his father's absence. An uneasy lull hung over Zanzibar until Seyyid Said's next step should become known. In due course instructions arrived from Oman naming Seyyid Said's fourth son, Majid, Acting Governor in Zanzibar and on the African coast until the Sultan's return. In effect this news implied the recognition of Majid as successor to Khalid's inheritance, a decision which could not have been universally popular in Zanzibar. Barghash's absence with his father left the dissidents without their natural leader, however, and Hamerton, by strengthening the Baluch guards at various strategic points, demonstrated to any would-be rebels that Britain was keeping watch over the island.

This brief moment of potential danger was soon to be overshadowed by the death, in October 1856, of Seyyid Said himself. Of Seyyid Said more justly than of many others it can be said that his passing marked the end of an era. As a soldier he had met with little success. But by diplomacy and perseverance and through his steady loyalty to Britain he had been able to build a commercial empire based on Zanzibar which had completely superseded the barren inheritance to which he had succeeded at the beginning of his reign. It was he who created Zanzibar, and from his death the importance of the island, and more particularly of its rulers, declined steadily. By his unwavering if sometimes unwilling support of the British anti-slavery campaign he laid the foundations upon which British humanitarianism could mount its attack upon the whole corrupt and cruel commerce in human beings throughout East Africa. Sir Bartle Frere paid Seyyid Said his rightful tribute when he said of his family that it was one to which civilization and the English Government in India were under considerable obligation.[1]

The logical separation of the Busaidi possessions in Arabia and Africa, upon which Seyyid Said himself had decided, took place upon his death without any immediate difficulty. Thwain became ruler in Oman and Majid succeeded his father in Zanzibar where he was immediately recognized as Sultan by the British and American Governments. Nevertheless, Majid knew that his position was far from secure. The French had not recognized him, and between the death of the British Consul, Hamerton, and the arrival of his successor, Captain C. R. Rigby, on July 27, 1858, there was a significant gap during which British contacts with Zanzibar were tem-

[1] Mrs. C. E. B. Russell: *General Rigby, Zanzibar and the Slave Trade.* Allen and Unwin, London, 1935, p. 104.

Dr. Ludwig Krapf

John Hanning Speke

Sir Richard Burton

Lord Cromer

Seyyid Barghash

Tippoo Tip

Sir Henry Morton Stanley

Mutesa of Buganda

porarily broken. Lacking his father's strength of character Majid could do little to restrain his subjects from taking part in the slave-trade. So freely did it flourish that Rigby remarked that Majid alone appeared to be taking no part in it. It was fortunate, therefore, for the young Sultan that the first real challenge to his authority was delayed until 1859, by which time Rigby had gained a fair grasp of the island's problems. In January of that year news reached Zanzibar that a powerful fleet was being equipped by Thwain for the invasion of Majid's dominions. Meanwhile, the island was being ravaged by cholera with a violence reminiscent of the plague. 'Men were seized with sudden illness in the streets and died in agony in one or two hours while ships in the harbour lost their entire crews,' Rigby recorded in his diary.[1] On February 24 the Sultan's four ships of war sailed to meet the invading force. The French Consul was jubilant at the news of Thwain's impending attack and admitted to Rigby that France was already negotiating with Thwain and that his seizure of the Zanzibar Government would meet with French approval. Barghash, too, was seeking to overthrow his brother and actually attempted to murder Majid by firing on him at night when the Sultan was passing his house in a boat.

The threatened invasion never took place. A solitary dhow belonging to the Omani fleet arrived in Zanzibar towards the end of February and all on board were immediately taken prisoner. On March 2 the steam frigate, *Assaye*, sailed into Zanzibar harbour to protect British subjects and bringing the news that Thwain's fleet had been intercepted and turned back by a British squadron from Bombay. Still the danger was not at an end. Prevented from taking an active part in the overthrow of Majid, Thwain now sent a sum of 40,000 dollars (c. £9,000) to the powerful El Harthi family in Zanzibar to assist them in stirring up revolt, while Barghash himself was in close touch with the El Harthi. To add to the difficulties of the situation the French schooner, *L'Estafette*, eight guns, had already arrived in Zanzibar and was joined on March 28 by the corvette, *Cordelière*, thirty guns, with Commodore Le Vicomte Fleuriot de Langle aboard. The Commodore and the Consul openly announced their support for Barghash and insulted Majid before his own people. The arrival of two further British ships of war, *Clive* and *Persian*, to join *Assaye*, more than restored the balance. With these

[1] Mrs. C. E. B. Russell: op. cit., p. 79.

powerful persuaders in the background Rigby was able to convince the French Commodore that he was meddling unwisely in the affairs of an independent ruler.

The departure of the *Cordelière* eased the tension only slightly, for the machinations of Thwain, together with the subversive activities of the French Consul, ensured the persistence of an undercurrent of intrigue. A further plot to assassinate Majid was manufactured by one of Thwain's agents but was discovered in time and the would-be murderer was captured and imprisoned. Convinced that Barghash was involved in the crime Majid ordered him to be conveyed to Oman on board the frigate *Piedmontese*. Barghash appeared to acquiesce in this decision then slipped away to a large country house which he barricaded in preparation for a siege and then announced his intention of seizing the government. Rigby's intervention now proved decisive. The British Consul urged the spiritless Sultan to take action and in response to Majid's request a handful of British naval officers joined the Sultan's forces in their attack upon Barghash's stronghold. The gates of the stockade were blown open by rockets and gunfire directed by the naval officers but the Sultan's forces refused to storm the house. The following day Rigby again intervened when, in answer to Majid's appeal for British troops, he asked the senior British naval officer to send a force sufficient to overcome Barghash's resistance. After the event Rigby justified his action on the ground that he had been supporting the lawful ruler at Majid's request against rebellious subjects. Whether or not his second intervention was necessary will never be known for, on the arrival of the sailors, Barghash was found to have evacuated his position. Rigby was secretly informed that he had taken refuge in his own house in the town. The Consul then set a guard upon the house pending the arrival of some of Majid's forces and the following morning he called upon Barghash to surrender. The latter submitted after a lengthy parley and was pardoned by Majid on condition that he left Zanzibar for ever, that he would never again plot against the Sultan and that he would always accept the advice of the British Government. Barghash agreed and was sent to Bombay. The El Harthi leaders made their submission and the rebellion was at an end. Barghash himself returned to Zanzibar eighteen months later with the Sultan's permission but never again caused any trouble for his brother whom he succeeded on the latter's death in 1870. Thwain, too, ceased to be a danger after 1861 when he was induced to submit his claim to Zanzibar to the arbitration of the Governor-General of India, Lord Canning. Again Rigby played an important part in the negotiations leading up to the Canning award, and the Commission appointed to investigate the rival claims was greatly influenced by the British Consul's advice. In the event, both Majid and Thwain agreed to recognize the territorial division made by their father. Majid also agreed to make an annual payment to Oman of 40,000 German crowns (c. £9,000), not as a sign of his subjection to Thwain but because of the greater wealth of Zanzibar.[1]

The part played by Britain in these exciting events marked a new stage in the relationship between that country and Zanzibar. Hitherto Britain's interest in the East African coast had been solely determined by the desire to promote the anti-slavery campaign and to check French strategic expansion. Now she was being forced by circumstances to intervene more positively in the political affairs of Zanzibar. The Canning Award had shown her to be the arbiter of Zanzibar's political problems and subsequent events were to confirm this position. Yet Britain had no desire to assume an official status as protector of the Sultan's territories, as events soon showed. In 1860 Rigby had complained that the French were again threatening the security of Zanzibar by establishing in the city itself a stronghold capable of being manned by a garrison of between 1,200 and 2,000 men, with a plentiful supply of water from the three wells enclosed within its walls. The French replied that their intention was to set up a mission station and a hospital for seamen, but Lord Russell, the British Foreign Secretary, complained to the French Minister, Thouvenal, stressing Britain's desire to maintain the Sultan's independence. After some delay the French Government came to the conclusion that the strategic and economic value of a foothold in Zanzibar did not justify a clash with Britain. On March 10, 1862, a joint declaration was signed by France and Britain that they would respect the independence of the Sultans of Zanzibar and Oman. The inclusion of the latter ruler in the agreement appears to have been due initially to an error in the drafting of the declaration but it was agreed that the arrangements should be extended to Oman when the declaration was made final.

France honoured the agreement without any further comment

[1] Mrs. C. E. B. Russell: op. cit., pp. 107–24.

and from this time French interest in Zanzibar declined along with French trade on the East African coast. By the joint action of the declaration and the Canning Award Majid's dominions were thus secured from outside intervention. Both instances, however, emphasized the importance of British intervention in Zanzibar affairs and although Britain made no direct attempt to extend her influence further the tide had already set against Zanzibar's independence. Majid himself lacked both the ability and energy of his father, and continued to feel insecure on the island in spite of the loyalty which most of his subjects had displayed during the tumultuous opening years of his reign. It was his uneasiness in Zanzibar and not in any sense his desire to assert a more direct sovereignty over the mainland which induced him to establish an alternative home on the coast to which he gave the name Dar es Salaam, the haven of peace. The Sultan's dependence upon Britain was, moreover, still further increased towards the end of his reign as a result of the strong personal influence exercised over him by Dr. (later Sir John) Kirk. Kirk arrived in Zanzibar as medical officer in 1866. On the illness of Rigby's successor, Playfair, Kirk became Acting Consul and was subsequently appointed Consul-General. Majid's uncertainty coupled with Kirk's determination began to mould Zanzibar's policy still more dramatically along British lines. Even when Barghash succeeded his brother in 1870 there was no marked change. Although Barghash was a man of livelier energy than Majid his basic interest was in trade and the wealth to be acquired from commercial activities. He had no desire to take upon himself the responsibilities of empire and it was Kirk who constantly drew his attention to the growing political challenge of the powers of western Europe.

Barghash's first experience of British intervention in the affairs of Zanzibar could have brought him little pleasure. In 1871 a Commission of Inquiry was set up by the British Parliament to report on the East African slave-trade. Early in 1873 Sir Bartle Frere arrived in Zanzibar to urge Barghash to close all slave-markets in his dominions and to forbid entirely the export of slaves from any part of the East African coast under his control. The Sultan, appreciating all too clearly the likely reaction of his subjects, procrastinated as long as he could. Finally he gave in under pressure from Kirk, backed by the presence in the harbour of several British warships. Inevitably Barghash's capitulation placed him still further under Britain's protection as a result of the discontent which it was bound to arouse among his own subjects. But Kirk insisted that the new regulations were observed. Attempts to avoid them by marching slaves along the coast instead of sending them by ship were checked when Barghash, on Kirk's advice, published further restrictions to forbid this practice and also to prohibit slave caravans from bringing their human merchandise to the coast. To enforce the new rules Kirk further induced Barghash to create a new armed force under a British Officer in addition to his personal bodyguard of Baluchis. The new body of troops was intended to supplement on shore the work of the naval patrol at sea. The officer selected to build up this force was a naval lieutenant, Lloyd William Mathews, who in 1877 had already had three years' experience of the naval patrol along the coast. In due course he created for himself a position of influence in the Sultan's dominions and eventually became the Sultan's first minister. The eldest surviving son of a hard-riding, adventurous father of remote Welsh descent and of Jane Penfold of Sussex, Mathews was born in Madeira on March 7, 1840. From his father he inherited an almost reckless courage in the face of danger and from his mother a pride in his beautiful home and gracious hospitality. While maintaining the principles taught him in the navy and above all the hatred of the slave-trade, Mathews completely identified himself with the well-being of the Sultans whom he served. To an exceptional degree he absorbed Arab ways of thinking and observed Arab courtesy, combining in himself the administrative powers of the west with a complete loyalty to the manners and customs of the east.

For Kirk, Mathews's appointment was opportune, not only as a further check to the slave-trade but also as a potential obstacle to the new threat to the Sultan's authority in East Africa arising from European interest in that area. Kirk, although an officer of the British Government, was as loyal an adviser to the Sultan as Mathews himself, and far more aware than Barghash of the need to protect Zanzibar's interests. A close associate of Livingstone, Kirk had absorbed his great friend's loathing of the sufferings imposed upon the African population by the slave-trade and was one of the chief contributors to its overthrow. At the same time he constantly urged upon the British Government their obligation to assist the Sultan in maintaining his position against foreign encroachment. Barghash, meanwhile, remained until too late sublimely indifferent to the political insecurity of his position. He had submitted to Britain over the slave-trade and, in so far as he felt competent to think of political matters, he relied upon Britain to protect him. In 1877 he freely offered to Sir William Mackinnon, founder of the British India Steam Navigation Company, a concession to develop his mainland territories between the coast and Lake Victoria in return for a share in the profits and a portion of the customs revenue. Mackinnon and his associates, meanwhile, would administer the region with complete authority. The British Government had little interest in such imperial ventures and rejected the proposal. Mackinnon, who in 1872 had started a monthly mail service between Aden and Zanzibar, did not lose interest in East Africa, however, and Barghash was always ready to surrender his administrative responsibilities to a promising collaborator.

If Barghash was indifferent to the exercise of sovereign power Kirk could not remain unperturbed by the growing interest in East African exploration among representatives of the European powers. On April 6, 1877, he wrote to the Foreign Secretary, Lord Derby, in answer to an appeal for help against Egyptian expansion from Kabaka Mutesa of Buganda, and in October 1880, to check a threat still nearer home, he induced Barghash to send a military force under the command of Mathews to Momboio on the mainland opposite Pemba. There Mathews established a post to act as proof of the Sultan's authority not only to the slave-traders but also to the European powers. It was Kirk's intention to set up a series of similar posts stretching to Ugogo, but the Foreign Office refused to give its sanction lest Britain should be committed to defining the extent of the Sultan's dominions. This action on the part of the British Government had serious repercussions. The Anglo-French Declaration of 1862 had recognized the Sultan's independence but had omitted to define the limits of his territory. The omission provided a wide loophole in the 1880s when the Germans tried to seize any territory over which no clearly defined sovereignty existed. Barghash's belated recognition of his danger was reflected in his attempt to induce Tippoo Tip to act as his agent at Tabora, but, as has been seen already, Tippoo was too involved in his own vast trading empire to take up the Sultan's cause in the less profitable centre of Tabora. Meanwhile, British help, so readily forthcoming to restrain the activities of the French slave-traders or to tumble down pretenders to the throne of Zanzibar who might strive to win the support of the island's slave-trading community, proved unreliable when other issues were predominant. The loyal observation by Britain of the 1862 Declaration was, in fact, a two-edged weapon as far as Zanzibar was concerned, for though it ensured the succession of Sultans loyal to British anti-slave-trade activities it did little to protect Zanzibar against the many pressures to which the island and its inhabitants became subject in the 1880s.[1]

The earliest attempts by Europeans to penetrate the East African mainland did not foreshadow the violent political activity of the closing years of the nineteenth century, although experience in other parts of the world suggested that great social revolutions might result. For the first Europeans to establish themselves on the East African mainland in the nineteenth century were Christian missionaries. Yet East Africa itself was not the attraction. Ludwig Krapf, the son of a farmer, was born near Tübingen in Germany, in 1810. As a boy he wanted to be a sea captain but his father was unable to afford the money for his training. Some little time later he was attracted by an essay which he read on the spread of Christianity. He offered his services as a missionary and at the age of seventeen became a student at the missionary college of Basle. Krapf later joined the Church Missionary Society in England and set out in 1837 on his first journey to Africa as an agent of that Society. Ethiopia was his objective and he joined a branch of the C.M.S. in Adowa. After a short stay there he moved farther south to work among the Shoa and it was then that he was attracted by the idea of trying to proselytize the Galla. He was under the mistaken impression that the Galla occupied a great part of central Africa and that a mission to them would have far-reaching effects. In 1842, therefore, he left his work in the kingdom of Shoa and after a hazardous journey to the coast made his way to Egypt. From there he returned to Aden to consider his future plans. Krapf's idea was to go to the East African coast and from there to make his way into the interior and so make contact with the Galla from a new direction. He reached Zanzibar in January 1844, after calling briefly in Mombasa which impressed him as a promising starting-point for his work.

[1] R. M. Lyne: *An Apostle of Empire*. Allen and Unwin, London, 1936. This biography of Lloyd Mathews gives a detailed picture of Zanzibar in the last quarter of the nineteenth century.

During his two months' stay in Zanzibar he received considerable assistance from Sultan Seyyid Said who showed a great interest in the missionary's tale of his adventures in Ethiopia and warned him against the dangers he would be likely to encounter on the mainland.

Krapf settled in Mombasa with his wife in May 1844, and set himself to learn the Swahili language. Soon malaria attacked his family and while the missionary was lying dangerously ill his wife died on July 13, 1844, four days after giving birth to a baby daughter. Five days later the child also died. Far from abandoning his work in circumstances which appeared so utterly hostile, Krapf redoubled his efforts. He travelled extensively around the outskirts of Mombasa, yet within the first five months of his stay there he found time to translate the whole of the New Testament into Swahili and to compile an outline grammar and dictionary of the language. The main object of his journeyings was to discover a suitable site for a mission station. This he found in the village of Rabai, only a few miles inland from Mombasa and standing on a raised piece of land which commanded a wonderful view of Mombasa town and the sea. On June 10, 1846, Krapf was joined in Mombasa by the Rev. J. Rebmann who, after overcoming the inevitable bout of malaria, travelled with Krapf to Rabai to obtain the permission of the local elders to found a mission station there. Both missionaries suffered from recurrent attacks of fever but as soon as they had established a firm foothold at Rabai they turned their attention to the west. In September 1847 Rebmann set out on his first long journey to visit the country of the Wateita. He carried with him a letter from the Governor of Mombasa calling upon any chiefs he met to give him whatever assistance he might require. This journey, which lasted about a month, was the forerunner of many great adventures of exploration by the two missionaries. In April 1848 Rebmann set out to visit the Chagga. On May 11 he saw what he took to be a white cloud in the sky. His guide told him that the cloud was cold and he came to the startling conclusion that what he saw could only be snow. He had set eyes on Mount Kilimanjaro. On the slopes of the great mountain he was met by Masaki, one of the leading Chagga chiefs, who received him with friendship and invited him to return and teach his people.

By June 11 Rebmann was back in Mombasa after making what

he regarded as a most satisfactory journey. He learned, however, that Masaki was not the greatest of the Chagga chiefs but that Mankinga was looked upon by the Chagga as the most powerful of their rulers. Later in the year, therefore, he set out again, determined to get into touch with Mankinga. Masaki tried to hold up his march but with the aid of some of Mankinga's soldiers Rebmann was able to reach the great chief's country. After being suitably sprinkled by a witch-doctor with a charm made of blood the missionary was allowed to make contact with Mankinga who seemed so well disposed towards him that he could have settled immediately in his country. But Rebmann thought it important to return first to Rabai which he reached once again in February 1849.

Rebmann's travels had opened up interesting prospects to him as a missionary but his most important achievement had been the discovery of Kilimanjaro. Yet, such was the fate of African explorers that, although he had seen the mountain clearly and had spent some time at its base, his reports of a snow-capped eminence standing on the Equator aroused violent opposition among some of the arm-chair geographers of England.[1] One of them even argued that Rebmann must have mistaken for snow a special, light-coloured type of rock, or quartz, which was likely to be found on the summit of equatorial mountains and which from a distance would look like snow. But Rebmann stuck to his view. He had discussed with the Chagga the white cap on Kilimanjaro and had been convinced that they fully understood the nature and properties of snow. Nevertheless, he was unable to convert his critics.

Kilimanjaro was not the only discovery of the missionaries of Rabai. Travelling north-westwards into the country of the Wakamba, Ludwig Krapf reached Kitui on November 26, 1849. The chief at Kitui, Kivoi, told him that he himself had been to the Chagga country and had seen the white mountain of Kilimanjaro and added that there was another snow-capped mountain some six days' journey from Kitui. He urged Krapf to ascend a small hill a little beyond the village, but as it was the rainy season the mountain was invisible. As Krapf was leaving Kitui on December 3, 1849, however, he suddenly saw Mount Kenya distinctly, rising up in two large pillars to the north-west.

[1] W. D. Cooley: *Inner Africa Laid Open.* Longman, Brown, Green and Longman, London, 1852, pp. 75–130.

Rebmann, in the meantime, had set out in April 1849, on his third visit to the Chagga, hoping to penetrate to the land of the Wanyamwezi. The Chagga chief, Mankinga, Rebmann's former benefactor, now showed himself in a different light. He did not want Rebmann to pass beyond his country, so he deprived the missionary of all the stock of goods which he had brought as presents, thus making his further advance impossible. Disappointed in his plans and with his health once again undermined, Rebmann made a weary journey back to Rabai in June.

During the previous year Krapf had also travelled to the west and south-west. It was in July of 1848 that he made his first visit to the powerful chiefdom of Usambara. Unlike Rebmann, Krapf met with no importunities from the chiefs on the route. So great was the authority of the ruler of Usambara, Kimweri, that none of his subjects dared to ask for tribute lest they should incur his anger. Kimweri himself received Krapf with dignity and friendship. He urged the missionary to send teachers to his country and offered gifts of ivory and slaves or cattle in return for the presents which Krapf himself had brought. Krapf refused the gifts, however, explaining that he was on a journey of goodwill and was not wishing to trade. Kimweri continued to treat him kindly and when he was due to leave suggested he should return by a much easier route to Pangani at the coast and thence by sea to Mombasa. On his homeward journey, therefore, Krapf was able once again to visit Zanzibar where he was received with great kindness by the Sultan who was greatly interested in the news about Mount Kilimanjaro.

Krapf's subsequent journey to Ukamba and Kitui in 1849 encouraged the hope of establishing among the Wakamba a mission station which would be the first of a series of posts penetrating into the interior of the continent and which would fulfil his ambition to get in touch once more with the Galla. In July 1851 he set out again from Rabai with the object of setting up a station in the highlands beyond the Athi River. The interest shown by the Wakamba, among whom he settled, soon became more of a burden than a subject for rejoicing. Scarcely for a moment was he left alone. His reading was an unfailing source of interest to them, and whenever he tried to write they wanted to know what he was writing about and whether what he had written contained any sorcery. Many also came to beg gifts from him or to see his various possessions which fascinated them with their novelty. Others brought him gifts of food but wanted far greater presents in return. Still others were merely curious and attended for their own entertainment. Eventually Krapf was driven to the conclusion that he must move on, via Kivoi's village in Kitui, and attempt to reach the Tana River. Kivoi was anxious to accompany Krapf to the river and set out with him in August. After some days the party was set upon by robbers and dispersed. Kivoi himself was killed and Krapf had a miraculous escape from the arrows of his attackers. His discovery of the upper reaches of the Tana was virtually an accident, for he stumbled upon the river in his search for water. He was fortunate, however, in getting in touch once again with the Wakamba and subsequently in returning to Rabai.

In the years which followed, Krapf and Rebmann, together with another recruit, J. Erhardt, who had joined the station at Rabai in 1849, made a number of journeys into the interior of East Africa, adding still further to the knowledge of the hinterland of Mombasa. The threat of the Masai and the Galla robber bands was ever present, but the peoples nearer the coast seem to have been consistently friendly and to have offered their help to the missionaries as they travelled about the country.

In setting out for the Tana River Krapf had had a distant hope of finding the source of the Nile. It was not, however, to the missionaries but to more professional explorers that this honour fell. While Krapf and Rebmann were the first to open up the hinterland of Mombasa, the main penetration of the interior took place farther south. Nevertheless, it was the publication in England in 1856 of a map drawn by Erhardt, showing the country between the coast and a great inland sea, which proved to be one of the most important factors in attracting the explorers, Burton and Speke, to East Africa in 1857. It was to the Arab traders that the early European explorers owed a debt of gratitude for blazing the trail into the interior, however. For it was along well established trade routes that the first Europeans travelled into Africa in search of geographical knowledge.

Both Richard Burton and John Speke were explorers of great experience when they arrived in Zanzibar on December 19, 1856. Both were officers of the East India Company's army and Burton had distinguished himself as a linguist and in particular as an Arabic scholar. In 1853 he had journeyed in disguise to Mecca and Medina, and in 1854, again in disguise, he had travelled to Harar. The idea of exploring the lake regions of central Africa appealed to his vivid imagination and challenged his courage and fortitude. In 1856 he proposed to the Royal Geographical Society that he should lead an expedition to the heart of the African continent and the Society agreed to sponsor his plan. The Foreign Office contributed a thousand pounds towards the expenses of the expedition and the Court of Directors of the East India Company allowed Burton two years' leave from their army. The flamboyant romanticism which coloured the boldest actions of his companion found no echo in Speke. Speke himself had spent many furloughs in India preparing himself for the great task of exploring the African continent by making journeys into unknown territory. Nevertheless, it was not so much the possibility of discovering unknown lands as the hope of adding to his father's collection of zoological specimens which attracted Speke to Africa. He had shared the hazards of Burton's expedition in Somalia in 1854 and 1855 although he had had little taste for disguising himself with a huge hot turban and 'baggy loose drawers', while the theatrical effect of a broad belt decorated with pistol and dirk might have damped his enthusiasm had he not been so determined to fulfil his aim of penetrating into the heart of the dark continent. In spite of these differences of character, the two men had appreciated each other's qualities of courage and determination in the course of their earlier expedition, and there seemed little reason to expect that their mutual respect would suffer in the course of their new venture.

Before starting out upon their main undertaking the two travellers first visited Mombasa where Burton was anxious to talk with Rebmann and to learn something about the details of his earlier travels. On their return journey they left their dhow at the mouth of the Pangani River and then travelled by canoe and on foot to Vuga, the headquarters of the state of Usambara. Kimweri, the former great chief of the Sambaa, was now an old man and his authority had been greatly circumscribed by the raids of the Masai. Returning from Vuga both travellers were attacked by fever but eventually reached Zanzibar in March 1857. Burton carried quinine with him but was reluctant to use it because he was not sure of the size of the doses nor of the times at which they should be taken. Subsequently both travellers suffered greatly from malaria and Burton used a compound of aloes, quinine and opium which he considered to be the best antidote.

Burton was now anxious to start for the interior as soon as possible. Early in June a half-caste Arab guide, provided by the Sultan of Zanzibar, was sent to the mainland near Bagamoyo along with a Hindu customs clerk, charged with recruiting porters, but they met with little success. Traders had spread rumours about the objects of the expedition which frightened away possible recruits. Donkeys were bought instead, but a considerable proportion of the stock of ammunition and trade goods had to be left behind under an arrangement whereby the more necessary items would be forwarded in ten days' time by the Hindu traders at the coast. In the event, these loads reached Burton eleven months later. The list of the provisions and equipment which Burton took with him is remarkable evidence of the immense preparations which preceded an expedition of this sort. Camp furniture had to be chosen with particular attention to its lightness and durability in all weathers. Instruments included chronometers, prismatic compasses, an azimuth compass, a thermometer, a portable sun-dial, a rain-gauge, sextants in boxes, a pocket lens, a mountain barometer and a variety of other important aids to observation and map-making. Clothing, bedding and shoes were also selected with care and provisions ranged from a box of cigars to the various spices so necessary to make palatable the food which they might be able to pick up on their way. In addition there were the loads of goods, particularly of cloth, to be given in exchange for food and hospitality on the journey.

The expedition was accompanied by an escort of twelve Baluch soldiers under a jemadar. They were armed with matchlocks, shields, swords, daggers and knives and had with them forty pounds of gunpowder and a thousand lead bullets. The explorers were also fortunate in the personalities of their two Yao gunbearers, Sidi Bombay and Mwinyi Mabruki, both of whom were later to have remarkable careers of exploration. After completing the expedition with Burton and Speke in 1858 they joined Speke's subsequent expedition in 1860 to Lake Victoria and down the Nile to Cairo, whence they returned to Zanzibar. In 1871 they joined Stanley on his expedition to Ujiji, where he met Livingstone, and returned with him to the coast the following year. Mabruki also returned to Livingstone at Tabora, and Bombay would have accompanied him if he had not been prevented by illness from leaving the coast. In 1873 Bombay crossed Africa with Cameron to the west coast at Benguela, returning by ship to Zanzibar in 1876. Their various employers were sometimes annoyed with them and sometimes angry, too, but the service they rendered to all the explorers was of infinite importance.

After all its preliminary organization the caravan got on the move on July 1, 1857. 'It was like driving a herd of wild cattle,' Burton wrote, for they covered only two miles on the first day. When they camped for the night desertions began as the porters' courage ebbed before the prospect of traversing unknown country and meeting strange peoples. Gradually, however, the caravan began to take shape, and each day greater distances were covered. In spite of frequent attacks of malaria which afflicted both Europeans the first 118 miles were covered in eighteen days, and the caravan cleared the country of the Wazaramo after twice buying their way past hostile parties of warriors. By July 25 they had reached Zungomero, an important caravan station immediately south of the Uluguru Mountains. Here they halted for almost a fortnight to reorganize. Both leaders were worn out by constant fever and several of the porters deserted. The quartermaster had proved to be dishonest and other porters were unwilling to carry their loads. When the caravan continued its journey on August 7 Burton and Speke were almost too weak to sit on their donkeys, but Burton's determination remained unshaken. An attempt by the Baluch escort to browbeat him only led to his threatening to push on without them. Faced with this stern attitude the Baluchis gave way. Farther along the route Arab caravans were encountered returning to the coast. The members of one of these had contracted smallpox but, by good fortune, the disease did not attack the whole of Burton's caravan, although a few of his party succumbed to it. Yet another Arab caravan helped the explorers with porters and donkeys, the mortality rate among the latter having been very heavy. Signs of the activities of African slave-raiders were also encountered in the shape of deserted villages, and the raiders themselves passed the explorers' caravan to attack other villages which Burton and Speke had only recently quitted.

Reaching the bare plains of Ugogo, the caravan was assailed in earnest by demands for *hongo* which made heavy inroads into the stock of trade goods. Fortunately, perhaps, for the security of the travellers Burton accepted these demands as reasonable customs duties and made no attempt to resist. It was in Ugogo, too, that Burton once again had reason to thank the Arab traders with whom he came in contact. At an earlier stage of the journey one of the porters had deserted, abandoning an important load which contained survey books. Burton's efforts to discover this load had been unsuccessful, but while he was in Ugogo a large, well-equipped Arab caravan arrived from the coast bringing with it the load which Burton had lost. The Arabs suggested that Burton and Speke should attach themselves to their caravan, an offer which the two explorers for a time were glad to accept.

On November 7 the caravan marched into Kazeh, the site of the modern Tabora. Here, Burton estimated, about twenty-five Arabs were in residence, although this probably did not represent the true Arab population since many of them would be away on journeys to the coast or farther into the interior. Those who were present proved both helpful and hospitable and it was while the travellers were resting at Kazeh that they learned that the large lake of which they were in search in fact comprised three lakes. This exciting news revived the tired men and after a month spent in reorganization and in collecting new trade goods Burton decided to push on in spite of the difficulty of recruiting new porters during the rainy season when the local population were engaged in cultivation. In any case, friction had begun to develop between the Baluch escort and the people of Kazeh so that further delay was inadvisable. On December 5, therefore, Speke went on ahead with an advance guard and Burton followed three days later. At this stage of the journey the latter had to be carried in a litter owing to the violence of the fever which had taken hold of him. The Baluch escort behaved badly, being under the impression that their leader was dying, and the situation was made serious by the constant fear of attack by the Watuta, a branch of the Ngoni, who were known to ravage the area between Kazeh and Lake Tanganyika. Although nothing was seen of these raiders the caravan proceeded nervously and the evidence of Watuta raids which was encountered in the devastated villages along the route did little to restore confidence.

On February 13, 1858, the explorers at length reached the shore of Lake Tanganyika. Speke was bitterly disappointed because he could see nothing but mist and glare owing to an affliction of the eyes. But the travellers had achieved the first stage of their journey and even the shabbiness of Ujiji could not detract from that. The town, which Burton had expected to resemble Zanzibar, turned out to be nothing more than a collection of hovels. The population were mainly Waha and the headman was both drunken and dishonest. During the first fortnight of the stay in Ujiji Burton and Speke stayed in an Arab house, too blind and ill to derive much pleasure from their success. Then, after failing to hire a dhow, they set out at length on April 10 in two canoes to explore the northern end of the lake. At this stage they were mainly anxious to discover whether the river which they had been told flowed out of the lake could be the source of the Nile. *En route*, however, they learned that the river ran into the lake rather than out of it, a piece of information which struck both as a bitter blow. In fact they never reached the northern end of the lake because their crews refused to carry them farther, and by May 13 they were back in Ujiji, and fortunately in better health.

With their stock of goods running low Burton came to the conclusion that they could not hope to explore the southern end of the lake. He therefore decided to return to Kazeh, and they embarked upon their journey on May 26 following a more northerly route than the one they had taken on the outward journey. Kazeh was reached on June 20 by which time relations between the two leaders had become seriously strained. Both men were cut out to be leaders, but as a result of the hardships and difficulties which they had undergone their differing personalities aroused feelings of animosity which grew more pronounced during their second sojourn in Kazeh. The events which followed emphasized still further the cleavage between them. Burton was anxious to make preparations for the return journey to the coast. Speke, on the other hand, was violently attracted by the idea of investigating the more northerly of the three lakes of which the Arabs had spoken. Burton was not sorry to see him go, and Speke set out early in July. Reaching the southern end of Lake Victoria on July 30 he followed the eastern side of the Mwanza Gulf until, on August 3, he experienced his moment of destiny. For here it was that he saw spread out before him the great expanse of Lake Victoria. With characteristic restraint he recorded the momentous decision to which this vision led him. 'I no longer felt any doubt,' he wrote, 'that the lake at my feet gave birth to that interesting river, the source of which has been the subject of so much speculation, and the object of so many explorers.'[1] In what proportion wishful thinking mingled with cool calculation to produce this conclusion it is impossible to say. Certainly Speke's character would lead one to think that the latter element must have played an important part. Yet there can be no doubt that it was a touch of inspiration which led him to state his opinion so convincingly and although it was totally out of character it proved to be fully justified. This day marked the turning-point in Speke's career. Almost at once there began a trickle of criticism which built up to a river of adverse comment in succeeding years. By August 25 he was back with Burton at Kazeh, where his news was received by his leader with a total absence of enthusiasm. Between Kazeh and the coast the bickering between them became more acute. Speke's decision to hurry back to England, leaving Burton sick in Aden, subsequently led to heavy criticism, for it was Speke who received the first acclaim for an expedition of which Burton had been the leader. But it was his theory as to the source of the Nile which had sped Speke's footsteps homeward and that theory was entirely his own.

Sir Roderick Murchison, President of the Royal Geographical Society, was enthusiastic about Speke's news and enlisted the aid of the Society and of the British Government in organizing a new expedition, to be led by Speke himself, in an attempt to prove beyond all doubt the truth of his claim. On April 27, 1860, Speke set out again from Portsmouth on board the steam frigate, *Forte*, accompanied by a new and more congenial travelling companion, Captain J. A. Grant, whom he had known well in India. Here was renewed that quest for the source of the Nile which had occupied the minds of geographers and dreamers for thousands of years. It was a quest which Speke was convinced he would be able to bring to a triumphant conclusion, but it was not for some fifteen years that the world accepted his claim.

Sailing around the Cape the two travellers landed in Zanzibar on August 17, 1860, and after six weeks' preparation the march into the interior began early in October. Although for some considerable distance Speke was covering ground he had traversed

[1] J. H. Speke: *What Led to the Discovery of the Source of the Nile*. Blackwood, Edinburgh and London, 1864, p. 307.

before, the journey was far from being an easy one. Meanwhile, Burton had published his account of their earlier expedition in which he had launched a thorough attack upon Speke's views on the size of Lake Victoria and upon his claim that it could be the source of the Nile.[1] Four thousand miles away, in the heart of Africa, beset by all the troubles to which travellers were subject, Speke could do little to vindicate himself. A communication reached England bearing the date September 30, 1861, and stating that Speke was still south of Lake Victoria. Then there was silence for more than a year.

A cable from Alexandria brought further news, later proved to be false, that Consul Petherick had died somewhere in the southern Sudan. It was upon Petherick that Speke was depending for supplies when he reached Gondokoro after one of the most difficult parts of his journey. Sir Roderick Murchison was gravely apprehensive about the explorers' fate. There followed further months of suspense. Then another telegram from Alexandria announced that Speke and his party had reached Khartoum. This was followed by a telegram from Speke himself stating simply, 'The Nile is settled!' How untrue this optimistic prognostication turned out to be Speke himself was to find when he returned to England. In the meantime he had the satisfaction of having achieved a great feat of endurance and determination. During the months which had elapsed since the last news of him had been received from Kazeh he had travelled round the western end of Lake Victoria, carefully mapping the north-western shore of the lake. He had met and stayed with the refined and gentle Rumanika, ruler of Karagwe, with the boisterous young Mutesa, Kabaka of Buganda, and with Kamurasi, the grasping chief of Bunyoro-Kitara. After several months' delay at Mutesa's capital, while the young monarch had resisted all his attempts to continue his journey, Speke had at last struck eastward and had come upon the Nile at Bulondoganyi, some thirty miles north of the lake. Marching upstream, he had reached the mighty 'stones', as the Baganda called the waterfall which marked the dividing line between the lake and the river emerging from it, and had named the cataract the Ripon Falls after the Earl de Grey and Ripon, who had been President of the Royal Geographical Society when he left England. It was here, too, beside the Ripon Falls, that Speke had conceived

---

[1] Richard F. Burton: *The Lake Regions of Central Africa*. Longman, Green, Longman and Roberts, London, 1860.

the idea of encouraging missionaries to come and settle in the land to the north of the lake, an idea which the Church Missionary Society, anxious to develop by gradual stages from the coast, considered to be visionary. He had been unable to sail down the Nile because of an encounter with hostile Banyoro which forced him to travel across country to Kamurasi's headquarters. This diversion was to result in adverse criticism in England, more particularly when, after further delays at Kamurasi's headquarters, he had crossed the Nile at the Karuma Falls and had then struck across country to Afuddu, near the present Nimule, instead of following the river. It was quickly pointed out by his detractors that there was no justification for assuming that the river which Speke had seen emerging from Lake Victoria was the same river which he met again at Afuddu. From Nimule Speke had gone on to Gondokoro where he was met by that great explorer and renowned sportsman Mr. (later Sir Samuel) Baker, who had come from Khartoum with his equally gallant wife to give what help he could. It was at Gondokoro, too, that Speke received the news that he had been awarded the Founder's Medal of the Royal Geographical Society for his discovery of Lake Victoria in 1858.

The joy of Speke's return was soon overshadowed by an attack upon the success of his journey. Burton and others stressed that Speke had touched the shores of what he claimed to be the great Lake Victoria only at the extreme south, during his earlier journey, and at its north-western corner more recently. This, it was argued, was no proof of the existence of a large lake, while the views of the Arabs to which Speke appeared to give much credit could not be relied upon. Scepticism of this nature would have been enough in itself to discourage Speke, but it was followed, soon after the publication of his *Journal of the Discovery of the Source of the Nile*,[1] by a vindictive and vituperative attack from James M'Queen, a fellow of the Royal Geographical Society, in which Speke's character as well as his scientific accuracy was called into question. 'It is with disgust,' M'Queen wrote, 'that we want proper words to express, to find the first names in Europe prostituted, and especially the name of our great and gracious Sovereign insulted and degraded, in giving names to places in this most barbarous and degraded country. . . . The eminent characters seized upon to give names to

[1] William Blackwood and Sons, Edinburgh and London, 1863.

Ripon Falls, Murchison Creek—a stagnant puddle—can scarcely feel gratified by the appropriation of their names.'[1] This was not all. Burton, alongside his own more scientific criticisms of Speke's journal, quoted M'Queen *in extenso* in his book *The Nile Basin*. Then, too, the work of Samuel Baker cast further doubt upon Speke's story. When the two explorers had met at Gondokoro Speke had attempted to assuage Baker's disappointment at being forestalled in his desire to discover the source of the Nile by telling him of another lake which he had heard existed to the north-west of Lake Victoria. After Speke had left to continue his journey northwards Baker had taken up the search for the new lake. The journey through what is now northern Uganda had proved to be most difficult and could never have been accomplished without the assistance of the ruthless Egyptian and Sudanese slavers who dominated the region. In spite of hardships Baker was eventually able to discover the lake which he named Lake Albert. He was also able to prove to his own satisfaction, by the evidence of his own eyes and from information which he obtained from Kamurasi, ruler of Bunyoro, that a river which flowed into the northern end of Lake Albert and almost immediately flowed out again was indeed Speke's Victoria Nile. This river was navigable from Lake Albert to Afuddu. Unfortunately Baker had been unable to circumnavigate the whole of the lake, but so impressed had he been by what he saw of it that he was convinced it must extend for a considerable distance in a southerly direction. This view was eagerly seized upon by Speke's critics who maintained that the Nile was probably fed from Lake Albert which in turn must draw its waters from a much greater river flowing into it from the south. The great explorer Livingstone had already advanced the view that the Nile rose far to the south, and Baker's activities seemed to support this theory. Livingstone himself wrote: 'Poor Speke has turned his back upon the real sources of the Nile. . . . His river at Ripon Falls was not large enough for the Nile.'

Now the tragedy approached its climax. It was thought that a debate between Speke and Burton in the presence of the British Association would provide an opportunity for scientific minds to hear both sides of the case and to reach a fair conclusion. A meeting

[1] Richard F. Burton: *The Nile Basin* (Part II Captain's Speke's discovery of the source of the Nile. A Review by James M'Queen, F.R.G.S., reprinted by permission from the *Morning Advertiser*). Tinsley Brothers, London, 1864, pp. 109–10.

was arranged in Bath for September 16, 1864. Burton and Speke met at midday on the 15th, but later in the day Speke, while out shooting, mishandled his gun and fatally shot himself.

This tragic accident did nothing to stem the attacks of Speke's critics. Even his staunch supporter, Sir Roderick Murchison, was forced to bow before the weight of opposition. On May 22, 1865, Murchison delivered an obituary oration to the Royal Geographical Society which was full of whole-hearted praise of Speke and his work. But he concluded his speech with the announcement that, with the approval of the Council, he proposed to send Livingstone to examine the country between Lake Nyasa and Lake Tanganyika in an attempt to dispel the doubts and uncertainties which still prevailed concerning the watersheds of central Africa. Among other things Livingstone was to try to discover whether any river flowed northward out of Lake Tanganyika to join the Nile.[1] The Nile quest was still on, and Livingstone's journey, which proved to be his last, still failed to solve the problems which confused the geographers. A map drawn by E. Stanford to accompany Livingstone's *Last Journals*,[2] published in 1874, still showed the shore of Lake Victoria from Mwanza westward round to the Ripon Falls as delineated by Speke, but the opposite shore was drawn generally parallel to it at a distance of only thirty to fifty miles. East of this lake, which was shown as Lake Okara, there appeared another lake, named Lake Kavirondo, sixty miles long and fifty broad, and connected with Lake Okara by the Kidette river.

Although ten years after his death Speke's discoveries still remained unvindicated the tide of opinion was beginning to turn. In the middle of 1874 Colonel Chaillé-Long an American, attached to the staff of Colonel Gordon, Governor of Egypt's Equatorial Province, was sent to visit Mutesa, the ruler of Buganda. In the course of his return journey in August he sailed down the Nile from Bulondoganyi, the point reached by Speke, as far as Lake Kyoga, and thus became the first foreigner to discover the lake. At the same time his journey verified one of the doubtful sections on Speke's map. Early in 1876 Colonel Gordon himself, with the assistance of two Italians, Gessi and Piaggia, surveyed the Nile

[1] *Journal of the Royal Geographical Society*, Vol. XXV, 1865, pp. clxxvi–clxxviii.

[2] H. Waller: *The Last Journals of David Livingstone in Central Africa*, 2 Vols. John Murray, London, 1874.

from Dufile to the point where it enters Lake Kyoga. Now the whole course of Speke's river had been verified. In April of 1876 Gessi also circumnavigated Lake Albert, proving that Baker's estimate of its size was unduly exaggerated and that the only river of any consequence which entered it, apart from the Victoria Nile, could not be regarded as a significant tributary of the Nile. There remained then the great question as to the size of Lake Victoria and its claim to be the source of the Nile.

It was to Henry Morton Stanley, perhaps the greatest of all the African explorers, that the honour of making these discoveries fell. Already Stanley had earned for himself a mixed reputation by a journey from the east coast to Ujiji to make contact with Dr. Livingstone in 1871. A newspaper man of humble origins he had to fight an unceasing battle not only against the hardships of the African continent but also against the vagaries of his own character. Conscious of his boundless energy and ability he suffered constantly from the conviction that he was being looked down upon by the aristocratic patrons of exploration and geographical research. But, however uncertain he may have been in the presence of members of the Royal Geographical Society, he was wholly at home among the jungles, mountains and plains of tropical Africa. Sent out in 1874 by the *Daily Telegraph* and the *New York Herald* upon yet another African odyssey he travelled with all the drive and organization of his adopted country, America. He made the 720-mile journey from the east coast to the southern shore of Lake Victoria in the amazing time of 103 days, compared with Burton's and Speke's time of 154 days from the coast to Kazeh. He took with him in sections a boat, the *Lady Alice*, which he launched on Lake Victoria, and in the course of the next few months he sailed round the whole lake. In a series of letters to the *Daily Telegraph*, accompanied by maps of his travels, he proved to the world that Speke had been right in his surmise that Lake Victoria was one great lake. Stanley himself had previously been among those who believed that there were probably several small lakes, but now, utterly convinced by his own experiences, he took up Speke's defence with all the journalistic skill at his command. There remained, however, still one further question to settle. Was Lake Victoria indeed the source of the Nile or was the lake itself fed by some great river? On this point Stanley still disagreed with Speke. At first he had been impressed by the size of the River Simiyu which flows into Speke Gulf at the southern end of the lake. Later, however, he changed his mind when he saw the greater river, Kagera, flowing into the lake from the west. The *New York Herald*, whose agent Stanley was, took up the theme of Stanley's discovery with enthusiasm. 'The grand problem of this geographical era,' the newspaper wrote, 'which may be said to have commenced with Ptolemy, has been the discovery of the sources of the Nile. To solve it, many explorers essayed and failed, leaving to Henry M. Stanley the palm of the victor, the glorious prize of success.' But the newspaper had strayed beyond the truth. Speke had already seen the Kagera, and after due consideration had decided that it was not large enough or important enough to be considered the true source of the Nile. Sir Rutherford Alcock, the President of the Royal Geographical Society, voiced the views of geographers throughout the world on May 26, 1877, when he said, 'One other remark regarding the Kagera. Mr. Stanley tells us that during the dry season it exceeds in volume the Thames and the Severn united . . . but whether this river or the Shimeeyu (Simiyu), or any other river flowing into the lake, is to be considered a source or not—among so many and all so distant from the Nile—the honour will still remain with the parent-mother Victoria.'[1]

The Nile quest was at an end. But, if geographers might relax and draw their maps with greater authority, other and more disturbing forces were beginning to work in eastern Africa as a result of the travels of the great explorers of the 1860s and 1870s. The outstanding figure in the new movement was David Livingstone, who drew together by his own adventures the strands of exploration and missionary endeavour. To appreciate the significance of his contribution it is necessary to turn back some thirty years or more. Livingstone had been posted to the London Missionary Society station in Bechuanaland in 1841 and had subsequently travelled northward across the Kalahari desert. Early in his career he recognized the peculiar problems of missionary work among primitive people who possessed so few of the material comforts of life and who, through the growing activities of the slave-traders, lacked even day to day security. The conclusions he reached were of the greatest importance to future missionary policy in Africa. For he became convinced that steady, step by step, evangelization could not succeed

[1] *Journal of the Royal Geographical Society*, Vol. XLVII, 1877, p. cxciv.

unless the way had been prepared by a more general civilizing campaign. For this purpose he believed it necessary to establish a mission station in the very centre of the territory where the missionaries could carry on their work, rather than at the coast, but the station must be linked with the coast by a reasonable line of communications. Along that line of communications would flow not only the word of God but also trade goods to improve the daily life of the African population.

It was in pursuit of this principle that, having found what he believed to be a suitably healthy site for a mission station, Livingstone started out upon the remarkable journey which between 1853 and 1856 took him across the continent to Loanda on the west coast and thence back again to Quilimane on the east coast in search of a satisfactory line of communication. In the course of this journey he discovered the Victoria Falls and also confirmed the views on policy which he had been formulating. His contacts with the slave-trade—which had not by any means developed to the limit it was to reach not very long afterwards—convinced him that only a legitimate form of trade could overcome the horrors perpetrated by the Arab slavers and their African accomplices.

Returning to England, Livingstone found himself a public hero. His appeal for help to bring commerce and Christianity to central Africa met with an enthusiastic response from all quarters. In the course of 1857 the Government of Lord Palmerston made available the sum of £5,000 to equip an expedition, to be led by Livingstone, with the object of exploring the possibilities of the River Zambezi as a highroad to the regions of the interior now beset by the slave-trader. In December 1857, before setting out on his expedition early in the following year, Livingstone made his famous appeal in Cambridge for missionary support. The result was the formation of a new missionary society, the Universities Mission to Central Africa. The Society was new, also, in its approach to its task, for its object was to set up centres of Christianity and civilization in central Africa at which the teaching of Christianity would go side by side with instruction in agriculture and with the encouragement of trade.

From the point of view of Livingstone the explorer the journey was a success, for Lake Nyasa was discovered as a result of his excursion up the Shire River, a northern tributary of the Zambezi. But as a means of preparing the way for missionary activities the expedition was a complete failure. The Zambezi was found to present serious difficulties as a gateway to Africa because the mouth was not navigable and rapids were located farther upstream. The Shire, too, was blocked by the Murchison cataracts, while the River Rovuma, farther north, had also proved to be impracticable for navigation. Nevertheless, when the first group of missionaries arrived at the mouth of the Zambezi in 1861 under the leadership of Bishop Mackenzie, Livingstone led them inland to the home of the Ma-Nyanja tribe, an area which had recently become the field of activity of the Yao slavers.

With precarious lines of communication behind them Mackenzie and his followers quickly found themselves faced by an even greater problem, the antagonism of the Yao. Inevitably too, and with Livingstone's approval, the bishop became involved in disputes with the slavers which made the position of the missionaries almost impossible. Three of their number died, and others, suffering from ill health, had to return to Britain. Mackenzie himself died from fever and was replaced by Bishop Tozer. The latter moved the mission headquarters to a new and healthier site, but not long afterwards and in the face of Livingstone's stern opposition he decided to transfer the station to Zanzibar. This retreat from the mainland might have been serious, for so far no other missionary societies had interested themselves in eastern Africa. Since 1840 the Roman Catholic Verona Fathers had been trying to reach the lake area along the River Nile, but their efforts had been restricted by sickness, by the hostility of the Sudan tribes and by the marshy country which was intersected by rivers choked with sudd. The Church Missionary Society, active in India since the second decade of the century, was fully occupied with the problems which followed upon the Indian mutiny, and its attention had not yet turned seriously to East Africa in spite of the pioneer work of Krapf and Rebmann. Even the problems of the East African slave-trade failed to attract the attention of the missions to the extent they had done on the west coast.

Nevertheless, the slave-trade did eventually play its part in arousing missionary interest in East Africa. In spite of the efforts which had been made to enforce the anti-slave-trade treaties, and in spite of the genuine co-operation of successive sultans of Zanzibar, the trade still continued along the east coast and many slavers escaped the watchfulness of the naval patrols off-shore. A few slaves were rescued annually, however, and the problem of maintaining and succouring these people was one with which the official British representative in Zanzibar had no machinery to deal. Bishop Tozer, therefore, agreed to accept responsibility for any released slaves passed on to him by the British Consul. The arrangement offered opportunities to Tozer and his fellow-missionaries which extended beyond the mere rendering of humanitarian services to destitute human beings. Already examples were available in India, Mauritius and the Seychelles of villages for freed slaves from which it was hoped that a few of the more able converts might later go forth into their own country to preach the gospel of Christ. The journey of Burton and Speke to Lake Tanganyika had shown that in spite of difficulties the route into the interior was not impassable, and Speke's later expedition had confirmed this information. This discovery was made at an opportune moment, for the abolition of slavery in the United States of America in 1863 had had such a startling effect upon the west-coast slave-trade that philanthropists and missionary societies could, for the first time, turn the full force of their interest upon East Africa. In 1868 the Holy Ghost Fathers from their station in Zanzibar founded a settlement for freed slaves at Bagamoyo on the mainland. The Church Missionary Society also began to urge the British Government to take much sterner measures to control trade in the Indian Ocean. The Government was not slow to respond, and on his way to negotiate an anti-slave-trade treaty with the Sultan of Zanzibar, Sir Bartle Frere called on Pope Pius IX to inform him that Britain would look favourably upon the strengthening of the Roman Catholic missions in East Africa. Frere was also charged with reporting to the Church Missionary Society on the most suitable site for a settlement to handle freed slaves in East Africa. He therefore took the opportunity provided by his visit to make a close inspection of the mission stations in the neighbourhood of Zanzibar, and in consequence of what he saw he firmly recommended that the British Consul should be authorized to subsidize them for their work for freed slaves irrespective of their nationality or denomination.

The seed had been sown, but it was the final adventure of Livingstone which brought it to fruition. On his return to England after his Zambezi expedition the great explorer met with an even warmer reception than before. In startling contrast to the suspicion accorded to Speke's report the account of Livingstone's activities[1] was read with enthusiasm, and geographers were as anxious as Livingstone himself that he should return to East Africa as soon as possible to consolidate and extend his achievements. The controversy over the source of the Nile was an added reason for Livingstone to give his authority to whatever story proved to be true. In the meantime two further explorers, Albrecht Roscher, a native of Hamburg, and Baron Carl von der Decken, had lost their lives exploring the east coast and its immediate hinterland. Roscher had reached the eastern shore of Lake Nyasa in October 1859, shortly after Livingstone had reached its southern end. Turning northwards early in 1860 he was attacked and murdered for the sake of the small amount of equipment that he carried. Von der Decken came to East Africa to join Roscher, but on his arrival in Zanzibar was met with the news of his colleague's death. His attempt to reach Lake Nyasa in the hope of rescuing Roscher's journals was frustrated by the opposition of the Arab slave-traders along the route from Kilwa to the interior. Von der Decken therefore abandoned this objective and instead, in 1861, set out to investigate the truth of Krapf's and Rebmann's claims concerning Mount Kenya and Mount Kilimanjaro. In the course of 1861 and again in 1862 he paid two visits to Kilimanjaro and on the second journey climbed the mountain to a height of 14,000 feet but did not reach the snow-line. In 1865, after a visit to Europe, he set out upon an expedition towards Mount Kenya, following the Juba River, but at the beginning of October he and the doctor who was accompanying his expedition were speared to death in the town of Bardera.

Only six months later Livingstone was once again on East African soil and striking into the interior from Mikindani near the mouth of the Rovuma River. As on his first great journey he was accompanied by only a small number of African porters together with, on this occasion, thirteen marine sepoys supplied by the Bombay Government. The expedition seemed ill-fated from the start. Several of the porters deserted and Livingstone soon found it necessary to dismiss the sepoys. He reached Lake Nyasa in August 1866, after testing to the uttermost his skill in negotiating with Afri-

---

[1] D. Livingstone: *Narrative of an Expedition to the Zambesi and its Tributaries*, 1858-64. John Murray, London, 1865.

cans. There, on the lake, he encountered further difficulties when the Arabs, remembering his attack on the slave-trade during his second expedition, prevented him from obtaining transport across the lake in a dhow. Moving southwards on foot round the lake shore Livingstone encountered a serious food shortage because the villages he passed through had been ravaged and destroyed by slave-traders. The loss of a box of medical stores shortly afterwards was an even more serious blow and when he reached Lake Tanganyika in April 1867, he was seriously ill for a month. Rumours were spread by some of his deserting porters that Livingstone had died, but letters reached England in January 1868 proving the tale to be untrue. With the aid of Arab traders who were more friendly and helpful than those near Lake Nyasa, Livingstone spent two years travelling in the region to the south and south-west of Lake Tanganyika, and it was during this period that he discovered Lakes Mweru and Bangweulu. He reached Ujiji in March 1869, only to find that the stores which he had ordered to be sent from the coast and upon which he was depending so heavily had been looted and little remained.

Livingstone rested in Ujiji for some months and then crossed Lake Tanganyika into Manyema. For more than two years he travelled laboriously about the country west of the lake in the hope of discovering whether the rivers flowing northwards were tributaries of the Congo or, as he hoped, of the Nile. Weakened by illness, and suffering from the hostility of the African peoples, who had recently begun to be oppressed by the slave-trade, he was able to cover far less ground than he had intended. What he saw still further convinced him, if such confirmation were necessary, of the horrors which the slavers were perpetrating. He returned to Ujiji in October 1871, in a weak condition, to find that a further supply of stores sent at his request by Kirk, the British Consul in Zanzibar, had completely disappeared. Eighteen days later help reached him unexpectedly.

Henry Morton Stanley, that other great name in the field of tropical African exploration, first came to East Africa neither as an explorer in the line of Burton and Speke nor yet as a missionary-explorer like Livingstone. Stanley, as has been seen, was a reporter, and for him to get in touch with the world-renowned Livingstone in the very heart of the African continent would be good copy for the newspapers which he represented. There were, however, those who possessed expert knowledge of East Africa and had a close personal acquaintance with Livingstone who openly decried Stanley's venture on the ground that Livingstone was almost certain to be safe in spite of their having received no recent news of him. They could not, of course, have known of the loss of his supplies and in particular of his medical stores. In the event, Stanley's encounter with Livingstone was most opportune although the latter was certainly not lost in the technical sense. For Stanley brought with him not only fresh supplies but also news from the outside world and the encouraging information that the Royal Geographical Society and the British public were vitally interested in Livingstone's activities and discoveries.

In the company of the shy yet bold young man who had come to meet him under such strange circumstances Livingstone took on a new lease of life. Together they explored Lake Tanganyika and Livingstone even returned with Stanley as far as Tabora where the two men stayed together for a month in February and March of 1872. Livingstone, however, refused to accompany Stanley to the coast and the latter set out alone on March 14 carrying with him the news of his friend's activities and achievements.[1] At the coast he met an expedition, equipped by the Royal Geographical Society, which had been sent to relieve Livingstone. On hearing Stanley's news the project was abandoned, but a further expedition, organized more carefully on the basis of the information which Stanley provided, was dispatched some time later under the command of Lieutenant V. L. Cameron, R.N. After spending almost two months in collecting porters Cameron set out from the coast on March 28, 1873. In Tabora, which he reached on August 2 after grave sufferings and difficulties, he learned that Livingstone was dead. He therefore decided to push on to Ujiji and to follow up Livingstone's exploration of Manyema. In the course of 1874 he mapped most of Lake Tanganyika and then, proceeding south-westward, he reached the Atlantic coast near Benguela in November 1875.

When the contents of Livingstone's diary became known to the world they provided both stimulus and justification to all those, missionaries and others, who believed that the challenge of the East African slave-trade must be met. Already the Holy Ghost Fathers were setting up self-contained Christian villages on the mainland, manned by Africans trained in their mission centre in

[1] H. M. Stanley: *How I Found Livingstone*. Samson Low, London, 1872.

Bagamoyo and supported by a European missionary. Following upon Sir Bartle Frere's advice the Church Missionary Society also established a settlement for freed slaves near Mombasa in 1875 and gave it the name of Frere Town. This was to become the most important settlement of its kind provided by the mission societies. Livingstone's own earlier scheme of establishing mission stations in the vicinity of Lake Nyasa was taken up in 1874 by the Free Church of Scotland. The moving figure in the scheme was Dr. James Stewart who had already founded a famous mission station at Lovedale in South Africa in 1861. It was decided that the new station should be sited at the southern end of Lake Nyasa and a small steamer was made available which should sail between the lake and the Murchison cataracts on the Zambezi. The first party of missionaries, under the leadership of E. D. Young who had led one of the Livingstone search parties, set out from London on May 21, 1875, and sailed up the Zambezi as far as the Murchison rapids where they dismantled their steamer to reassemble it on the Shire River and sail into Lake Nyasa on October 11. The mission was accompanied by Harry Henderson, a representative of the established Church of Scotland, whose duty it was to find a site for a sister mission station on behalf of his own church. Henderson eventually selected a position in the Shire highlands, to the south of the lake, and there established the settlement of Blantyre. The Free Church mission settled at Mandala on the southern shore of Lake Nyasa. The question of supplying the two societies was solved when Mr. James Steven of Glasgow, convenor of the Free Church sub-committee dealing with the mission at Mandala, personally founded the Livingstonia Central African Trading Company. In addition to providing regular supplies for the missions the company hoped to export ivory at a price which would undercut the Arab merchants using slave-porters. At a later date and under the new name of the African Lakes Trading Corporation the company was able to extend its operations to Tanganyika with the financial support of the British South Africa Company.

The Universities Mission also extended its field of activity soon after Livingstone's death. In 1873 Bishop Tozer was succeeded by Edward Steere, a man of great versatility and boundless energy. In 1875 a new permanent base on the mainland was founded at Magila, in the Bondei country, and in 1876 Steere set out with a number of former Makua and Nyanja slaves who had been freed and maintained by the U.M.C.A. and whom he now hoped to restore to their own country in the vicinity of Lake Nyasa. Having travelled 100 miles inland from Lindi the freed slaves refused to go farther and a new settlement was made for them at Masasi with two missionaries to assist. From this base one of the missionaries, W. P. Johnson, extended the activities of the society inland among the Yao and then, in 1881, still farther inland to the eastern shore of Lake Nyasa where he continued his work among the Nyanja tribe.

The London Missionary Society, of which Livingstone himself had been a member until 1856, undertook a startling project in 1877. This was in part a response to the journeys of Burton, Speke, Livingstone, Cameron and others, and in part was due to the recent interest in the use of steamships. A citizen of Leeds, Robert Arthington, offered the Society £5,000 towards the purchase of a steamer for work on Lake Tanganyika. To make use of this offer called for the establishment of a base 850 miles from the coast, a remarkable undertaking and one which must inevitably attract criticism. Nevertheless, the first expedition set out in 1877 following the well-trodden trade route, and reached Ujiji very swiftly. During the next five years stations were opened at Ujiji and at other points on the lake shore, but the mission was not a success. Deaths were numerous and there were many resignations due to the great strain imposed upon the health and characters of the missionaries. The problem of keeping open the route to the coast was unduly heavy and took up too much of the missionaries' energies. Eventually a group decided to open up a road to the south and south-east, via Lake Nyasa, making full use of the waterways of the region. Although this route was then generally adopted, wisdom soon demonstrated the advisability of moving the mission centre to Northern Rhodesia and of abandoning the posts along the shores of Lake Tanganyika. Sixteen years after the first expedition had started out the transfer took place.

Of more lasting importance not only to the evangalization of East Africa but also to the political development of that region was the expedition which set out under the auspices of the Church Missionary Society in 1876. The instigator of this new scheme was Henry Morton Stanley. In the course of his second great African journey Stanley spent some time in 1875 at the court of Kabaka

Mutesa of Buganda. There, like Speke, he was impressed by the organization of Buganda and, unlike Speke, he found Mutesa no longer a foolish youth but a skilful diplomatist. In the course of his stay Stanley broached the subject of Christianity with the Kabaka and found in him a ready listener. Stanley, whose own Christian faith was of a strong if uncomplicated character, saw in Mutesa's interest the possibility of establishing a sound missionary station in an organized and prosperous country. On the other hand, it is more than probable that Mutesa looked upon Stanley's suggestion that the Kabaka should call for missionary help as a tentative offer of assistance against Bunyoro and against an even greater threat to his country from an expanding Egypt. There was probably, therefore, little religious interest behind Mutesa's preoccupation with Christianity,[1] but Stanley himself had no doubts. He dispatched a message by Linant de Bellefonds, an agent of the Egyptian Government whom he found at Mutesa's court, calling upon the missionary societies of England to answer Mutesa's request for aid. His appeal created a greater impression than had the earlier proposal by Speke which the Church Missionary Society had rejected. In view of the state of public interest aroused by Livingstone's death it would indeed have been difficult for the missions to have resisted Stanley's call. Nevertheless, the C.M.S. would still have preferred to abide by their established policy of steady progress, step by step, from the coast. Their position became untenable, however, when, a few days after Stanley's letter had been published in the *Daily Telegraph* to startle its receptive readers, an anonymous offer of £5,000 was made to the Church Missionary Society for the purpose of establishing a mission station on the shores of Lake Victoria. Other contributions were also received for the same purpose, and the Church Missionary Society found itself unable to offer further resistance. Many wise counsellors would have preferred to pursue the old system. Although it had been proved that the road to Lake Victoria was less difficult than earlier thinkers had believed, to get there was still a cumbersome and frequently a hazardous undertaking. The more direct route from Mombasa was not so well known and the likelihood of an attack by the Masai could not be overlooked. The longer route from Bagamoyo through Tabora and round or across Lake Victoria was safer but took many months and was liable to interruption

[1] Sir John Gray: 'Mutesa of Buganda.' *Uganda Journal*, Vol. 1, 1934, p. 33.

Dr. David Livingstone

Emin Pasha

Mwanga of Buganda

Mukama Kabarega

Dr. Carl Peters

from the tribes along the way. Fully alive to the magnitude of the undertaking the C.M.S. selected a party of six to form the first expedition, and in spite of many difficulties the first two members, who formed the advance guard, were received by Kabaka Mutesa in July 1877. At the end of the following year three more missionaries entered Uganda from the north, following the Nile route.

In 1879 yet another missionary society struck boldly into the interior. This was the White Fathers Mission, founded in 1868 by Cardinal Lavigerie to work among the Muslims of Algeria and more particularly to provide homes for children orphaned by famine. The order had grown in strength and Lavigerie had begun to look for further fields of activity. He was attracted by the schemes of King Leopold of the Belgians' International African Association for the exploration and civilization of Central Africa, and considered that the missionaries might well follow up the work of Leopold by carrying Christianity into the heart of the continent.[1] Pope Leo XIII accepted Lavigerie's proposals and so quickly did the Cardinal move that a letter from the Church Missionary Society requesting him not to send agents to Buganda was received only when the first expedition was on its way. The party of missionaries set out from Bagamoyo in June 1878, and on reaching Tabora divided into two parts, one going on to Ujiji and the other turning northwards to cross the lake to Buganda.

Buganda appeared to offer an excellent starting-place for missionary activity. The country was apparently well-organized under a strong government. It had a ruler who seemed to be intelligent and who appeared to be interested in the civilizing force of Christianity. Moreover, his influence was so great that most of the leading chiefs were constantly in attendance upon him so that missionaries established at his headquarters were in daily contact with men who could influence the people throughout the length and breadth of the country. Nevertheless, the position was fraught with danger. As the Kabaka gradually came to realize that the missionaries had no intention of helping him with arms or military aid against his enemies his friendship cooled. At the end of 1879 the withdrawal of Egyptian garrisons from Bunyoro removed the fear of Egyptian intervention

[1] R. M. Slade: *English-Speaking Missions in the Congo Independent State* (1878–1908). Académie royale des Sciences coloniales, Brussels, 1959, pp. 35–37, and J. Perraudin: 'Le Cardinal Lavigerie et Leopold II. *Zaire*, Vol. XI, No. 2, 1957; Vol. XII, Nos. 1 and 2, 1958.

and for a while Mutesa was actively hostile, openly encouraging a revival of the cult of Buganda's national gods. Inevitably, too, the missionaries were drawn into the political life of the country on account of their knowledge and skill. The existence of two missionary societies, one consisting of Britons and the other of Frenchmen, each expounding a different version of Christianity, led to further confusion. Inevitably, too, the missionaries' teaching tended to undermine the peoples' unquestioning attachment to their Kabaka who hitherto had attracted to himself the absolute loyalty and willing subservience of the whole country. Under the strong hand of Mutesa the dangers inherent in this situation were reduced, yet his unfriendliness became so marked that the Roman Catholic mission decided in 1882 to abandon their post in Buganda and to join their friends to the south of the lake. The C.M.S. missionaries persevered in spite of constant difficulties, but when Mutesa died and was succeeded by his much weaker son, Mwanga, the real problems of the new age in Africa began to make themselves felt in Buganda.

CHAPTER FOUR

EAST AFRICA AND INTERNATIONAL DIPLOMACY

AT the opening of the last quarter of the nineteenth century East Africa was still an almost completely unknown territory so far as the outside world was concerned. The Arab slave- and ivory-traders probably knew more about the interior than anyone, but they had no desire to attract commercial rivals or the attention of humanitarians by communicating their knowledge to others. European explorers had added greatly to the accuracy of the geographers' maps and had told something of the lives of the peoples of the interior to interested listeners. But they had inevitably been restricted in their travels to the well-trodden routes of the traders, and vast areas were unknown to them. A clearer picture of conditions in the heart of the continent was beginning to be collected by missionaries, but their work had barely started. African society, although on the verge of a revolution, was unaware of the fact. Some tribes, living along the slave routes, had seen their normal life disrupted by the constant threat of raiding parties or by their own active participation in raids, and at the coast traditional tribal hierarchies had been replaced or overlaid by Arab authorities. Elsewhere, although the shrewd Mutesa of Buganda might scent danger, the tribes of East Africa lived as they had lived for generations. Change, if change occurred, came so slowly as to pass unnoticed. In some areas the fertile soil produced all that men needed and destroyed any motive for improvement. In other districts the barren, sunbaked dust offered little but the prospect of annual famine and endemic shortage, and in its own deadening way destroyed men's will to better their lot. Change could only come from without, and the forces of the outside world were poised for attack.

Almost all the journeys of exploration in East Africa started at the east coast and worked westward into the interior, but the first threat of annexation came from the north. The Albanian adventurer, Muhammad Ali, who, ostensibly in the name of the Sultan of Turkey, had established his family as the ruling dynasty of Egypt at the beginning of the nineteenth century, had extended his authority up the Nile as far as Gondokoro. His rule, however, had never penetrated the sudd of the southern Sudan. For all his vast ambitions Muhammad Ali, like the soldier he was, had always retained a stern sense of reality. His equally ambitious but largely irresponsible grandson, Ismail, who came to office in 1863, allowed no consideration of realism to impose restraints upon his imperialist schemes. It might also be said that he was encouraged in his fantasies, albeit for very good reasons, by a number of able Europeans whom he employed, and, less directly, by the humanitarianism then exercising a powerful influence in Britain.

Since Muhammad Ali's day the Sudan, under Egyptian administration, had become a scene of corruption and oppression, where the Sudanese people were treated simply as a source of taxation or of private wealth for the administrators. Underlying all was the deadly destructive force of the slave-trade from which officials benefited freely and openly. Said Pasha, who was governor of Egypt from 1854 to 1863 and under whom the Suez Canal project was initiated, visited the Sudan in 1857 and proclaimed the abolition of the slave-trade and the reduction of taxation. No doubt this was pleasing to the anti-slave-trade campaigners in Britain and elsewhere, but the practical result was nil. For Said, a polished voluptuary, had neither the personality nor the willing agents to make his proclamation effective. Ismail made a more spirited attempt to reform the evil in the Sudanese administration, for he was genuinely anxious to see improvements even if only to catch the eye of the powers of Europe and in spite of the fact that his popularity among his own subjects would not be enhanced by his actions. He therefore appointed European governors to the provinces of the Sudan, men of ability and physical determination. But their efforts met with little success for they were surrounded by hordes of corrupt assistants.

His failure to achieve improvement within what might by a stretch of imagination be termed his own jurisdiction did not deter Ismail from evolving grandiose imperialist schemes which took in not only the Red Sea coast but also the land stretching beyond the sudd to the great lakes and to the very sources of the Nile. His aims were given a great fillip by the appointment of Sir Samuel Baker as Governor-General of Egypt's Equatorial Provinces in 1869. Baker's experience as an explorer in the southern Sudan was of great value, and not least his awareness of the tremendous influence wielded by the slave-traders, half-Arab, half-Egyptian, who ravaged and dominated the land as far south as the Victoria Nile. His tremendous physical vitality and dauntless will fitted him better than any other man to struggle against the slavers' evil influence and to impose some form of order in the terrorized regions. Having been forestalled by Speke in his hope of discovering the source of the White Nile he sought fulfilment for his ambitions in extending Egyptian rule, in fact his own rule, over the whole basin of the Upper Nile.

Some indication of the nature of the slave-trade was given by Baker himself in his book, *Ismailia*,[1] in which he wrote: 'These people [the slave-traders] had deserted their agricultural occupations in the Soudan and had formed companies of brigands in the pay of various merchants of Khartoum. The largest trader had about 2,500 Arabs in his pay, employed as pirates or brigands, in Central Africa. These men were organized after a rude military fashion and armed with muskets; they were divided into companies, and were officered in many cases by soldiers who had deserted from their regiments in Egypt or the Soudan.

'It is supposed that about 15,000 of the Khedive's subjects who should have been industriously working and paying their taxes in Egypt were engaged in the so-called ivory trade and slave-hunting of the White Nile.

'Each trader occupied a special district, where, by a division of his forces in a chain of stations, each of which represented about 300 men, he could exercise a right of possession over a certain amount of assumed territory.

'In this manner enormous tracts of country were occupied by the armed bands of Khartoum, who would make alliances with the native tribes to attack and destroy their neighbours, and to carry off their women and children, together with vast herds of sheep and cattle . . . an individual trader named Agād assumed the right over

---

[1] Sir Samuel W. Baker: *Ismailia*. New edition. 1 Vol, Macmillan, London. 1890, pp. 2–3.

nearly ninety thousand square miles of territory . . . Thus the seeds of anarchy are sown throughout Africa, which fall among tribes naturally prone to discord.'

As far as the great powers were concerned Ismail's ambitions were viewed with a mixture of benevolence and indifference; indifference since none of them was interested in territorial acquisitions in equatorial Africa, benevolence due to Ismail's instructions to Baker to eliminate the slave-trade. Baker was therefore free from external interference and its inevitable complications, but the task he faced was enormous. The slave-traders resisted as strongly as their varied resources would allow, and roused the tribes against him. Yet, through his powerful personality and unflagging energy, Baker achieved a considerable measure of success. In Acholiland he established defensive posts at a number of strategic points and gar-risoned them with Egyptian and Sudanese troops. From these bases he imposed order within the radius of his soldiers' marching powers. Advancing southward he entered the kingdom of Bunyoro-Kitara, no longer ruled over by the slothful and acquisitive Kamurasi who had preyed upon Speke and Grant and upon Baker himself during the latter's journey to discover Lake Albert. In 1869, Kamurasi had been succeeded by his son, Kabarega, a man of a very different character, warlike, aggressive and given to open opposition rather than to pernicious importunity. Kabarega had had to fight for his position against his brother, and it was the arms of slavers from the north that had turned the balance in his favour. But now that he was in power he was no man's servant or tool, although he still eyed the guns of the slavers with suspicion and caution. When, therefore, Baker arrived in 1872 and announced that Bunyoro would form part of the Egyptian empire Kabarega's response was clear and decisive. Threatened by Kabarega's spearmen, Baker was forced to retreat hastily across the Nile to Fatiko, near Gulu, in Acholi country.

Baker was now in an unenviable position. His term of office had only eight more months to run and his task, even as far as Acholi-land was concerned, was far from finished. He therefore adopted an expedient which, feasible so long as his powerful personality dominated the scene, was disastrous from a long-term viewpoint. In order to speed up the pacification of the country he enlisted the support of some of the slave-traders themselves. He used them to garrison his posts so as to augment the troops he had brought with him and through his own terrifying strength he imposed upon them some vestige of order. Before he left the country to return to Egypt he also insisted that the garrisons should grow corn to satisfy their own needs so that they would not be a burden upon the local tribes. But, although Baker's name is still honoured in the legends of the Acholi, his departure brought disaster to his work. Freed from the restraining force of his presence the ex-slavers reverted to their former practices, fortified by the semi-official status Baker had given to them.

Ismail's expansionist aspirations did not come to an end when Baker quitted his service. Baker himself was succeeded by a man who, although wholly different in character, was no less determined in his intention to strike at the heart of the slave-trade. Colonel Charles Gordon had already won a heroic reputation in China as a fearless and unorthodox fighter. Faced with the task of attacking the slave-trade in equatorial Africa he brought to the work a crusader's zeal and unbounded nervous energy which enabled him to cover vast distances, under almost inhuman conditions, at a speed which made his unexpected arrival in the midst of a slave-raid seem like the intervention of some avenging fury.

Gordon's ideas were drafted on a wide canvas. To check the traffic in slaves he felt it necessary to extend Egyptian authority not only to the great lakes but also along the east coast to the neighbourhood of Zanzibar itself. The Egyptians did, in fact, occupy Kismayu, but a protest on behalf of the Sultan by the British Consul in Zanzibar put a stop to further Egyptian ambitions in that direction. Meanwhile, the advance from the north was meeting with less success than Gordon had hoped. In 1874 he reached Gondokoro with his American chief of staff, Chaillé-Long, the first of a number of emissaries to Mutesa, Kabaka of Buganda. Gordon's hope was that he might be able to use Buganda as a stepping-stone in his campaign to establish a link with the east coast. Mutesa, however, was extremely wary.[1] He had sent warriors to assist Kabarega's brother in his bid for the throne of Bunyoro, but they had arrived too late to assist although not too late to bring news of the part played by the slavers from the north in Kabarega's success. He had also been

[1] Chaillé-Long's account of the journey is contained in his book *Central Africa*. Sampson Low, London, 1876.

fully informed of Baker's abortive attempt to plant the Egyptian flag in Bunyoro. Not surprisingly then, he was suspicious of all approaches from the north be they through the official channels of Egyptian government representatives or through the less official agency of 'Turkish' slavers. In any case, the difference between the two was not easily distinguishable. Although, therefore, Chaillé-Long claimed on his return that Mutesa had agreed to put an end to his trade with Zanzibar and to send all ivory to Gondokoro, it seems certain either that the Kabaka had failed to understand what Chaillé-Long had been proposing or, more likely, that he had understood all too well and had sent the American away with soft words in the hope of diverting Egypt's ambitions for a little longer. Certainly his behaviour towards Linant de Bellefonds, Gordon's French assistant, and towards the Egyptian, Nuehr Aga, whom he kept in virtual captivity, clearly indicated that he would go to considerable lengths to maintain his independence, even if he shrank from outright war against such a potentially powerful adversary. Gordon himself, on learning of the treatment meted out to Nuehr Aga, appears to have concluded that co-operation with Mutesa was impossible, while outright conflict would be premature with Acholiland and the southern Sudan in such an unsettled condition. For Gordon had discovered all too soon that the good work done by Baker had been largely undone during the brief period since his departure. The oppressive behaviour of Baker's garrisons had reaped its reward of resistance from the Acholi tribesmen. Only the post at Fatiko remained intact, and even there the garrison scarcely dared to emerge from the security of their stockade. Gordon therefore made no further attempt to extend Egyptian influence as far south as Buganda.

Gordon was faced with three chief difficulties, the corrupt behaviour of his own Egyptian agents, the opposition of the slavers and the deeply rooted suspicion extended to all Egyptians and Arabs by the tribes which had suffered so much at their hands. The one man who appeared to meet with any real success in allaying the fears of the Uganda tribes was the inscrutable German doctor, Eduard Schnitzer, later known to the world as Emin Pasha. Emin, one of Gordon's recruits, visited both Kabarega and Mutesa, and although he achieved little more than a state of armed neutrality in his relations with the Kabaka of Buganda he seems to have been on fairly friendly terms with Kabarega, which was no small achievement for a European.[1]

When Gordon left Khartoum in November 1876, after deciding to sever his connection with Ismail, he left no more lasting impression upon the tribes of northern Uganda than Baker had done. Even when he returned unexpectedly as Governor-General of the Sudan on behalf of Egypt in 1877 he was unable to devote much attention to the southernmost part of his territory, being too deeply involved in trying to cleanse the administration in Khartoum, in suppressing risings in Darfur and in negotiations with Abyssinia. Before long he came to the conclusion that it would be advisable to draw in his southern frontier to Dufile, but Emin, who became Governor of Equatoria in 1878, was reluctant to abandon the south. In accordance with Gordon's orders he withdrew the garrisons from Bunyoro in 1879; but following Gordon's resignation from the Khedive's service he had a freer hand and was able to reoccupy the area as far south as the Somerset Nile.

In 1881, however, events in the Sudan brought Egyptian imperialism to a halt. Tormented by years of oppression by government officials who neither wished nor were able to protect them from the slavers, the Sudanese lacked only a leader to bring them to the stage of revolt. In 1881 that leader emerged. Muhammad Ahmed, son of a Dongolese boat builder, was both a religious reformer and a national commander. In August he proclaimed himself to be the Mahdi, the expected Messiah. He was immediately joined by hundreds of willing followers in the northern Sudan, and the feeble and incompetent attempts of the government to restrain him only strengthened his hand. Gordon had already left the Sudan in January 1880, and had been succeeded as Governor-General by Raouf Pasha, an Egyptian whom Gordon himself had dismissed for malpractices two years earlier. Under Raouf's evil leadership the administration was helpless. By 1883 Emin was cut off in Equatoria where for six years he attempted single-handed to maintain a semblance of administration in the face of constant threats of Mahdist aggression.

So ended Egypt's imperialist claims in Uganda. Among the Acholi and Madi the aftermath took the form of revengeful attacks

[1] G. Schweitzer: *The Life and Work of Emin Pasha.* Constable, London, 1898, 2 Vols. Vol. 1, pp. 46–52.

upon the slavers and Egyptian garrisons alike as soon as it was realized that they were cut off from assistance. Food supplies were withheld and the personal influence of Emin was the only restraining factor in the area. As far as Buganda was concerned Egyptian aggression had had far-reaching effects. The shrewd Mutesa had been deeply perturbed by what he had seen and, more inclined than Kabarega to diplomacy, had looked for allies against the threat from the north. He had welcomed the overtures of friendship made by Seyyid Majid of Zanzibar in 1869 and had responded by sending presents of ivory and a baby elephant which were received by Seyyid Barghash who in the meantime had succeeded Majid. As has already been suggested it was the threat from Egypt which had also induced Mutesa to show friendship towards Stanley and to demonstrate such apparent enthusiasm for the explorer's proposal that missionaries should be invited to Buganda. The refusal of the missionaries to comply with the Kabaka's request to supply arms and to co-operate with him in his military ventures had proved a disappointment to Mutesa, however, and this feeling became tinged with suspicion on the arrival of reinforcements for the C.M.S. mission, not by the traditional route from the east coast but from the north, from the land of Mutesa's potential enemies. The main results of Khedive Ismail's aspirations, therefore, bore no relation to his hopes. He was able to build no far-flung Egyptian empire for he lacked both resources and determination. Instead, it was through his activities, if only indirectly, that Christian missionaries began their work in Buganda which was to be followed soon afterwards by European political intervention.

If Ismail's contribution to the opening up of Africa was indirect, the influence of two other men was both direct and decisive. Those two men were David Livingstone and Henry Morton Stanley. Livingstone's life had lit the fires of missionary interest in East and Central Africa, but the circumstances of his death fanned the flames of enthusiasm and created the atmosphere suited to active intervention. The long journey of his body from Lake Bangweulu to the coast, whither it was carried by his faithful African followers, seemed to sympathizers in Britain like a symbolic appeal from Africa to the civilized nations of the world. For had not Livingstone's men braved the enmity and superstitious fears of their fellow-countrymen by transporting their master's remains through regions where a corpse was thought to bring the gravest ill luck? Distinguished leaders from all walks of life attended Livingstone's funeral service in Westminster Abbey. England was alert for action. Yet, just as it was Stanley who, by his letter to the *Daily Telegraph*, was responsible for canalizing the missionary fervour aroused by Livingstone into the direct channel of intervention in Uganda, so too it was Stanley, rather than Livingstone, who demonstrated the possibility of realizing the desires of geographers, philanthropists and traders alike. His great journey from the east coast to the west between 1874 and 1877 was made more significant by the constant flow of exciting dispatches to the newspapers which he represented. His accounts of Mutesa of Buganda spoke of a chief more powerful than any who had been thought to exist even by the geographers who had read the works of Burton and Speke. His journey down the Congo River both settled many of the problems of the geographers and at the same time aroused the interest of the traders. Above all, the efficiency with which he prosecuted his journey impressed those who, if they had formerly thought about Africa at all, considered it to be an impenetrable territory of lowering jungle and scorching desert.

Even more important than Stanley's impact upon public opinion was the influence of his success upon Leopold II, King of the Belgians. Leopold had been on the throne ten years in 1876 when Stanley's letters began to startle the world. A young man of liberal interests and lively ambition, the King found his energies unduly constrained by the limits imposed by the small, neutral state of Belgium. While still heir to the throne he had travelled extensively in the Middle and Far East and his imagination had been stirred by what he had seen. When he became king, however, he had little scope for his abilities until the steady flow of news from Africa awoke in him new hopes of action. From 1876 the story of East African development must turn away for a time from Africa itself to Brussels and later to Berlin.

On September 12, 1876, Leopold summoned a meeting in Brussels of geographers, explorers, philanthropists, merchants and any others who might be interested in contributing to the task of opening Africa to the influence of western civilization. An attack upon the slave-trade was one of the operations envisaged and was particularly designed to appeal to the humanitarians. But this was only one aspect of the grand concept which, although scarcely formulated as yet in Leopold's mind, was to lead ultimately to the partitioning of almost the whole African continent among the leading powers of Europe. Leopold's plan took time to mature and the first result of the three-day conference was the formation of the International African Association with its headquarters in Brussels and with Leopold as its President. The distinguished people present at the formation of the Association attended as private individuals and not as representatives of the seven great nations to which they belonged. Even Leopold himself acted in a personal capacity and in no way committed the Belgian Government to supporting his project.

Inevitably the eyes of the Association turned first towards East Africa where Burton, Speke, Livingstone, Cameron and Stanley had blazed the trail into the interior. By 1877 an expedition was fitted out with the object of establishing a chain of posts from the east coast to Lake Tanganyika in order to facilitate the work of later explorers. Other expeditions followed, but they achieved very little. The Belgian officers who led them were astonishingly ignorant of the problems before them and appear to have done nothing to acquaint themselves with the nature of the country from the various sources of information made available by earlier travellers.

An experiment with Indian elephants to provide transport in 1879–80 proved a complete failure, but a number of posts of a temporary character were founded and a rather more important base was opened at Karema on Lake Tanganyika in the latter year. Nevertheless, the Association met with little success in East Africa and already Leopold's attention had been diverted to another, more promising field of action. At the same time the Association was rapidly losing its international character as the philanthropic motives with which it started became steadily subordinated to hopes of imperial expansion. Yet, although the emphasis now switched from the east coast to the west, the influence upon East Africa of the scramble for African dependencies in which the European powers indulged in the late 1870s and 1880s was all-important.

The achievements of Stanley opened up visions of greater developments to follow. His arrival at the mouth of the Congo in August 1877, presented Leopold with the twofold idea of using the mighty river as a highroad into Africa and of employing Stanley to open up that highroad. With this vision there also began Leopold's territorial ambitions. The national committees which had sprung up as a result of the conference organized by Leopold had quickly rejected their status as auxiliaries of the main Association and had demonstrated their interest in promoting national rather than international aims. They had subscribed little money to the parent body which was, in consequence, largely maintained from Leopold's private resources. Leopold's new project, therefore, although maintaining the appearance of an international undertaking, was fundamentally a private gamble.

No sooner had Stanley stepped ashore in Marseilles in January 1878, than he was met by emissaries from Leopold. But it was not until June that Stanley was able to visit the Belgian King while plans for the fulfilment of Leopold's new scheme were not formulated until a meeting was held in November which was attended by members of the International Association and at which there was formed the *Comité des Etudes du Haut Congo*. The plans were adopted and the necessary money subscribed at a further meeting held in January 1879. The scheme appeared to consist, primarily, of an investigation of the commercial possibilities of the Congo Basin in the light of the available geographical information and of the reactions of the tribes along the river. This objective was not intended to conflict with the philanthropic aims of many of the members of the International Association. In fact, there was no likelihood of any tainted accusation of economic imperialism being levelled against the committee in that age. The Association itself was a strong advocate of free trade principles, and the development of the resources of a stagnating continent was universally regarded as a laudable motive in the late nineteenth century. It seemed impossible that the people of Africa should not benefit directly from the exploitation of the country's economic resources and, less directly but none the less fruitfully, from the civilizing influences radiating from the trading centres. This was Livingstone's own doctrine and Livingstone, even in the mid-twentieth century, has never been accused of having been driven by base motives to undertake his journeys of exploration.

No one appeared better suited to the task of implementing the Committee's scheme than Stanley himself, who set out in 1879 under the flag of the International Association, a gold star upon a blue field. But he had not even reached the mouth of the Congo before the Committee decided to return the subscriptions of all contributors. Then, by assuming the title of the International Association of the Congo in 1882, the Committee declared its virtual independence of the original Association while only thinly diguising its Belgian composition.

Stanley's early success in making treaties with the chiefs living far upstream was largely a triumph for his own ability and personality over the inexperience and differences of opinion of his colleagues. It was, however, sufficient to convince Leopold of the feasibility of his plan for opening up the Congo and perhaps for taking control of the river. The King was not alone in his dreams of territorial annexation in the Congo region. France, through the agency of an able young explorer, Pierre Savorgnan de Brazza, who was backed by the far-sighted statesmanship of an overt economic imperialist, Jules Ferry, was already staking its claims along the Ogowe River, north of the Congo, and along the north bank of the Congo itself. It was, in fact, the openly acquisitive character of Ferry's policy which was responsible for the sudden outburst of mutual distrust among the European powers which led to the Berlin Conference of 1884 to 1885 and to the deliberate partition of Africa.

The country which reacted first to the aggressive nature of French colonial policy was the oldest and the weakest of all the colonial powers. Portugal had for many years laid claim to the West African coast between 5° 12′ and 8° south latitude which included the mouth of the River Congo. This claim had never been recognized by the other powers, however, and British, French and Dutch traders had operated freely along the lower Congo for more than a century without seeking permission from Portugal, but at the same time without themselves laying any claim to ownership of the region. In these circumstances the Portuguese were no more troubled by Leopold's international activities in the Congo basin than they had been by the operations of any other private individuals. Leopold, however, had aroused in France a spirit of emulation, and France was openly a colonizing power, at least when Ferry held office. Consequently, French penetration along the Congo seemed to Portugal to constitute a serious threat to her claims, whether justified or unjustified, to the West African coast and its hinterland. Portugal, unaided, could not hope to resist French ambitions if they turned deliberately southward nor, indeed, did it seem to the Portuguese

126

that Leopold would be in any stronger position. Throughout the nineteenth century Britain had been the chief scourge of the Portuguese slavers along the West African coast, but she had shown little interest in territorial annexation as long as her trade was unimpaired. Now, under Gladstone's Liberal Government, it was clear that she had no plan to seize territory in the Congo area. Indeed, Britain had enough troubles in Egypt in the early 1880s to turn her against other acquisitive ventures in Africa. So it was to Britain that Portugal turned in 1882 in defence of her claims.

Lord Granville, the Foreign Secretary, was no more anxious to recognize Portuguese fictions than his predecessors had been. But, fearing French expansion with its inevitable trading monopolies and adverse influences on British commerce, he was prepared to negotiate an agreement which would be advantageous to both Britain and Portugal. He rejected the Portuguese suggestion that their country should have jurisdiction along the Congo River for an undefined distance, but in return for many concessions, including Portuguese recognition of the rights of the Congo Association, Britain eventually agreed in February 1884 to acknowledge Portugal's claim to the coastline and to a limited hinterland. A compromise was also reached regarding the navigation of the Congo River. Britain's original suggestion that this should be controlled by an international body was reluctantly modified at Portugal's request so as to place it under the control of an Anglo-Portuguese Commission.

The publication of the treaty caused an outburst of criticism. Portugal had been secretly negotiating with France while her diplomatists had been holding discussions with Britain, but the revelation of her perfidy was less surprising to France than were the terms of the treaty. More serious from Britain's point of view was the fact that the agreement provided the occasion for a temporary *rapprochement* between France and Germany. For some time Bismarck had been encouraging French aspirations in Africa in his desire to divert French attention from ideas of revenge over the loss of Alsace and Lorraine in the Franco-Prussian War. He had not, however, until very recently, shown any hostility towards Britain. In spite of shrill objections from France he had approved of British intervention in Egypt in 1882. But during the early part of 1884 his attitude towards Britain had changed abruptly as a result of the slowness amounting to virtual if unwitting discourtesy on the part of Lord Granville in replying to Bismarck's inquiries concerning Britain's status and aims in south West Africa. This appears not only to have sparked off an intense desire to humiliate Britain but also to have demonstrated to Bismarck that an interest in imperialism might assist him in defeating his liberal critics in Germany. Hitherto, historians, philosophers and economists had emphasized without avail the importance of a profitable outlet for Germany's excess population and for her increasing industrial production and also the need for a symbol of her new-found unity and strength.

With the energy and determination which characterized all his actions Bismarck became an imperialist almost overnight. Taking advantage of Granville's dilatoriness he made haste to declare protectorates over the Cameroons and Togoland in 1884. Simultaneously he demonstrated Germany's new-found official interest in colonies and her leading position in the colonial field by summoning a conference to meet in Berlin in November 1884 to discuss the future of the Congo basin in the light of Portuguese claims, of the Anglo-Portuguese treaty and of the activities of the Congo Association. In Granville's defence it must be said that he had constantly urged Portugal to keep in touch with Germany over her negotiations with Britain. That he had not insisted upon Germany's being taken fully into the confidence of the negotiators now had extremely serious results, for Germany and France began the conference firmly linked in their opposition to Britain. Fourteen powers were represented, including the United States, but the International Association sent no official delegate since its exact status had never been defined. The activities of the Association were at the root of the conference and at the end of the deliberations it emerged as the recognized governing body in the Congo with Leopold as sovereign. But the latter achievement was incidental to the conference as a whole which, in fact, was mainly taken up with the interplay of the great powers and in particular with the conflicting and sometimes confused objectives of Britain, France and Germany.

The opening discussions quickly revealed that, in spite of earlier alignments, Britain and Germany were in agreement with the International Association in wishing to maintain free trade in the Congo basin while it was France and Portugal who wished to restrict that freedom. The false association of France and Germany had, in fact, already been demonstrated by their rival ambitions in West Africa had not Bismarck been too blinded by his distrust of Britain to see it. It was still further confirmed when discussion turned to the question of freedom of navigation along the Congo and Niger Rivers. Once again it was Britain and Germany who drew together while France drew apart. Britain was strongly opposed to the appointment of an international commission on the Niger in view of her historical claim to control the delta, while France was only too anxious to assert herself in any part of West Africa. Bismarck now began to appreciate France's territorial appetite as he had not previously done and his *entente* with France weakened accordingly. He was, moreover, particularly anxious to obtain British recognition for the International Association as a sovereign power and with this end in view he brought pressure to bear upon France to ensure that the Niger and Congo problems were treated separately in accordance with the wishes of Britain.

The third question which was discussed at the conference, that of effective occupation, was to have more direct repercussions upon East Africa than did the two problems already mentioned. Again this issue orginated in a misconception on the part of Germany concerning British intentions and ended in Bismarck's accepting drastic modifications to his original proposals. Germany's object in trying to insist that any power occupying territory in Africa should have no legal claim to that territory unless it exercised strong and effective political control was intended as an attack upon the numerous but vague imperial claims made by Britain as a result of her trading activities. It was one of these claims, in south West Africa, which had caused Bismarck's earlier annoyance. Britain as the most important colonial and commercial power in the world had two basic reasons for opposing Germany's suggestion. In the first place she was anxious to minimize the obligations imposed upon occupying powers in view of the vast areas in which her traders claimed pre-eminence and, secondly, she wished to avoid restrictions upon the commercial activities of her subjects by the declaration of monopolies over any region by rival powers. Germany, still at that time a minor colonial power, had much to gain by pressing for a more severe policy. She was anxious to assert her claims to territory before they could be forestalled by the active British and, having done so, she wished to be in a position to protect the trade of her own subjects. In this issue France, already an important colonial power, was closer to Britain than to Germany, and it was due to French influence that Bismarck agreed, even before the conference began, to limit the application of his proposals to the coastline. This restriction virtually invalidated the whole scheme, a result which Bismarck does not appear to have appreciated. He was not alone in his confusion, for the first British reaction to the modified proposal was that Germany was deliberately restricting the obligations to the coastline in order to give herself a free hand in seizing unlimited territory in the hinterland. Fortunately these mutual suspicions did not permanently cloud the perceptions of the leading statesmen of the two powers. The British Lord Chancellor, Lord Selborne, quickly recognized that, even in its modified form, Bismarck's scheme might still cause inconvenience to Britain. In the face of powerful opposition from the Foreign Office and from British experts in Berlin Selborne persisted in calling for a distinction to be drawn between territories actually annexed, in which Bismarck's rules might justifiably be enforced, and protectorates which in his opinion should be exempted from these obligations. Faced by Bismarck's apparent intransigence the British Cabinet thought it advisable to override the advice of the Lord Chancellor. Instructions were sent to the leading British spokesman at the conference, Sir Edward Malet, Ambassador in Berlin, to accept Bismark's terms. Before this information was transmitted to him, however, the German Chancellor had himself decided to give way to Selborne's demands. The reason for this change of front was probably twofold. In the first place, the unnatural character of his *en ente* with France was becoming increasingly embarrassing and secondly, he had become interested in schemes for planting German authority in East Africa and with this object in view he wished to avoid placing too many restrictions upon German activities.

The result of these laborious negotiations was that in future any power taking possession of a tract of land along the African coast was merely required to notify the other signatories of the Berlin Act to give them an opportunity to make good any prior claims which they might have. Thenceforward it was only necessary for the annexing power to ensure the establishment of sufficient authority to protect existing rights and the freedom of trade and transit.

Selborne had won his point. Administrative obligations in African dependencies were reduced to a minimum.[1] In so far as East Africa was concerned, however, it was Germany who was to make the most of the British victory and Britain was to regret the freedom of action which she herself had virtually guaranteed to Germany.

Bismarck's decision to lead Germany officially into the colonial field marked a turning-point in history, but he himself, as has already been shown, only became the spearhead of the German colonial movement in the 1880s. The movement, in so far as it transcended the simple desire for expansion in Europe itself, was of nineteenth-century origin. It was in no way related to the minor efforts of the Hanseatic League or to the rather more ambitious activities of Brandenburg merchants on the West African coast in the seventeenth century. Stirred by the conquests of Frederick the Great, Prussian colonial energies were for a long time directed exclusively towards the unification of the German people and the creation of a German empire in Europe. It was therefore the success of this campaign for unification which later provided the incentive to further expansion overseas. Nevertheless, there had been a number of advocates of German colonial expansion beyond the seas even before unification was achieved. Some of these, like the economist, Friederich List, a disciple of Adam Smith who was born in 1789, believed that unity could only be achieved by a comprehensive programme of economic development which would forge bonds of mutual interest among the German peoples and which must involve the acquisition of colonies as an outlet for the excess population. The question of making provision for German emigrants was an important one. Many Germans were finding new homes in the United States, at the Cape and in Australia and were being lost to the Fatherland. If German colonies could be founded the colonists would then maintain their association with their homeland. In 1843 a society was founded in Düsseldorf to encourage emigration to Brazil, which at that time was a more promising field of enterprise than Africa. Colonies, in the true sense of the word, could not be founded there because the territory belonged to the Brazilian Government; but southern Brazil continued to be extremely popular as a place in which to establish German settlements, in spite of the

---

[1] The best account of the Berlin Conference is contained in S. E. Crowe: *The Berlin West Africa Conference* 1884–85. Longmans, Green, London, 1942.

formation of a number of other societies interested in a variety of countries.

It was, however, the upsurge of national fervour resulting from the events of 1866 and more particularly of 1871 which, in the last analysis, gave momentum to the inchoate ideas and movements supporting German colonial expansion. Heinrich von Treitschke, thundering out his views on German greatness and his hatred of Great Britain to the students attending his professorial lectures in the universities of Freiburg-im-Breisgau, Kiel, Heidelberg and Berlin, became for the intellectuals the mouthpiece of aggressive Prussianism in the 1860s and 1870s. Vice-Admiral Livonius, in the more restrained language which befits a naval officer on duty, urged in his dispatches the importance of Germany's acquiring territories overseas. Chambers of Commerce, which had everything to gain from a wider expansion of German markets, followed the example of the intellectual leaders and called for colonial enterprise. Bismarck, meanwhile, was keeping an eye upon European politics and took no action in response to these appeals although he was not indifferent to the various arguments put before him. He was particularly interested in the economic standpoint of the Chambers of Commerce, but he was biding his time.

It was therefore events in Africa which proved decisive in changing Bismarck's outlook. In 1875 Livonius had recommended the declaration of a protectorate over Zanzibar.[1] Eleven years earlier still, in 1864, von der Decken had also written while exploring the Juba River, 'I am persuaded that in a short time a colony established here would be most successful, and after two or three years would be self-supporting. It would become of special importance after the opening of the Suez Canal. It is unfortunate that we Germans allow such opportunities of acquiring colonies to slip, especially at a time when it would be of importance to the navy.'[2] But in 1864 Germany had been too interested in her own immediate destiny to feel any enthusiasm for colonial enterprise in so remote a region as East Africa and even when Bismarck received Livonius's dispatches he was still unconvinced that Germany was sufficiently secure in Europe to turn her attention elsewhere. None the less, the operation set on

[1] E. Lewin: *The Germans and Africa*. Cassell and Company Ltd., London, 1915, p. 30.

[2] Quoted in J. Scott Keltie: *The Partition of Africa*. Edward Stanford, London, 1895, p. 108.

foot by Leopold II and the part played by German explorers in enlarging upon the arterial exploration of Burton, Speke, Livingstone and Stanley aroused more than a casual interest in Germany. The German Society for the Scientific Exploration of Equatorial Africa was founded in 1873. Germany was also represented at Leopold's Conference in Brussels in 1876 by Baron von Richthofen, President of the Geographical Society of Berlin, and by the eminent explorers, Dr. Gustav Nachtigal, Dr. Gerhard Rohlfs and Dr. Georg Schweinfurth. As a result of the conference the German African Society was founded as a branch of the International Association and two years later it united with the earlier German Society to form the influential German African Society of Berlin. In 1881 the German Colonial Society was founded and was able through public meetings at many of which leading explorers were among the speakers, and by the publication of information about hitherto unknown territories, to arouse the interest and support the general public and in particular of the merchant community. None of these societies was able to implement its views as long as Bismarck remained in opposition and their caution seemed irksome to the more active colonialists. Among this latter group Carl Peters quickly achieved prominence. A young man of only twenty-eight in 1884 Peters had had a university education and had spent some time in England, a country for which he developed an intense hatred. Impetuous, ruthless and impatient, he assembled a number of other young men of a similar outlook in Berlin early in 1884 and founded the Society for German Colonization. His object was to put into effect the ideas which the less adventurous German colonial societies had been promulgating. The older societies did not welcome the activities of the new association but Peters was undeterred. To the German people he proclaimed, 'The German nation finds itself without a voice in the partition of the world which has been proceeding since the fifteenth century. . . . To remedy this deplorable state of affairs a society has been founded at Berlin which will resolutely and energetically undertake the execution of colonial projects and will support the efforts of associations having the same aim.'[1]

Zanzibar was Peters's goal, for it provided the most suitable base at which to prepare expeditions into the interior of East Africa.

[1] Quoted in E. Lewin: op. cit., p. 171.

Nevertheless he had to proceed with the utmost secrecy. German trading interests were firmly established on the island but British influence with the Sultan was paramount. Britain herself had consistently refused to declare an official protectorate but Sir William Mackinnon, Sir John Kirk and General Lloyd Mathews were virtually in charge of Zanzibar's affairs and they were a formidable triumvirate for the young Peters to challenge. Skill and deception would be needed to avoid their watchfulness and Peters lacked neither of these qualities. He arrived in Zanzibar in November 1884, together with two companions, Count Joachim Pfeil and Dr. Carl Jühlke, all three disguised as mechanics. The German Consul had received instructions from Berlin to discourage the young adventurers, but Peters having once set out did not easily surrender. With his two friends he crossed to the mainland and signed his first treaty with an African chief on behalf of his society. Now for the first time the German flag was hoisted in East Africa. Pushing up the Wami River, the three adventurers made further treaties in Usagara, Uzigua, Nguru and Ukami. Mangungo, 'sultan' of Msovero in Usagara, was reported to have agreed to offer 'all his territory with all its civic and public appurtenances to Dr. Carl Peters . . . for all time', while Peters in his turn undertook to 'give special attention to Msovero when colonizing Usagara'.[1] These treaties were clearly never understood by the chiefs who appended their marks, but they were probably no worse than other agreements made by the pioneers of empire of many nations. Their main purpose was to serve as proof to other powers that Germans had a prior claim in the area concerned.

Carl Peters had stolen a march on Sir John Kirk who was anxious to maintain the authority of the Sultan of Zanzibar over as much of the mainland as he could possibly control. Peters therefore hastened to Berlin to consolidate his achievement. On February 12, 1885, he founded the German East African Company and ceded to it all the treaty rights he and his party had acquired. He also obtained a charter from the German Emperor granting his protection over all territories acquired by the Society for German Colonization in East Africa and recognizing the sovereign rights of the society in those areas. These actions immediately provoked a loud protest from a number of British merchants who had themselves become interested

[1] R. N. Lyne: op. cit., p. 75.

in East Africa only a short time before. In September 1884, Mr. H. H. (later Sir Harry) Johnston, had already obtained treaties in the vicinity of Taveta and on the slopes of Kilimanjaro with the Sultan of Zanzibar's permission. These concessions he had handed over to the President of the Manchester Chamber of Commerce. A group of merchants had then planned to acquire territory between the coast and Lake Victoria with a view to building a railway and exploiting the trade of the area. This group now formed itself into the British East African Association in order to resist the German invasion of their proposed field of enterprise.

To Kirk, the upholder of the claims of the Zanzibar Sultan, the attitude of the British Government throughout this period appeared disastrous. It is true that Lord Granville had requested Sir Edward Malet in May 1885 to draw the attention of the German Government to the plans of the British East African Association. He had added, however, that Her Majesty's Government would not support the Association if its activities appeared likely to conflict with the interests of the German Protectorate.[1] Britain's policy in East Africa was less concerned with the well-being of the Sultan of Zanzibar than with her own problems in Egypt. Having been drawn to intervene in Egypt in 1882 by her interest in the Suez Canal route to the Far East, Britain now found it necessary to remain there in order to maintain orderly government in what had always been an area of the greatest strategic importance to British commerce. For some not very clearly defined reason the protection of Egypt was also thought to involve the control of the Upper Nile. Britain therefore was anxious to retain the friendship of Germany since her activities in the Nile Valley were being watched with suspicion and jealousy by France, Egypt's long-term, if unreliable, ally. In any case Britain's interest in Zanzibar had mainly centred upon the campaign against the slave-trade. Long before 1885 successive Sultans had done all that could be done from Zanzibar to assist in the campaign and Britain's interest in the island had now waned considerably. In these circumstances Sir John Kirk was doomed to see the work, to which he had devoted so much energy, deliberately set aside in order to permit Germany to pursue her policy of expansion unhindered. For the British Government, which was reluctant to thwart the Germans in defence of the commercial interests of British merchants, was

[1] E. Lewin: op. cit., p. 176.

equally unwilling to intervene to protect the Sultan of Zanzibar's claims upon the mainland. The Sultan protested to Bismarck and subsequently to the British and American Governments against the declaration of a protectorate over the areas claimed by Peters, but Britain in reply merely ordered her representative to co-operate with the German Consul-General in promoting German aims.

Meanwhile, the race for treaties was still going on. With Peters in Berlin, his colleagues planned a second expedition with Kilimanjaro as their objective. Determined to resist to the limits of his power in defence of the territories which he believed to be his own, the Sultan sent troops to Usagara and dispatched an expedition under the leadership of General Mathews to Kilimanjaro to forestall Jühlke, a task which Mathews with his greater knowledge and experience of East African travel was able to undertake successfully. In Teita Mathews collected together the remnants of the tribe who had survived a recent famine and explained to them the object of his mission. He obtained from them a promise of loyalty to the Sultan and he hoisted the Zanzibar flag. On May 30, 1885, in an assembly of Chagga chiefs brought together by the principle chief, Mandara, Mathews then signed a further twenty-five treaties before setting out on his return journey to the coast. Only a few days later Dr. Jühlke arrived among the Chagga, entered into blood brotherhood with Mandara, and signed a treaty by the terms of which the Chagga chief placed himself under the protection of the German East African Company and ceded sovereignty over his state to Jühlke as representative of the Company.[1] Such was the durability of treaties in East Africa.

The Sultan, meanwhile, had refused to recognize German protection over the district of Witu, at the mouth of the Tana River, where the ruler, Simba, had rejected his authority and had assembled around himself a band of malcontents and scoundrels who were prepared to support him in his rebellion. On April 8, 1885, Simba had readily granted to the Germans a concession of his chiefdom, an area of 500 square miles, in return for gifts of arms and ammunition, for he saw in the Germans a less immediate threat to his independence than that arising from the Sultan's hostility. On May 27, 1885, then, the district was placed under imperial protection, and a few years later it became the northern base for a two-pronged

[1] R. N. Lyne: op. cit., pp. 69–71.

German advance into the continent which threatened to restrict British claims in East Africa to a small coastal strip with an unimportant hinterland. In 1885, however, the British Government could not foresee these developments and appeared naïvely satisfied with a German offer to recognize the independence of the Sultan's territories as acknowledged by Britain and France in 1862 in return for a commercial treaty with Zanzibar.

The success of the Conservative party at the polls in June 1885, made no noticeable difference in British policy in East Africa. A German squadron sailed into Zanzibar harbour on August 7, 1885, and threatened the Sultan's palace. The Sultan, abandoned by Britain, was forced to recognize all the German claims including that of a protectorate over Witu. Even the Germans' promise to recognize the independence of the Sultan's territories took on an ironical significance, for to do so involved in the German view a prior investigation of the limits of those dominions. England and France had never looked upon this step as being of any importance, but now they fell into line with Germany's wishes and a joint commission comprising representatives of the three powers was appointed to carry out the task. The commission asked for the assistance of the Sultan, and General Mathews was appointed to represent him. Mathews was given little opportunity to state the Sultan's case, however, and the British representative on the Commission, Lieut.-Colonel H. H. Kitchener, was unable to induce his colleagues to give Mathews a better hearing. Even after the appointment of the commission German agents continued to press forward in the Kilimanjaro area, the one region in which British interests were involved. Their action called forth a stern protest from the Earl of Rosebery, the new British Foreign Secretary, this being the first indication that the British Government was prepared to intervene seriously on behalf of British interests in East Africa.

The work of the Commission led to the signing of an Anglo-German Agreement towards the end of 1886. The Sultan's mainland possessions were declared to be limited to a coastal belt stretching from Tunghi Bay in the south to Kipini at the mouth of the Tana River in the north and extending inland to a depth of ten nautical miles from high water mark. In addition his dominion was recognized as extending over the more northerly towns of Kismayu, Brava and Merka, each surrounded by an area of land covering a ten-mile radius from the town, and also Mogadishu with a five-mile radius of land. Simultaneously, the hinterland was divided into British and German spheres of influence, the British sphere to the north and the German sphere to the south of a line running north-westward from the mouth of the Umba River to skirt the northern foothills of Kilimanjaro and to run thence to the eastern shore of Lake Victoria at a point 1° south latitude. Harry Johnston's treaties with the Chagga, therefore, had served no more purpose than those of Mathews, but the British East African Association at least had the satisfaction of seeing some limit imposed upon German expansion. As far as the Sultan was concerned the treaty probably gave him all that he could effectively claim. Yet the replacement of the Arab trading empire, based though it was on the slave-trade, by the activities of European and Indian traders seemed an ungenerous return for the enterprise shown by Seyyid Said, his subjects and his successors.

According to the Anglo-German Agreement Zanzibar's territory extended as far south as Tunghi Bay where the Sultan had a customs house. But on December 30, 1886, Germany and Portugal, without the previous knowledge of either Britain or Zanzibar, made a declaration recognizing the Rovuma River as the northern boundary of Portuguese territory. The Sultan who had acquiesced in the earlier Anglo-German Agreement protested at this violation of what had been recognized as his territory. The issue was settled by discussions between General Mathews and a Portuguese representative, Senhor Capello, but not before villages on Tunghi Bay had been bombarded by the Portuguese. Cape Delgado, immediately south of the Rovuma River, was then declared to be the southern boundary of the Sultan's territory.

In spite of having become committed to intervention in East Africa the British Government continued to be reluctant to take responsibility for the administration of any part of the British sphere. Indeed, such was Britain's lack of interest that when Emin Pasha, cut off from Egypt by the Mahdist rising, offered to make Equatoria a British province, the British Prime Minister, Lord Salisbury, replied that the matter was one for the Germans to deal with since Emin was himself a German subject. In these circumstances the use of the vague term 'sphere of influence' admirably suited the British Government's book. The task of opening up eastern Africa on behalf of British interests then fell to a group of men who, under the chairmanship of Sir William Mackinnon, had formed themselves into the British East African Association. Whatever his achievements as chairman of the British India Steamship Company, Mackinnon was no great empire-builder. Nevertheless, he soon found himself involved in an issue which aroused a lively protest from the rival German company. The predicament of Emin Pasha may have aroused no acquisitive instincts in Lord Salisbury but it certainly captured the imagination of the British public. A committee was formed under Mackinnon's chairmanship to finance a relief expedition and Henry Stanley was chosen to be leader. Mackinnon saw in the project the hope of performing an act of the greatest humanity and at the same time of staking a claim to the rich supplies of ivory in Equatoria. For, until a railway had been built and had encouraged speculation in land, ivory provided the only form of trade goods which could cover the high cost of human porterage from the interior and make a profit for the company. The Germans, however, jealous for the security of their own protectorate, did not wish Stanley to follow any of the well-established routes from the east coast, all of which now lay, at least in part, within their sphere of influence. Even when Stanley decided at the instigation of Leopold II to follow the Congo into the interior from the west coast it was still believed that he would emerge from Africa by the eastern route. The Germans were afraid that he might make treaties in the region which they claimed as their hinterland. In the meantime, however, Lord Salisbury had given an assurance that no annexations would be made by Britain in the area of the German hinterland and Germany was to have a free hand in the country south of Lake Victoria.

The retention of the coastal belt by the Sultan of Zanzibar now appeared to be an unrealistic arrangement in view of the British and German activities in the interior, although the customs dues collected at the mainland ports were of vital importance to Zanzibar's revenue. Mackinnon, who had great influence with the Sultan, had no difficulty in overcoming this problem. On March 24, 1887, he obtained a concession of the ten-mile coastal belt between the River Umba and Kipini for a period of fifty years. His Association thereby agreed to administer the territory in the name of the Sultan while the latter was to receive the same customs dues that he was getting at the date of the concession, together with 50 per cent of any additional net revenue. The Germans were anxious to follow this example and in 1888 they induced Sultan Khalifa, who had succeeded his brother, Barghash, on the latter's death in March of that year, to lease to them the coastal strip fronting on their own sphere for a similar period of fifty years. The concession conferred no territorial ownership but the Germans immediately began to concentrate their activities in the coastal area. They increased the number of customs posts and abandoned to the missionary societies the unprofitable stations established by Peters in the interior. In March 1887 the German East African Company had been incorporated by Imperial Charter, and with a zest which characterized all German economic activities in East Africa investigations had been set on foot to discover everything possible about the soil, climate, vegetation and other features of the territory under the Association's control. Subordinate companies were founded to encourage the development of plantations and various crops including coffee, tobacco and maize were tested in an attempt to assess their suitability to East African conditions. But the Germans were not equally conscientious in their relationships with the African people, and their behaviour in the coastal region soon reaped a reward of violence. Careless of the religious feelings of the Muslim population, disrespectful to the Sultan's flag and brutal in their treatment of the African tribes, they stirred up universal hatred.

The rising which began in August 1888 in Bagamoyo and Pangani, was instigated by Arabs but it was carried out with the support of the African coastal peoples. With these latter the Arabs had established a friendly relationship through years of close association and this friendship had been cemented by mutual opposition to the excesses committed by the Germans. A half-caste chief, Bushiri of Pangani, rallied the Arab resistance and the German company found itself faced with a rebellion which it lacked the resources to quell. Plantations were abandoned before the advancing rebels and even the British Indian subjects on the mainland were forced to take refuge in Zanzibar. British warships helped the Germans to blockade the coast and the Imperial German Government sent troops to suppress the rising. Captain Hermann von Wissmann, a traveller and explorer of great experience and high reputation, was sent by the German Government to take up the appointment of Imperial

Commissioner in command of the company's agents. Bushiri, meanwhile, was harassed from place to place until he was finally captured and executed in December 1889, but the insurrection in the more southerly areas was not finally suppressed until the middle of 1890.[1]

Two events of importance are to be noted in connection with the rebellion. The first was Britain's readiness to co-operate with the Germans in handling the insurgents. Whatever the rivalries existing between the nations Britain continued to look upon Germany as a civilized power anxious, as she herself was, to introduce the benefits of western culture into tropical Africa. Although individual examples of friction between British and German subjects in East Africa were by no means rare, it was not until the war of 1914–18 that doubts were cast by Britain upon Germany's civilizing mission in her African dependencies. The other event of importance was the German Government's decision to intervene directly in the affairs of East Africa. The rebellion demonstrated clearly the inability of the German company to administer the territories which it claimed. In May 1889, therefore, the company was incorporated by an Imperial Charter as a purely commercial concern, and when peace was restored the Imperial Government itself took over responsibility for the administration of German East Africa. The coastal strip which had been leased from the Sultan was now bought for a sum which started out at four million marks but which was subsequently considerably reduced.

While these events were taking place Carl Peters had again thrown down the gauntlet in the face of the British. On the strength of a number of treaties made with chiefs in the British sphere and of the concession of the coastal strip by the Sultan of Zanzibar, the British East African Association had been granted a royal charter as the Imperial British East Africa Company on September 3, 1888. The charter empowered the company to administer those parts of the British sphere where it could acquire treaties of protection, approved by the Secretary of State. Although a post had been established at Machakos, some 250 miles from the sea, the directors did not, however, contemplate penetrating much further as yet in spite of

[1] A valuable Arab version of the motives underlying this rising is contained in Hemedi bin Abdallah bin Said el Buhriy's *Utenzi wa Vita vya Wadachi Kitamalaki Mrima*, translated by J. W. T. Allen. Supplement to the *East African Swahili Committee Journal*, No. 25, June 1955.

the attractions of Buganda which, superficially, appeared to offer a profitable market for British goods. The company was, in fact, in a far from adventurous mood. With an initial capital of only £240,000 it faced a task for which this sum was wholly inadequate. Undoubtedly some of the directors had high hopes of the ivory trade and believed that at some future date a more varied trade would develop, while the highlands, now remotely hidden in the interior, might prove an irresistible attraction to speculators. In the meantime, the Germans controlled all the established routes into the continent except those travelled by Swahili caravans through little-known and climatically hazardous country. There were, however, other directors whose philanthropic interests outweighed their business acumen, and it could not be long before the call of the missionaries from troubled Buganda would awaken in them a desire to respond. As an interim measure a gentleman-hunter, Mr. (later Sir Frederick) Jackson, was dispatched by the company in August 1889 to investigate the country in the direction of Lake Victoria, but with instructions not to get involved in the troubles in Buganda about which information had recently reached the coast. In any case, the news of Stanley, who had made contact with Emin Pasha only to find him reluctant to abandon his province and his troops, suggested that if the company wished to extend its activities farther inland Equatoria would provide greater scope than Buganda.

The news of Stanley was a matter of concern to the Germans as well as to the British company. All their former fears about his trespassing upon their hinterland were revived and there were rumours that Wissman was to lead an expedition to Lake Victoria to counter Stanley's activities. What eventually happened was that in July 1889 Carl Peters evaded British patrol vessels, landed in Witu, and set out with a small party up the Tana River, ostensibly to the relief of Emin, in fact to try to seize the hinterland behind Witu. Had he been successful he would have effectively limited the British sphere to a coastline tapering off in an unprofitable triangle extending at best to the point on Lake Victoria where the British and German boundaries reached the eastern lake shore. The Imperial German Government denied Peters's claim that he had their support, but with Peters at large the British company could not afford to be complacent. Indeed, only events in Europe saved Buganda from falling under the influence of Germany.

The land of the Kabakas was passing through evil times. During his reign the strong-willed Mutesa had been able to retain some control over the new forces at work in his country. Arab traders had been admitted freely, but their activities had been carried on under the strict supervision of the Kabaka himself. And if many of his subjects had become interested in Islam, Mutesa himself had also paid it some attention, with the tolerant outlook of one who knew his own ability to check excess. The Christian missionaries, too, had been able to arouse a deep concern for their teachings in the minds of some Baganda and had attracted a wider circle of those who hoped to benefit materially from the new religion. The missionaries' success had, indeed, been enhanced by their being confined to the centre of the kingdom where the life of the people flowed more fully. But under the watchful eye of Mutesa they could not hope to be too successful, lest they should challenge his own pre-eminence. Mwanga, who succeeded Mutesa on the latter's death in October 1884, was of a different calibre. A young man of weak character he was unable to dominate the situation in which he found himself, save for brief periods and by ill-considered acts of violence. Although he induced the Roman Catholic missionaries to return to his country the pattern of events in Buganda soon began to change. The Arabs cannot yet have been disturbed by German annexations nearer the coast since the news of Peters's earliest activities would not have reached Buganda until the early months of 1885. They may, it is true, have been suspicious of the interest shown in East Africa by representatives of Leopold II's International African Association. More probably, however, they now saw their opportunity to gain the sort of dominant position behind the Buganda throne that they already enjoyed in Tabora.

Mwanga's first outburst of violence against the Christians, the cruel slaughter of his pages, followers of the C.M.S. mission, on January 31, 1885, was almost certainly due to purely personal motives. Meanwhile, however, the Arabs began to play upon Mwanga's sense of insecurity and his dislike of the Europeans by telling him of the achievements of the explorer, Joseph Thomson, who had recently become the first European to penetrate through the Masai country almost to the borders of Buganda. Then came the news of the German activities near the coast which stirred up the Arabs' campaign to such an extent that, in May 1885, Alexander Mackay thought it advisable to write to Kirk, in Zanzibar, warning him that the first Bishop of Eastern Equatorial Africa, James Hannington, who was about to start his journey to Buganda, would be walking into grave danger. Recognizing the growing hostility of Mwanga, Mackay also created a Church Council consisting of some of the leading Baganda Christians to carry on the work of the Church if the European missionaries were driven out of the country.

In spite of the Kabaka's anger, many still sought baptism. Some, indeed, were drawn to the new faith by the courageous death of the first three martyrs. In October, however, Mwanga struck his next blow. Advancing by the little travelled northern route, Bishop Hannington reached Busoga. There he was seized by a chief, Lubwa, who, acting on Mwanga's instructions, put him to death. The lives of the missionaries at Mwanga's capital were now in grave danger, for the Kabaka, having commanded the death of their leader, was afraid to try any compromise with the Europeans. In November 1885 a Catholic chief was executed and six months later came the great persecution. In one huge pyre over thirty victims were burnt alive, some of them mere boys, pages who confessed before Mwanga himself that they were readers of the missions but refused to recant. Perhaps two hundred others also perished, among them some of the leaders of both mission churches. But others escaped and the work continued, although often it had to be carried on at night and in secret. Three Roman Catholic missionaries remained in Buganda, while, on the departure of the Rev. R. P. Ashe for Europe in August 1886, Alexander Mackay was left alone to represent the C.M.S. mission until he was replaced a year later by the Rev. Cyril Gordon. Both Mackay and Ashe were anxious for the British Government to make strong representations to Mwanga, but it was not easy for Britain to intervene effectively when Buganda lay in so remote a region. The C.M.S. disliked making an appeal to the Government and eventually it was left to the Rt. Rev. Henry Perrott Parker, second Bishop in Eastern Equatorial Africa, to explain the missionaries' aims to the Kabaka. Parker met Mackay at Usambiro at the southern end of Lake Victoria in November 1887, and from this new station he wrote to Mwanga on December 28. On March 26, 1888, however, the Bishop died without ever setting foot in Buganda.

Left to rely increasingly upon their own resources the Baganda

Lord Lugard

Alexander Mackay

Mgr. Hirth

Sir Apolo Kagwa

Christians found themselves forced into something closely resembling political activity in their need to counter the Arabs' struggle for power. Buganda began to divide into four groups; the numerically strong pagan group, who did not wish to see the old traditions and the old political systems swept aside by a transfer of loyalty from the Kabaka to a divine ruling spirit, the Muslims, the Catholics and the Protestants.

Although it had been the Muslims who had first stirred up Mwanga against the Christians it was to the conservative pagans that the Kabaka naturally turned in defence of his position. He was constantly in fear of reprisals for his anti-Christian activities and was deeply if uncomprehendingly conscious of the challenge to his authority which was embodied in the new religions. In September 1888 he conceived a naïve plot to rid the country of the foreigners and of their supporters of all denominations by marooning them on an island in Lake Victoria and leaving them to starve. Inevitably the plan leaked out and Mwanga was forced to flee the country. There then followed a brief alliance between Christians and Muslims under the rule of Mwanga's brother, Kiwewa, but after only a few weeks the Arabs made a bid for power. The Christian chiefs were driven from the country. The missionaries were seized and dispatched in a boat across the lake. The mission stations were destroyed. Kiwewa himself, refusing circumcision, was deposed and starved to death, and his place was taken by a younger brother, Kalema.

The fleeing Christians found refuge in Ankole, 200 miles to the south-west, where they were seen by Stanley in the course of his journey to the coast with Emin Pasha who had at length agreed to abandon Equatoria. The missionaries, meanwhile, joined their respective mission stations south of the lake. Mwanga, expressing penitence, soon sought refuge with the Catholic mission, and the Baganda Catholics proposed to their Protestant brethren a campaign to restore him to the throne. At first the latter hesitated, but, supplied with firearms and ammunition by the trader, Charles Stokes, the Christians eventually joined together, with Mwanga in their midst, to carry the war back to Buganda. Kalema was defeated in two battles, but in a third succeeded in driving the Christians back to the Sese Islands in the northern part of Lake Victoria. It was during the short lull which followed that news reached the Christians of the approach of Jackson's caravan from the east.

Mwanga and Stokes both wrote to him asking for help. Stokes then left for the coast and the Christians launched a further attack in October, twelve months almost to the day after the expulsion of the missionaries from Buganda. Kalema and his supporters were driven from the capital and nearly all the Arabs were killed. Mwanga, promising complete religious liberty, was restored. Apolo Kagwa, the leader of the Protestants, became Katikiro, or chief adviser, and the other offices were divided amicably between Catholics and Protestants.

Gordon of the C.M.S. at once wrote to Jackson explaining the changed circumstances but adding that help was still necessary. Jackson found all the letters awaiting him on his arrival at Mumia's in November but his caravan was too weak to intervene effectively in such a complicated situation. In any case, his instructions were to avoid Buganda. He replied, therefore, that since his help appeared no longer to be required he could only agree to enter Buganda if Mwanga was prepared to make considerable concessions to the company. At this stage the political division between the two missions emerged in a different light. Hitherto their political struggle had been an internal one to counter the challenge of Islam and paganism. Now they were faced with intervention in the affairs of Buganda by outside powers, and their relations with these powers needed to be clarified. The C.M.S. did not wish to plead for the help of the British Government to promote their campaign. Nevertheless, recent events had shown how precariously balanced was the country's political system and the defeated Muslims still hung threateningly on the borders ready to overthrow the government at the first opportunity. Nor was Mwanga a tower of strength even with the support of the temporarily united Christian parties. If the British company could be induced to help in the maintenance of order and security the C.M.S. missionaries would naturally welcome its intervention. The French White Fathers had different views. Their attitude towards the problem of maintaining order was the same as that of the Protestants. They did not, however, relish the idea of the British company's influence reaching out to Uganda since this might give an advantage to the C.M.S. at their expense.

Mwanga himself inclined more towards the Catholic party than to the Protestants so that under the influence of Fr. Lourdel he replied to Jackson in terms which the latter regarded as ambiguous.

146

In the belief that nothing was to be gained by further correspondence Jackson then turned northwards to Mount Elgon leaving Buganda to its own devices. Immediately the crisis feared by both missions arose. The Muslims re-entered the capital in November 1889, and Mwanga was once more a fugitive. Lourdel forgot his doubts. Letters were dispatched at once to Jackson agreeing to all his demands if only he would give his help. The letters fell into the hands of Peters who arrived at Mumia's early in February 1890, while Jackson was still away to the north. Peters wasted not a moment. Here was a perfect opportunity to steal a march on the British company. Hastening to Buganda he found that Mwanga had again been restored but that the defeated Muslim army was still threatening the western border. In these circumstances Mwanga was ready to sign an agreement with Peters, and Lourdel was glad to support him. The C.M.S. missionaries agreed, although reluctantly, and Peters hurried away with considerable jubilation having, apparently, added Buganda to Germany's East African dependencies.

Finding on his return to Mumia's that his letter had been opened by Peters, Jackson made his way with all speed to Buganda to undo what he feared Peters must have done. The intervention of the Germans had shown the Buganda situation in a new perspective. Jackson, therefore, arrived at Mwanga's headquarters soon after Peters's departure but was unable to extract a treaty from Mwanga. Disappointed, he started out for the coast, taking with him two envoys from Buganda to whom had been given the task of discovering whether their country fell within the British sphere or the German sphere.

The Buganda question was being settled in Europe at that very moment without any reference to the treaty made by Peters or to the activities of Jackson. The news of the persecutions in Buganda had had varied and violent effects upon public opinion in Britain. There were some who, despairing at the apparently unbending opposition of Mwanga and horrified by the high cost in lives to the C.M.S. mission, argued as had often been done in the past in the face of setbacks that the difficulties must be an indication of God's displeasure at the work of the Society. When the news of the overthrow of Mwanga and the expulsion of the Christians from Buganda reached England the chorus of despair became louder. But louder still was the voice of those who saw in the courageous death of the

Baganda martyrs a vindication of the missionaries' work and a summons to still greater efforts. *The Times*, in a leading article on October 30, 1886, quoted the old saying that 'the blood of the martyrs is the seed of the Church', and went on to state: 'On the success of the Uganda experiment, with its alternation of favourable and adverse circumstances, depends the happiness of the interior of the vast continent for generations.[1] Opinion in the Press and at missionary meetings had not yet mustered the force which it was to wield in 1892, but Salisbury's reluctance to annex new territories in an arbitrary fashion undoubtedly brought him under heavy criticism from missionary societies as a result of events in Buganda. By the time that Stanley had returned to England to add the weight of his unique experience of Africa on the side of intervention Salisbury was already engaged in careful diplomatic negotiations with Germany over that very issue. Through the part he played in assembling the Brussels Conference of 1889–90 the Prime Minister was laying the foundations of a more active British policy in tropical Africa.

On July 1, 1890, a further Anglo–German Agreement was signed which laid down that the boundary between the British and German spheres of influence in East Africa would be extended westward across Lake Victoria and then on to the Congo border along the 1° south latitude. Germany abandoned her claim to Witu and thus relieved the British company from the threat in the north. The northern boundary of the British sphere was now loosely described as following first the Juba River and then extending onwards to the Nile. A British protectorate was recognized over Zanzibar and Pemba and over the Sultanate of Witu, and a satisfactory boundary was agreed upon between German East Africa and Rhodesia and Nyasaland to the south. Germany obtained from Britain the barren, but strategically desirable, island of Heligoland in the North Sea and Salisbury, unmoved by the Cape to Cairo railway dream of Rhodes and Stanley, formally abandoned any claim to the areas south-west of Lake Victoria.

In an important sense the Anglo–German Agreement marks the end of an era in East Africa. Henceforward the hinterland rather than the coast would be the dominant element. With the declaration of a Protectorate over Zanzibar the decline in importance of the

[1] E. Stock: *The History of the Church Missionary Society*. C.M.S., London, 1899, Vol. II, pp. 415–16.

Sultanate was confirmed. Although British attention was not transferred immediately to the mainland, and the efforts of Sir Gerald Portal as Consul-General helped for a time to sustain the importance of Zanzibar as a port, the features which had attracted Britain and other powers to the clove-scented island became steadily less significant. The campaign against the slave-trade, still incomplete, could now best be waged in the interior of the continent. The Brussels Act of 1890, which laid upon the signatories the obligation to do all in their power to suppress the slave-trade, pointed its finger at the mainland. The attractions of Zanzibar as a harbour and as the great entrepôt of East African trade also were soon to be challenged by the new German harbour of Dar es Salaam and not long afterwards by the British port of Kilindini, each of which became the terminus of a great railway serving the very heart of Africa.

CHAPTER FIVE

THE EUROPEAN
CONQUEST OF EAST AFRICA

THE road to action was now clear as far as diplomatic considerations were concerned, and moral obligations remained as strong as ever. But the British Government appeared to think it had done enough. It was now left to the Imperial British East Africa Company to shoulder the burden. The company, however, still lacked the financial resources to enable it to intervene usefully in the remote interior, while the best route to Buganda through the British sphere had still to be discovered. There were some who thought it might be possible to avoid the arid country immediately to the west of the coastal strip which proved such a severe test to travellers for the first few days of the journey and which made the use of animal transport difficult if not impossible. Their idea was to follow the River Tana in the early stages, but after that the going was extremely uncertain. In Buganda itself the restoration of Mwanga had not made for an easier situation although the company was not to know this. Formerly the undisputed head of his people, Mwanga now held his power by the grace of the Christian faction, with the Muslims still occupying a threatening position. Within the Christian group itself the division between Catholics and Protestants was growing steadily more acute. Mwanga himself still inclined towards the Roman Catholics because he saw in the Protestants a party which, in alliance with the I.B.E.A. Company, might continue to threaten the tattered remnants of his supremacy. It was, therefore, an incendiary situation which the company was called upon by the British Government to control from a base over eight hundred miles away in Mombasa.

Even before the news of the Anglo-German Agreement had reached East Africa the company's energetic Administrator, George Mackenzie, had been prevailed upon by Kirk's successor in Zanzibar,

Colonel Charles Euan-Smith, to try to thwart the German thrust into the interior and he had therefore planned to dispatch a caravan to Buganda under the leadership of a young army officer, Captain F. D. (later Lord) Lugard. The plan was delayed by the arrival of Sir Francis de Winton to replace Mackenzie and de Winton was anxious to lead this important expedition himself. He was eventually overruled by the directors of the company and Lugard set out from Mombasa on August 6, 1890, with the unenviable task of trying to make an agreement with Kabaka Mwanga and of imposing his authority impartially upon the rival religious parties in Buganda.

Almost at once the company became involved in a dispute which was to jeopardize the whole of Lugard's work during the next two years. Mackinnon, the chairman of the company, argued that the advance to Buganda had been undertaken at the wish of the Foreign Office in order to fulfil national obligations and that it was contrary to the interests of a company whose limited capital made a cautious policy essential. In fact, the company had gone forward willingly enough. For, pending the opening up of the country by the construction of a railway, the only commodity which would survive the long journey to the coast by human porterage while still offering profit to the trader was ivory, and ivory came from the interior, from Toro, Bunyoro and the upper Congo. Nevertheless, Mackinnon approached the problem by asking the Government to guarantee the interest on the capital needed to build the railway and Lord Salisbury, although never openly admitting the Government's responsibility, was willing to raise Mackinnon's proposal with the Treasury. The latter body was sympathetic, admitting that the effective occupation of the interior might be a better means of checking the slave-trade than the relatively expensive and not wholly successful activities of the naval patrol along the coast. But Salisbury's confidence ebbed away before the prospect of bringing the scheme to Parliament and eventually he adopted the more cautious approach of asking for money for a preliminary survey. This would cost £25,000 of which the company was to supply £5,000. Even this limited proposal was postponed under pressure from the Liberal, anti-colonial Opposition and the company was asked to put up all the money. This was more serious than a simple matter of delay, for the Government's hesitation was liable to discourage potential investors and the company felt itself compelled to decide upon withdrawal from Buganda. With the long-term objective of territorial annexation still in view, however, Salisbury urged the company to finance the railway survey until Parliament could be induced to vote the money. Captain J. R. L. Macdonald of the Royal Engineers was put in charge of the survey and started work towards the end of 1891.

Unaware of the clouds which were banking up in Britain, Lugard pushed on confidently to Buganda. When he arrived there in December 1890 his force consisted of about fifty Sudanese and Somalis who had had some military training and 270 porters of whom he regarded a third as being reliable men, a third as indifferent and a third as useless. They were all undisciplined. His ammunition was low. He put little faith in his old Maxim gun. He was harassed by having to disperse his forces to forage for grain since his followers disliked the basic local diet of plantains. His line of communication with the coast was protected only by a handful of isolated and lightly-manned posts and at any time Stokes might arrive with further supplies of arms and ammunition to strengthen the position of the already well-armed politico-religious factions. The attitude of the White Fathers and their followers was also obscure. The missionaries themselves could not but be disturbed by the arrival of the representative of a British company with the implication that support was to be given to their Anglican rivals. The Baganda Catholics outnumbered the Protestants and they had the sympathy of Kabaka Mwanga. Mwanga himself, descendant of a long line of autocratic rulers, and secure at least for the time being upon his throne, could scarcely be expected to welcome any further limitations upon his authority imposed by the agent of a chartered company.

In spite of the adverse conditions in which he found himself Lugard acted quickly and boldly. Having made cordial approaches to both missions and having paid a formal visit to Mwanga himself, he called again upon the Kabaka on December 24 with an agreement for his signature. By the terms of the agreement the company offered its protection to Buganda in return for the recognition of the company's suzerainty and the appointment of a Resident with control over all Europeans. The Resident would also be required to give his approval before any negotiations took place with other powers and he would be president of a committee controlling taxation and finance. In addition there should be freedom of religion and trade. The slave-trade must be stopped and the supply of arms was to be strictly controlled. It is clear that Mwanga was being asked to concede much in return for a very slender prospect of aid from the company. Not unnaturally he hesitated to sign and Lugard was running a grave risk when he tried to insist upon the Kabaka's acceptance of the agreement. During the next two days, however, the Catholic missionaries prevailed upon the chiefs who were their followers to accept the agreement, subject to confirmation by their delegates who had gone to the coast with Jackson that Buganda was now accepted by the European powers as a British sphere of influence. With his main supporters prepared to accept the agreement Mwanga was able to hold out no longer. He signed on December 26.

Lugard's position was now formalized, but effectively it was no stronger than it had been before. Alarms and disturbances between the English and French factions continued unabated. Lugard did his utmost to convince both sides of his friendship and impartiality but the weakness of his military position made a mockery of his claims to suzerainty on behalf of the company. Mwanga, meanwhile, was still far from willing to concede the status of overlord to the company's agent. In these circumstances Lugard could influence events only by the strength of his own personality or by acting as a make-weight to one or other of the Baganda parties. His position in this latter respect was strengthened on January 31, 1891, by the arrival of Captain Williams with seventy-five Sudanese soldiers and one hundred Swahili porters. Even now, however, it required all Lugard's diplomacy as well as the military force at his disposal to maintain the balance between the religious factions. That balance was threatened among other things by the unusual allocation of chieftainships made at the time of the reconquest of Buganda by the Christians. To satisfy both parties the chief offices of state had been shared equally between Catholics and Protestants. Below these, the minor officers had been distributed in descending order to Catholics and Protestants alternately. If a man then changed his religion he lost his office. This meant that he also lost the land which went with the appointment. Because Mwanga himself was regarded as the leader of the Catholic party there was a tendency among the more nominal Protestants to transfer their allegiance and the Catholic party grew stronger accordingly. The Catholics were therefore anxious to change the system of allocating posts equally between the parties. The numerically weaker Protestants were equally anxious to maintain the *status quo* so as not to lose their grip upon the chieftainships. In order to maintain the precarious balance of power and consequently to protect his own position, Lugard tended to favour the Protestant attitude to the existing arrangement. He was thus laid open to the charge of failing to honour the terms he himself had laid down in his Agreement with Mwanga with regard to the importance of upholding religious freedom. The French priests, zealous to promote their religion, were not slow to criticize his behaviour.

In these difficult circumstances Lugard must have found consolation in the knowledge that he had the warm support of de Winton, the company's administrator at the coast, and of the directors in London. At the same time he must have been increasingly baffled by the lack of any clear definition of the company's objectives in Buganda. For it was being borne in upon him that the value of that region to the company as a potential trading centre had been greatly overrated, while if the company wished to intervene effectively in the affairs of Buganda it would require the aid of a number of British administrative officers backed by a trained military force of at least 500 men. It was, in fact, with the problem of obtaining an armed force adequate for maintaining order as much as with the hope of gaining access to a valuable source of ivory that Lugard began to turn his attention to the west. Somewhere in the region of Lake Albert were the Sudanese troops, under the command of Selim Bey, whom Emin Pasha had left behind when he marched to the coast with Stanley. Between Lugard and the Sudanese lay the force of Baganda Muslims who, more numerous than the Christian Baganda, continued to threaten Mwanga's security and the stability of the country. Fortunately for Lugard, the Baganda envoys to the coast returned in March with a company's caravan to confirm that the region was a British sphere of influence. Although he was dismayed to find no reference to himself in the letters from the Consul-General in Zanzibar, Lugard was consoled by the fact that the envoys' news at least removed the Baganda's fear that the negotiations he had undertaken with Mwanga might be challenged by the Germans or by some other power. He felt free, therefore, to turn his attention whole-heartedly to the Muslim threat which would have to be faced sooner or later. If all went well the task of dealing with the Muslims might act as a rallying-point, if only a temporary one, for the rival Christian factions. At the same time, Lugard was not unaware of the possibility that Mwanga and the Catholic party might unite with the Muslims to get rid of him. In the event, however, the Baganda Christians rallied willingly enough to the prospect of loot, and after Mwanga himself had rejected Lugard's proposal that he should lead the Baganda forces it was agreed that the Protestant Katikiro, Apolo Kagwa, should be the commanding general.

The company's Sudanese troops played little part in the subsequent campaign on the borders of Bunyoro. In spite of the persistent disunity between the Christian parties their spearmen and musketeers overran the Muslim forces. With victory assured, however, they refused to agree to Lugard's proposal that they should follow up their success with an advance against the capital of the Muslims' ally and Buganda's enemy, Kabarega of Bunyoro. While the Baganda abandoned themselves to looting, therefore, Lugard decided to pursue his plan of travelling to the west. Leaving Williams to return to their base in Kampala with a handful of troops, he himself marched southward in May to Buddu, one of the south-western districts of Buganda. He was joined by a young man named Kasagama, a descendant of the ruling house of Toro which, some years previously, had been overthrown by Kabarega in his campaign to restore the former boundaries of the empire of Bunyoro-Kitara. Lugard took Kasagama with him with the object of reinstating him as ruler of Toro and, at one stroke, of weakening the power of Kabarega while extending the range of the company's suzerainty.

During the first stage of his journey to the west Lugard passed through the northern borders of Ankole, the territory of the Mugabe Ntare, with whose deputy Stanley claimed to have made a treaty. This agreement had been made before the Anglo-German agreement which made Buganda a British sphere so that Lugard determined to take steps to confirm Ntare's friendship. The Mugabe proved to be nervous of meeting a white man, however, and Lugard had to be content with making blood-brotherhood with one of Ntare's representatives. At this ceremony the Mugabe agreed, through his representative, to accept the company's protection. In return he would put an end to the slave-trade and do all in his power to check the traffic in arms and ammunition through his country. Once again Lugard could do little to honour his side of the bargain nor yet was he in a position to ensure that Ntare carried out his obligations. But he could delay no longer and he hurried on to the west, harassed alike by the shortage of food for his caravan and by the fear that Emin Pasha, now in German service and ostensibly in charge of Bukoba district, was travelling ahead of him in the hope of contacting Selim Bey and possibly of seizing his old province of Equatoria on behalf of Germany. Whether Equatoria fell within the British sphere or not would not be easy to prove, and if Emin took possession of it first the Germans' case would be a strong one.

In the vicinity of the narrow Kazinga Channel, which links Lake Edward to Lake George, Lugard made his first contact with the Banyoro outposts. These he brushed aside to cross the channel and seize the valuable Katwe salt lake beyond. Here he built the first of his western forts, on a high neck of land between the Salt Lake and Lake Edward, and gave to it the name of Fort George. His first attempt to locate Selim Bey by skirting the south-western slopes of the snow-topped Ruwenzori Mountains was a failure. He returned to Fort George, therefore, and then advanced northwards, this time along the eastern flank of the Ruwenzori range. The full might of Kabarega's army barred his way, but the startling effect of Lugard's Maxim gun, for once firing effectively, scattered the Banyoro host, leaving its camp to the victor. A further stockade, which Lugard named Fort Edward, was built on the borders of Toro to protect the southward route to the Salt Lake. The Batoro themselves were still afraid of reprisals from Kabarega but gradually plucked up courage to rally round the young chief, Kasagama. The moment seemed opportune for re-establishing Kasagama as ruler of Toro and Lugard now entered into an agreement with him which was similar in terms to the treaty made with Ntare. There was one additional provision which laid down that all ivory collected in Toro would be the property of the company, for Lugard never lost sight of the fact that he must make a profit if the company was to maintain itself in the interior.

This first Toro Agreement was signed in August 1891, and once again the offer of the company's protection appeared extremely tenuous, although without Lugard's aid Kasagama would certainly never have gained the throne. Mindful of the increasing obligations he had incurred in the company's name, Lugard now wrote once more to England asking for European administrators and troops. He then recommenced his northward journey on August 26. Another large Banyoro army was defeated by resolute action and the caravan crossed the Semliki River to come upon Selim Bey's forces at Kavalli on the south-western shore of Lake Albert. It was some time before Lugard was able to induce Selim Bey to accept service with the company and then only on the understanding that efforts would be made to obtain his formal release from the service of the Khedive of Egypt. Here Lugard learned that Emin Pasha had indeed been ahead of him but had failed to induce Selim Bey to accompany him on his further travels to the north-west. Emin's remarkable career did not, in fact, last much longer. Only a little over a year later, in October 1892, he was murdered by Arabs in Manyema, a victim of their last desperate stand against the advance of European influences in Africa.

The troops with Selim numbered several hundreds, but the whole party which marched out from Kavalli with Lugard amounted to almost nine thousand, and many of them were women and children. The majority of these recruits Lugard posted out in a series of stockades which he constructed in the course of his return journey. The object of these posts was to protect Toro against the vengeance of Kabarega, and the Sudanese fulfilled their task successfully although in time they themselves became almost as severe a scourge to the Batoro as Kabarega himself had been. Lugard then left the affairs of Toro in the hands of Fenwick de Winton, the son of the company's administrator. De Winton's instructions were that he should work through Kasagama and he was given no authority over the Sudanese garrison. His task was an unenviable one and shortly afterwards he succumbed under the strain of his work and the climate and died. Meanwhile, Lugard began his return journey, having opened up a route to the west with its resources of ivory and salt and having in the process struck numerous blows against the power of Kabarega. He had also entered into agreements with the rulers of Ankole and Toro and, not least among his achievements, he had strengthened the military force at his disposal.

In Lugard's absence Captain Williams had tried to maintain cordial relations between the rival parties in Buganda in a situation which was becoming increasingly difficult to control. He had sympathized with the Catholic missionaries in their criticism of the system of allocating chieftainships and in so doing he had brought upon himself the resentment of the C.M.S. missionaries. He did not, however, obtain the consolation of winning the sympathy of the Catholics who were busily attempting to propagate their religion, nor yet of Mwanga who, in July, had flown his own flag once again in defiance of the company. Skirmishes between the two parties were frequent. In December 1891, for reasons which it is difficult to assess, Mwanga told the Anglican missionaries that he wished to join their church. In spite of the temptation to seize such an important ally the C.M.S. representatives referred the Kabaka to Williams assuming, probably correctly, that political rather than spiritual considerations lay behind Mwanga's action. Williams, too, behaved with circumspection and before any further action was taken Mwanga returned to the Catholic fold.

It was to this disturbed state of affairs that Lugard returned on the last day of 1891. Only a few days earlier he had received for the first time the shattering news that the company, awed by the unexpected expenses incurred by its Uganda venture, had decided to withdraw him and his force with all speed to the coast. In total ignorance of the true situation the directors had stated that this step was a temporary one and Lugard was requested to obtain an extension of the treaty with Mwanga before leaving and if possible he was to leave a volunteer to act as Resident at Mwanga's court at the Kabaka's expense. The missionaries might leave with Lugard if they wished.

Lugard's reaction was to resist the company's decision by every means in his power and on January 7, 1892, he received news of a brief respite. As a result of the efforts of the C.M.S. in Britain money had been raised to enable the company to retain an interest in Uganda for a further twelve months until the end of 1892. Fortified by this stay of sentence Lugard turned to face the immediate problems by which he was surrounded. Tension had been mounting in and around Kampala and on January 24 fighting broke out between the two Christian parties. Lugard, who had sensed the approaching climax and had issued arms and ammunition to the Protestant party, now intervened briefly but effectively with his Maxim gun and Sudanese troops. The Catholics were put to flight and Mwanga himself took refuge on Bulingugwe Island in Lake Victoria, some six miles from his capital. The Catholic mission was overrun and destroyed, but the missionaries were unharmed and were able to take refuge in Lugard's fort. Lugard realized all too clearly that no lasting peace could be guaranteed without the assistance of Mwanga and he did his utmost to induce the Kabaka to return to Kampala. Mgr. Hirth, the Catholic Bishop, was allowed to go, at his own request, to see Mwanga and to ask him to return, but he did not fulfil his mission. Renewed fighting broke out in which Mwanga's party took the initiative. Led by Williams an attack was launched against Bulingugwe Island but Mwanga and Mgr. Hirth escaped and eventually reached Bukoba in German territory. The Catholics then began to collect in Buddu. Lugard, however, continued his campaign to induce Mwanga to return, and on March 30 the Kabaka capitulated.

As a basis for peaceful relations in the future Buganda was now divided so as to give the fertile province of Buddu to the Catholic chiefs while the remaining five-sevenths of the country were given to the Protestant chiefs. This arrangement did not prevent Catholics and Protestants from living in each other's territory. A new treaty, very similar in terms to the previous agreement of 1890, was also signed by Lugard and Mwanga. It contained one additional clause, however, stating that, save by mutual agreement, the treaty should continue in perpetuity. Lugard, it is true, was still very conscious of his dependence upon Mwanga's co-operation, but the Kabaka must equally have realized that he could no longer rule over the whole of his people without the support of the company. Buganda had not been conquered by the British in the January battle, but without the company's troops to aid the Protestants Mwanga might well have reasserted his authority on that day. So long, however, as the company could exercise the power of decisive military intervention in a divided country the ruling house of Buganda was no longer sovereign. Next, Lugard turned to solve the Muslim issue and again, largely through the impact of his strong personality, he induced Mbogo, the Muslim leader, and the other chiefs to return in peace to Buganda. They signed the new agreement between Mwanga and the company and took up residence in three small districts within easy reach of Kampala.

At last Lugard felt he could leave Buganda and return to England to wage a campaign for the retention of the country in which he had striven so hard. His task was a formidable one. The debate on the vote of money for the railway survey had taken place in March 1892, and had been the occasion of a trial run for some of the leading arguments against retention. The Liberals maintained that the

Government had no obligation to shoulder the responsibilities entered into by the company. Britain, they said, had no claim to sovereignty in an area which was no more than a sphere of influence defined so as to prevent its seizure by other powers. To adopt a forward policy in these circumstances would be an act of injustice to the native population. The argument that Britain was responsible, through its participation in the Brussels Conference, for campaigning against the slave-trade in what was no more than a sphere of influence was therefore untenable. In any case all available information, including Lugard's own reports, suggested that the slave-trade scarcely existed in Uganda, while the construction of a railway would meet with the steady opposition of the natives. In reply, the Government was hesitant, but the vote went in their favour. Almost immediately news of the fighting near Kampala had begun to arrive in England to disturb the political field still further. It had had no effect upon the company's determination to withdraw from Uganda, however, and in May it was decided to order Lugard to quit the country with his followers by the end of the year. Lugard, in fact, had started for England long before the letter reached Kampala.

In England the situation became still further complicated by the resignation of Salisbury and his party in August, to be succeeded by the ageing Gladstone and his Liberals. The main hope of the retentionists now rested in Lord Rosebery, the Foreign Secretary, who alone in the Cabinet appeared to have any interest in holding Buganda. From a variety of sources Rosebery was plied with arguments in favour of retention to which he was ready enough to pay heed. Gladstone and Harcourt, the Chancellor of the Exchequer, were violently opposed to Rosebery's policy. In the forefront of their minds was the memory of the recent disaster in Khartoum when a Liberal Government's interference, even to assist in evacuation, had led to a feeling of national disgrace over the death of Gordon. Rosebery therefore played for time, in the hope that the growing popular feeling in favour of retention might in due course swell to a flood which would enable him to sweep aside the opposition of his leader and colleagues. He even hinted at resignation if the other members of the Cabinet would not at least bear with him in his delay. This threat to the ministry enabled Rosebery to extract from the reluctant Government an undertaking to refund to the company the costs of a further three months' occupation. On this understanding the company continued to shoulder the task until March 31, 1893.

On October 3, 1892, Lugard arrived in England where he was immediately subjected to a heavy barrage of criticism for his actions in Buganda and particularly for his part in the events which had culminated in the short battle between the Baganda Christian factions. The Catholic missionaries, with highly-coloured accounts of Lugard's alleged partiality towards the Protestants, had enlisted the support of the French Government in their claim for compensation for their losses during the fighting. The British Government, already reluctant to admit any responsibility for the actions of a private company, even though the company was acting as their agent, were further embarrassed by a report on the events in Buganda, submitted at their request by Captain J. R. L. Macdonald, the engineer officer who had been engaged to carry out the railway survey. Macdonald, who had arrived in Kampala only a short time before Lugard's departure, had become Lugard's great enemy. His report therefore gave particular weight to the evidence of Lugard's detractors. But its critical nature, coupled with the vehemence of the French attack upon Lugard played into the latter's hands. Bishop Tucker of the C.M.S. and Captain Williams, Lugard's old colleague, both spoke up in his defence and eventually, although he never had any formal acquittal by the Foreign Office of the charges brought against him, he could rest assured that he had the sympathy of a large section of the British public.

Fortunately for Lugard, during the period of strain his thoughts were taken up less by the vilification levelled against him than by his concern for the future of Uganda. Like Rosebery he looked to public opinion to win the case against Cabinet resistance and in Lugard Rosebery found a most powerful advocate of retention. The nation's leading newspapers, with the exception of the liberal *Manchester Guardian* and *Daily News*, were turning against evacuation. The Church Missionary Society was actively urging retention in the interests of the security of a young Christian people who through their martyrs had proved their claim to consideration. The Anti-Slavery Society, which for some years had been rather in the background, now came to the fore with its moral arguments for retention. Lugard, himself, in the first of a series of lengthy letters to *The Times* set out the various grounds for retention. The commercial possibilities of East Africa which he had previously denied were now stressed, although the fact remained that without orderly administration and the investment of considerable capital there was no genuine hope of profit or of any of the developments which would ultimately lead to a flourishing trade. On the political side he pointed to the geographically strategic position of Uganda at the head-waters of the Nile, again an exaggerated argument but one which the French were thought to believe in, and the rivalry of the French strengthened Lugard's case. In the face of Liberal denials he reiterated his belief that Britain had an obligation to shoulder the responsibilities he had undertaken on behalf of the company. But the argument which probably won most emotional support was the fate of the Christians and missionaries in the event of withdrawal. To one after another of the leading personalities of the land Lugard stated his case. In a barn-storming series of lectures in both England and Scotland in November, he appealed to a sense of honour, to philanthropic zeal, to commercial enterprise and to national pride. The presence of memoranda submitted to Parliament was already being felt in October and it became more pronounced under the impact of Lugard's confident but unemotional exposition of the Uganda problem. The judicial voice of Lord Herschell, the Lord Chancellor, added weight to the campaign with the view that where the Government had not specifically dissented from the acts of the company it was responsible for them to foreign powers.

Early in November the first signs of the influence of public opinion upon the policy of a worried Cabinet were to be seen in the decision to send a Commissioner to Buganda to report on the situation there. The choice of Commissioner was left to Rosebery and he selected Sir Gerald Portal, the young British Consul-General in Zanzibar, whose support for a policy of retention was as strong as Rosebery's own. The supporters of evacuation still pretended that Portal's report would leave the issue to be decided by the Government, while the more radical supporters of the Government, led by Labouchere, still argued that if money and effort were to be expended they would be better employed in improving the material condition of the poor of England. But theirs was a rearguard action. The tide of battle was already running in favour of Rosebery. Lugard, however, was not wholly satisfied with the progress of events. A suggestion had been frequently made, in part, it is true, to cover the fact that the Liberals were giving ground, to the effect that Uganda and the interior should be administered from Zanzibar. This idea undoubtedly appealed to Portal who had himself striven hard to revive the declining influence of Zanzibar. It did not appeal to Lugard, who had little time for Zanzibar where slavery was still permitted although the slave-trade was forbidden.[1]

Portal started for the interior on New Year's Day, 1893. He was accompanied by his younger brother, Captain Raymond Portal, by Mr. E. J. L. Berkeley, the company's administrator, by Brevet-Major Roddy Owen, a distinguished soldier and gentleman-rider, and by a number of others. The difficulties which the company's men had had to face were revealed all along the route. The inefficiency, apart from any moral considerations, of human porterage disturbed the Commissioner greatly. At Machakos, where the company's able representative, John Ainsworth, was in command of a strongly stockaded post, there was a lull in the endemic struggle against the Wakamba. Fort Smith, the company's equally strong post in Kikuyu territory, was found to be virtually in a state of siege. Small parties out foraging for food were liable to sudden attack and only a few nights earlier there had been an attempt to burn the fort itself. Both Wakamba and Kikuyu had experienced a certain amount of harsh treatment at the hands of caravans and this had undoubtedly contributed to the distrust which they exhibited towards Europeans. The Kikuyu in particular had been given a bad name by travellers, and strangers arriving in their country tended to treat them accordingly. Portal noted, however, that they seemed to be industrious and careful agriculturalists. He also noted that the climate and fertility of their country appeared admirably suited to European farmers.

But Buganda was Portal's goal and he pushed on with all speed across the prairie country of the Masai. These latter were recovering by dint of their own courage from the decimation of their cattle by disease some two years earlier. This had resulted in the Masai themselves being reduced to the verge of starvation, yet their resilience was already enabling them to take up their former ways again.

[1] The best accounts of Lugard's work in Uganda and his subsequent campaign for retention are to be found in his own book, *The Rise of our East African Empire*. Blackwood, Edinburgh and London, 1893, Vol. 2, and in M. Perham: *Lugard—The Years of Adventure*, 1858–98. Collins, London, 1956.

Farther west, deserted villages gave their silent witness to recent Masai raids upon the Kabras people of northern Kavirondo. The Kabras themselves had simply migrated still farther westward to plant their well-tended fields of millet, maize, beans and sweet potatoes beyond the reach of the Masai. The caravan halted for a day to rest the porters at the village of Chief Mumia where the company had established a small storehouse. The village had become a favourite stopping place for caravans and the inhabitants had responded quickly to the advantages of exchanging food for trade goods. Mumia himself lived on until 1949, a remarkable link with an earlier age. Busoga, when the caravan reached it, proved to be a land of plenty, a region of endless banana gardens and fine shade trees inhabited by a people fully clad, unlike the naked Kabras, in toga-like garments of bark-cloth. Advancing through the rolling, green-clad countryside Portal reached the Nile, the threshold of Buganda, on March 12. Two long, light canoes, made of planks sewn together with fibres of aloes and plantains, transported the caravan across the 500 yards of water separating Busoga from Buganda. On the farther bank Portal, like Speke thirty years earlier, was startled by the well-dressed appearance and confident bearing of the people as much as by the excellent roads, it being the dry season, and by the clean, well-kept villages for which even his journey through Busoga had not prepared him.

Kampala itself was reached on March 17. The company's fort which had recently won such fame appeared to the Commissioner, with its mud huts, to be 'absurdly small and insignificant'. From longer acquaintance with the Baganda Portal also found them to be a friendly people but possessing no outstanding qualities. Of Mwanga and his sycophantic supporters and of the oppressive system of administration prevailing in the country he formed a very low opinion.[1] He spent ten weeks in Kampala and its immediate neighbourhood. On April 1, 1893, the company's flag was hauled down in the fort and replaced by the Union Jack. By this gesture Buganda, Busoga, Kavirondo and the Masai country to the Kedong River was transferred at least for the time being from the control of the I.B.E.A. Company to the British Crown. So, too, it must be assumed, were Ankole and Toro by virtue of their agreements with Lugard,

[1] Some of Portal's more condemnatory remarks about the Kabaka which are contained in the original MS. of his 'Mission to Uganda' now in the library of Makerere College, were omitted from the published version.

although Portal himself does not appear to have been clear on this point. The country to the north of these areas, stretching to the borders of the Sudan and Ethiopia and to the Juba River, still remained within the British sphere of influence but could not by any stretch of imagination be said to be under British control.

Portal next set to work to collect information on the subject of his commission and to try and settle some of the difficulties by which Buganda was still heavily beset. The Anglican Bishop, Tucker, and the Roman Catholic Bishop, Hirth, were now at least agreed that the withdrawal of the British from Buganda would be followed by grave disturbances.[1] This confirmed Portal's own opinion, but the two churchmen were still very anxious about the claims of their respective parties and did not hesitate to press their views upon the Commissioner. In a letter to his mother, dated April 7, 1893, Portal wrote, 'All's well that ends well, but I don't wish ever again to have a three and a half hours' skirmish with two angry bishops— one not understanding English, and the other knowing no French. The whole history of Uganda for the last ten years is more worthy of the Middle Ages, or the days of the Edict of Nantes, than the end of the nineteenth century; but I don't think either side is more to blame than the other.'[2] Portal was unduly optimistic in this assessment of the outcome of the interview he described, the main result of which was a new distribution of land, announced on April 22, which gave to the Catholics a larger share of the country than they had had under Lugard's scheme. Needless to say, neither side was satisfied by the new arrangement, and the Muslims were disgruntled because they had been given no further extension of territory. A further attempt by the Commissioner to induce the Bishops to divide the country into separate spheres of activity was rejected completely. All that emerged from his negotiations was a purely temporary arrangement by which the Catholics agreed that their main line of expansion would lie to the west while the Protestants were to concentrate upon the east. Even less satisfactory was Portal's proposal that there should, henceforward, be two Katikiros, one Protestant and one Catholic, two commanders-in-chief and two officers in charge of canoes. This arrangement baffled the Baganda

[1] Entebbe MSS. Inward, 1893. Bp. Tucker to Sir G. Portal, Namirembe, March 30, 1893, and Mgr. Hirth to Consul-General, Rubaga, April 27, 1893.
[2] Sir Gerald Portal: *The British Mission to Uganda in* 1893. Edward Arnold, London, 1894, p. 226.

and merely formalized the division between the two parties. Fortunately this system of duplication came to an end in 1900.

On May 27 Portal suffered a grave personal blow. Soon after his arrival in Kampala he had sent Major Owen and Captain Portal to Toro with instructions to reduce Britain's commitments by calling into Kampala the Sudanese garrisons along the Toro-Bunyoro border. Portal seems to have had little interest in western Uganda and does not appear to have taken into account the likely result of his orders. Captain Portal, however, contracted a fever and arrived back in Kampala on May 20 in a weak condition. Seven days later he died. The Commissioner was overwhelmed by the loss. He had been busy writing his report and was himself in poor health. Now he hastened to obtain Mwanga's signature to a new agreement on May 29 and set out for the coast the following day. In theory this agreement could be no more than a provisional one since Britain was ostensibly awaiting Portal's return before reaching any decision on Uganda. By its terms Mwanga accepted the protection of the British Government instead of that of the company. In return the Kabaka agreed not to enter into negotiations or hostilities with other powers without the consent of Britain and he also transferred to Her Majesty's Government the control of the assessment, collection and disposal of his country's revenue and taxes. This arrangement envisaged a protectorate in its most limited form, granting Britain the right to intervene in the affairs of Buganda without imposing upon her any responsibility for the government of the country. It could scarcely have been satisfactory to Mwanga but he was in no position to argue with the greater military force at Britain's disposal. Buganda had not been conquered by Britain but she had no greater freedom of manœuvre in these negotiations than a conquered state would have had. The limited nature of Britain's intervention in Buganda reflected only her desire to avoid assuming unnecessary administrative responsibilities.

Portal reached the coast on October 19 and was in Zanzibar by the evening of October 22. There he found his acting deputy, Rennell Rodd, lying seriously ill. He did not spend long in Zanzibar, however, but left for England on November 4. He lived for only a short time after his arrival there, for on January 25, 1894, he succumbed to a chill which his constitution, weakened by his stay in the tropics, was unable to withstand. The heavy death-roll among the pioneers who laid the foundations of European administration in East Africa is some indication of the trying conditions under which they carried on their tasks and must not be overlooked when assessing the weight of their achievement.

It is unlikely that Portal's recommendations were the deciding factor in the British Government's decision to declare a protectorate over Buganda for that decision had virtually been taken already. Nevertheless his report provided a justification for the waverers who did not wish to appear to be abandoning their position too easily. The report itself was presented to Parliament on April 10, just over ten weeks after Portal's death. As was to be expected, the retention of Buganda was strongly urged although the means advocated involved some vague connection with Zanzibar for administrative purposes. The need for a railway was also emphasized. Lord Rosebery, who on March 6 had succeeded Gladstone as Prime Minister, found Parliament prepared to accept the declaration of a Protectorate over Buganda but the Government, anxious to avoid excessive financial commitments, stated its intention of appointing a Commissioner responsible for Buganda alone with only a Sub-Commissioner to administer the line of communication to the coast. The company was to be bought out but it was decided that a railway would not be built. This plan was approved by the Liberals with Conservative and Unionist support although the Radicals continued in opposition. British public opinion had won a great victory and Lugard, whose determination during the period of stress in 1891 and early 1892 had made retention possible, had himself played a vital part in converting public opinion to Rosebery's view.

Meanwhile, events in Africa had once again taken on a serious aspect. Macdonald had been left by Portal to act as British Representative but had been given instructions not to interfere in the internal affairs of Buganda except to prevent gross injustice or cruelty. Away to the west Owen, who was reluctantly withdrawing the Sudanese from the Toro frontier posts, was only too keenly aware that by fulfilling Portal's orders he was exposing Lugard's protégé, Kasagama, to the attack of his rival, Kabarega. The Muslims, already discontented over the land question, were growing restless and were seeking, unsuccessfully, to enlist the aid of Selim Bey and the Sudanese troops stationed in Kampala and in Port Alice some twenty-five miles away. In the middle of June 1893,

Macdonald began to suspect the loyalty of Selim Bey who was then at Port Alice. He therefore took the precautionary measure of disarming the garrison in Kampala in spite of protestations of loyalty from the Sudanese officers. On the same day the Muslims in Kampala revolted, but were driven away to the west by a force of Protestant Baganda organized by Macdonald. As a further precaution Macdonald then arrested Selim Bey who was tried and deported. He died at Naivasha on his way to the coast. These decisive and necessary actions probably saved Kampala, but they made nonsense of Macdonald's instructions to keep outside Kiganda politics. Moreover, his treatment of the Sudanese troops and especially of their leader was to have repercussions a few years later when it played a minor but significant part in causing the mutiny of 1897.

Although the Muslims had been defeated in the first clash they now lay astride Macdonald's communications with the west and some of them were trying to get in touch with the Sudanese garrisons in Toro. The Muslim problem, which had largely been settled by Lugard, was once more inflamed. Kabarega, too, was threatening Toro, encouraged as was only to be expected by signs of the withdrawal of the Sudanese garrisons. He was strengthened by a lively middleman trade in guns and ivory between Acholi and German East Africa, and Arab traders had established themselves in Bunyoro. Ntare of Ankole also appeared to be permitting caravans of gun-runners to pass through his territory in spite of his agreement with Lugard. In these circumstances Owen inquired reasonably enough as to what provision had been made to protect the Batoro when he withdrew and if Kasagama moved to the safety of Singo as had been suggested. He could see neither reason nor justice in his orders for, having met and defeated the dissident Baganda Muslims, he was confident that he could resist Kabarega also. Macdonald, harassed by Catholic demands for a further distribution of land and worried by the inability of the Muganda chief placed in charge of Busoga to maintain order or to collect taxes along the main line of communication to the east, was angered by Owen's procrastination. From Koki only there came the more cheerful information that its ruler, the Kamuswaga, formerly involved in Bunyoro's trade in arms and slaves, had agreed to become a tributary of Buganda.

In September 1893 Macdonald was at length driven to recognize the need for a campaign against the aggressive Kabarega. Owen was authorized to prepare for an advance from the south while Macdonald gathered his forces for the main attack. In November Colonel Colvile arrived to take over from Macdonald and with instructions to check a rumoured Belgian advance into the British sphere in the direction of the Nile. Macdonald's proposed campaign fitted in well with these orders and Colvile took command of the expedition which consisted of the Sudanese troops together with a vast number of Baganda. The advance began in December. Within a month Kabarega's capital near Hoima was occupied and although the Mukama continued to wage a guerrilla campaign for nearly a year he was finally driven to take refuge north of the Nile in November 1894. A small occupation force was left in Bunyoro to prevent any revival of Kabarega's influence, but no official annexation was contemplated. As a reward for their part in Kabarega's overthrow the Baganda annexed large areas in the east and south-east of Bunyoro, the most important of these being Mubende, the former centre of the Kingdom of Kitara and the burial place of many former rulers of Bunyoro. To recover Mubende, which was to become famous in subsequent history as 'the lost counties', has been the chief goal of Bunyoro ever since and has resulted in a backward-looking rather than a progressive policy among the Banyoro as a people.

After the first successes against Kabarega Major Owen had been sent on an expedition down the Nile. He advanced as far as Wadelai where he induced the local chief, Ali, to accept protection, at that time a very slender offer. Returning thence to Toro, he restored to office Mukama Kasagama who had been driven by Kabarega to seek refuge in the foothills of the Ruwenzori Mountains. He then made another agreement with the young ruler which guaranteed British protection in return for the acceptance of a British Resident in Toro. A similar agreement was made in August between Major Cunningham and the Mugabe of Ankole. Both treaties were ostensibly signed on behalf of the British Government yet neither had been authorized by that Government. In fact, the British decision to declare a protectorate over Buganda was announced in June and was formally proclaimed in Mengo by Colvile on August 27, 1894. But this decision affected Buganda alone, which at this date did not even include Koki.

Although Britain was still far from clear as to her exact relationship with Buganda, the age of extreme caution in imperial matters was beginning to wane. The ambitions of imperialists like Cecil Rhodes were already making their impact upon public opinion. The Liberal Government, under Lord Rosebery, now repeatedly declared that it had no intention of abandoning the British sphere of influence in East Africa and in 1894 a step was taken which demonstrated a growing consciousness of the importance of Africa in world affairs. Leopold II, sovereign of the Congo Free State, was anxious to extend his territory to the Nile. To do so, he maintained, was in no way exceeding the limits previously agreed between himself and Sir William Mackinnon on behalf of the I.B.E.A. Company. Rosebery, like Salisbury before him, rejected Leopold's right to extend his frontiers in this way. There was, however, little immediate hope of effective British occupation in that area so that, faced with French ambitions in the same direction, Rosebery decided to use the Congo State as a buffer between the British and the French spheres. On May 12, 1894, an agreement was signed by Britain and Leopold as a result of which Leopold recognized the right of Britain to the territories assigned to her by the Anglo-German agreements. Simultaneously the boundary between British territory and the Congo Free State was fixed along the 30th meridian of east longitude from the north of the German sphere to the watershed of the Nile and Congo, from which point it would follow the watershed in a northerly and north-westerly direction. In return Leopold leased from Britain for his own lifetime a considerable strip of land on the west bank of the Nile and stretching from Lake Albert to beyond Fashoda. With the object of fulfilling at least a part of Rhodes's Cape to Cairo railway dream, Rosebery then obtained from Leopold the lease of a strip of land sixteen miles wide, running from the most northerly port on Lake Tanganyika to the most southerly point on Lake Edward, thus linking Rhodesia with the British sphere in East Africa.

The treaty was not well received by the other colonial powers in tropical Africa. France resented the attempt to thwart her violent policy of annexation and in August Leopold agreed to renounce all right to occupy territory leased by Great Britain north of 5° 30′ north latitude. The area south of this line became known as the Lado Enclave. Germany, with equal firmness if with less obvious indignation, protested against the lease to Britain of a strip of territory along the western frontier of her East African possessions, particularly without any prior consultation. Britain therefore agreed to the cancellation of the lease.

The decision which had been taken in Britain to accept officially the responsibility for intervention in Buganda's affairs, automatically raised the question of what should happen to the company's territories lying between the Kedong River to the west and the coastal strip leased from the Sultan of Zanzibar to the east, all part of the vital line of communication with Buganda. Although the Buganda venture had strained beyond their limits the resources of a body in which philanthropic motives predominated over the desire for commercial profit, the company had not been inactive nearer the coast. Mr. Ernest Berkeley, who became Administrator in 1891, had had considerable experience in the consular service and he had brought to his new post both energy and sound commercial control. The possibilities of the Tana as a commercial waterway were explored and found to be inadequate. In Witu, which was placed under the control of the company in March 1891, the legal status of slavery was abolished. Unfortunately the company became so dissatisfied with its treatment by the British Government that it renounced its control on July 31, 1893. The state was placed under the sultanate of Zanzibar and slavery again became legal. Simultaneously a punitive expedition was launched by Zanzibar forces against the Sultan of Witu, Fumo Omari, whose stockade was stormed in August. The ruling dynasty was deposed, but a guerrilla war was carried on for some time by the Sultan's supporters. The company in the meantime was establishing friendly relations with the chiefs along the coast as far north as the Juba River, the boundary between the British and Italian spheres which had been agreed upon by the two powers in March, 1891, while the river itself was explored and found to be navigable for a distance of 400 miles. The advice of specialists was sought on the agricultural possibilities of the coast area and in 1891 the lease of the coastal strip itself was converted from fifty years to a grant in perpetuity in return for a payment of 80,000 dollars (c. £17,000). At Mackinnon's own expense a road was constructed across the Taru plain, while at Machakos the company opened an industrial institution for the training of Africans. Investigations were also made into the possibility of inducing Indians to settle along the main river banks, but the numbers willing to participate in this scheme were small.

Even in the area nearer the coast, however, the limitations imposed upon sound development by the company's financial stringency, were all too evident. There they were dealing with societies which depended heavily upon the institution of slavery, which the company could not but deplore, and which were ruled over by semi-independent chiefs whom the company could scarcely hope to control. Subsidies paid by the company to some of the leaders of the Mazaria near the coast and to the Somali near the Juba River, in the hope of gaining their assistance in administering the country, were treated virtually as tribute and encouraged aggression rather than co-operation. A premature attempt to impose a hut tax upon the Wagiriama not only failed as a result of the company's inability to enforce its collection but also gave the impression that the company was prepared to be oppressive but was too weak to command respect. More important fundamentally, however, was the endemic feeling of unrest due to the conviction that the company, though lacking the resources to impose order, would before long endeavour to put an end to slavery. The company brought upon itself the scorn of missionaries and Arabs alike through having to compromise with the latter when their fugitive slaves took refuge with the C.M.S. in Rabai and Frere Town. Moreover, although it felt itself bound to discourage an active campaign of Christian proselytization among the Muslims, it was, at the same time, obliged to try to enforce the anti-slavery legislation which successive British Agents had wrung from the sultans of Zanzibar.[1] Against this impossible background any positive achievements by the company were not without merit.

All this effort was brought to an abrupt end on July 1, 1895, when the British Government, having taken upon itself the protection of Buganda, decided to take control all the way to the coast. Zanzibar, where a regular administration under British auspices had been introduced by agreement in October 1891, was arbitrarily called upon to buy out the company's lease of the coastal strip. This seemed unduly harsh as far as Zanzibar was concerned although the country's revenues were now wholly administered by British officers under the direction of the Consul-General while the Sultan retained

[1] Sir A. H. Hardinge: *A Diplomatist in the East.* Jonathan Cape, London, 1928, pp. 161, 164, 217.

his private estates and received a fixed annual grant. Nor did the annual revenue of £17,000, which the Sultan was to receive from the British Imperial Government as Administrator of his mainland territories, offer much consolation since he knew all too well that it would not be placed at his disposal but would be used by his English officials for the development of the island of Zanzibar.[1] At the same time the sum paid to the company could scarcely be considered adequate compensation for all its expenditure of money and effort. But the British Government persisted. Its protection was extended over the coastal strip as part of the existing Zanzibar Protectorate while the hinterland between the coastal strip and the Kedong River became the British East Africa Protectorate without further inquiry and without any agreement such as was made in Buganda. This action was accounted for, although no legal justification was needed in the mid 1890s, by the apparent absence of any chiefs with whom to negotiate and by the urgent need to control the main line of communication with the lake region.

It is certain that the British Government had no clear idea as to the nature of the relationship thus established with the lands and peoples of East Africa although the declaration of a protectorate may have contained some intimation of Britain's acceptance of a degree of responsibility greater than had been intended when the spheres of influence had been determined. But the character of the indigenous organization of the peoples of the East Africa Protectorate, as well as the way in which the Protectorate was declared, inevitably led, within a very few years, to the need for Britain to take upon herself the direct responsibility for administering the country. In this way, three very different versions of the term Protectorate were to develop in British East Africa. In Zanzibar, where a unified if not very efficient system of government existed, British influence simply percolated into the offices of state, leaving the Sultan as ruler. In the East Africa Protectorate the variety and looseness of the political systems called for direct administration. Buganda on its own might have followed the Zanzibar pattern, but in the years following upon the declaration of the Buganda Protectorate several other areas were added, to form the Uganda Protectorate, thereby making impossible the simple structure introduced into Zanzibar. In due course the organization of the Uganda Protectorate came to

[1] Sir A. H. Hardinge: op. cit., pp. 132–3.

lie between the two extremes of Zanzibar and the British East Africa Protectorate and resembled more closely the pattern which was developing in German East Africa.

The decision of the British Government to take over from the company was unpopular with the Sultan of Zanzibar, Hamed bin Thwain, on more than financial grounds. He had been led to hope that with the withdrawal of the company at least the nominal rule of the territory on the mainland would be transferred to himself. When the news of the British Protectorate was communicated to him he accepted it with the dignity and fatalism of his race. Possibly, too, there was a touch of irony in his reply. 'I am like a little bird in the claws of a powerful eagle,' he said. 'The eagle can either drop the bird and let it die, or he can carry it to a place of safety.' His faith in the goodwill of the British Government was shaken and his disappointment was fostered by Arabs at his court who disliked the influence of Mathews and the other British administrators who now, in the name of the Sultan, were the virtual rulers of Zanzibar. Prominent among the Sultan's unofficial counsellors was an Omani Arab named Sheikh Hilal bin Amr, who was already suspected by the Government of India of having intrigued against the domestic peace of Oman. Hardinge frequently warned the Sultan against him and eventually, in 1896, Hilal was moved to Aden where he was treated as a political exile.

The real clash with Zanzibari opinion soon followed. In August 1893 Lord Rosebery had urged upon Rennell Rodd, the Acting Consul-General, the importance of putting an end as soon as possible to the legal status of slavery in the Sultan's dominions. On September 13, 1889, Seyyid Khalifa, who succeeded Sultan Barghash, had been prevailed upon by Gerald Portal to make a number of concessions in return for the lifting of the naval blockade imposed by the British and Germans to check the rising in the German coastal territories. Among the points agreed by Khalifa was one which said that all persons entering his dominions after November 1889 should be free, although they would become his subjects. All children born in his dominions should also be declared free. A year later, in August 1890, Khalifa's successor, Seyyid Ali, confirmed Khalifa's anti-slavery measures but found himself quite unable to enforce them owing to popular feeling. Rennell Rodd therefore considered it reasonable to point out to Rosebery that in the existing state of society in Zanzibar, and more particularly in view of the vital part played by slaves in maintaining the economy of the country through their work in the clove plantations, to destroy slavery at one swoop would be bound to cause serious disruption. The slaves themselves, free now to grow their own food, would be landless and starving if severed from their masters, and the Arab slave-owners' property was so heavily mortgaged to Indian moneylenders that they would be in no position to maintain paid labour even if they wished to do so.

Although Rodd's reply convinced the permanent authorities in the Foreign Office the weight of philanthropic opinion in Britain was still great. Lord Kimberley, the Foreign Secretary, wrote to Arthur Hardinge, Rodd's successor, on November 27, 1894, asking for a full report. Hardinge's views were very similar to those of Rodd, but the opportunity for bold action was suddenly provided through unforeseen circumstances. In the latter part of 1896 Sultan Hamed bin Thwain died unexpectedly, and not without some suspicion of poison. Seyyid Khalid, a son of Barghash, immediately seized the throne and defied the Acting Consul-General, Mr. Cave, who held office while Hardinge was on leave. The new Sultan was not the obvious successor. Nor was he well disposed towards the protecting power, for he believed that with Germany's help it had dismembered his father's dominions. Cave was fortunate in that, a day after Khalid's seizure of power, a British naval squadron commanded by Admiral Rawson arrived off Zanzibar. When Khalid still resisted, the squadron fired on the palace. Khalid fled to the German consulate and subsequently took refuge in Dar es Salaam. Khalid's cousin, Hamed bin Muhammad, was chosen by the British Government to be Sultan. The manner of Hamed's succession demonstrated the overriding power of the British, while Hamed himself, stout, elderly, greybearded and dignified, had no desire to challenge that supremacy.

By this chance Britain was presented with a good opportunity to attack the legal status of slavery. The futility of resistance had been impressed upon the citizens of Zanzibar by the recent bombardment. Many of the slave-owners of Pemba fled at once with their slaves to Oman where, however, by an agreement between the Government of India and the Sultan, every slave arriving by sea could claim his freedom. Hardinge, nevertheless, was anxious that if the Arabs were to be required to swallow this bitter pill they should receive compensation. He argued, with some justification, that England had compensated the former British slave-owners in the West Indies and to do less for the Arabs would savour of extreme injustice. His view was not shared by the British Anti-Slavery Society, but the Government was prevailed upon to agree. On April 6, 1897, therefore, the formal abolition of the legal status of slavery in the Sultan's dominions of Zanzibar and Pemba was proclaimed. Now any slave who so wished could claim his freedom and his master might demand pecuniary compensation, while the preamble to the decree was carefully drafted so as to lay emphasis upon the Sultan's desire to fulfil the religious law of Islam by bestowing freedom from servitude upon such of his subjects as desired it.

A temporary effect of the decree was the depreciation in value of real estate, more particularly in Pemba, since labour was not readily available to develop the land. For some time, however, there were few applications for freedom and a number of slave-owners refrained from asking for compensation. The vagrancy which resulted from the freeing of slaves, some of whom preferred stealing to work, was firmly suppressed, and as a result of the gradual way in which the decree was implemented the clove crop, even in Pemba, was higher in 1898 than in the previous three years. The Arabs now began to pay all their labourers, whether free or not, thereby stimulating their efficiency and increasing the crop. So, while some slave-trading still continued illegally in the British protected territories on the mainland, the root of slavery had been cut in Zanzibar itself without the fearful consequences, either social, political or economic, which many had foreseen.[1]

Throughout the latter half of the nineteenth century naval supremacy had played a decisive part in establishing British control over the affairs of Zanzibar, and Britain had not hesitated to demonstrate her naval strength when a sultan appeared hostile to British designs. In Uganda,[2] too, where the altruistic motives which had induced Britain to take a close interest in Zanzibar were to some extent blended with more selfish aims, Britain's military prowess had played a vital part. If Britain's position in Zanzibar rested as much upon naval strength as upon the goodwill of the Sultan, in Buganda and Toro the efficacy of the agreements still rested very

[1] Sir A. H. Hardinge: op. cit., pp. 187–207.

[2] Henceforward the name 'Buganda' will refer to the Kabaka's kingdom while 'Uganda' will be used to indicate the whole of the British sphere north of Lake Victoria.

Sir Albert Cook

Laying the first railway line, Mombasa 1896

Old trolley lines, Mombasa

First train to leave Kilindini

heavily upon the power of British arms. More blatant, however, because based upon a more positive and urgent desire for empire, was Germany's conquest of Tanganyika.

Perhaps the most detailed study of Germany's struggles to conquer and subdue the tribes of East Africa is to be found in a report submitted by Mr. (later Sir Charles) Dundas at the request of the British Government in 1923.[1] The object of the report, as Dundas himself admitted, was to provide positive indication of Germany's unfitness to rule over undeveloped peoples,[2] and it undoubtedly contained a formidable tale of guerrilla warfare ranging over the greater part of German East Africa. Nevertheless, to look upon this catalogue of battles and skirmishes as evidence of Germany's mismanagement of the administration of her East African dependency is to post-date the fighting in the brief story of Germany in East Africa. For these struggles in almost every case were due to the efforts of the African tribes to resist conquest rather than the revolts of an already conquered people. One can follow the pattern of these struggles along the lines of German penetration. The earliest battles were fought in the coastal area in the region of Bagamoyo and in the country of the Wazaramu between 1891 and 1893. Then along the main lines of communication the struggle continued. The Chagga along the northern route into the interior made their last attempt at organized resistance to German control under the leadership of Meli, the son of Chief Mandara, in 1892. For a few months the Germans were able only to maintain themselves in the area by diplomatic negotiations until a strong force under the command of Colonel von Schele attacked and defeated Meli, where he had taken refuge in thick bush country. Henceforward the Chagga became the most docile of the Germans' subjects.

Along the great central trade route the Wanyamwezi, ever ready for new experiences and new contacts, were friendly towards the Germans until they realized that the latter came to eat up the land and to subjugate the people, then they, too, took up arms. Under their aggressive leader, Siki, they attacked a German column in 1892 and in spite of a number of expeditions against their fortified stronghold they were able to close the caravan route for several months. They were eventually defeated by a German force led by Lieutenant

[1] Sir Charles Dundas: *A History of German East Africa.* Government Printer, Dar es Salaam, 1923.

[2] Sir Charles Dundas: *African Crossroads.* Macmillan, London, 1955, p. 106.

von Prince, and Siki committed suicide. The Wagogo, also, resisted the German advance. Truculent at all times, their hostility remained a constant threat to the security of communications and several expeditions were necessary to intimidate this aggressive but disunited people. By 1894 and 1895 Germany was probing even further inland although her forces were still to some extent occupied in suppressing the resistance of the slave-traders near Kilwa. Three chiefs in the Bukoba area and Tagaralla, ruler of Ujiji, also felt the weight of German arms. About the same time the Germans launched an advance against the Wahehe in the Iringa area. These latter had already shown their prowess in defeating a small German force and this had given them a reputation for invincibility which encouraged them to take bold action against caravans travelling through their country. They were well led by Mkwawa who had been largely responsible for welding the tribe into a conscious unit. Mkwawa's fortress near Iringa was surrounded by stone walls which in places were twelve feet high and which were strengthened at intervals by powerful bastions. The Germans launched an attack against the Wahehe stronghold in October 1894 and after heavy fighting Mkwawa fled. He left behind him booty which included 30,000 lb. of gunpowder and 2,000 head of cattle. Simultaneously the more northerly section of the tribe also suffered defeat and the power of the Wahehe was broken. Nevertheless, Mkwawa exerted so powerful an influence over his people that he was able to sustain a guerrilla war lasting several years which threatened the ultimate annihilation of the whole tribe. The Germans therefore established two stations among the Wahehe in the hope of isolating Mkwawa from his followers. They attempted to pacify the people while maintaining a constant pursuit of their chief but because of the reputation he had created Mkwawa was able to evade capture for more than three years. In July 1898 his hiding-place was betrayed to the Germans and the warrior chief, already sick, committed suicide to avoid capture.[1]

While the Germans were thus engaged in subduing the Wahehe their attention was already being diverted to the north-western region where their advance still continued. Beyond the borders of the German sphere the Belgians were meeting trouble from Manyema tribesmen. In 1898 they were forced to evacuate the country east

[1] G. G. Brown and A. McD. Hutt: *Anthropology in Action*. O.U.P., London, 1935, pp. 36–37.

of Lake Kivu and the Germans took advantage of this withdrawal to establish three posts in Ruanda. A year later, when the Belgians attempted to reoccupy the region they found it in the hands of German troops. It was agreed as a temporary measure that the district should be held by equal forces of Germans and Belgians until it was finally decided in Europe that the region so arbitrarily claimed by the Germans should, in fact, form part of the German sphere. The ruler of neighbouring Urundi, Muesi Kisabo, continued to reject any advances from the Europeans. Backed by a population of about half a million people and fortified by a reputation for supernatural powers Muesi appeared a formidable obstacle to further German expansion. Captain Bette, then in command of Usumbura, decided to put the powers of the chief to the test. Advancing into Urundi with a strong force he occupied Muesi's capital after a short skirmish and active patrol measures at last induced Muesi himself to surrender in 1903.

With virtually the whole of the German sphere now conquered, there broke out a rising both different in nature and more devastating in its effects than any previous struggle. From the outset the Germans had been anxious to exploit the resources of their new East African dependency and this may well have accounted for the ruthless manner in which they set about the task of bringing the country under control. They had certainly been attracted by the economic possibilities of the south-eastern region, and between 1890 and 1899 a number of expeditions had been sent into the hinterland behind Lindi and Mikindani to try to destroy the hostile power of the Yao chief, Matschemba. These undertakings had met with varied success until, in July 1899, Matschemba was forced to take refuge in Portuguese territory. Most of his people submitted and a German post was established on the Rovuma River to prevent any attempt by Matschemba to return to his country. It came, therefore, as a surprise when the Maji Maji rising broke out in the Matumbi hills north west of Kilwa in July 1905. The first conspirators were chiefs and medicine men of the Wapogoro and Wagindo, but the movement was dangerous because it soon spread to a number of other tribes. It took its title from the use of a 'medicine' concocted with water, maize and sorghum seed which was said to make the recipient immune to bullets and which therefore deprived the Europeans of the advantage which their weapons had formerly given them. A number of explanations have been given for the rising and for its widespread character. The Germans had alienated certain sections of the population by levying forced labour in their all-out attempt to develop the country's resources. With the same end in view they had compelled large numbers of peasants to plant cotton seed irrespective of the peasants' inclination. At the same time the rigid administrative system which the Germans had introduced made it difficult for the German officers to get in touch with the African population. When a district administrator was forbidden to sleep away from his headquarters without the Governor's permission it is not surprising that little was known of public reaction to official policy.[1] Nevertheless, although the reasons mentioned undoubtedly played their part, the discontent of the people was almost certainly due to deeper motives. Some understanding of these can be gained from an Arab account of the Maji Maji rising entitled *Utenzi wa Vita vya Maji Maji*.[2] Although this poem deals with only a small part of the rebellion and is far from sympathetic towards the rebels, it raises two significant points. The first is that the systematic way of life imposed by the German administration was contrary to local traditions and practice and proved extremely irksome to the easy-going peoples of East Africa. The second emerges from a conversation said to have taken place between the young men engaged in the fighting and an elder to whom they had turned with complaints about the hardships of war. The chief's reply condemned them for their weakness and pointed out that, fundamentally, they had gone to war to regain their manhood which they had lost when they had surrendered the direction of their lives to the Germans. These two factors were to prove a basic source of discontent in the territories ruled over by the European powers who frequently could not understand why their well-meaning attempts to improve the material conditions of African life appeared to give rise to so much resentment.

In the opening stages of the rebellion the Germans were worried lest the Wanyamwezi, who could put between thirty and forty thousand warriors into the field, all carrying firearms, together with thousands more armed with native weapons, should join in the

[1] Sir Horace Byatt: An address delivered to the African Society, July 9, 1924. *Journal of the African Society*, Vol. XXIV, No. xciii, pp. 2–5.

[2] Abdul Karim bin Jamaliddini: *Utenzi wa Vita vya Maji Maji*. (Translated by W. H. Whiteley.) Supplement to the *East African Swahili Committee Journal*, No. 27. June 1957.

struggle. The spirited and courageous Wahehe might also be drawn in, for the rising spread rapidly until the whole land was in ferment from Songea to Lindi in the south and from Dar es Salaam to Kilosa in the north. Mahenge became a centre of particularly heavy fighting as the Germans exerted every effort to check the spread of the rebellion westward to the Wahehe. Casualties were heavy on both sides and the Germans were hard-pressed to provide the reinforcements and replacements needed to meet an attack on so many fronts. Gradually, however, the systematic campaigning and deadly machine-gun fire of the Germans took its toll until, in January 1907, the last flicker of rebellion was quenched among the Ngoni who had fought longest and hardest of all. The failure of the Maji Maji rebellion was followed by a period of relative peace although there was a brief revival of trouble in 1908 which was quickly suppressed. The casualties during the fighting and the famine which followed the rebellion taught the tribes a terrible lesson. The Germans, too, had learnt a lesson and from 1907 onwards far more attention was paid to administrative policy.

The appointment of Mr. Ernest Berkeley as British Commissioner in Uganda in 1895 marked Britain's official acceptance of her responsibility for the affairs of Uganda in a more practical fashion than had the declaration of a protectorate over Buganda the previous year. Thrusting behind her the anti-imperialist outlook which had dominated nineteenth-century policy Britain now began a process of annexation in Uganda, wherever possible making use of agreements but employing force where necessary. Berkeley himself quickly became conscious of the incomplete nature of the existing agreement with Buganda and the tentative arrangements with neighbouring peoples. In December 1895 he wrote to the Foreign Secretary asking permission to negotiate with other chiefs in order to extend Britain's official relationship with the other tribes of Uganda. He was authorized to proceed as he thought fit and in July 1896 the Marquess of Salisbury himself took the step of extending the Protectorate to Bunyoro, Toro, Ankole and Busoga.[1] What lay behind Salisbury's action is not clear. It may well have been that Berkeley's request had indicated that Britain must soon take a more active part in the administration of these lands lying on the borders of Buganda and, as in the case of the East Africa Protectorate, the new declaration

[1] F. O. 2/111. F.O. to Berkeley, July 17, 1896.

thus gave formal notice of the British Government's intentions. In any case the agreements previously made with Ankole and Toro were now regularized and already Ankole had taken steps to improve her relationship with the British through the initiative of Nuwa Mbaguta, the able and far-sighted adviser of the new Mugabe, Kahaya. It was on Mbaguta's recommendation that a request was sent to the British Commissioner to post an administrative officer in Ankole, and Kahaya then established his headquarters in the vicinity of the British station. This was a shrewd move, for Kahaya's authority was limited in its extent, but his proximity to the British post attracted the attention of the Protectorate authorities and thereby prepared the way for his assumption of control over chiefs who hitherto would never have accepted his authority.

The situation in Bunyoro was still unsettled. Disputes arose over the claims of the Baganda to occupy the land they had been allotted when Kabarega was defeated. Successive British administrators adopted contradictory attitudes and the Foreign Office, when appealed to by Berkeley, vaguely commented that since both Buganda and Bunyoro now formed part of the British Protectorate there appeared to be no problem to solve.[1] In an endeavour to introduce some more recognizable form of order Yosiya Kitahimbwa, the twelve-year-old son of Kabarega was declared Mukama in 1898, but in the following year his powers were declared to be in abeyance during his minority. All authority was then wielded by a British Sub-Commissioner acting through an African katikiro whom he himself appointed. Late in 1898 also, a number of prominent Baganda chiefs claimed that Buganda was traditionally sovereign over Bunyoro, Toro, Ankole and Busoga.[2] Their announcement was addressed to George Wilson, Sub-Commissioner in Buganda, whose wisdom in handling African affairs was outstanding. Wilson investigated the claim with characteristic thoroughness and impartiality. His conclusion was that while Busoga had been, intermittently, a tributary of Buganda for a considerable period, a few isolated gifts from Kabarega to Mutesa had little significance and the claim of the Baganda chiefs had no historical foundation in respect of Bunyoro, Toro or Ankole.[3]

[1] J. W. Gregory: *The Foundation of British East Africa*. Horace Marshall, London, 1901. pp. 216–18.

[2] Entebbe MSS. Apolo Kagwa, Stanislas Mugwanya and others to the Sub-Commissioner, Uganda District, November 8, 1898.

[3] Entebbe MSS. Wilson to Berkeley, February 8, 1899.

Two events of far greater seriousness had marred British efforts at orderly control of the affairs of the new Protectorate. In July 1897 Mwanga, who had never settled down happily under British tutelage, escaped from his capital and raised the standard of revolt. He was able to rally a considerable force to his cause since the loyalty of the Baganda to their Kabaka was deeply ingrained. Among many of the leading chiefs, however, Mwanga's own evil habits had aroused severe distaste, and their regular contact with British administrators and missionaries at the capital had undermined the unquestioning awe in which the simpler peasantry still held their ruler. A force of Sudanese troops was sent in pursuit of Mwanga and when he took refuge in German East Africa he was officially deposed by the British Acting-Commissioner, Colonel Trevor Ternan, who summoned the leading chiefs to Kampala to proclaim the accession of Mwanga's infant son, Daudi Chwa. That Ternan was able to achieve such a revolution with little difficulty was an indication of the change in attitude of the influential Baganda towards the Kabaka and even more of the tremendous power and influence now wielded by the British. The succession of a child only one year old to the office of Kabaka still further strengthened that position, for while many of the chiefs held the British in great respect for the knowledge they had brought to Uganda, others recognized that their own positions and status had been largely achieved through their adherence to the white invaders. The appointment of three regents to rule the kingdom during the Kabaka's minority only underlined the changes which had taken place. The senior regent, Apolo Kagwa, created for himself such a position of authority by his co-operation with the Protectorate Administration, coupled with the strength of his own character, that Buganda never became truly united under its Kabaka until after Kagwa's death. Without British support Kagwa could not have succeeded, for, although the regents' power was great, they could not hope to win the unwavering loyalty which a kabaka could command, more especially if there was a suggestion, as indeed there was bound to be in Kagwa's case, that he was ruling as much in his own interests as in those of the youthful Daudi Chwa. Mwanga, meanwhile, escaped from his exile early in 1898 and sought refuge with his former enemy, Kabarega, north of the Nile among the Lango. The two former rulers were betrayed and captured in April 1899, and were in due course deported. Mwanga died in exile, but Kabarega was allowed to return to Uganda in 1923 only to die in Jinja before he could reach Bunyoro.

The second event which disturbed Uganda in the later 1890s was a revolt among the Sudanese troops, and the companies affected were those which had been engaged in the campaign against Mwanga. Almost immediately afterwards they were ordered to march to Eldama Ravine where they were to come under the command of Major J. R. L. Macdonald who had instructions to lead an expedition to counter a rumoured advance by the French towards the Upper Nile. The Sudanese reached Eldama Ravine but once there refused to proceed farther. Their pay was in arrears owing to the difficulty of obtaining adequate supplies of the cloth which formed the normal currency of East Africa. In addition they had not been allowed to bring with them the women who normally accompanied them to minister to their comfort on long marches. Perhaps, too, it would not be wrong to suggest that their memories of Macdonald's treatment of their former leader, Selim Bey, made them less amenable to reason. Having unsuccessfully stated their case, therefore, the troops retreated to Lubwa's in Busoga where they were welcomed by the Sudanese garrison which had already seized three British officers who had been unfortunate enough to find themselves at the mercy of the troops when news of the mutiny reached the camp. The mutineers were hotly pursued by Macdonald and there followed a lengthy siege of Lubwa's during the early stages of which the three imprisoned officers were killed. In Kampala there was great apprehension lest the remaining companies of Sudanese soldiers should follow the example of the rebels. Prompt action was taken to disarm them, however, and no trouble ensued. Mainly due to the influence of George Wilson the Christian Baganda also remained calm, although it was the refusal of their leader, Mbogo, to break his agreement with Lugard which alone prevented the Muslims from taking advantage of the unsettled state of the country to stage a revolt. The Christian Baganda, on the other hand, rallied to the aid of the Protectorate authorities. Under the leadership of Apolo Kagwa a large force marched to Lubwa's to take part in the siege and many lost their lives in the skirmishes which took place outside the stockade. Early in January 1898 the mutineers made good their escape and after a fierce engagement with pursuing forces the survivors took refuge north of the Nile where some of them joined Kabarega. Henceforward they caused no further trouble and they were eventually dispersed by an expedition which followed them into the swamps beyond Lake Kyoga in 1901.

The mutiny had two important results. In the first place the loyalty of the Christian Baganda demonstrated clearly the allegiance of the leading chiefs to the new authority of Britain. But perhaps even more important was the reaction in Britain to the prolonged military operations in Uganda. Considerable sums of money had to be sent by Britain to assist in putting down the revolt, and the expenditure of this money, more effectively even than humanitarian sentiments, convinced the British Government that a more decisive policy was necessary in the Protectorate. In 1899, therefore, Sir Harry Johnston was commissioned to go to Uganda and to make recommendations on the future administration of the Protectorate.

While Britain was thus reluctantly awakening to her responsibilities in East Africa those responsibilities were being still further extended. Macdonald, in furtherance of his original mission and Lieut.-Colonel Cyril Martyr, commanding the troops in Uganda, hastened to take advantage of the restoration of peace in Buganda by starting out independently to the north, beyond the Nile, where they made a number of treaties with the local chiefs. The British Government gave official recognition to these agreements in 1899, but little could be done at that stage to maintain communications with such remote regions. The territory fell within the British sphere by agreement rather than in reality. No protectorate was declared over this region until, along with the rest of Uganda, its status as a Protectorate was assumed by the Uganda Order in Council of 1902.

But the first steps were already being taken in the 1890s to link up the protected territory south and west of the Victoria Nile with the lands of the Nilotic and Nilo-Hamitic tribes to the north. The chief agent in this important development was the Muganda general, Semei Kakunguru. Kakunguru had already won military distinction in the campaign against Bunyoro in 1893–94 and he increased his reputation by the part which he played in the capture of Kabarega five years later. In the meantime, rivalry sprang up between the successful general and the great Katikiro, Apolo Kagwa, which decided the former to concentrate his energies upon the chiefdom of Bugerere, to the north-east of Buganda, which had been granted him as part of the spoils of war against Bunyoro. Bugerere soon proved too small to contain Kakunguru and he began to extend his authority beyond Lake Kyoga among the Kuman and Iteso tribes. He was encouraged in his venture by Colonel Ternan who placed him in charge of the land north of the lake which Britain was not yet ready to administer. Step by step, then, he advanced eastward, establishing forts in which he placed Baganda garrisons and linking these strongpoints by good roads. As his control of the area increased he began to distribute chieftainships among his Baganda followers as if he were himself a kabaka, and in this way he unwittingly gave birth to a system of ruling new areas through the agency of trusted Baganda which was to be adopted in a modified fashion by the British administrators who followed on his heels. Indeed, Kakunguru's whole relationship with the British was to prove a most complex issue when the latter tried to treat him simply as their agent and not as the conqueror which he saw himself to be.

A forward policy in Uganda would have been both pointless and dangerous without adequate protection for the main line of communication with the coast, and the appointment of a Sub-Commissioner or indeed the declaration of a protectorate over the territory along the route between Uganda and the coast was a meaningless gesture so long as the tribes remained hostile. The Nandi in particular provided an almost constant threat to the security of the link with the outside world for a full ten years after the declaration of the British East Africa Protectorate. Indeed, until 1902 the Nandi were the responsibility of the inland Protectorate and not of the East Africa Protectorate, and a number of expeditions had to be set on foot before their resistance to European intrusion in their territory was broken. In 1896 the whole Nandi region was up in arms. A mail party was attacked and the caravan route became unsafe for travellers. Considerable damage was inflicted upon the tribesmen by a military expedition and a post was established in Nandi country to try to maintain order. The Nandi were not subdued, however, and although friendly relations were established between the British administrators and the headmen the behaviour of the warriors remained unpredictable. Tribes living on the borders of Nandi territory complained of cattle raids and in 1900 a convoy of ox-carts with a small police escort was ambushed near the top of the Nandi escarpment. A few days later the coastward-bound mail which was trying to avoid Nandi country was also attacked and the escort killed. A second punitive force consisting partly of Indian and partly of African troops spent several weeks chasing the elusive tribesmen with little success, for the Nandi were anxious only to avoid a pitched battle. The arrival of Sir Clement Hill, Superintendent of the African Department of the Foreign Office, led to an attempt being made to come to terms with the Nandi so as to enable railway construction to go ahead, and a temporary peace was arranged. A feature of this second campaign had been the assistance rendered to the British by a Luo chief named Odera Olala, and it should be noted that the Luo caused no difficulty at any time to the Protectorate authorities. But the Nandi settlement was of a very tentative nature, and the construction of a railway through Nandi country provided a further occasion for opposition which was only brought to an end by the diplomatic intervention of Mr. C. W. Hobley, Sub-Commissioner in Kavirondo.[1]

In 1902 the territory of the Nandi was transferred, along with a considerable region on all sides of it, to the East Africa Protectorate. This change in no way reduced the antipathy of the Nandi towards European authority and there was some suggestion that the British administrative officer in charge of the district was handling the difficult situation badly.[2] In the middle of 1905 news was received that the Nandi Laibon was plotting once again against the Protectorate Administration and this was followed almost immediately by an outbreak of raiding and murder over almost the whole district. The elders complained that they could not hold the impetuous warriors in check and British opinion was divided over the method to be employed to restore order. Some maintained that the best approach lay through peaceful negotiation with the elders while others considered that anything short of a devastating campaign would be looked upon by the warriors as a sign of weakness. After some delay a military expedition was decided upon in September, and African troops assisted by Masai warriors and Somali levies were entrusted with the task of subduing the warlike Nandi. The decisive blow was struck, however, when the Laibon was shot as a result of his treachery while taking part in negotiations. Several columns continued to range over Nandi country for some weeks afterwards, but the

[1] C. W. Hobley: *Kenya from Chartered Company to Crown Colony*. Witherby, London, 1929, pp. 109–16.
[2] R. Meinertzhagen: *Kenya Diary*, 1902–1906. Oliver and Boyd, Edinburgh, 1957, pp. 194–6.

backbone of resistance had been broken. An armistice was agreed in November and a new Laibon was appointed in December.[1] Land was set aside, but not yet demarcated, as a Nandi reserve, and after initial difficulties the Nandi were driven by the troops into the area allotted them in 1906.

Elsewhere the early attempts at establishing a nominal form of administration in the East Africa Protectorate met mainly with opposition which was greatly weakened by the lack of unity among the tribes involved. The main exception to this occurred in the first year of the Protectorate when the new authorities inherited from the I.B.E.A. Company the revolt of Mbarak bin Rashid, one of the Mazaria chiefs at the coast. Although a naval force successfully stormed Mbarak's stronghold at Mweli, some fifteen miles from the coast, it was unsuited to the bush warfare to which the Mazrui chief and his supporters then resorted. There was a delay of four months while reinforcements were sent from India and during that time numerous supporters flocked to Mbarak's aid. The Wagiriama also took courage and rose in arms. Malindi was attacked by Mbarak's forces and although the attackers were repulsed they succeeded in setting fire to the town. The arrival of further Indian reinforcements, in March 1896, made possible a more systematic campaign and before long Mbarak and his men were forced to take refuge in German territory where they were disarmed and interned. Negotiations followed between the British Commissioner, Sir Arthur Hardinge, and the German Governor, Major von Wissmann, as a result of which an amnesty was signed enabling all but ten of the leaders of the rising to return to the British Protectorate. The campaign had caused considerable delay in the establishment of British administration in the vital coastal area, but at the same time it had resulted in the subjugation of a number of influential Arab chiefs who had hitherto been an endemic source of trouble to the Sultan of Zanzibar and, in turn, to the I.B.E.A. Company. It was fortunate, too, that the origin of the struggle had been a disputed succession over which Arab opinion had been divided, so that even in this campaign the British had not been faced with a united opposition. From this time it was clear to all that British influence had completely superseded that of the Arabs in a region which had formerly been a stronghold of Arab individualism. The Wagiriama

[1] R. Meinertzhagen: op. cit., pp. 194–251.

were also induced by Hardinge to submit and the instigator of their rising, a blind old headman and magician named Ngonyi, who was also chief organizer of the illicit ivory trade in the area, was removed from the district. For some years thereafter there was little trouble, although this was due more to the perfunctory nature of the administration than to any deep-seated acceptance of the British Protectorate. A number of lawless characters gathered round Ngonyi in his exile, awaiting only an opportunity to create further trouble, but their opportunity did not come until 1914 when, on the outbreak of war, the Germans got in touch with the malcontents who had been further incensed by the demand for porters made by the British military authorities. A company of King's African Rifles had to be diverted from the main struggle to restore order and from that time the Wagiriama ceased to stir up trouble.[1]

The Somali of Jubaland Province also resisted the imposition of Protectorate control. There were two sultanates within the province, one of which had its headquarters some distance inland at Afmadu, which was not so much a town as a collection of villages consisting of mud huts surrounding a number of wells. From 1896 it was ruled over by the young Ahmed bin Murgan who, although he had sworn allegiance to the British Queen before taking office, soon began to behave in a manner which was far from reassuring to the Protectorate authorities. News of his participation in a slave-raid against the Galla gave warning that all was not well, and in 1898 some of his followers were involved in raids in the vicinity of Kismayu in retaliation for injuries which they believed to have been inflicted upon one of their number by the Protectorate authorities. Hardinge would have liked to launch a full-scale attack against Afmadu, being convinced that nothing short of an overwhelming display of strength would make the Somali amenable to British control. He was restrained, however, by Lord Salisbury who was concerned at the number of expeditions which seemed necessary in East Africa. A more limited attack was undertaken and Ahmed sued for peace. But Hardinge's estimate had been correct. Some two years later the Sub-Commissioner of Jubaland, Mr. Jenner, was murdered while travelling through the Province and the Acting Commissioner of the East Africa Protectorate, Colonel Ternan, found it necessary to launch a costly campaign against Afmadu to restore order.

[1] C. W. Hobley: op. cit., p. 166.

That the large tribes of Kikuyu and Wakamba were easily subdued was mainly due to their lack of a central organization. Mr. John Ainsworth, Sub-Commissioner at Machakos and one of the Protectorate's most able administrators, nevertheless had numerous skirmishes with the Wakamba while trying to introduce British control into their territory. The Wakamba were cunning hunters, and with their deadly poisoned arrows they could be dangerous opponents. But their sectional interests and mutual jealousies prevented them from taking united action. Much the same was true of the Kikuyu who were slow to abandon their opposition to the white intruders. Numerous expeditions were launched against different units of the tribe before they were induced to abandon their practice of ambushing caravans and to submit to British administration.[1]

Most striking of all was the reaction of the Masai to the Protectorate. This warlike tribe which had caused the Protectorate authorities considerable misgivings put up no military resistance. This was due in part to the ravages the tribe had suffered from smallpox and cattle plague and in part to the influence of the Laibon, Lenana, who appears to have realized the futility of opposing the power of Britain. Indeed, Lenana entered into a bond of mutual respect with some of the British administrators, including Frank Hall, founder of Fort Hall, and John Ainsworth himself. Hall employed Masai warriors to maintain order among the Kikuyu around the station at Dagoretti and on a number of occasions Masai spearmen assisted the Protectorate authorities. There were occasions, too, when the warriors indulged in cattle-raiding to demonstrate their prowess in war, but as administration took a firmer hold upon the country it became increasingly difficult for them to revert to their warlike ways. So it was that the most aggressive of all the East African tribes submitted more readily than most to the overwhelming military strength of the European conquerors. Yet, by completely ignoring the ways of the Europeans, the Masai, more successfully than any other tribe, contrived to remain impervious to the changes which the Europeans attempted to introduce into the lives of the people of East Africa.

[1] R. Meinertzhagen: op. cit., pp. 48–50, 60–75, 100.

CHAPTER SIX

THE FOUNDATION OF SYSTEMATIC ADMINISTRATION

SYSTEMATIC administration was introduced into East Africa by the Germans almost, it would appear, as an afterthought. The era of German occupation divides itself into three phases. The first was a period of all-out effort to establish German imperial claims before they could be curtailed by the expansionist ambitions of other powers. The second was a period of simultaneous conquest of the African tribes and economic exploitation of the country's resources. The third followed upon the shock dealt to German sentiments by the Maji Maji rising and the Herero revolt in German south-west Africa and was a period in which a new assessment of administrative problems was made, accompanied by an intensification of economic development.

It was towards the end of the first phase, on April 26, 1890, that Emin Pasha, now in German service, set out from Bagamoyo with instructions to proceed to Lake Victoria and forestall British activities in that area. From the point of view of establishing Germany's claims in the Lake region the expedition proved to be unnecessary for little more than two months after Emin's departure the Anglo-German Agreement of July 1 defined the limits of both British and German expansion in that area. To some degree the activities of Emin and his party became an embarrassment to the Imperial Commissioner, Hermann von Wissmann, who recognized that Emin's gesture in hoisting the German flag in Tabora and building a station in Bukoba might seem merely provocative to the African people at a time when German communications between the coast and the interior were both slender and insecure. When Emin left Bagamoyo, Mpwapwa was Germany's most westerly station and beyond there lay miles of barren, dry territory before Tabora was reached.

Wissmann, therefore, sent orders to Emin to return to the coast, but the latter decided to ignore them and proceeded still farther westward.

Wissmann's sensible caution was more than counterbalanced by the urgent desire of others to exploit the resources of East Africa to the utmost and without delay. It was this desire which was largely responsible for the speedy and ruthless conquest of German East Africa described in the previous chapter and it was this concentration upon economic development which led to the reduction of administration to the bare minimum necessary to keep the tribesmen in subjection. In so far as humanitarian motives lingered on they amounted to little more than the rejection of existing African customs as barbaric and the conviction that contact with Europeans and association with European methods of economic development would inevitably be beneficial for the African peoples. It was therefore with some justification that Dr. Heinrich Brode, writing towards the end of the first decade of the twentieth century, was able to boast that German East Africa was ten years ahead of British East Africa in its economic development.[1] This was due far less to the four or five years' start gained by the Germans through the earlier declaration of a protectorate than to the different approach which Germany had towards her East African possessions. For, while Britain was anxious to make the new protectorates pay their way so as to avoid any drain upon the Imperial Treasury, Germany had a much more positive desire to make her East African territory a profitable area, capable of producing the raw materials needed by the industries of the fatherland.

With this end in view, far greater effort was expended in investigating the economic possibilities of the German dependency than in its two northern neighbours. Considerable sums of money were also invested in the territory both by the German Government and from private sources. Between 1894 and 1906 imperial appropriations to a total of £4¼ millions were voted to assist in the development of German East Africa while many private financiers invested substantial sums very largely, it would appear, on patriotic grounds since there was little immediate likelihood of a profitable return.[2] Faced with a country of which a large proportion consisted of

[1] H. Brode: *British and German East Africa.* Edward Arnold, London, 1911, p. 97.

[2] O. T. Hamlyn: *An Historical Sketch of the Tanganyika Constitution.* Unpublished MS.

unpromising soil, where communications were both limited and slow and where the sole ambition of the vast majority of the population was to eke out a meagre subsistence from agricultural or pastoral pursuits, the German authorities avoided any preconceived plans for a basically settled or basically African form of development and set themselves to exploit the latent resources of the territory by whatever means came to hand. Unfettered by lengthy traditions of colonial administration they were ready to experiment, to learn from their British neighbours and, if necessary, to be completely ruthless. Much of the legislation promulgated by the Germans to assist in the economic exploitation of the country was based upon similar laws passed by the British in the adjacent territories. Some of it was of an extremely liberal character and improved upon the British prototype. At the same time, the administration of those laws was frequently harsh and entirely contrary to the spirit in which they had been drafted simply because local officers were anxious to achieve results rather than to observe principles of behaviour.

The handling of the land question illustrates the division between intention and implementation. By an Imperial Decree of November 26, 1895, the whole of the land in German East Africa was declared to be Crown Land and the ownership was vested in the Empire. The existing rights of private individuals, of chiefs and of tribes were to be recognized none the less and commissions were appointed to discover which areas were available for alienation and to set aside land for native reserves. In the latter connection it was recognized that the shifting agriculture practised by the native population made it necessary to make liberal provision for their needs. The commissions were therefore required to reserve for African use four times the area of land actually under cultivation. In spite of these extremely reasonable precautions the more readily accessible and more fertile areas, such as the hinterland of Tanga stretching to Kilimanjaro, soon attracted so many settlers that the African population was deprived of land which was vital to its needs.[1]

In the early days of German occupation, however, the absence of adequate internal communications limited the area of development to the coast, and this, in turn, restricted the type of crops which could be grown in such a hot, low-lying region. The importation

[1] C. K. Meek: *Land Law and Custom in the Colonies.* O.U.P., London, 1949, p. 101.

of sisal plants from Florida in 1892 marked the beginning of what was to become Tanganyika's most valuable product. The plants flourished even better in their new setting than in their homeland, taking only four years to mature instead of five to eight years in the western hemisphere. Further, at the beginning of the twentieth century political disturbances in the West Indies resulted in a fall in the production of sisal in that area with a consequent rise in world prices which made it possible for the Germans to establish the crop more firmly in East Africa. Because of the need for expensive equipment for processing sisal a large output was necessary to make it profitable, so that sisal-growing became, almost inevitably, an occupation for European planters. Provided, too, that adequate capital was available, subsequent fluctuations in world prices never permanently undermined the industry. The value of sisal produced in German East Africa rose from 1,368,000 marks in 1906 to 7,359,000 marks in 1912,[1] and the construction of the central railway westward from Dar es Salaam to Morogoro in 1907 and on to Tabora in 1912 and to Kigoma on Lake Tanganyika in 1914 opened up vast new areas of land ideal for sisal-growing and little suited for anything else.

Coffee also was first grown as a plantation crop in the Usambara region behind Tanga. In order to foster this development work was begun in 1896 on the construction of the Usambara Railway, later to be known as the Tanga Railway. The private company which undertook the project soon stopped work through lack of funds and the line was taken over by the German Government. It reached Korogwe in 1902 and Moshi in 1912. In spite of improved communications, however, coffee-growing did not prove successful in Usambara. The shortage of labour in the plantations, the unsuitability of the soil and high overheads due to the attractive salaries paid to their administrative staff by the large companies which started up the plantations, soon rendered the work unprofitable.[2] As development ceased in Usambara it began in the Kilimanjaro region where the soil was more promising and where the numerous Chagga provided a more ample labour supply. The Greek and Italian cultivators who were responsible for pioneering coffee-growing in this area began on a rather less ambitious scale

[1] E. Lewin: op. cit., p. 300.

[2] H. Brode: op cit., p. 58.

than the Germans in Usambara and so avoided the crippling expenses of the experimental years. The extension of the Tanga Railway to Moshi in 1912 was as much a recognition on the part of the Government of the success achieved by the planters of Kilimanjaro as an encouragement to further development in the same region. In 1906 the value of the coffee crop was 531,000 marks and by 1912 it had risen to 1,903,000 marks.[1] Of this latter sum, however, less than half was produced from European-owned plantations. For, by the end of the German period, African peasant-grown coffee had outstripped the European-grown crop. A few Chagga took an example from the planters and began to grow *Arabica* coffee themselves but they were not encouraged by the German Administration. More important was the *Robusta* coffee produced by the African inhabitants of the Bukoba district where the soil and climate was more suited to this rather poorer quality crop. In both areas the coffee was grown under the shade of the plantain trees which provided the main food of the Chagga and of the Bahaya of Bukoba, and the double use of the same land enabled the growers to produce a valuable economic crop without endangering their food supply. The wealth which coffee-growing brought to the Chagga and the Bahaya enabled both tribes to draw ahead of many others in Tanganyika in their material prosperity and in their political self-reliance.

Cotton was also grown by the Germans as a plantation crop and, like coffee, was later taken up to a limited extent by African peasant growers. When the Germans occupied East Africa they found the coastal peoples already growing Indian cotton for household purposes and in the region of the great lakes Peruvian cotton was also being produced. The earliest attempts made by the Government to encourage further cotton-growing in the late 1880s and in the 1890s met with little success, but a change took place at the beginning of the twentieth century. The cotton famine caused by the American Civil War had been followed by a rapid increase in the consumption of raw cotton by European factories. This increase was not accompanied by a similar growth in the output of American cotton. Consequently, towards the end of the nineteenth century European textile manufacturers were beginning to fear that they bould soon be at the mercy of American cotton producers and would we defeated by the competition of American manufacturers. To

[1] E. Lewin: op. cit., p. 300.

counter this threat the mill-owners of Europe took steps to provide alternative supplies of raw cotton. The British Cotton Growing Association and the German Kolonialwirtschaftliches Komitee were formed to promote this objective and in 1902 the K.W.K. sent some samples of Egyptian cotton grown on the coast to Hamburg. The German markets approved the quality of the cotton, and backed by this incentive every effort was made to induce Africans living in suitable districts to grow more. At the same time regulations were passed and other steps taken to maintain a high quality.

Cotton-growing required considerably less care and skill than coffee-growing and therefore appeared to be a suitable crop for African peasants to produce. None the less, in 1905 the K.W.K. founded a school in Mpanganya on the Rufiji River to give Africans instruction in the best methods of cotton cultivation. The school was taken over by the Government in 1910 and became the model for other Government cotton-stations in the Lindi and Kilosa districts. In August 1904 an ordinance was passed prohibiting the import of all seed from America, and in July 1910 this prohibition was extended to all cotton seed except Egyptian seed imported direct from Egypt and the Upland variety which had been actually grown in Uganda or Nyasaland. The K.W.K. supplied seed free to District Officers for distribution to African growers while European planters could obtain the seed at a moderate price. The latter could also purchase machinery at manufacturers' prices while the cost of freight was regulated and space made available for the cotton crop in ships bound for Europe. Textbooks on cotton-growing were published in a number of vernacular languages and the Government contracted with a Bremen firm to keep District Officers informed as to the state of the home market. In spite of all these efforts, however, the African population were slow to show enthusiasm for cotton-growing and they were quick to lose interest when prices fell in 1909. To counteract a possible reduction in the amount of cotton produced, the K.W.K. in 1910 guaranteed a minimum price to African growers if other buyers proved unwilling to purchase the crop or if the price they offered was unduly low. This policy was so effective that in 1912 it had to be abandoned owing to the rapid increase in cotton production which, coupled with the fluctuation in world prices, made the undertaking given by the K.W.K. far too expensive. Nevertheless a sound beginning had been made and the output remained steady even if it was not very large. In 1913 the area planted by Africans amounted to 15,000 hectares, compared with 12,941 hectares planted by Europeans. Between 1902 and 1912 the amount of cotton exported annually rose from half a ton to 1,882 tons, valued at 2,110,000 marks,[1] while the K.W.K. estimated that the 1913-14 crop would amount to 3,000 tons.[2]

As early as 1893 the large number of wild rubber trees which the Germans found growing in East Africa encouraged them to experiment with plantation rubber, while simultaneously taking steps to encourage Africans to collect wild rubber for sale. The first export of plantation rubber in 1907 amounted to about fifty tons. In 1910 there was a sudden rise in the price of rubber produced in Ceylon and Malaya which encouraged the formation of a number of companies in London. These companies were prepared to buy plantations anywhere in the world and German East Africa proved a tempting area of investment. There was some criticism among German settlers of the Government's policy of allowing Englishmen to establish plantations in German territory. It was, therefore, a clear indication of the German Administration's readiness to adopt every available means of developing the Protectorate that these criticisms were not permitted to deter British speculators. The value of the rubber produced rose from 2,386,000 marks in 1906 to 8,390,000 marks in 1912,[3] by which time rubber was challenging sisal as German East Africa's most profitable crop. After this promising start, however, the industry crashed completely in 1913 owing to overproduction in the east. The large plantations with their correspondingly greater running expenses were hard hit, but even the smaller growers employing only a handful of local labourers were facing grave difficulties when war intervened to bring even more overwhelming problems.

A further source of revenue of considerable importance was the export trade in hides and skins. The millions of cattle, sheep and goats which the Germans found when they arrived in East Africa were of uniformly poor quality. Their African owners showed little interest in upgrading their stock which were mainly kept as a form of

---

[1] E. Lewin: op. cit., p. 300.

[2] *Tanganyika Territory: Report from the Armistice to the end of 1920.* H.M.S.O., London, 1921, pp. 53-56.

[3] E. Lewin: op. cit., p. 300.

currency rather than for their value as meat or as dairy cattle. The large number of animals caused serious overgrazing in some districts while in others cattle owners were forced to adopt a nomadic existence in order to find fodder for their herds. Unfavourable climatic conditions would have made it difficult for the Germans to introduce any marked improvement in the stock in most areas even if the owners had been willing to co-operate, but the value of hides and skins largely compensated for the absence of any other commercial value for the animals. In 1912 hides and skins were exported to the value of 4,067,000 marks. In 1909, also, the *Wollschafzucht-Syndikat* was founded in an attempt to meet the heavy demands of the German woollen industry by starting large-scale sheep farming in German East Africa, although there were far from favourable reports from British East Africa where experiments had already been made.[1]

One of the most striking examples of the Germans' thoroughness in investigating every possible means of exploiting their East African dependency was the foundation in 1902 of the Amani Biological and Agricultural Institute. This centre, established in the fertile Usambara mountains, was the home of intensive investigations into plant diseases, insect pests, soil and plant chemistry and many other problems confronting farmers in the tropics. The Germans' aim was to create an institution which would in time become a worthy rival of the British Institute at Pusa, in Bihar, or the centre founded by the Dutch at Buitenzorg, in Java, and which would serve the same purpose in respect of Germany's tropical African possessions as the others had done in the Far East. From the results obtained during the short period before the outbreak of war this aim proved far from being too ambitious.

The all-out emphasis upon production put a heavy strain upon the territory's labour supply. Until the railways were built, and even afterwards in the regions distant from the main lines, transport depended almost entirely upon porters. In addition, labour was required in considerable quantities for public works, so that when European planters were crying out for labour while the African population was simultaneously being pressed by the Government to cultivate the land more intensively a difficult situation was bound to arise. Rechenberg, who was Governor of the Protectorate from 1906

[1] H. Brode: op. cit., p. 130.

to 1912, was also anxious to avoid the creation of an insecure and discontented proletariat relying solely upon wages, and this attitude had still further repercussions upon the labour supply. The settlers were angered by the Governor's policy and Herr Bernard Dernburg, who became Germany's first Secretary of State for the Colonies in 1907, remarked after a visit to Africa in the same year that 'The Planters are at war with everybody, with myself, with the Government, with the local officials, and finally with the natives'.[1] The planters themselves were gravely concerned about the future of German East Africa as a settler territory if Rechenberg's policy was allowed to prevail. But, following on the heels of the Maji Maji rising which had demonstrated the failure of Germany's relations with the African population, it was clear that a more enlightened approach was necessary in dealing with the African population. Dernburg, too, had profited from his African visit by studying the manner in which the British Administration had handled a still more acute labour problem in the neighbouring East Africa Protectorate, and the results of his observations were embodied in two labour regulations published in February 1909. The legal position of the labourers was defined in accordance with the pattern already adopted in British East Africa in 1906 which ensured that contracts were clearly understood and, except in the case of very short periods of employment, must be in writing. Recruiting was placed under official control, and a number of Commissioners for Native Affairs were appointed with the specific duty of acting as intermediaries between employers and labourers and of settling differences between the parties involved. These arrangements appeared to work satisfactorily although the planters, who now found labour even more difficult to obtain, complained that there was a deliberate plan on the part of the Government to put them out of action so as to encourage native production. It was also claimed that the Commissioners favoured Africans rather than their employers.[2]

It was true that both Rechenberg and Dernburg set great store by native production as a sound basis for developing the economy of the country in the interests of its inhabitants and of the German nation. Nevertheless, it was impossible for them at that stage to ignore the importance of plantation agriculture. In spite of the

[1] F. Lewin: op. cit., p. 281.

[2] H. Brode: op. cit., p. 90.

criticisms levelled against him it was Dernberg himself who, after 1907, was largely responsible for encouraging German investment and activity in East Africa by his enthusiasm and by his gift for propaganda. When the autocratic and implacable Rechenberg was succeeded by Dr. Schnee in 1912 the increasing prosperity of the country, coupled with the Governor's more diplomatic handling of the settlers, brought the dispute to an end.

The German policy of developing the country by every available means had, in fact, always been based upon the assumption that the presence of at least some European settlers would be of benefit to the territory. As has already been seen, in 1895 the whole country was declared Crown Land and there was no hesitation about alienating suitable land to Europeans. By the end of the German period 3,005 square miles were in European hands and although this comprised less than 1 per cent of the total area of the Protectorate a land problem had already been recognized. The Chagga of Kilimanjaro, for example, had been gradually pushed up the mountain as the lower slopes were taken up by European plantations. The Administration admitted that further settlement in such areas would provide a legitimate cause for grievance and the alienation of additional land was forbidden in the oversettled regions, but this caused no hardship since by 1913 less than a fifth of the alienated land had been cultivated.[1]

One field in which remarkable advances were made was in the provision of educational opportunities for the African population. The bulk of this work was in the hands of the missionary societies, and to the U.M.C.A., the C.M.S., the White Fathers and the Holy Ghost Fathers there were added during the period of German administration a further Roman Catholic mission and a number of Protestant missions which divided the country between them so that the work of evangelization was extended over almost the whole of the Protectorate. In addition to their more spiritual labours the missionary societies paid considerable attention to the education of their potential converts and at the outbreak of war in 1914 they were providing primary education for more than 100,000 children and a more advanced literary and practical education for a smaller number of pupils. With an eye to future benefits a school founded in Tanga by the German Colonial Society in 1892 was taken over by

[1] C. Leubuscher: *Tanganyika Territory.* O.U.P., London, 1944, p. 29.

the Administration in 1895 and other schools were established in the more important stations in the interior. The first object of the official schools system was to produce junior clerical workers who, for a very small salary, would assist the administrative officers in their routine work. Nevertheless, carpentry and other useful crafts were also taught in the more senior schools, and in the Tanga school 48 teachers were in training in March 1912. In its essence education in German East Africa was as experimental in character and as practical in its objectives as the whole of the Government's economic policy of which, indeed, education formed a part. This was largely dictated by circumstances and the good intentions of the Colonial Secretary, Dr W. H. Solf, should not be overlooked. In a speech in the Reichstag in 1913 he said 'Colonizing means missionizing and missionizing in the lofty sense of education towards culture . . . the natives have a right to demand that they should be regarded by the more highly developed races as an end and not as a means.'

Over the question of slavery, also, the Germans adopted a practical rather than an idealistic attitude. As a signatory of the General Act of the Anti-Slavery Conference in Brussels in 1890, and of other international treaties relating to the suppression of slavery, Germany was faced with considerable obligations in East Africa. Public opinion in Germany supported the Protectorate Administration and in 1892 representatives of the German Anti-Slavery Committee were sent to East Africa to assist in the suppression of the slave-trade and in the care of rescued slaves. In 1895 measures were taken to make slave-raiding and slave-trading an offence in German East Africa and for some years the Government contemplated bolder steps to prohibit slavery itself. Particularly along the coast, however, domestic slavery was firmly entrenched, and the Government was reluctant to contemplate the payment of the large sums of money which it would be necessary to offer to slave-owners as compensation. Still more disturbing in view of the restless years which had succeeded the declaration of a Protectorate was the fear of the political upheaval which might result from any drastic action in this field. Thus, while the Government of the British East Africa Protectorate struck a blow at the secret trade which still lingered on in the tidal creeks and mangrove swamps of the coastal area by abolishing the legal status of slavery on the mainland in 1907, the Germans continued to proceed with the greatest caution. In 1901 legislation was promulgated permitting the termination of household slavery by purchase and in 1907 a further compromise was reached through a decree which announced that all children born of slave parents after 1906 should be automatically free. The results of these various enactments were not immediately seen, however, and it was left to the British to take the final step by abolishing slavery in the former German territories after the First World War.

Fully occupied as the extremely limited number of German officers undoubtedly were with the problem of economic development, they had little time to evolve any theory regarding administrative policy. Indeed, until the shock of the Maji Maji rising startled the Government into the realization of the need to consider its relations with the African population, administration was largely an *ad hoc* affair. Nor could the Imperial Chancellor devote much attention to such a remote problem although until 1907 he was responsible for the over-all supervision of the territory. In East Africa itself the control of affairs was in the hands of a Governor who had an advisory council which met twice a year but which appears to have had little interest in the formulation of policy. Anxious as the Government was to bring the whole country under control as quickly as possible, local administration took the most handy form in each area. This led to the adoption of a variety of methods of administration although in the early stages it was customary to construct a well-sited *boma*, or fort, garrisoned by a handful of troops and capable of resisting attack. The District Officers were frequently men seconded from the army and their methods savoured of their military background. In the north-west, in the districts of Bukoba, Ruanda and Urundi, German opportunism took advantage of the existence of fairly well organized tribal systems of government by retaining the indigenous local authorities under the supervision of a Resident. Yet they did not hesitate to replace the ruler of Karagwe by a chief of their own choosing, and any possibility of union between different African communities which might threaten German overrule was defeated by encouraging rivalry instead of co-operation between the different chiefs.[1]

The Maji Maji rising, with the loss of life involved and the demands it made upon the Imperial Treasury, forced the Germans to think more constructively about administrative problems. In

[1] O. T. Hamlyn: op. cit.

202

May 1907 a separate Colonial Department was created with Dr. Dernburg at its head. Dernburg's visit to East Africa resulted in a considerable improvement in the higher levels of administration, although Iringa and Mukenge continued to be administered as military districts. A Judicial Commission was appointed under the chairmanship of Dr. Kleine to investigate charges of misgovernment during the early years of German rule and its report, which was submitted to the Reichstag in April 1907, aroused a strong feeling of indignation in Germany. Where acts of cruelty and brutality were proved the offenders were heavily punished, and, although similar acts were not unknown in the years which followed, the work of the Commission undoubtedly had a salutary effect upon the manner in which the majority of German administrative officers approached their task. Even now, however, much depended upon the character and personality of individual officers and although in some areas officials made whole-hearted attempts to understand the people whom they were governing,[1] such an attitude was by no means uniform. There still remained an acute shortage of European officers to fulfil the many tasks of administration and in general the Germans remained content to employ the system introduced by the Sultan of Zanzibar of appointing akidas. These men were government servants and were rarely natives of the districts over which, under European supervision, they exercised control. The system had the dual weakness of reducing the opportunities for direct contact between European officials and the people they administered and of depriving the existing indigenous authorities of an opportunity to develop under European guidance. This latter weakness was to some extent avoided by the appointment of a number of more influential village headmen as jumbes. Yet the significance of this policy must not be overestimated since the additional authority vested in the jumbes added nothing to their importance in the eyes of their own people. Indeed, since that authority was of alien origin it sometimes served to undermine the loyalty of the villagers to their traditional leader.

The influence of the akidas was perhaps the most important element in the German administrative system. Many of them were men of ability but almost all of them were imbued with Islamic culture and were therefore unsympathetic to local customs and

[1] F. H. Melland and E. H. Cholmeley: *Through the Heart of Africa*. Constable, London, 1912, pp. 64, 93.

203

habits. The authority they wielded was considerable. They were responsible for law and order, they exercised certain magisterial powers and they collected the three rupees poll tax which was the only direct tax imposed by the Germans upon the African population. The latter function gave particular scope for the akidas to oppress the people under them. The burden of the tax itself upon the tribal population varied considerably. In areas where economic crops had been introduced or where a man might easily obtain paid labour, the tax did not weigh heavily. But in other areas even such a small sum as three rupees was difficult to come by, and the opportunity for extortion given to the tax-collectors inevitably resulted in the burden being more severe where an unscrupulous akida held office.

Although the many campaigns which the Germans waged against the tribes in the course of establishing their authority had a disruptive effect upon the social life of the people, which was confirmed by the akida system, the extent to which social organization was destroyed was far less than has often been suggested. Faced by an alien and apparently irresistible authority, the tendency of most of the African tribes was to observe such regulations as they could not avoid, while at the same time continuing to regulate the rest of their day to day lives according to traditional standards. When the German rule became too oppressive the people revolted, as in the case of the Maji Maji rising, and when this occurred they made no distinction among their victims between the administrators and the missionaries. They were simply resisting the unbearable intrusion of an alien way of life in all its aspects. Yet it would be wrong to suggest that the missionaries made no distinctive impression. The number of their converts is difficult to assess but was probably small. Some of the latter, however, the adherents of the British and French missions, loyally submitted to hardship and cruelty for their faith during the First World War. It is interesting, too, that when war came to the land the majority of the African peoples remained steadily loyal to their German overlords. That this should have been true of those who enlisted as soldiers is not surprising since they were given considerable latitude in regard to foraging for food and other necessities which amounted almost to looting rights. But the rest of the population continued to supply food and labour until they eventually disappeared into the bush before the fighting overwhelmed them. Perhaps it was that the war appeared as a happy reversion to the former, less restrained way of life which the rigid and alien regulations imposed by the Germans had tended to repress. Certainly the Germans left behind them many memories, but their years of rule made no lasting changes in the lives of the people. This may be attributed to the relatively short period of German control and even more to the devastating effects of the war, since the British troops advanced across German East Africa with the obliterating effect of a duster over a blackboard. More fundamental, however, was the fact that the Germans never really made human contact with the African people, to whom they seemed like a machine to be avoided if possible and to be borne only if there was no way of escape.

Unlike their German neighbours the British administrators in the East Africa Protectorate were slow to introduce measures for the development of the area under their control. For the first seven years of the Protectorate the country was looked upon as little more than a supply route to Uganda. Such life as it possessed was limited to the coast with a few scattered stations along the caravan route. It is some indication of the lack of importance attached by the British to the East Africa Protectorate that until 1900 it was placed under the supervision of the British Agent and Consul-General in Zanzibar to whose salary of £1,800 was added an allowance of £200 a year in respect of his responsibilities on the mainland.[1] It was not until 1900 that the Protectorate was given its own Commissioner who, however, still maintained his headquarters in Mombasa.

Yet even a supply route had to be protected and so it was that in the East Africa Protectorate administration preceded the introduction of any economic programme. Sir Arthur Hardinge, the first Commissioner, divided the Protectorate into four provinces. Each of these was placed under a Sub-Commissioner and was further divided into districts. But the administration did not extend across the parched deserts of the north to the Abyssinian border. Even the whereabouts of the frontier were unknown and the only official along the five-hundred-mile-long border was a Greek agent appointed by the British Minister in Addis Ababa. He was stationed at a remote water-hole named Moyale along with a small Abyssinian bodyguard to turn back Abyssinian raiding parties. A trade route linking

[1] Sir Arthur Hardinge: op. cit., p. 132.

British East Africa with Addis Ababa was opened up through this difficult region by the Boma Trading Company, a group of adventurers with their own private army who traded in cattle and sheep, beeswax, ivory and hides. From time to time the importance of opening up this northern region both for the sake of what the country might produce and in order to protect the tribesmen against Abyssinian raiders was argued by a variety of people. Early in 1909 an administrative officer with a small force of King's African Rifles relieved the Greek agent in Moyale and shortly afterwards another administrative officer, Mr. (later Sir Geoffrey) Archer established the post which still bears his name. But it was not until Sir Percy Girouard became Governor later in 1909 that the Northern Frontier District came into being, and even then the district remained closed to European traders and no attempt was made to develop commercial links with Abyssinia. In consequence there could be no taxation, so that for many years a vast area of territory remained as an administrative responsibility without producing any revenue.[1]

Even in the region through which the main line of communications passed, administration developed slowly. Owing to the shortage of administrative officers the Government was anxious to employ any indigenous authorities who might appear suited to their needs. The Native Courts Regulations of 1897 simply empowered administrative officers to supervise the procedure and punishments of indigenous courts presided over by chiefs or elders in the various tribes. It soon became clear, however, that responsibility could not be avoided in this way, for there were virtually no chiefs or councils of elders who possessed authority which was recognized over a sufficiently wide area to make them competent to administer the country under a minimum of supervision. The Village Headman Ordinance of 1902 marked the Government's recognition of the need to intervene more directly to control the tribesmen. Even this measure, however, was strictly limited in scope and simply appointed official headmen in charge of a number of villages who were paid a small salary from a rate levied on the inhabitants of the villages. The headmen's duties consisted in delivering criminals to justice, in helping with the collection of the hut tax and in supplying labour for public works. The Ordinance envisaged that existing chiefs or

[1] E. Huxley: *White Man's Country*. Chatto & Windus, London, 1935, Vol. I. pp. 241-5.

clan leaders should be appointed as headmen wherever possible and in some cases this was the policy adopted. Inevitably the nature and source of the authority exercised by the headmen resulted in their being regarded by the people simply as government officials. The Amending Courts Ordinance of 1907, however, indicated that the Government had no desire to destroy indigenous systems of organization either directly by abolishing them or indirectly by ignoring them. By the terms of this Ordinance the Governor was empowered, in setting up native courts, to recognize the jurisdiction of a tribal chief or of a court of elders. The Native Authority Ordinance of 1912 was also intended, wherever possible, to enable the tribes to be governed by their acknowledged chiefs and elders and according to their own customs.[1] That tribal institutions which persisted in spite of, rather than with the aid of, the British administrators was, however, the result of other factors, initially economic but ultimately racial, which revolutionized the whole of administrative policy.

The transfer of Uganda's Eastern Province to the East Africa Protectorate in 1902 seems to have been the result of a clash of wills rather than of a carefully conceived plan. The effect of the transfer upon both Protectorates was far greater than those responsible for it could ever have imagined. Sir Harry Johnston, sent to East Africa in 1899 to make recommendations upon the future administration of Uganda, concluded at an early stage that the two Protectorates were in fact complementary. The Uganda Protectorate appeared to have by far the greater economic potential while Mombasa would inevitably continue to be the outlet for Uganda's produce. In effect the two Protectorates formed one economic unit which could be most suitably administered jointly. Difficulties of communication might render it necessary to retain Commissioners in Entebbe and Mombasa but there should be a High Commissioner who would have supreme control over policy and finance.[2] This proposal was not at variance with Johnston's instructions but the Foreign Office appears to have been taken aback by its boldness. An alternative suggestion was presented to the Foreign Secretary by Sir Clement Hill who, as a civil servant of high rank, had been jealous of the

[1] Lord Hailey: *Native Administration in the British African Territories.* H.M.S.O., London, 1950, Vol. I, p. 92.

[2] F.O.2./462. General Report by Sir Harry Johnston on Uganda, July 10, 1901.

appointment of Johnston, a man with no official status, as Special Commissioner in Uganda. That alternative was the transfer of Uganda's Eastern Province to her sister Protectorate. Hill's main argument appears to have been that the unity of interest between the Protectorates postulated by Johnston had been exaggerated and that in any case the area was too big to be administered by one central authority.[1] The strength of Hill's case, however, would appear to have rested very largely on the fact that Hill himself was in England to present it while Johnston did not return until a decision had virtually been reached. The Marquess of Lansdowne, who made the decision, does not appear to have ruled out the amalgamation of the Protectorates at some later date. It is significant, too, that Sir Charles Eliot, Commissioner in the British East Africa Protectorate, only gave his approval to Hill's scheme on the understanding that it did not prejudice the amalgamation of the Protectorates in the future.[2] Eliot himself was convinced of the advantages which would accrue from amalgamation and with prophetic insight he noted that while such a measure was well within the bounds of possibility at the beginning of the twentieth century divergent developments in the two territories might well make it impossible twenty years later.[3]

The importance of the transfer of territory so far as the East Africa Protectorate was concerned was that it presented the country with a considerable area of land possessing, in appearance at least, the qualities needed for profitable farming, and blessed with a climate which could not fail to attract Europeans. Here was the genesis of the decision to establish a settler economy in the East Africa Protectorate. It is true that the land occupied by the Kikuyu possessed a temperate climate and was extremely fertile, but there was little land to spare in that neighbourhood. Elsewhere, between the Kikuyu territory and the coast, there was little prospect of profitable farming for either Europeans or Africans. There was, of course, the alternative of encouraging more extensive farming by the African population. That this policy was not adopted was probably due to two factors, the need to obtain quick results financially

[1] F.O.2./519. Memorandum by Sir Clement Hill, July 25, 1901.

[2] F.O.2./456. Telegram from Eliot to Lansdowne, November 8, 1901.

[3] Sir Charles Eliot: *The East Africa Protectorate*. Edward Arnold, London, 1905, pp.180–2.

First coffee crop, St. Austin's Mission, 1902

Sir Hesketh Bell

George Wilson

Sir Charles Eliot

and the attractions of the apparently limitless and virtually empty highlands beyond the Rift Valley.

That money was needed to pay for the administration of the Protectorate was obvious, but since the administration was of a limited character the amount involved was not great. The new factor which made the economic development of the Protectorate imperative was the construction of the Uganda Railway. During the first half of 1895 the Conservative Opposition in Britain had been urging upon the Liberal Government the importance of constructing a railway to Uganda in order to develop the economic resources of the country over which a Protectorate had been declared. The logic of this argument seemed irrefutable and when the Conservatives came to office later in the year they quickly started work on a line from the coast to Lake Victoria. In September 1895 a committee was appointed under the chairmanship of Sir Percy Anderson of the Foreign Office to supervise the construction of the railway and the chief engineer, Mr. George Whitehouse, and his staff arrived in Mombasa in December. Preliminary investigations soon demonstrated that Macdonald's earlier estimate of the cost of such a railway had been inadequate. In June 1896 the Chancellor of the Exchequer asked Parliament for £3,000,000 without committing himself to any estimate of the final sum needed. It was probably as well for the Conservative Government that the Liberal critics of the scheme could not foresee that the final cost to the British taxpayer would be £7,909,294.[1]

Owing to the lack of interest shown in the railway by the African population, labour had to be largely imported from India, and at one point 15,000 men were engaged on constructing the line. A variety of exotic problems caused the engineers continual anxiety. Jiggers attacked the bare-footed coolies, causing lameness, and in many cases making it necessary for toes to be amputated. For the greater part of 1898 two man-eating lions waged their own effective war against the labourers in the neighbourhood of Tsavo and in December they succeeded in bringing work to a standstill for three weeks.[2] In June 1899 the railhead reached Nairobi, a site chosen rather for its suitability as a base for further railway construction

[1] M. F. Hill: *Permanent Way*. East African Railways and Harbours, Nairobi, 1950, pp. 242–3.

[2] J. H. Patterson: *The Man-Eaters of Tsavo*. Macmillan, London, 1907 *passim*.

than for its attractions as the site of the future territorial capital. When Sir Arthur Hardinge paid his first visit it was nothing but a Masai kraal, and the surrounding country, open and undulating, seemed like a zoological garden, teeming with rhinoceros, zebra, antelope, lion and giraffe.[1] Even three years later the town was inhabited mainly by railway employees. The only shop was a tin hut selling everything from cartridges to beer, sardines, jam and paraffin, and the only hotel was a structure of wood and tin. The firm of Boustead and Ridley carried on its work as general merchants, and a soda-water factory provided an early intimation of future industrial development. A few score yards from the handful of bungalows, game still abounded, but by 1906 a rapid increase in settlement had driven the zebras from their earlier haunts.[2]

From Nairobi the onward route necessitated a plunge into the Rift Valley, and here a rope incline had to be constructed to provide a temporary diversion while the main line gradually descended by easier gradients to the floor of the valley. Pushing onward past the isolated cone of Mount Longonot the railway had then to climb once again to a height of 9,000 feet to the crest of the highlands beyond, and from there it traversed the Nandi Plateau before descending once more to the low-lying land of the Luo on the shore of Lake Victoria. Major J. W. Pringle submitted a report on his final inspection of the railway in October 1903, and in the same month responsibility for the railway was transferred from the Foreign Office Railway Committee to the Administration of the East Africa Protectorate. By this time the Uganda Railway, built to open up the inland Protectorate, no longer touched Uganda at any point owing to the recent transfer of territory. Although the railway continued thenceforward to act as Uganda's lifeline, its construction probably had even greater influence upon the East Africa Protectorate. For it was the need to make such an expensive investment pay its way that precipitated the economic exploitation of East Africa.

Sir Charles Eliot, Commissioner for the East Africa Protectorate from 1901 to 1904, was a cold but scholarly man who saw in the problem presented by the railway, which passed through largely empty country, not simply a task for the economist but also an opportunity to promote the advancement of East Africa's indigenous

[1] Sir Arthur Hardinge: op. cit., pp. 234–5.
[2] R. Meinertzhagen: op. cit., pp. 9, 12, 301.

population. He weighed the needs of the African people with care and came to the conclusion that the greatest benefits for the future would be derived from the introduction of European settlers. Upon the efforts of this latter group the Protectorate would be compelled to rely heavily for its economic prosperity for some considerable period, but Eliot was convinced that the Africans themselves would derive considerable benefit from the opportunity to learn the ways of western civilization and from intermingling with the settlers and watching them at work.[1] His view was typical of his age, when no one had as yet questioned the right of civilized men to develop the resources of the world and their long-term duty to teach primitive peoples the code of behaviour and scientific knowledge of the civilized world.

The possibility of developing the East Africa Protectorate as a new dominion by means of British endeavour had already deeply stirred another man whose influence upon East Africa was to be almost as great as that of Cecil Rhodes upon Central Africa. Hugh Cholmondeley, third Baron Delamere, hunter and adventurer, had trekked southward from Somaliland through the highlands and valleys between Lake Rudolf and Mount Kenya until he reached the Aberdare Mountains in 1897. So captivated had he been by what he saw that his pleasure-seeking life became filled with a new ambition, as a result of which he spent the whole of his fortune and the whole of his energy in his attempt to convert his dream of a white man's country in the highlands along the Equator into a reality. Delamere returned to England in 1898 but was back in Africa the following year and in 1903 he committed himself whole-heartedly to the project which had taken so powerful a hold upon him.

The number of Europeans in the Protectorate was still small but there were already several thousand Indians settled there. These latter were not the coolies who had come to work on the railway, most of whom had already taken their discharge and returned to India. They were commercial men or petty traders, many of whose forebears had traded at the coast for generations and had financed the caravans which had travelled into the interior. These Indians had followed the railway as it advanced towards the lake and their shops and trading posts had been pushed out beyond the sphere of effective administration. Some were anxious to acquire land but

[1] Sir Charles Eliot: op. cit., pp. 105–6, 173–5.

were uncertain as to their status in this respect. The Deputy Commissioner of the Protectorate, Mr. (later Sir Frederick) Jackson, gave them some reassurance in a letter to the Secretary of the Indian Association on February 28, 1902, in which he wrote: 'You are in error in supposing that the Government has any intention of drawing a distinction between Europeans and Indians as far as rights of mining, settling and acquiring land are concerned.' In August, while serving as Acting Commissioner, Jackson took the further step of issuing a Government notice inviting Indian agriculturalists to come to the Protectorate.[1] Eliot, however, was not prepared to confirm this open-handed policy. He fully appreciated the benefits provided by Indian traders and he saw possibilities for useful farming along the shore of Lake Victoria or near the mouth of the Tana River by Indians accustomed to growing cotton or other tropical crops. At the same time he thought it unwise to permit any large-scale acquisition of land by Indians in the cooler parts of the Protectorate. In his view there must be no competition between two dissimilar races in the colonization of East Africa.[2]

The question still remained as to how to attract European settlers, for in 1902 there were less than a dozen Europeans cultivating land in the Protectorate and all of them had farms on the edge of Kikuyu territory. The Indian Lands Acquisition Act had been applied to both British Protectorates in East Africa so as to enable the Government to purchase land for official purposes, and in 1897 regulations had been published which permitted the lease of land by Europeans. More tempting terms would be required, however, if colonists were to be attracted in large numbers. The British Government had therefore sought advice in 1899 with regard to its powers over land after the declaration of a Protectorate and had come to the conclusion that, subject to the recognition of existing rights, it might claim sovereignty over all other areas. Moreover, so small a proportion of the East Africa Protectorate appeared to be occupied by Africans that there seemed little danger of injustice if settlers were allowed into the country. In 1901 the East African (Lands) Order in Council attempted to place the alienation of land to Europeans on a sound basis by laying down that any land alienated must be Crown Land,

[1] W. Macgregor Ross: *Kenya from Within.* Allen and Unwin, London, 1927, p. 301.

[2] Sir Charles Eliot: op. cit., pp. 178–9.

that is, land not already occupied by Africans. The East Africa Order in Council then set out the terms upon which Crown Land could be alienated and a Land Department was created. The Department, in due course, produced an Ordinance which was based mainly upon the Canadian pattern of land control. It now became possible to purchase land and not just to lease it, a change which would undoubtedly prove attractive, but in other respects the Canadian system was not ideally suited to East African conditions. Under the new Ordinance an applicant might first buy 160 acres at two rupees an acre, and when he had fulfilled certain stipulations regarding the development of his land he became entitled to buy a further 480 acres. Payment could be spread over sixteen years and when completed a freehold title would be given.

There was still considerable uncertainty as to the suitability of the climate for Europeans, the nature of the crops which would grow in East Africa, the diseases to which both crops and animals might be prone and the whereabouts of markets for East African produce. Nevertheless, settlers began to make their way to East Africa early in 1903 and by April there were nearly a hundred in the country. Lord Delamere, meanwhile, had been refused pastoral land on the Laikipia Plateau because it was too far from the railway and from administrative control. He was finally granted 100,000 acres in the Rift Valley at an annual rent of rather less than £200 which at the time was thought to be excessive. The Government then offered grants of 640 acres for agricultural purposes or 5,000 acres of grazing land in the vicinity of Delamere's concession, free of charge, in order to attract other settlers. Not a single request was made for pasture land, however, and in September 1903 Sir Charles Eliot sent the Commissioner for Customs, Mr. A. Marsden, to South Africa to publicize the opportunities offered in the Protectorate. The response to this mission was extremely good, so much so that early in 1904 a wholly unprepared Land Office was besieged with requests for land from several hundreds of South Africans, few of whom had money to waste on waiting in Nairobi until land could be surveyed. This hold-up was accentuated by the Government's insistence upon the whole paraphernalia of British practice in regard to survey and registration of titles. An administrative officer, J. O. W. Hope, was instructed to demarcate as swiftly as possible a line to the south of Kikuyu country defining the unoccupied area available for settlement. The land granted in this area proved to be among the richest in Kenya, but the grants marked the beginning of the clash between European and African claims on land which was to extend over a much wider area and which in due course was to be one of the main sources of dispute between the two races. In spite of a sincere attempt to reach a fair decision Mr. Hope had insufficient time to investigate historical rights in land, many of which had been further complicated by the recent decimation of the Kikuyu of the Kiambu district as a result of a smallpox epidemic.

Although the Germans had encroached upon African-owned land on Kilimanjaro the area affected was relatively small and Germany was never faced with the competition for land between Africans and Europeans which was to be one of the basic features of British East Africa's development. For, while the problem of Kiambu might presage an outburst of intense feeling in the future there was a still more immediate problem in regard to the Masai. These predatory nomads had denied vast areas of country to the other tribes without making much use of it themselves. Sir Charles Eliot saw no reason why this state of affairs should continue, more particularly in the land adjoining the railway which was not, in any case, vital to the Masai and which could be used more profitably as grazing ground by European settlers. Before he could make his views effective, however, the Commissioner resigned as a result of a dispute with the Foreign Office over grants of land and over the policy of creating a Masai reserve, an approach to the question of racial relationships to which Eliot was opposed. He was succeeded by Sir Donald Stewart who, in pursuance of the tactics to which the Foreign Office was now committed, announced that two reserves would be created for the Masai, one in Laikipia and the other between the railway line and the German border. They would be linked by a road half a mile wide. The Masai accepted this arrangement which was embodied in a formal treaty signed in August 1904 by Stewart and Lenana, the Masai Laibon, together with representatives of all the clans. The treaty was ratified by the Secretary of State. The majority of the Masai then gradually moved from the Rift Valley to Laikipia although a few remained where they were while others roamed over land allotted to the European farmers. Twice the northern reserve had to be enlarged but still the Masai wandered beyond its borders. Then the track between the two reserves had to be closed to prevent the spread of cattle disease and it became increasingly difficult for Lenana, who lived in the southern reserve, to maintain order. The proposal to concentrate the tribe in an adequately enlarged southern reserve had the double advantage of re-uniting the Masai under Lenana's control, which Lenana himself and the other elders were anxious to achieve, and at the same time of making available the excellent land on the Laikipia Plateau for European farmers. The northern Masai agreed to move, but the manœuvre became unnecessarily complicated as a result of the intervention of the Secretary of State who wanted to draw up a new agreement. Twice the move began and twice it was checked, causing the Masai to turn against the plan, but eventually the transfer took place in spite of an attempt by the new Laibon, Legalishu, to contest the Government's powers in the law courts.

It was the inefficient handling of the whole problem rather than any injustice in the proposal to limit the Masai grazing grounds which drew attention to this one tribe in particular. But, as an introduction to the policy of creating African reserves which the Protectorate Government had adopted in principle in respect of all the tribes soon after Eliot's departure, the Masai issue was unfortunate. It appeared to have created a pattern which would at all times favour the claims of European settlers at the expense of the needs of the African population. In 1906 four reserves were established for the Kikuyu, Kitui, Kikumbuliu and Ulu tribes in addition to the two created for the Masai, but this did not act as a protection for the tribes concerned as it was said to do. For occupied as well as unoccupied land within the reserves might still be alienated if the Governor obtained the consent of the Secretary of State. This latter provision was felt to provide adequate protection for the tribes, although the reserves had not been gazetted even as late as 1914, and the rights of the occupants had never been defined. To the Africans, however, the creation of reserves seemed to bring only insecurity, a state of mind which the treatment of the Masai did little to reassure. Furthermore the limited information upon which the creation of the reserves was based led unwittingly in a number of cases to tribes being deprived of essential grazing grounds or watering places, while certain tribes were given land which was already claimed by others. Since the right to use enough land to supply his family's needs was such an important factor in the life of every African tribesman the ill-feeling which was often involuntarily created formed the basis for much future unhappiness as far as Africans and Europeans were concerned.

If, at this early stage, the relations between Africans and European settlers were already being jeopardized by ignorance and misunderstanding, yet another source of racial friction was already emerging. The Foreign Office, having been slow to recognize the importance of encouraging settlers, became suddenly prolific in its ideas for the development of the territory while still failing to comprehend the true needs of the situation. One proposal was to plant a colony of Finns in East Africa while from the fertile mind of Joseph Chamberlain sprang the suggestion that East Africa should provide a home for the Zionists who were unable to obtain the approval of the Sultan of Turkey for the establishment of a Jewish National State in Palestine. These various proposals came to nothing but not so the recommendation that Indian settlement should be encouraged. But the presence of several thousand Indians in the East Africa Protectorate soon gave rise to serious disagreement between the Indian community and some of the white settlers who feared for the sanctity of their claim to land in the highland zone. During his brief period of office as Commissioner, which lasted barely a year, Sir Donald Stewart appointed a committee under the chairmanship of Lord Delamere to inquire into the Protectorate's land problems. The committee had not yet reported when Stewart unexpectedly died on October 1, 1905. His successor, Sir James Hayes Sadler, was well-disposed towards the Indian community, a fact which contributed to the growing opposition towards the Indians displayed by some of the European settlers, so that now relations between the settlers and Government servants also became strained.

Recognizing the challenge with which they were faced the Indian community, in April 1906, subscribed 20,000 rupees to enable them to present their case over the right to acquire land in the highlands to the Governments of the Protectorate, of India and of the United Kingdom. Not surprisingly, in view of the composition of the Land Committee and the climate of opinion at that time, the Committee's report when published came out firmly in support of reserving land in the highlands for European settlement. This view gained the approval of the Secretary of State for the Colonies, Lord Elgin, who sent a dispatch in July 1906, setting out his opinions. This subsequently became known as the Elgin Pledge. The Under-Secretary of State, Mr. Winston Churchill, was far from certain that the exclusion of British Indian subjects from the highlands could be regarded as a valid policy and in 1907 felt constrained to say so both in Britain and in East Africa. Elgin himself subsequently modified his earlier statement in a dispatch of March 19, 1908, in which, while maintaining that as a matter of administrative convenience land in the highlands should be granted to Europeans only, he added that there should be no restriction to the subsequent legal transfer of land simply upon racial grounds.

The year 1908 was the high-water mark of immigration. Labouring ox-wagons transported many Dutch families of South African origin across the plains and over the mountains of the East Africa Protectorate to the highlands beyond the Rift Valley. From 1910, however, the preponderance of South African settlers began to be challenged by the arrival of men from Britain, bringing with them considerable capital which most of the South Africans had lacked. It is interesting, too, that the men of British origin were to play a far more prominent part in the political life of the territory than did the Boers. There was still some controversy over the terms on which the settlers could obtain land and various bills intended to clarify the situation met with criticism from so many quarters that when war broke out in 1914 the situation was still unsettled. The increase in the number of white settlers, however, strengthened the view of those who believed that Africans should not be exposed simultaneously to the influences of western and eastern civilizations. The comparative poverty and the lower living standards of most of the Indian population also encouraged the European settlers to decry the contribution which Indians could make to the civilizing mission in East Africa. Just as the competition for land caused a rift between Europeans and Africans, so too did competition between Europeans and Asians over land and the right to a place of influence in the Protectorate exacerbate relations between the two groups of immigrants.

The increase in European settlement, with the consequent demand for large supplies of labour, provided further grounds for friction between white and black. The settlers, it must be admitted, did not see the issue in this light. The Government had encouraged them to take up residence in East Africa in order to develop the territory and it was therefore only reasonable that the Government should guarantee the availability of an adequate labour force. The climate might be attractive to Europeans but it was not clear that it would be suitable if they were to indulge in manual labour. In any case the introduction of European labourers would seem pointless with so many Africans apparently employed on their own farms for only a small proportion of the year. Nor would it seem justifiable to miss the civilizing opportunity presented by the employment of Africans on European farms where they might learn the benefits of regular work. Thus ran the settlers' argument and it was one which the Government found difficult to refute. It was true that on the traditional basis of subsistence farming the African population saw no reason why it should labour for foreigners. At the same time, the Government had deliberately founded its economy upon settler enterprise and most of the settlers had obtained land in areas which were virtually uninhabited and where labour was not readily available.

In 1906 an Ordinance was promulgated to regulate relations between employers and employees but in general Sir James Hayes Sadler was extremely reluctant to commit himself to a policy of compelling Africans to work for private persons. In the circumstances of the time his reticence virtually amounted to opposition, since to the Africans official silence over the labour issue implied that the Government did not want them to work. In December 1907 Sadler announced further rules which were intended to improve the situation but which only convinced the settlers that he wished to make the recruitment of labour still more difficult. Sadler agreed to hear the settlers' case, but after attending a public meeting at which Lord Delamere urged that methods of compulsion be legalized the Governor reaffirmed that in his view the rules he had introduced were justified. If the Government was to help to supply labour it must be prepared to protect the labourers. The settlers were deeply disappointed by this reply. On the afternoon of the same day some of them decided to go to Government House and request the withdrawal of the rules and the acceptance of a variety of proposals to protect employers against broken contracts and higher wages. Government officers would also be directed to encourage Africans to work and to assist in recruitment.[1] Under such direct pressure the

[1] *Correspondence Relating to Affairs in the East Africa Protectorate*, Cd. 4122, H.M.S.O., London, 1908, pp. 6-22.

Governor refused to give an immediate reply. The following day he stated that he would not withdraw the rules but was prepared to adjust them after discussions in the Legislative Council.

In March 1908, when the dispute was at its height, the Labour Inquiry Board, which Sadler himself had appointed, published its findings. The recommendations were similar in character to those put forward by the settlers with the added proposals that a tax rebate should be granted to Africans who worked for Europeans and that land set aside for native reserves should be limited to the existing requirements of the African population since larger reserves would reduce the labour supply available to the settlers.[1] Two months later the Governor did concede that the introduction of a poll tax, supplementing the already existing hut tax, might be desirable to tap the supply of young, unmarried men, who, in his opinion, would provide an adequate supply of labour if they could be induced to leave the reserves.[2] The following year, however, the Secretary of State issued instructions forbidding Government officers to recruit labourers for farmers.

The problem was still unsettled, and in 1912 the report of a further commission sitting under the chairmanship of Mr. Justice (later Sir Jacob) Barth compelled the Colonial Secretary, Mr. Harcourt, to state clearly his opposition to any suggestion that Government should compel Africans to work and to stress that taxation must be clearly divorced from a policy of labour recruitment.[3] He was prepared, on the other hand, to accept the Commission's recommendations regarding the introduction of a system of personal identification for Africans and the reorganization of reserves so as to limit them to the current needs of the African population. But still the attempt to introduce a satisfactory labour policy was delayed and the settlers' exasperation was diverted only by the outbreak of war in 1914.

The severe struggle which the settlers had to wage against a variety of difficulties, coupled with their own pioneering character, stirred in them the spirit of resistance against any suspected encroachment upon what they believed to be their rights. Thus, even at their most aggressive, they were firmly convinced that they were acting on the

[1] W. Macgregor Ross: op. cit., p. 92.

[2] *Report of the Committee on Emigration from India to the Crown Colonies and Protectorates*, Cd. 5194, 1910, pp. 49–50.

[3] M. R. Dilley: *British Policy in Kenya Colony*. Thomas Nelson, New York, 1937, p. 222.

defensive, a paradox which did not contribute towards the ready achievement of compromise either in their relations with the Government or with the African or Indian communities. The very sense of their isolation strengthened their belief in their civilizing mission and their attachment to western traditions of independence, and the apparently unbending officialdom of the Administration provided a ready target for their criticisms. The Government undoubtedly faced great difficulties through lack of personnel but it made up for this weakness to some extent by the width of its powers. The whole of the Protectorate's economic life, land, minerals, railways, roads, lake steamers and harbours were owned by the state.[1] To challenge this all-powerful machine the Farmers and Planters Association, founded in January 1903, to market the settlers' first economic crop of potatoes in South Africa, soon began to take an interest in politics. Its object in so doing was to guarantee the reservation of land for Europeans in the highlands and as an earnest of its intentions it adopted the new name of the Colonists Association. By 1905 the Association was petitioning the Secretary of State against the British pioneer's traditional enemy, taxation without representation, and was calling for the appointment of a legislative council which would include representation for the settlers . In the same year, British administration in the Protectorate having been greatly extended since its inception, control of the territory was transferred from the Foreign Office to the Colonial Office, and on his appointment as Governor, Sir James Hayes Sadler was instructed to set up a Legislative Council. The Council held its first meeting in the tin-roofed railway institute in Nairobi on August 17, 1907. It was no elaborate affair, consisting as it did simply of five official members and three unofficial, the latter being nominated by the Governor. Nevertheless, since one of the unofficial members was the redoubtable Lord Delamere the views of the settlers were unlikely to pass unheard.

With the appointment of a Legislative Council containing settler representation it might seem that the need for the Colonists Association had ceased to exist. The Association itself, comprising as it did so many individualists, had already begun to split without any external assistance, and a number of local associations had blossomed in areas as far apart as the coast and the Rift Valley. But

[1] E. Huxley: op. cit., Vol. I, p. 181.

the settlers did not consider that their political activities could be limited to the formal sessions of the Legislative Council. Delamere himself complained that in its original form the Council permitted the unofficial members to do nothing more than listen to a statement of policies already decided upon by the Government. If the latter body was to be kept alert to the true needs of the country some association of settlers would be necessary to give voice to those needs. In 1908 a central committee consisting of representatives of some of the local associations was set up to co-ordinate policy. From this there emerged in 1911 the Convention of Associations, the object of which was to hear views from all parts of the country and to forward to the Government those which won general approval. Appropriately enough the Convention soon carned the title of the Settlers' Parliament and its first object was to achieve elected representation of the settlers in the Legislative Council. This claim was submitted in a petition to the Secretary of State in 1913 and the unofficial members of the Council resigned in order to emphasize the force of the Convention's argument. It should be added that the old cry of 'no taxation without representation' was also raised to strengthen the settlers' case. For, with the passing of the Imperial grant-in-aid, in 1913 a poll tax was imposed upon non-Africans, the first direct taxation to which they had been subjected. It is quite possible that the Colonial Secretary might have agreed to this proposal but before he could take any action the outbreak of war pushed the issue into the background.[1]

Behind the façade of political and economic skirmishes considerable efforts, often of a wholly unselfish character, were being made to exploit the limited resources of the territory. The African population continued to be self-supporting as far as food was concerned, except in famine years, but owing to the Government's policy of developing a preponderantly settler economy, African agriculture contributed far less than it might have done towards the increased output of economic crops. A certain amount of official encouragement was given to the cultivation of cotton by Africans near Lake Victoria and of copra in the coastal region. There was also some increase in the output of maize and simsim for local consumption. At the same time, hides and skins from African-owned cattle, sheep

[1] E. Huxley: op. cit., Vol. I., pp. 210–12, 276–80, and G. Bennett: 'The Development of Political Organizations in Kenya'. *Journal of Political Science*, Vol. V, No. 2, June 1957, pp. 1–2.

and goats provided a valuable source of revenue to the Protectorate during the experimental years when European farming had as yet little to show. These hides and skins found a ready market in America and Germany, and largely as a result of their success the African population was still producing by its own efforts about half the total value of the territory's exports in the years immediately preceding the outbreak of war.[1] The Protectorate also continued to produce a certain amount of ivory, formerly its most important export, but most of that exported from Mombasa now came from Uganda or farther west from the Congo.

The settlers, meanwhile, accepted the challenge of their new environment with enthusiasm and courage although they were vividly conscious of the difficulties to be overcome.[2] In all the qualities needed by the pioneer Lord Delamere was pre-eminent and agriculture in the Protectorate owed much to him. Experiments with varieties of wheat encountered a number of setbacks due to rust until careful scientific research, sponsored mainly by Delamere, evolved a successful species named, appropriately, Equator, after Delamere's farm on which it was bred. Then came the problem of milling the grain. In 1908 Delamere formed a small company along with a few other settlers and himself subscribed half the capital. A mill was started in Nairobi and an expert miller was brought to the country. But for the intervention of the war flour might have been exported within a very few years. In any case the firm of Unga Limited was founded not as a profit-making concern but mainly to encourage wheat-growing. When this policy was criticized by his fellow-shareholders Delamere demonstrated his confidence in the plan by buying out the shares held by the other directors, an action which enabled wheat-growing to survive a number of difficult years.[3]

A start had been made in growing other produce and as has already been seen potatoes were the first crop to be exported. Probably as early as 1893 *Arabica* coffee had also been planted almost simultaneously by a Roman Catholic missionary in the Teita hills and by a Scottish missionary at Kibwezi. The trees were little cared for as long as they supplied the immediate needs of the mission and

[1] *Kenya Colony: Annual Report for 1912–13.* Cd. 7050. H.M.S.O., London 1914, p. 17.

[2] J. F. Lipscomb: 'Kenya's Agriculture, Pt. I. The Start of the Venture. *Kenya Weekly News*, February 15, 1957, p. 14.

[3] E Huxley: op. cit., Vol. I, pp. 117–18, 171–2, 177.

they soon became infested with borer beetle. From Teita, however, some seed was sent to St. Austin's Mission near Nairobi in 1900 and the following year other seed was obtained from Mauritius. Before long the mission began to supply settlers in the neighbourhood and coffee-growing began to spread. Between 1907 and 1913 the value of coffee exported rose from £270 to £18,000. In 1910 the secretary of the Coffee Planters' Association, which had been founded two years earlier to improve the standard of coffee-growing and to ensure a regular supply of labour, was able to boast that from its first introduction the coffee industry had suffered not a single setback. His claim was premature, however, for in 1912 a leaf disease broke out due to rust fungus and this was followed in succeeding years by a formidable variety of pests and diseases which taxed the skill of both growers and Agricultural Department alike. In spite of these difficulties the acreage under coffee increased rapidly, surviving the disappointment which resulted from the failure of the hopes of further expansion which had been raised by the discovery of wild coffee growing in the Nandi forest.[1] Rubber, again much of it wild, also raised high hopes as it had done in German East Africa. But after reaching an export value of £31,963 in 1910–11[2] it declined abruptly in importance. Sisal, on the other hand, which was introduced from German East Africa in 1902, became steadily more profitable in spite of the prohibitive export duty on bulbils and suckers imposed by the alarmed Germans.[3]

At an early stage a number of settlers, among whom Delamere was prominent, recognized the territory's potentialities as a stock-raising country. The hazards which faced the would-be ranchers, however, were if anything greater than those encountered by the agriculturalists. One settler, who chose to take up land on the borders of Nandi country in the very early years of the century, lost much of his stock through theft and was almost poisoned by the Nandi in the course of 'friendly negotiations'.[4] More common, however, was the devastation wrought by East Coast Fever which

[1] J. F. Lipscomb: 'Kenya Agriculture, Pt. IV. The Start of Coffee.' *Kenya Weekly News*, March 8, 1957, p. 17.

[2] *Kenya Colony: Annual Report for 1910–11*. Cd. 6007. H.M.S.O., London, 1912, p. 11.

[3] J. F. Lipscomb: 'Kenya Agriculture, Pt. III. The Weather, Labour and Sisal.' *Kenya Weekly News*, March 1, 1957, p. 15.

[4] E. Huxley: op. cit., Vol. I, p. 155.

was first met with near Nairobi in 1904. The establishment of a Government farm at Naivasha provided a reservoir of pedigree stock and experiments were carried out to discover which breeds would withstand the numerous diseases prevalent in the country. Sheep of many varieties were imported, merinos from Australia, Tasmania and South Africa, Shropshires, Suffolks, Cheviots, Lincolns, Welsh Mountains, King Hills and Romneys, while crosses between English mutton breeds and native ewes developed into good size animals producing good mutton although no attempt was made to export it. Pigs were also imported from 1904 onwards although the delay in erecting a bacon factory caused by financial difficulties discouraged a number of people who had hoped to take part in this project.[1]

These many experiments and setbacks imposed a great strain upon the courage and resources of the earliest settlers and it says much for their persistence that developments were as remarkable as in fact they proved to be. Although exports were not high by 1914 the nature and quantity of the Protectorate's imports suggested that the country was coming to life and that Africans as well as Europeans were beginning to feel some material benefits from the change in the country's economic structure. Cotton piece goods to the value of more than half a million pounds were imported in 1912–13 and a high proportion of these were bought by Africans. In the same year the hut and poll taxes amounted to £157,614[2] and much of the money spent on imported goods and paid in taxes had been earned on European farms. Little of the country's revenue was spent on services directly benefiting the African population, however. Although a Government industrial school was opened in Machakos in 1914, for example, the education of Africans, as in Uganda, was left in the hands of the missionaries.

In spite of the increasing prosperity of the Protectorate, heavy reliance was still placed upon the income from the railway, although hut and poll tax and customs duties were the next most important sources of wealth. Both the railway revenue and the customs duties gave an inaccurate impression of the Protectorate's prosperity. A considerable proportion of the income from the railway was raised

[1] J. F. Lipscomb: 'Kenya's Agriculture, Pt. II. The Start of Animal Husbandry.' *Kenya Weekly News*, February 22, 1957, p. 26.

[2] *Kenya Colony: Annual Report for 1910–11*. Cd. 6007. H.M.S.O., London 1912, pp. 5 and 11.

by charges on goods and produce travelling to and from Uganda. From the time when the control of the railway was transferred from the Foreign Office to the East Africa Protectorate Administration the whole of the revenue was credited to the Protectorate and was used to finance the general development of the territory and not just to carry out improvements on the railway. A similar procedure existed in regard to the customs duties collected at the coastal ports until the year 1909–10 when, for the first time, a small proportion of the income was handed over to the Uganda Administration. There was, therefore, a double reason for criticizing the satisfaction which was generally felt at the cessation after 1912 of the Imperial grant-in-aid without which the administration of the Protectorate could not previously have been sustained. In the first place Uganda fairly claimed that her neighbour was living on income rightly due to the inland Protectorate. More important still was the fact that the satisfaction felt because the Protectorate was so quickly paying its way was misguided, since the continuation of capital aid in those early days might well have laid the foundations of a far more thriving economy than could be achieved with the money available to the Protectorate Administration from its internal source of revenue and to the relatively small group of European and Indian investors living in East Africa.

In spite of the unorthodox practice of the East Africa Protectorate regarding railway and customs revenue, Uganda also basked in the unfortunate complacency resulting from having achieved freedom from Imperial grants-in-aid by the outbreak of war. This achievement was due to a much more rapid development of economic crops than had been achieved in the neighbouring territory, yet it was a surprising result in view of the change in attitude of the British in Uganda since the over-enthusiasm of the first European travellers had painted in glowing colours the potential wealth of the Buganda kingdom and of the country extending eastward to the highlands overlooking the Rift Valley. The numerous wars and the absence until 1902 of any adequate communication with the coast had made the development of the country's economy and the regular flow of trade virtually impossible. By the time the Uganda Railway reached Lake Victoria, moreover, the pleasing tracts of land between the lake and the Rift Valley were in the process of transfer to the East Africa Protectorate.

Of Uganda, as of its eastern neighbour, it might fairly be said that it was the desire to relieve the Imperial Government of financial responsibility rather than any positive policy of development and exploitation which aroused official interest in the economic growth of the Protectorate. The suppression of the Sudanese Mutiny had led to an increase in grants-in-aid from £89,000 in 1897–8 to £339,000 in 1898–9 and £397,000 in 1899–1900. This upward leap had caused the Imperial Government no little concern, and the need to put forward proposals which would have due regard to economy was stressed upon the Special Commissioner, Sir Harry Johnston, in his terms of reference. Uganda, therefore, illustrates in both its economic and administrative development what Britain really meant by the declaration of a Protectorate. For Britain's view was that a Protectorate should give her powers of interference without any reciprocal obligation beyond that of defence against external aggression. This attitude was not so overbearing as it might seem, for a minimum of interference was intended. It was, in fact, a product of the conflict and resulting compromise between those who, like Joseph Chamberlain, saw in the expansion of the Empire, and the close co-operation of its members, untold prospects of economic prosperity and military strength and those supporters of free trade on the other hand who wanted no more than the right of uninhibited access to any part of the world, coupled with unfettered competition between traders of all nations. With the swift increase in the imperial expansion of the European powers in the closing years of the nineteenth century, and the growing habit of imposing tariffs on foreign competitors, the objects of the free traders could only be secured, and then incompletely, by Britain's laying claim to territory in the regions where imperial expansion was taking place. It was in this spirit that British protectorates were declared in East Africa, and in these circumstances it is not surprising that the Government found some difficulty in winning enough support to enable it to promote a more active campaign of development within its new dependencies. There was thus no clear-cut policy as regards the form which administration should take in the new Protectorates or the lines along which economic exploitation should be encouraged, a situation which was clearly reflected in the piecemeal nature of the extension of British control in Uganda and one which was to complicate greatly the subsequent political development of the country.

On his arrival in the Protectorate it was to Buganda that the Special Commissioner, Sir Harry Johnston, first directed his steps. This was to be expected for it was with Buganda that the closest British links already existed and many of the other parts of the British sphere were still virtually unknown. Nevertheless, Johnston's action was to have a profound effect upon the future for, during the next few months, he took part in negotiations which not only extended but also strengthened and helped to perpetuate the special position of the Buganda kingdom. Economy, as has already been noted, had been impressed upon Johnston and he had no desire to disrupt the generally effective organization of Buganda in order to introduce a new and expensive hierarchy of British administrators. It was therefore to economic considerations that he first turned his attention, since in his terms of reference he had been instructed to investigate means of developing the Protectorate's resources so as to relieve the financial burden upon Britain. The system of land tenure, which depended entirely upon the whim of the Kabaka and his subordinate chiefs, seemed to the Commissioner to be the first item in need of reform. His initial proposal was to stabilize land ownership so as to encourage improvements in land usage. To do this he recommended that all occupied land should be granted to the occupier in freehold while the rest should be retained as Crown Land for distribution in any manner which seemed likely to encourage the Protectorate's development. This plan did not win the approval of the chiefs who saw in it the destruction of the whole scheme of patronage enjoyed by the Kabaka and his subordinates. Nor was the alternative of granting land only to the most senior chiefs likely to find favour with the lower ranks in the hierarchy. The final arrangement whereby it was agreed that many smaller chiefs also should receive land in freehold was therefore a compromise which Johnston felt he was justified in making on two accounts. In the first place it won for him the backing of the influential Baganda in his future negotiations, while at the same time more than half the estimated area of the Kingdom was recognized as Crown Land, thereby ensuring that there would be land available for the peasantry if the demands of the newly-created land-owning class threatened to become too severe for their tenants' comfort.[1]

[1] R. Oliver: *Sir Harry Johnston.* Chatto and Windus, London, 1957, pp. 300–02.

If the land settlement put the chiefs in the mood for further negotiations they were not prepared to make concessions without any return. While they agreed to Buganda's being formally described as a province equal in status to other provinces within the Protectorate, it was a Buganda with its borders laid down in writing of which they spoke. They were prepared, too, to forgo their claims to tribute from the neighbouring tribes, but their new boundary included the disputed areas recently annexed from Bunyoro. Revenue collected in Buganda was to be merged into the Protectorate's income, but no further direct taxation, in addition to the existing hut and gun taxes, might be imposed upon the Baganda without the consent of the Kabaka and Lukiko. The laws of the Protectorate would have effect in Buganda so long as they did not conflict with the terms of Johnston's Agreement; but the Lukiko, now formally constituted for the first time, with, as its members, the three regents, twenty *Saza* chiefs and sixty-six other notables nominated by the Kabaka, was given something akin to legislative power in that it might forward for the approval of the Kabaka and the Commissioner any majority proposals for the better administration of the kingdom. The office of Kabaka Johnston handled with respect, appreciating the reverence in which it was held by the Baganda as a whole. Yet, perhaps because the Kabaka at the time was only a child, less formal attention appears to have been paid to him in the agreement than was accorded to the chiefs. So long as he remained loyal to the protecting power he would continue to be recognized and would be given the title of His Highness.[1] But in spite of the fact that the Kabaka played no part in the signing of the agreement it was upon him that, in due course, the whole relationship between Britain and Buganda was to turn. He was no longer sovereign in Buganda, nor had he been since Lugard's time, but he was the link without which the chain of control would have been useless.

Three aspects of the Buganda Agreement of 1900 were to have lasting effects. In the first place the very existence and the nature of the agreement placed Buganda in a special position in relation to the rest of the Protectorate as Johnston himself appears to have intended. Secondly, the transformation of the sycophantic agglomeration of chiefs of Mutesa's day into the neo-parliamentary, though not wholly unsycophantic Lukiko of the twentieth century, created a focus for the political interests of the Baganda which inevitably complicated any attempt to create a legislative body representative of the Protectorate as a whole. Finally, the land settlement which was also embodied in the agreement created a powerful vested interest which, when an exchange economy began to replace the early subsistence economy, caused envy among those who had been excluded from grants of land in freehold. And not only envy, but a genuine sense of injustice was felt in some quarters, since it was left to the members of the Lukiko, themselves the chief beneficiaries of the settlement, to decide which land the various chiefs might claim.

Later in the year Johnston made a further agreement with the ruler of Toro which was much simpler in form and amounted primarily to the recognition of the Mukama as ruler over the group of principalities at the foot of the Ruwenzori range as long as he remained loyal to Britain. All the land was declared to be Crown Land but grants of freehold were made to the Mukama and a few of his leading chiefs. The simple form of the agreement reflects both the haste with which it was drafted and the relative unimportance of Toro in Johnston's estimation. The haste with which the treaty was prepared, however, gave rise to discontent in that its terms appeared to give less than his just status to the Mukama in relation to the other chiefs. This difficulty was cleared up in 1906 through the intervention of the able and sympathetic Deputy Commissioner, George Wilson.[1] More serious, however, was the absence of any definition of the system under which the peasantry would henceforward occupy their land. Johnston himself assumed that, since the leading chiefs had received grants of land in freehold and there was no shortage elsewhere, the existing right of the peasants to use such land as they needed for subsistence purposes would remain untouched. With the example of Buganda as their prototype, however, the Batoro chiefs began to make claims upon the peasantry which could be justified neither by tradition nor by the new agreement and the land issue continued to trouble Toro for several decades. In Ankole Johnston came to the conclusion that the Mugabe did not exercise sufficient influence over the cluster of neighbouring chiefdoms to warrant the formulation of an agreement. By the following year, however, and due mainly to the efforts of the

[1] Entebbe MSS. S.M.P., R. 125.

powerful Nganzi, Nuwa Mbaguta, the chiefs of the tribes round about Ankole had consented to acknowledge the paramountcy of the Mugabe. A limited agreement similar to that already made with Toro was then signed by George Wilson acting on behalf of the Commissioner.

By this time Johnston had already started on his return journey, leaving behind him three types of relationship between the peoples of Uganda and the single Protectorate authority. At the one extreme there existed a complicated agreement with Buganda, while at the other stood the conquered territory of Bunyoro and the districts lying to the east of Buganda which were directly administered by Protectorate officials. Between the two lay Toro and subsequently Ankole, differing little in status from Bunyoro and the rest yet rejoicing in the possession of agreements, the existence of which undoubtedly added to the confusion already existing in the Protectorate's administration. In the years before the First World War direct administration was also introduced among the Acholi, Lango, Iteso and other tribes to the north and among the Bakiga and their neighbours in the extreme south-west. For the greater part the extension of British rule was achieved without resistance although here and there some local chief tried to oppose the encroachment upon his powers and in Kigezi, to the south-west, witchcraft disturbed the early days of British administration. In the absence of chiefs with anything more than a purely local authority, the British made use of Baganda agents in minor administrative posts to put into effect the policy of the Central Government very much as Kakunguru had done and was still doing among the Iteso. The main difference, however, was that the agents employed by the British were looked upon as a temporary expedient, functioning only until local chiefs had learnt something of the demands of British rule. It would probably be true to say that the Baganda agents were withdrawn from most areas even before local men had emerged who were qualified to take their place. Kakunguru's followers, however, regarded the country they administered as conquered territory and did not expect to be replaced, while the policy they enforced was the policy laid down by Kakunguru rather than by the Protectorate Government. Kakunguru himself was one of the tragic figures of the early twentieth century for he had laid the foundations of British administration north of the Nile and had, probably quite genuinely, formed the opinion that he was to be kabaka of the region under his control. The British, however, had no intention of creating new, autocratic African rulers, so that what began as a fruitful relationship between an able leader and the Protectorate authorities ended in disappointment and bitterness for the former. Kakunguru held a number of posts under the British administration but his proud spirit could not accept a subordinate place, and he ended his days as a private citizen waging a covert and semi-religious campaign against the Protectorate's policy of inoculating animals against the diseases to which they were prone.[1]

Until the outbreak of war the Protectorate Administration was not unduly affected by the variety of relationships which it enjoyed with the tribes under its control. Indeed, at this stage the differences were scarcely noticeable. The Baganda chiefs, happy in the status assured them by the 1900 Agreement and in many cases genuinely anxious to learn from their British advisers, accepted readily enough the comments and criticisms of the Protectorate authorities. The British, on their part, treated the young Kabaka with the ceremony befitting his office and thereby satisfied the Baganda peasantry. Over all loomed the dominating figure of Apolo Kagwa rejoicing in the great power he wielded and glad as yet to give his allegiance to the Protectorate Administration which supported him in his office and would, if necessary, uphold his status as senior regent against the rivalry, real or suspected, of his co-regent, Stanislas Mugwanya.

While the administration of the Protectorate was being gradually consolidated the boundaries were simultaneously being confirmed or amended. Between 1907 and 1912 the difficult task of delimiting the Uganda–Congo boundary was taken in hand while farther north, adjustments became necessary on the death of Leopold II in 1909. The Lado Enclave created by the Anglo-Belgian Agreement of 1894 passed to the Sudan on June 16, 1910. By the Brussels Agreement of the same year the western side of Lake Albert was transferred to the Belgians thereby achieving permanently what the lease of the Mahagi Strip had set out to do as a temporary measure in 1894. On January 1, 1914, the area now known as the West Nile District of Uganda and previously forming part of the Lado Enclave was handed over to the Protectorate by the Sudan. In return Uganda transferred

[1] H. B. Thomas: 'Capax Imperii: The Story of Semei Kakunguru.' *Uganda Journal*, Vol. VI, 1939, pp. 125-36.

to its northern neighbour the territory north of Nimule and there was some adjustment of the border to the north of Rudolf Province which was administered by Uganda until 1926.[1]

That the economic development of Uganda came to depend upon peasant agriculturists acting on the advice of government scientific and administrative officers, and selling their products to European and Indian traders, was due to a variety of factors and to the influence of two people in particular. Those two were Sir Hesketh Bell, Commissioner and later Governor from 1905 to 1910 and Mr. S. Simpson, Director of Agriculture from 1912 to 1928. Although both Lugard and Johnston had believed that Uganda would provide opportunities for European agricultural enterprise, Sir James Hayes Sadler, who succeeded Johnston as Commissioner in 1902, frankly admitted that the Protectorate without its former Eastern Province could not be regarded as potentially a white man's country. Nevertheless, there were those who continued to insist that the economic future of Uganda would ultimately come to depend upon plantation agriculture financed by European capital. Nowhere was this view more firmly expressed than by Chief Justice Sir William Morris Carter and the committees over which he presided to investigate systems of land tenure and to make recommendations for the future control of land. In 1906 Carter himself presented a carefully considered statement on the traditional systems of land tenure in Buganda. The following year the report of the first land committee was submitted. The Buganda Land Law of 1908 was based on its recommendations, and provided a sound legal basis for freehold tenure in Buganda. Moreover in keeping with Carter's desire to make land available to European planters *mailo* owners were permitted to alienate a percentage of their land under official supervision. For the rest of the Protectorate the committee recommended the enactment of an ordinance declaring all unoccupied land to be the property of the Crown unless evidence was brought to the contrary. The object of this proposal was not to deprive the peasantry of their rightful use of the land but rather to define the area available to the Protectorate authorities for distribution to the European planters whom the committee regarded as being essential to the Protectorate's development.

[1] H. B. Thomas and A. E. Spencer: *A History of Uganda Land and Surveys*. Government Press, Entebbe, 1938, pp. 29–37.

Shortly afterwards, in 1911, another committee was appointed under Carter's chairmanship which laid down as its objects the protection of the natives in the possession of land adequate to their requirements while ascertaining the areas available to Europeans and others for development. The committee submitted its first report on January 15, 1912. It was a disappointing document for, having reached the astounding conclusion that only the chiefs owned the land, it went on to recommend the allocation of estates to two or three hundred chiefs in each district as in Buganda, while the peasant occupiers would become rent-paying tenants. This would release considerable areas of land for alienation to prospective planters. Mr. R. C. Allen, the Land Officer, who was a member of the Committee, submitted a minority report opposing the grant of freehold and recommending that the land should be regarded as a native reserve. Subsequently two further reports were presented in which the comments of the Provincial Commissioners were included. Mr. F. Spire, Provincial Commissioner of the Eastern Province, was the only one to show any awareness of the danger of creating a landless class among the African peasants. He it was who suggested that as far as Busoga was concerned the whole district should be declared Crown Land, of which the greater part would be made available for the use of the African population. The first three reports were then assembled and the proposals were transmitted to the Secretary of State. On January 13, 1916, he sent a brusque reply in which he stated that the arrangements suggested did not appear to be in the best interests of either the peasants or the development of the Protectorate. Instead he preferred a system under which all land would be held in tenancy of the Crown while the chiefs would be given salaries.[1]

The Secretary of State's decision did not bring to an end the campaign for European plantation development in Uganda. Experiments were carried out with varying success on coffee, cocoa, rubber and a variety of other plantation crops. But from the very outset of his career Sir Hesketh Bell made it clear that so long as he held office European planters would not be welcomed in Uganda in any large numbers.[2] In fact, the lack of available land proved a deterrent

[1] Ibid. pp. 52–57.

[2] Sir Hesketh Bell: *Glimpses of a Governor's Life.* Sampson Low, London 1946, pp. 121–2.

to large-scale European plantation development in spite of the efforts of Chief Justice Carter. At a time when the East Africa Protectorate was trying to encourage European settlement in a country whose climatic conditions offered considerable attractions, Uganda had little to offer by comparison. Communications, except in Buganda and more particularly in those parts near the lake, were poor, while the neighbouring Protectorate, situated nearer the sea, had now got a railway. In Buganda itself the survey of *mailo* land was a slow process which inevitably delayed any firm offer of the large areas needed for plantation agriculture. Consequently, few inquiries were made by Europeans from outside Uganda although a few officials, better acquainted with the country's potential or at least believing themselves to be so, resigned the service in order to acquire land at the end of the first decade of the century. Even these latter, however, were discouraged by the sharp rise which took place in the price of land when the Baganda *mailo* owners recognized that they possessed something with an economic value. In 1912, for example, prices rose from 4s. to 30s. an acre.[1] At the same time Mr. S. Simpson, who became Director of Agriculture in 1912 and who remained in office until 1928, undertook an all-out campaign to encourage cotton-growing. His view was that it was the duty of the Government to encourage African agriculture so that although he was not hostile to European planters, as some of his critics suggested, the planters themselves received little assistance from the Government.

Carter's campaign to encourage plantation agriculture met, therefore, with little success. While his committee was still engaged in its deliberations peasant-grown cotton had already asserted its position as the main source of Uganda's wealth. Cotton had been found growing wild in Uganda by early explorers from Speke onwards, and Sir Samuel Baker had himself experimented briefly with some Egyptian seed. No one had fully recognized the economic possibilities of the crop, however, until 1903 when the Protectorate Government, casting around for some saleable product to replace ivory which no longer appeared to offer a sound basis upon which to build the country's economy, imported 1½ tons of three different kinds of cotton seed. This was distributed for trial cultivation by peasants in all likely and accessible parts of the Protectorate early

[1] *Uganda Herald*, May 2, 1913.

in 1904. About the same time Mr. K. Borup of the Uganda Company imported 2½ tons of five different kinds of seed and distributed it to twenty-seven chiefs in eight districts in Buganda. Later in the year Bunyoro and Busoga also received some seed.[1] The results of the tests showed that cotton grown by African peasants had considerable economic possibilities. But the experiments with several varieties of seed, although reasonable enough since little was known of the suitability of different types to Uganda's conditions, soon threatened to destroy the prospects of success. In 1907 adverse reports were received from the British Cotton Growing Association on the mixed quality of Uganda's cotton. In that year, therefore, the Uganda Protectorate Administration entered into an arrangement with the association whereby the two parties each agreed to contribute £1,000 annually for a three-year period to enable the association to carry out experimental work in Uganda. The association then entrusted the spending of the money to the British East Africa Corporation, a commercial concern. Fortified by this direct interest in the progress of cotton-growing in Uganda the association then urged the Uganda Administration to take firm action to check the cause of the complaints against the quality of the Protectorate's cotton. After consultation with local advisers Sir Hesketh Bell decided upon drastic measures. Of all the varieties so far tested, American Upland had proved most satisfactory. As soon as the season's crop had been harvested, therefore, Bell determined that every plant of any other variety must be uprooted and burnt and that all seed in the ginneries must be destroyed. Henceforward only approved seed should be made available, supplied from plots established by the Administration in various centres. On March 19, 1908, the Uganda Cotton Ordinance was promulgated, giving the Governor extensive powers to control the quality of cotton produced. The social and economic implications of this policy might have been disastrous but for the authority exercised by the Baganda chiefs. Bell, however, was confident of their support, and through their loyal co-operation the danger of discouraging the peasant growers at this early stage of development was averted, and only a temporary brake was applied to the output of lint cotton.

The task of expanding the area in which cotton was grown now

[1] C. Ehrlich: 'Cotton and the Uganda Economy, 1903–1909.' *Uganda Journal*, September, 1957, pp. 162–75.

presented two further problems. In the first place if the cotton was to find a market there must be an adequate number of ginneries to process the crop. At the same time more transport was needed, since peasant growers could not be expected to carry their produce on their heads over long distances from their fields to the ginneries. Until 1908 practically all the cotton produced was still being handled by the Uganda Company's ginnery in Kampala. In that year two further ginneries started work in the town while the British East Africa Corporation opened another ginnery in Kisumu mainly to deal with Uganda cotton. Yet even when the number of ginneries had increased in 1913 to twenty, all but one were still located in a few centres in Buganda and Busoga. The question of transport, therefore, had still to be tackled, and progress was greatly hampered by the shortage of funds. Sir Hesketh Bell was prepared to invest every available cent in establishing a good system of motor roads and he did his utmost to encourage the introduction of motor wagons so as to rid the country of the uneconomic and debasing practice of head porterage. But the impetus he gave, and which began to bear fruit in 1909 in a marked improvement in the roads in the immediate vicinity of Kampala, was lost again in 1910 owing to financial stringency and little more could be done before the outbreak of war. But Bell's plans did not end there. He evolved a variety of schemes for extending the Uganda Railway, the most practicable of which, the construction of a line from Jinja to Lake Kyoga to open up the cotton-growing districts of Busoga and to a lesser extent of Teso and Lango, was undertaken in 1910 with the assistance of a loan from the Imperial Treasury of £160,000. It was completed as far as Namasagali in the time of Bell's successor, Sir Frederick Jackson, in 1913.

These developments in communications came none too soon, for at the instigation of the Governor, administrative officers were encouraging growers everywhere to put greater acreages under cotton. Mr. Lloyd George's announcement that a loan of £500,000 was to be made to the East Africa and Uganda Protectorates for the improvement of communications also came at an opportune moment. The money was to be used to provide deep-water wharfage accommodation at Kilindini, the ocean terminal of the Uganda Railway and to develop communications in the interior. A sum of £25,000 was allocated for the construction of a railway link between

Kampala and the lake at Port Bell, named after the former Governor, and a further £100,000 was to be devoted to the development of feeder roads joining up with the Busoga railway.

As a result of the varied encouragement given to African peasants, cotton became, by the outbreak of war, far and away the most important export of the Uganda Protectorate and made it possible to dispense with the grant-in-aid from the Imperial Treasury in April 1915. The organization of the industry had also divided itself, apparently satisfactorily, with the African peasant growers on the one hand and European and Indian ginners and exporters on the other. The importance of the part played by the non-African ginners and traders cannot be over-emphasized. Without their initiative and experience the cultivation of cotton could have had little point, since the growers themselves had no knowledge of the later stages through which the cotton passed. As in the East African Protectorate, Indian traders penetrated into the remotest regions, living under the most primitive conditions yet contriving to encourage local production by the incentive of their trade goods. The Department of Agriculture also contributed its share to the success of the cotton crop with its free distribution of cotton seed, with the advice it offered on planting and cultivation and, not least, by providing the impetus which encouraged peasants to move away from a simple subsistence economy to a money economy. In this latter respect the chiefs also played their part, being quick to recognize the financial benefits they would derive from an increased output of cotton from their land.

The concentration upon cotton production had its repercussions upon the availability of labour for the non-African plantations and added its quota to the obstacles standing in the way of success for the planters. Until the immediate post-war years, however, this was not a very serious issue since the number and size of the plantations was small. The failure of cocoa, after a brief initial success, together with the fall in the world price of rubber, practically limited planters' hopes to coffee and as the coffee trees did not bear for several years the question of labour proved not to be so pressing an issue as it was in the East Africa Protectorate or even in German East Africa. Some complaints were lodged against the Director of Agriculture for encouraging Africans to grow cotton in areas where plantations of coffee already existed but there was no serious clash between the planters and the Government even in the brief boom period immediately after the war.

The prosperity which cotton brought to the Protectorate was mainly enjoyed in Buganda and the Eastern Province since the scarcity of communications made the spread of cotton-growing in other areas a slow process. Yet prosperity there undoubtedly was and it was reflected in the steady increase in the import of trade goods for the African market. Imports, like exports, owed much to the steady development of communications and above all to the Uganda Railway and to the ships on Lake Victoria which carried on where the railway for the time being left off. For, if a bulky crop such as cotton could never have become profitable until a relatively inexpensive means of transport had been provided, so too, goods from Europe which might be sold at a reasonable price in Mombasa became impossibly expensive after being carried nearly a thousand miles as head loads.

Yet the influx of trade goods was not such as to change the appearance of Buganda and the Eastern Province overnight. The Baganda had long been noted for the smartness of their dress and the neatness of their houses. Moreover, they were not greatly attracted by the tawdry products which found a ready market in less sophisticated regions. Textiles were more plentiful and their bright colours gradually replaced the more sombre hues of the dresses formerly worn by Baganda ladies of fashion. The white, smock-like, cotton kanzu, inherited from the Arabs, became more popular among the men. Those who could afford it used the more serviceable if less picturesque corrugated iron instead of grass thatch as roofing material for their houses. Chiefs in particular, as landowners and therefore as heirs to the new wealth, were able to take advantage of the supply of new amenities, thereby demonstrating to others something of the far-reaching character of Johnston's land settlement.

It was the chiefs, too, who were the first to take advantage of the educational opportunities provided by the missionary societies. These latter bodies, although still wielding an important influence in the affairs of the country, no longer in the twentieth century stood in the forefront of political events. Instead they exercised their influence largely through their schools. Not until the 1920s did the Protectorate Government play any part in the provision of education in Uganda. Before that date, and due entirely to the efforts of the missionaries, a widespread system of schools had been built up in the Protectorate and more particularly in the southern half of the territory. Most of these were primary schools concerned only with teaching the rudiments of reading and writing, yet within a few years of the opening of the new century the Church Missionary Society, the White Fathers and the Mill Hill Mission all had more advanced boarding-schools in the vicinity of Kampala. These latter aimed in the first place at attracting the sons and even the daughters of chiefs and great emphasis was laid upon character formation. All of them, moreover, stressed the importance of agricultural education and the inculcation of elementary technical skills. To the Uganda Company, which was itself formed in 1903 to take over the industrial side of the C.M.S.'s work, also fell the organization of the society's industrial school. The success of the missionaries' educational work was particularly marked in Buganda and proved to be one more factor in the more rapid progress of that kingdom in comparison with the other provinces of the Protectorate. The leading part played by Buganda in the affairs of the Protectorate was also due to its indigenous system of centralized, autocratic and bureaucratic government. This position had been strengthened by the 1900 Agreement and by the early success of cotton growing although in the latter field the Eastern Province was already challenging Buganda's leadership before the war in 1914. Yet virtually all parts of the country were showing some evidence of growing prosperity even if only in their ability to pay the poll tax which in 1909 completely replaced the hut tax as the chief direct imposition upon the African population.

This progress was all the more remarkable in view of the background of sleeping sickness against which it was made. The disease was first diagnosed towards the end of 1900 by Dr. (later Sir Albert) Cook of the Church Missionary Society[1] who had established a mission hospital near Kampala in 1897. The epidemic spread rapidly all around the shores of Lake Victoria, affecting German East Africa almost as much as Uganda. The missionaries did their utmost to relieve the sufferings of those who contracted the disease but they were handicapped by their lack of understanding of its origin and by the terrible fear which it evoked among the African population.

[1] Sir Albert Cook: 'Further Reminiscences of Uganda.' *Uganda Journal*, Vol. 2, 1934-35, p. 112.

For some time it was thought to be contagious, and families cast out any person suspected of being a carrier. Thousands died and it was not until 1903 that Colonel (later Sir David) Bruce, who had been sent to Uganda by the Royal Society to investigate the outbreak, discovered that it was caused by the bite of the *glossina palpalis*. This news was far from encouraging, for although the fly rarely travelled more than two miles from water the infested area stretched virtually round the whole of the lake. A German doctor, Professor Koch, was sent to make investigations in German East Africa in 1905 and for a time the scientists concentrated upon seeking a cure for the disease, since the task of eradicating the fly appeared to be beyond the resources of the respective Governments. It was Koch who discovered that atoxyl had some remedial effect, although it was soon recognized that no permanent cure could be achieved by these means.[1]

Characteristically it was Sir Hesketh Bell who seized upon and put into effect the one method of checking the spread of the disease. Bell had been concerned about the effects of sleeping sickness even before setting out for Uganda, and soon after his arrival in East Africa he came to the conclusion that if the fly could not be exterminated the people must evacuate the infested zone. He put his proposal to the Colonial Office where it was received with considerable caution. A committee was set up to consider the possible effects of his plan, but without waiting for its comments Bell put the scheme into effect. He had the support of his Principal Medical Officer and was confident of the co-operation of his administrative officers and of the Baganda chiefs. The move was made easier by the fact that, owing to the 1900 Agreement, only chiefs actually owned land, while the vast majority of the people affected were simply tenants. The chiefs were therefore offered alternative holdings of Crown Land in uninfested areas in order to enlist their support for the move. Nevertheless the task was enormous and did not end even with the evacuation of the hundreds of miles of lake shore. The inhabitants of the Sese Islands were moved to the mainland, and shortly afterwards the Buvuma Islands were also evacuated, projects which involved over 25,000 people. Subsequently the shores of Lake Albert and the islands in the lake, together with the islands

[1] H. Brode: *British and German East Africa*. Edward Arnold, London, 1911, pp. 78–80.

John Ainsworth

Lord Delamere

C. W. Hobley, Sir Percy Girouard (seated)
and Col. John Ainsworth

British troops embarking for the front—Nairobi

General Paul von Lettow-Vorbeck

Dr. Heinrich Schnee

in the River Nile and, later still, the east bank of the Nile in Acholi were all evacuated.[1] It is some indication of the respect in which the British administrative officers were held that these huge transfers of population were carried out with virtually no resistance whatsoever.

The British and German Governments also entered into an agreement which took effect on January 1, 1909, to prevent natives of their respective East African territories suspected of carrying the disease from moving from one Protectorate to another. Segregation camps were set up by both powers on their borders in which were detained any persons suspected of suffering from sleeping sickness, and officers from the two territories maintained regular consultation with their counterparts on the other side of the border. The result of all these activities was a swift decline in the number of cases reported and before the outbreak of war the disease had been reduced to negligible proportions. For this achievement full credit must go to Sir Hesketh Bell who had the courage to take the drastic step of uprooting scores of thousands of people in order to save their own lives.

While the three mainland territories were laying the foundations upon which their future development was to be constructed, Zanzibar, although no longer the focus of European interest in East Africa, was undergoing a number of important changes. The accession of Seyyid Ali bin Hamoud in 1902 at the age of seventeen led to the appointment as Regent of Mr. A. S. Rogers, his British First Minister. Seyyid Ali's minority then became the occasion for the introduction of a number of reforms. With a view to placing the territory's finances on a sounder footing a financial adviser to the Zanzibar Government was appointed in 1903. A more important change took place in 1904 with the promotion of the British Consul in Zanzibar, Mr. Basil Cave, to the office of Diplomatic Agent and Consul-General. Since 1900 Zanzibar had been the responsibility of the Commissioner and Consul-General for the East Africa Protectorate, and the increasing responsibilities of that office, together with the transfer of its headquarters from Mombasa to Nairobi had resulted in the Commissioner's being unable to pay much attention to Zanzibar. The promotion of Cave and the severance of Zanzibar from the East Africa Protectorate thus enabled the Foreign Office to maintain more direct relations with Zanzibar itself.

[1] Sir Hesketh Bell: op. cit., pp. 163–4.

Seyyid Ali attained his majority in June 1905, and two months later Rogers retired. Relations between the two had not always been very cordial, mainly because the Sultan resented the restrictions imposed upon him by his First Minister. Rogers's retirement, therefore, provided an opportunity for the reorganization of the Zanzibar Administration. Mr. E. Clarke, head of the African Department of the Foreign Office, was entrusted with the task of investigating Zanzibar's problems and of making recommendations. Clarke's report was submitted early in 1906, the most important proposal being that, in addition to a First Minister, there should be a Secretary for Finance and Trade and an Attorney-General. The Consul-General, meanwhile, should be authorized to call for reports from the three officials and should have the power of veto over their recommendations. The Protectorate's annual estimates should also be submitted to the Foreign Office for approval.

The Foreign Office accepted Clarke's proposals and the new scheme came into effect on July 1, 1906. The new Secretary for Finance and Trade, Mr. C. E. Akers, quickly came to the conclusion that in spite of the apparently comfortable situation of the country's finances, due to the revenue from a 25 per cent export duty on cloves and a 5 per cent import duty, the position was likely to deteriorate owing to competition from the mainland Protectorates. He considered that drastic economies could and should be made in the Protectorate's administration and that there should be a proportionate increase in expenditure on the improvement of communications and on the provision of education. In addition the import duty should be increased to $7\frac{1}{2}$ per cent from January 1, 1908.

Akers's proposals involved a radical reorganization of the civil service, but most of them were agreed upon and put into effect. In 1908 the Consul-General, Cave, left Zanzibar and was succeeded by Mr. Clarke who had already had both direct and indirect experience of Zanzibar's affairs in his capacity as a member of the Foreign Office. It was fitting that the originator of the new administrative system should now be responsible for putting that system into effect, and Clarke soon made it clear that as Consul-General he would exercise complete control over the Protectorate. The Sultan was suffering increasingly from ill health and found it necessary to make trips to Europe for ever longer periods each year. In December 1911 he decided to abdicate and was immediately succeeded by his brother-in-law, Seyyid Khalifa bin Harup, a great grandson of Seyyid Said. Although Seyyid Ali had exercised little influence over the administration of the Protectorate his reign had been an eventful one. One of the chief problems had been solved with the gradual relinquishment of extra-territorial rights by the Great Powers who had made trading treaties with Zanzibar in the nineteenth century. Attempts at increasing the variety of the country's agricultural products had failed owing to the conservatism of the clove and coconut-palm growers so that the newly-formed Department of Agriculture had decided to concentrate upon the improvement of those two staple crops and of the island's communications. An Education Department had been set up in 1908 to provide elementary education in reading, writing and arithmetic and in the Koran, and slightly more advanced education had been provided in the town. This was an addition to, and improvement upon, the Koran schools held by private teachers. Missionary attempts at providing education meanwhile had been less successful than had been hoped owing to suspicions on the part of the Muslim population. In 1908, too, a further revision of the judicial system resulted in the introduction of British magistrates into the Sultan's courts while all the courts of Zanzibar were placed under the ultimate control of British judges.

The creation of a number of new departments led inevitably to an increase in the number of British civil servants in the Zanzibar Administration. This aroused considerable criticism from some of the Sultan's supporters although the number of British officers involved was not, in fact, large. The increase in efficiency which their presence ensured went a long way towards justifying the additional expenditure on salaries and in any event the earlier system of administration had been far from economical since the Sultan had always been beset by a large number of dependants who thronged his court. Nevertheless one important reform had still to be introduced. In spite of the determination of Mr. Clarke to assert the authority of the Consul-General his relationship with the First Minister had not been a satisfactory one. On the death of Clarke on February 14, 1913, the British Government decided to make a complete change in its relationship with Zanzibar. Responsibility for the Protectorate was transferred from the Foreign Office to the Colonial Office on July 1, 1913. The office of First Minister was abolished and the duties of the Consul-General were thenceforward carried out by a British Resident. At the same time the Governor of the East Africa Protectorate was appointed High Commissioner for Zanzibar with general powers of supervision. The Sultan's anxiety about his position was met with reassurances from the British Government and as a practical indication of Zanzibar's autonomy, a Protectorate Council was established over which the Sultan presided while the Resident acted as Vice-President. The Council was to have three official members together with three unofficials, the latter to be appointed by the British Resident with the approval of the High Commissioner. Although the Council's functions were purely advisory there was in them the germ of a future legislature for the Protectorate.[1]

By 1914, therefore, each of the four East African Protectorates had begun to develop its own characteristics and already the truth of Sir Charles Eliot's forecast of 1905 was being demonstrated, that any amalgamation of the British territories must come soon if it was to come at all. Zanzibar, proud of her earlier position of pre-eminence, had no desire to be swallowed up in one of the mainland Protectorates. Uganda with her Buganda Agreement and her small but independent group of European unofficials was already beginning to look with some distrust at her eastern neighbour whose settler population seemed able to exercise a disproportionate amount of influence upon British public opinion. German East Africa, meanwhile, was being developed with characteristic Teutonic thoroughness and looked to the adjoining territories only for examples and experience upon which she could seize and which she could mould to suit her own requirements and to promote her own economic development. Then, suddenly, because of events in Europe, the Protectorates were thrown together in 1914 in the close embrace of military conflict.

[1] L. W. Hollingsworth: *Zanzibar under the Foreign Office*. Macmillan London, 1953, pp. 177–216.

CHAPTER SEVEN

EAST AFRICA AT WAR

ALTHOUGH the prospects of war had been kept alive in Europe throughout the first half of 1914 it was not expected that the European crisis would spread to East Africa. Sometimes German visitors to the British East Africa Protectorate had behaved in an arrogant fashion and even on occasion had declared that they would soon take over the British territory. But in East Africa generally Europeans found it difficult to believe that British and Germans, faced by such similar problems and administering large African populations, would go to war with each other. In addition, Articles X to XII of the Berlin Act of 1885, dealing with the neutrality of the territories comprised in the conventional basin of the Congo, gave an added sense of security. Neither British nor Germans were prepared for war. They had few troops and these were trained mainly in the art of warfare against ill-equipped and primitive tribes rather than in battles against opponents with modern arms. Furthermore, their ammunition was limited and their supply organizations nonexistent.

When the warning telegram from the Colonial Office, ordering precautionary measures to be put into force, reached Entebbe and Nairobi late on July 29 the slender forces of the two Protectorates were widely scattered. They consisted of the third (British East Africa) K.A.R., the fourth (Uganda) battalion and four companies of the first battalion from Nyasaland. The second battalion had recently been disbanded. Of the available seventeen companies, six were engaged in operations against the Marchan tribe on the Juba river, while others were on garrison duty on the northern border and on the point of mounting an expedition against the Turkana. One of the remaining companies was in Zanzibar and there remained only two companies in Bombo, twenty miles north of Kampala, and in Entebbe, and one and a half companies in Nairobi. To reassemble all these units would take time even if it were possible to disengage them from the operations to which they were already committed. There was no reserve except for a group of European volunteers in Uganda which amounted to little more than a rifle club for the entertainment of its members. In addition there was no headquarters staff to organize a general campaign.

The Germans were scarcely in any greater state of preparation. The territory's protective force consisted of 216 Europeans and 2,540 askaris. There were, in addition, forty-five Europeans and 2,154 Africans in the police force which was not, however, trained in military tactics. The combined force was undoubtedly stronger than that available to the British but any further reinforcements would have to come from within the territory itself. The Germans, nevertheless, had two great advantages over the British. First, they possessed a commander of determination. General Paul von Lettow-Vorbeck had been convinced since taking command in January 1914 that war was imminent and had toured the country extensively to assess the resources at his disposal and to make himself known to his subordinate commanders. Their second advantage lay in von Lettow's appreciation of the task of German East Africa in the event of a world war. He recognized that Britain would dominate the waterways of the world and that Germany could give virtually no support to her African possessions. Britain, on the other hand, free to maintain communication by sea, would wish to do all in her power to protect her overseas possessions if they were challenged. At the same time she would undoubtedly prefer to declare her African dependencies neutral so as to avoid dissipating her forces in distant parts of the globe. It was in Germany's interests, therefore, to wage a war in Africa which, although it could not hope to be victorious, would divert large numbers of British troops from the European front where the decisive actions of the war would be fought.

Von Lettow-Vorbeck had read his Berlin Act but saw no reason why treaty considerations should prevent two powers at war from extending their scene of action to the Congo basin. His difficulty lay in convincing the German Governor, Dr. Schnee, of the wisdom of this point of view since Schnee was the supreme military authority. It was the General's opinion that the best way in which to protect the colony and to damage his opponents was to threaten the British on their own soil. To achieve this purpose the most suitable base for launching operations would be the highly settled Kilimanjaro area. There, supplies of food would be adequate, the Usambara railway would provide a ready communication with the coast and fairly good roads ran southward to the Central Railway. In addition it would be possible from that base to threaten the Uganda Railway, the one line of communication linking the two British Protectorates with the outside world. To make the best use of this plan it was necessary to assemble the scattered German forces and concentrate them in the Kilimanjaro area as quickly as possible. Yet, even when orders for mobilization reached East Africa early in August, Dr. Schnee was still opposed to von Lettow-Vorbeck's plan. The General therefore had to be satisfied with concentrating his troops at Pugu, about twelve miles from Dar es Salaam. Even then, future action remained uncertain owing to the Governor's anxiety to avoid any British bombardment of Dar es Salaam and Tanga where the large civilian populations included a number of women and children.[1]

The British in East Africa were as aware of the vulnerability of the Uganda Railway as von Lettow-Vorbeck himself was and the outbreak of war aroused immediate concern lest the enemy should launch an attack in that direction. The Governor of the East Africa Protectorate, therefore, issued an appeal to all Europeans to give their services in the defence of the Protectorate, but before they had even received the appeal numbers of settlers left their homes to make their way to Nairobi. Many of these had invested all their capital in their farms and had devoted considerable labour to getting them into working order. But personal considerations were forgotten in the urgent need to meet the threat of a German attack. A regiment of mounted rifles and a regiment of infantry were raised, and a number of scout corps were formed to operate along the frontier and to give intelligence of German movements.

The possibility of a German attack upon Uganda appeared less serious. The Anglo–German frontier in the south-west, a mere line of latitude, had no strategic value and would be almost impossible to defend. On the other hand it was known that the German forces in the Bukoba area were relatively small so that any campaign would

[1] P. von Lettow-Vorbeck: *My Reminiscences of East Africa.* Hurst and Blackett, London, 1920, pp. 3–21.

be almost certainly of a limited nature. Uganda, in fact, learned of the outbreak of war in the middle of the celebrations leading up to the coming-of-age ceremony of the young Kabaka, Daudi Chwa. Most of the leading Baganda chiefs were already assembled in Kampala and were at once dispatched to their districts to raise forces whose task would be to defend the southern frontier. From other parts of Uganda, many of them only recently brought under effective administration, a proportion of the administrative officers had to be withdrawn with the possibility of local disorder to follow. The K.A.R. companies available for fairly immediate action, four in number, were at once sent to assist the troops in the East Africa Protectorate where the danger seemed greatest. Two further companies were withdrawn from Karamoja to replace them, leaving only one company to maintain order among the primitive north-eastern frontier peoples. The armed African police from all over the Protectorate were assembled in Kampala, Masaka and Mbarara, and from these an Active Service Company, two hundred strong, was dispatched on August 6 to the south-western border. Masaka was decided upon as the concentration area and thither later in the month and in September came the two companies of K.A.R. from the north, followed by the police and in due course by a body of levies which was later given the title of the Baganda Rifles.

While these preparations were being made the Governor of the East Africa Protectorate, Sir Henry Belfield, had appealed to the Colonial Office for assistance, since the Colonial Office, not the War Office, was still responsible for the defence of the Protectorates. In response to this appeal a request was made to India to provide forces to capture Dar es Salaam from the sea and to reinforce the land forces in East Africa.[1] Long before this help could be sent, however, the British navy struck the first blow of the war in East Africa. To the surprise of Dr. Schnee two British light cruisers, *Astraea* and *Pegasus*, opened fire on the wireless tower in Dar es Salaam on August 8. The tower was blown up by the Germans themselves but before the cruisers sailed away a truce was made on condition that the Germans in Dar es Salaam refrained from hostile acts during the war. On August 17 *Pegasus* raided Tanga and there, too, a truce was made subject to the Germans agreeing that their

---

[1] C. Hordern: *Military Operations East Africa*. H.M.S.O., London, 1941, Vol. I, pp. 15–31.

armed strength in the town should not exceed fifty African police. The British Government refused to ratify either of these agreements and the unfortunate result of the proceedings was to convince Dr. Schnee of the advisability of letting von Lettow-Vorbeck conduct the war in East Africa as he thought best.

Von Lettow-Vorbeck then moved his headquarters into the Kilimanjaro area and began his campaign against the British by sending out a series of flying columns against the Uganda Railway. The railway itself, running almost parallel to the German border and for many miles through thick scrub, was extremely vulnerable. Patrols could not hope to protect the whole line nor to intercept all the attacking forces launched against it. On the other hand the dry bush country made movement as difficult for the Germans as for the British so that the amount of damage done to the line was not so great as had been expected. Von Lettow-Vorbeck's strength, however, lay in the fact that at some time, if the railway was to be deemed safe, the British would have to advance across the parched country separating the two forces in order to dislodge him from the fertile slopes of Kilimanjaro. Until such time as the advance was made the initiative remained completely in his hands since he had already decided not to try to defend any of the remaining part of the interior of German East Africa, his main object being to keep his military force intact as a constant threat to British security.

Meanwhile, on September 1 the first Indian reinforcements reached Mombasa and in spite of the heavy demands made upon India in various theatres of war preparations went ahead for the creation of a second, larger force to attack Dar es Salaam. This plan had to be modified, however, in the light of the activities of von Lettow-Vorbeck's forces in the north. It was decided, therefore, to launch the first attack against the port of Tanga. This would bring the outlet of the Usambara railway into British hands, and at the same time a land force advancing round the western slopes of Mount Kilimanjaro would take von Lettow-Vorbeck's forces in the rear.

The action in Tanga was a complete failure for the landing force. The Indian troops had suffered severely from their voyage across the Indian ocean and were far from fighting fit. Furthermore, the element of surprise was lost owing to an attempt to negotiate the surrender of the town without bombardment since it was unprotected. This gave the Germans time to bring in two companies from the north who were able to resist a preliminary landing made on November 3. Early on November 4 the main force was landed but by then von Lettow-Vorbeck had poured reinforcements down the Usambara railway from Kilimanjaro and throughout the whole day hard fighting took place. Neither side was able to tell what was happening in the dense undergrowth but casualties among the attacking troops were very heavy and on the morning of November 5 the British force began to re-embark. The Germans had won an overwhelming victory, not only on account of the heavy casualties inflicted at relatively small loss to themselves but also because of the blow they had delivered to the morale of the British forces. Perhaps the most surprising event in the whole battle was a personal reconnaissance of Tanga township carried out on a bicycle by von Lettow-Vorbeck on the night of 4–5 November when neither side was sure of the other's movements. While the British were meeting with disaster in Tanga the troops advancing on von Lettow-Vorbeck's positions to the west of Kilimanjaro were also repelled in the neighbourhood of Longido Mountain so that the first large-scale offensive by the British forces was completely broken up.[1]

After the uncertainties of early August the campaign on the south-western border of Uganda, at the furthest extremity of the battlefield, had settled down into a series of patrol activities along the Kagera River. The withdrawal of administrative officers from outlying districts, and the threat of a German advance, had provided unruly elements with the opportunity to create trouble for which they had been looking for some time. Kigezi, where an administrative post had only recently been established and which itself bordered upon German territory, became an immediate source of trouble and the Chief Secretary authorized the officer-in-charge to withdraw if he thought fit. The German threat never materialized, however, and the position in Kigezi was gradually restored. Along the Kagera itself the Uganda police detachment struck the first blow on September 14, 1914, by seizing Kyaka Fort which dominated one of the crossings of the river some thirty miles from its mouth. The Germans were slow to bring up reinforcements but in November they launched a sharp attack on the fort which, although repulsed, induced the British forces to withdraw across the river to the north.

[1] P. von Lettow-Vorbeck: op. cit., pp. 35–48, and C. Hordern: op. cit. pp. 60–105.

The Germans followed up quickly and for a few weeks they menaced the south-western region of the British Protectorate. In December, however, they were driven back across the Kagera which from then onwards became a fairly static boundary across which patrol activity continued sporadically for nearly a year and a half. Henceforward Uganda was in no danger of invasion.

Foiled in their attack on Tanga by sea the British troops began preparations for an advance along the coast south of Mombasa towards the end of 1914. As a first step the small German town of Jassini, surrounded by its coconut and sisal plantations, was occupied as an outpost. In January, therefore, von Lettow-Vorbeck launched a counter-attack on Jassini hoping to induce the British forces to advance southwards to the support of their garrison before they had planned to do so, and then to ambush them en route. Von Lettow-Vorbeck's scheme was not wholly successful, but after hard fighting from the 17th to the 19th January four companies of Indian troops surrendered at Jassini and the threat of an advance on Tanga along the coast came to an end. Once again the Germans had scored an overwhelming moral victory, but on this occasion the loss in men and ammunition convinced von Lettow-Vorbeck that he must at all costs avoid such heavy encounters in future if he was to prolong the war as he wished to do. He therefore withdrew his forces to Kilimanjaro where supplies were still plentiful and where the troops could recover in the healthy climate.

The next twelve months resolved themselves into a period of guerrilla warfare in which the two most striking actions were carried out by naval forces and once again the actions were as widely dispersed as the fighting on land had been. On Lake Victoria no armed vessels existed before the war. The British possessed a flotilla of nine small steamers which had maintained a goods and passenger service between the Uganda Railway terminus at Kisumu and the principal ports on the lake. The Germans had only one vessel, the tug *Muansa* of forty tons. During the first fortnight of the war normal services were maintained by the British vessels but when it was reported that the *Muansa* was being armed it was decided to mount the only available gun, a saluting piece at Kisumu, on board the s.s. *William Mackinnon*. In January 1915 five of the ships on the lake were organized into a naval flotilla mustering a somewhat sketchy armament. During the rest of the year the flotilla bombarded various posts on the German shore and conveyed raiding parties which landed briefly at various strategic points. The most important action in the latter category was a large-scale raid carried out on Bukoba in June 1915, when the German station was briefly occupied and the fort and wireless station destroyed before the raiding force was re-embarked.[1] None of these actions was of particular military significance but they helped to maintain the morale of the British forces at a time when successes were rare in the skirmishing against the main German force in the Kilimanjaro area.

The Bukoba raid was followed by further good news from the Indian Ocean. On July 11, 1915, the German cruiser, *Königsberg*, was destroyed in the Rufiji River where it had taken refuge. The *Königsberg* had been in Dar es Salaam harbour just before the outbreak of war but had sailed away on July 31 to reappear off Zanzibar on September 20 where she took the British cruiser, *Pegasus*, by surprise and destroyed her. The *Königsberg* did no further damage but was lost to view until found in the Rufiji delta in October. Various attempts to destroy the vessel were unsuccessful until July 1915, when the British brought two shallow-draught gunboats armed with heavy guns to the river and these, assisted by four cruisers, launched a series of attacks which so damaged the German vessel that her severely wounded captain ordered the ship to be blown up. Ten 4.1-in. guns and two 3.5-in. guns were salvaged from the vessel, however, and in spite of their unsuitability for rapid movement proved of great value to the German forces in the subsequent campaigns.

The main front began to show signs of revival early in 1916. The problem faced by the British had been to supply adequate numbers of troops to make possible a large-scale advance into German territory. The demands of the holocaust in Europe made reinforcements from Britain impossible. South Africa was more promising because of the speedy and successful conclusion of the fighting in that area. The East Africa force which came into existence in November 1915, therefore, embraced all the troops already in East and Central Africa, African, Indian and British, together with further forces to be raised in South Africa. It was originally intended that the command of the new formation should be given to a South

[1] C. Hordern: op. cit., pp. 23–24 and 149–53, and A. Buchanan: *Three Years of War in East Africa*. John Murray, London, 1919, pp. 19–25.

African General but neither Botha nor Smuts was available owing to political problems at the Cape. The honour therefore fell to General Sir Horace Smith-Dorrien, a commander whose reputation was high both in Britain and South Africa owing to his generalship in the Boer War. Severe ill health forced him to resign his appointment before reaching East Africa, however, and the situation in South Africa being now more favourable it became possible to revert to the original plan. Lieutenant-General Smuts was appointed to succeed to the command and he landed in Mombasa on February 19, 1916. The South African contingent received the news of Smuts's appointment with mixed feelings. The Boers were delighted but the English South Africans were not so enthusiastic. The remainder of the East African force knew very little of Smuts's capabilities as a general although he was well known for his political achievements.[1] The new commander was therefore faced at once with the need to secure an important victory in order to win the confidence of his troops. Preparations for the big advance had already been made. An extension of the railway had been pushed forward from Voi in the direction of Taveta. In addition the road from Nairobi to Longido had been put into order so that troops could more readily skirt the western slopes of Kilimanjaro. Concentration areas had been prepared for the fresh troops expected from South Africa and by the time of Smuts's arrival a considerable force had been assembled ready for action.

Smuts's immediate plan aimed at defeating von Lettow-Vorbeck's forces in the Kilimanjaro area before the rains of mid 1916. To do this his main force would attack Taveta and then advance round the eastern slopes of the mountain while a large outflanking force would endeavour to push forward from Longido round the west of the mountain and cut off the Germans' retreat. The advance of the main force began in February and met heavy resistance. In March, however, when the main attack began to make headway the Germans were forced to withdraw. The outflanking force could not follow quickly enough to cut off the Germans' retreat and von Lettow-Vorbeck was able to rally his forces at Kahé. After further fighting he withdrew again across the Pangani River and although a South African force pressed on to Kondoa-Irangi to the south-west the

[1] C. P. Fendall: *The East African Force*, 1915–1919. H. F. and G. Witherby, London, 1921, pp. 39–59.

campaign was halted by heavy rains. Smuts's strategy had been sound but its execution had lacked drive.

Meanwhile events in the extreme west were beginning to threaten the German position along the Kagera. Throughout 1915 the Belgians had been looking for an opportunity to occupy some portion of German territory as a bargaining point in the event of peace. When the main attack was launched on the Kilimanjaro front von Lettow-Vorbeck could spare little thought and still less equipment for other fronts. In fact, he moved an appreciable force away from the Lake Kivu area in the west in order to be able to harass the South Africans in Kondoa-Irangi throughout the rainy season. On April 25, 1916, therefore, a Belgian force under Colonel Molitor crossed the German frontier and occupied Ruanda. This marked the beginning of the Belgian advance which was directed towards the south-western extremity of Lake Victoria with the object of cutting off the limited German forces west of the lake and preventing their retreat to the main base at Tabora. The plan which was put into effect at the end of May was not wholly successful, since the Belgian mesh was too great and the German forces were able to slip through. But the region west of the lake was quickly cleared and the British forces on the Kagera River also began their advance. In June an attack was made across the lake to seize Ukerewe Island, just north of Mwanza, while the fall of Mwanza itself in July marked the beginning of a change in British policy. Until the Belgians started to advance in April they had been repeatedly warned that the British were unlikely to take part in any considerable force in a combined offensive in the west. The successes of both British and Belgian forces in this area, however, convinced the British of the importance of maintaining the momentum of the advance upon the western section of the German Central Railway line. The capture of Mwanza, therefore, was followed by a southward advance from Lake Victoria.

Towards the end of May 1916 a further attack was launched against German territory, this time from the south-west. On November 12, 1915, Brigadier General E. Northey had been appointed commander of the combined forces on the Rhodesia–Nyasaland front of German East Africa. His role was intended to be a defensive one but Northey quickly came to the conclusion that the best way of ensuring the security of the border would be by fighting the Germans at every opportunity. Heavy rains early in 1916 gave him the respite he needed to organize his forces without molestation from the relatively weak German detachments opposing him. In May, therefore, and with the approval of Lieutenant-General Smuts, Northey's forces advanced into German territory and invested the German frontier posts. These were occupied with little difficulty and Northey then continued his advance to Neu Langenburg (later known as Tukuyu) which was captured on May 29. From there he was ordered to proceed in the direction of Iringa, 170 miles to the north-east, to cut off the retreat of the main German forces.

In spite of these diversions von Lettow-Vorbeck still conceived his main task to lie in the north. By mid May the rains had ended and Smuts's advance had recommenced. Von Lettow-Vorbeck had still no intention of being drawn into a decisive battle, however. Wherever the country gave him an opportunity to inflict casualties on the British forces with relatively little loss to himself he made a brief stand. But always when the pressure became too great he withdrew at nightfall and made good his escape. Smuts gave the retreating Germans little time to rest, pressing on by forced marches through thick bush country which tried the endurance of his troops and strained his ever-extending communications to the limit. The whole of the Usambara railway line was in British hands by June although there was some delay in bringing it into use owing to the damage which the retreating Germans had done to the vulnerable bridges and culverts. In any case the advance was too swift for the northern line to be of great importance to the British forces as a means of supply. By June 19 Handeni had been occupied and on August 28, after overcoming stubborn resistance at Turiani, the leading troops occupied Morogoro without any opposition. The Central Railway line was now cut. Misjudging the Germans' strategy, Smuts had expected von Lettow-Vorbeck to make his main stand in defence of the Central Railway and he had looked upon Morogoro, backed by the steep slopes of the Uluguru mountains, as the probable key point of the German defensive system. He was surprised, therefore, to meet no resistance, and when Tabora fell to the Belgian forces at the end of September he concluded that the campaign in East Africa was virtually at an end. He therefore pushed forward beyond the Uluguru Mountains in the hope of achieving a decisive victory. But his troops were exhausted. They had hoped for a rest when the Central Railway was captured and this further advance to the Mgeta River tested their endurance beyond its limits. By the end of September the advance had lost its momentum and heavy rains made communications through the Uluguru Mountains extremely difficult. A large proportion of the European and South African troops were therefore withdrawn to recuperate.

Farther to the south, Iringa was occupied at the end of August and Northey's forces swung southwards to take up a line along the Ruhuje River. This advance was of considerable importance because it deprived the Germans of valuable food-producing country so that Major Kraut's forces opposing Northey had to exert themselves to develop the resources of the fertile Mahenge area to the full. In October Kraut received surprise reinforcements when Major-General Wahle's patrols from the west linked up with him. Wahle had been placed in command of all the German forces in the west and had retreated before the British and Belgian advance to Tabora where he concentrated his forces. Recognizing the importance of the Mahenge region to von Lettow-Vorbeck's main body of troops retiring southwards, he decided that his own further withdrawal must be directed towards the control of the Mahenge area. From July he had been out of touch with the main body of German troops so that his arrival in the vicinity of the Ruhuje was as much a surprise to the Germans as it was to the British outposts which he took in the rear at a critical moment.

In the north every effort was made by the British forces to bring the Central Railway into action as soon as possible, but every bridge and culvert had been destroyed, although not as effectively as might have been expected, and there was little rolling stock available. Dar es Salaam, doubly important as the seat of German civil government and as the terminus of the Central Railway, was captured early in September, Tanga having fallen in July. For a time motor vehicles had to be adapted to run on the rails and act as tractors for the few vans which were available. With the capture of Tabora by the Belgians, however, more rolling stock became available, some of which was handed over to the British in exchange for spare parts of which they had a surplus. In due course, therefore, the railway became a main supply line for the advancing army.

Smuts was still dreaming of a final decisive engagement. Reinforcements of Nigerians and K.A.R. companies had arrived and he decided to advance to the Rufiji River at the end of the year.

The movement was planned once again as a frontal attack supported by an encircling movement, but after heavy fighting von Lettow-Vorbeck extracted his forces. The British were now across the Rufiji but the decisive campaign was still to be fought. Unfortunately this was not Smuts's interpretation of the situation. In January 1917 he handed over command to General Hoskins, his Chief of Staff, announcing that the East African campaign was at an end. Hoskins was thus placed in the difficult situation of taking command of an exhausted army with the main task of destroying von Lettow-Vorbeck's forces still to accomplish but with little likelihood of obtaining immediate reinforcements. To add to his troubles he was unable to weaken his garrisons along the Rufiji if he was to protect the newly-occupied territory from German counter-attacks. Throughout four months of torrential rain he had to maintain strong forces in unhealthy country with an almost insuperable supply problem created by the impassability of the roads in the rainy season while the strong currents of flood water made it equally difficult to send supplies along the rivers.

Von Lettow-Vorbeck had his difficulties too, although by ruthlessly cutting down his forces to the absolute minimum required to maintain battle efficiency and by employing considerable ingenuity in extemporizing food, clothing and medical stores he was able to keep his main force in being without any serious decline in its fighting strength. The vital stock of quinine was maintained by boiling Peruvian bark of which there was an adequate supply, the resulting vile-tasting liquid being known as Lettow schnapps. Bandages were also made from bark, and bread was made from every available type of grain improved by the addition of boiled rice. Experiments in shoemaking with the hides of game proved to be not as necessary as was at first expected since existing footwear could usually be patched up with leather taken from captured saddles. General Wahle, however, came to the conclusion that the supplies in his theatre were inadequate for the size of the force under his command. Two detachments led by Major Kraut and Captain Wintgens were therefore ordered to explore the resources of the mountains south of Songea. Kraut carried out Wahle's orders but attempts to capture British supply dumps along the lines of communication were unsuccessful and the harvest in the open country was not ripe so early in the year. Kraut, therefore, turned eastward and ultimately rejoined von Lettow-Vorbeck's main force. Wintgens in the meantime had decided upon an enterprising buccaneering expedition. Turning northward he hastened towards Tabora. Near the town he contracted typhus and was taken prisoner, but Captain Naumann took command and led his troops northward until they were finally forced to surrender in the neighbourhood of Kilimanjaro towards the end of 1917.[1] This original stroke created a lively diversion and drew the attention of a small section of the British and Belgian forces from their main task. In von Lettow-Vorbeck's opinion, however, the exploit served little real purpose and it weakened the main force for the vital struggle in the south-east.

In the difficult circumstances in which he now found himself von Lettow-Vorbeck had already been thinking about the Portuguese territory south of the Rovuma River. From chiefs who had crossed over into German territory he was able to gain some idea of the resources of the fertile region beyond the bare zone which extended for some days' march beyond the border. An expedition led by Major von Stuemer crossed the Rovuma south of Tunduru towards the end of 1916 and explored the banks of Lake Nyasa, sending back information which confirmed the reports of the fertility of the area. But von Lettow-Vorbeck had no intention of quitting German territory yet.[2] The British forces in the vicinity of the ports of Kilwa and Lindi, which they had captured in September 1916, were being steadily reinforced, and in May 1917 General van Deventer took over command from General Hoskins who had built up the army into an attacking force once again. In spite of being overwhelmed in numbers von Lettow-Vorbeck turned to face the threat from the east with considerable confidence. Although communications were still difficult owing to the heavy undergrowth, now that his forces were concentrated in one area, he was more directly in command of his troops than he had ever been at any other time in the campaign. From June the twofold advance from Kilwa and Lindi pushed on relentlessly. Against von Lettow-Vorbeck's seasoned troops and bold but skilful generalship British casualties were heavy and even the more intensive use of aircraft for bombing as well as for observation was not enough to overwhelm the Germans completely. Von Lettow-Vorbeck, on the other hand, could not

[1] P. von Lettow-Vorbeck: op. cit., pp. 188-9, 193-5.

[2] P. von Lettow-Vorbeck: op. cit., pp. 190-2.

afford the losses which the almost constant fighting made inevitable. Although the supplies of food were plentiful he was being compelled to fight more and more frequently as the British forces closed in upon his ever-shrinking position. In November, therefore, he began to withdraw up the Rovuma and on the 25th his advance-guard waded across the river on to Portuguese soil.

While the Germans were still some distance to the north the Portuguese had spoken confidently of being able to resist them, but when von Lettow-Vorbeck crossed the Rovuma their confidence ebbed rapidly. Appeals for assistance were made to Britain and since von Lettow-Vorbeck free might continue to be a danger the British Government decided that further action should not be limited to a defence of the Rovuma to prevent the Germans from recrossing. The Indian and Nigerian forces were withdrawn and the white regiments also were sent away, however, and the prosecution of the new campaign was left entirely to the K.A.R. The British Commander was convinced, though wrongly, that the move into Portuguese territory had been ultimately forced upon von Lettow-Vorbeck as much by lack of food as by military considerations and therefore expected him to try to return when the opportunity offered. In the meantime the best way to carry out instructions and destroy the German force was to attack with as strong an army as possible. It was useless to pursue the Germans across the barren waste of northern Portuguese territory, so bases were opened at Port Amelia and at Mozambique on the Indian Ocean. The plan was to form two lines running across the country from these two points and then to try to confine the enemy between them. But von Lettow-Vorbeck refused to be trapped and crossed the southern or Mozambique line with little difficulty.[1]

The pursuit continued southward through the early part of 1918 without ever resulting in a full-scale action. Reaching the outskirts of Quilimane von Lettow-Vorbeck turned suddenly northeastward, then westward and then northward again, and before the British forces had fully grasped the situation he was heading for the Rovuma with the pursuing columns either outdistanced or held off by rearguard actions. On September 28 he once more crossed the river. Fearing that the enemy would head rapidly northward the British quickly reinforced Mahenge and Iringa and

[1] C. P. Fendall: op. cit., pp. 121–2.

prepared to halt an advance on Tabora. But von Lettow-Vorbeck turned north-westward and then veered to the west and when news of the armistice was received he was well over the border into Northern Rhodesia. He was at once informed that the armistice terms included unconditional surrender of the German force in East Africa within a month, but this was subsequently found to be untrue. The correct wording stated that the German force was to be evacuated within the time mentioned. Von Lettow-Vorbeck emphasized the difference between the two expressions but agreed upon the inadvisability of allowing the askaris to return to their homes with their arms. He therefore used his influence to induce them to hand over their weapons and the force was then conducted to Tabora where the askaris were dismissed to their homes.

Von Lettow-Vorbeck had achieved his main object. With a relatively small fighting force he had occupied large numbers of African, Indian, Belgian and British troops for over four years, while the decisive war was being fought in Europe, the war which lost Germany her colonial empire. In so doing he had outwitted Smuts who believed the Germans had been fighting to defend their territory. It is true, however, that Smuts's attempts to encircle and destroy von Lettow's forces might have defeated the German commander's object if only the territory had not been so strongly in favour of the German's strategy of withdrawal and if only some of Smuts's forces had on occasion shown a little more determination. If the East African territories could have been declared neutral all von Lettow-Vorbeck's warlike instincts might have been nullified. Once war was declared the lines of the campaign were almost foredoomed, given a German Commander with von Lettow-Vorbeck's perception and determination. Any attempt simply to defend British territory would have left the initiative so completely to the Germans that both the British Protectorates would have been in the gravest danger. The only hope of an early British success rested in a much more decisive outflanking movement in March 1916 or in a similar manœuvre at the crossing of the Rufiji towards the end of the year. Von Lettow-Vorbeck had to be driven out of the Kilimanjaro area because his supply position there was so good that no amount of siege warfare would have forced him to withdraw. If, at the time of his first advance, Smuts had been able to infuse a more aggressive spirit into his outflanking force he might have been able to destroy the main German force instead of simply capturing a portion of the German territory. Similarly, if von Lettow-Vorbeck had had to cross the Rufiji under the fire of an outflanking force this, too, might have proved decisive. But at all times the supply and communication problem favoured the smaller force withdrawing on its own lines, and if Smuts played into von Lettow-Vorbeck's hands the German commander deserved some good fortune in reward for his own unquenchable spirit.

During the first years of the war the productive powers of German East Africa suffered very little, but external trade was brought to a standstill and the troops stationed in the Kilimanjaro area made heavy demands upon the food supplies of the district. When the British advance began in 1916, however, the situation changed rapidly. The German administrative system crumbled and the retreating army was forced to abandon the agricultural achievements of the years of peace. Stocks of rubber, cotton, sisal and coffee fell into British hands, together with hundreds of miles of territory, some of it cultivated but much of it barren. In March 1917 a Custodian of Enemy Property was appointed and in July of the same year his department absorbed that of the Controller of Enemy Merchandise. With the area north of the Central Line safely in British hands all the enemy property in the northern region was vested in the Custodian in May 1917. This officer had all the powers of a manager, collecting debts, selling off perishable goods and granting temporary leases of business premises and estates. The sisal estates were put out to public tender with the proviso that a tenant must clean and replant an area equal to that from which sisal was cut. The majority of potential British lessees were already employed in one way or another in the military forces, but there was a fair demand for leases from Greeks, and to some extent at least the output of the estates was maintained. The plantations of the central and southern regions were freed from military occupation only towards the end of the war and by that time they had in most cases fallen into serious neglect. Such produce as was available in this area was collected, but little could be done before the end of the war to restore the estates to order. The most effective policy for increasing production appeared to be to lease land for cotton growing for one season at a time and this plan did, in fact, yield fairly satisfactory results.[1]

[1] G. F. Sayers, ed.: *The Handbook of Tanganyika*. Macmillan, London, 1930, pp. 96–97.

Provision for the administration of captured German territory was of as makeshift a character as were the methods employed to handle the country's economy. A caretaker authority was established, using whatever sources happened to be available. When the British advance began a Chief Political Officer and four other senior officers had been seconded from the Government of British East Africa to accompany the military forces and to advise the army commanders in their dealings with the natives of German East Africa. But from March 1916 until almost the end of the year only martial law was in force in the captured areas. Meanwhile Mr. (later Sir Horace) Byatt, formerly Lieutenant-Governor and Chief Secretary of Malta, had been appointed Administrator of the Occupied Territory. As a result of Smuts's optimism it was widely believed that the campaign would have been brought to an end before Byatt ever set foot in East Africa. In the event he had to wait almost two years from the time of his arrival, in December 1916, before hostilities ceased. This period was not wasted. Late in December General Smuts delegated his powers to the Administrator in respect of the area north of the Central Railway and of a line continuing on from Tabora to Mwanza and thence along the southern border of the Bukoba District to the Kagera River. The Belgians, meanwhile, had taken over the administration of the provinces of Ruanda and Urundi and of Ujiji district and part of Ufipa. Such administrative officers, settlers and chiefs, as could with difficulty be spared from the two British Protectorates, whose resources of experienced officers were already strained to the limit, were then drafted into the occupied territory to try and restore some sort of order. German ordinances were frequently used to augment the Regulations for Peace and Good Order issued by the Administrator who, together with his small staff, spent much of his time studying the country and examining the copious German records in the hope of being able to formulate an administrative policy which could be adapted to the needs of the country when peace was restored.

The headquarters of the British civil administration was set up in Wilhelmstal, later renamed Lushoto, but accommodation was so restricted that some of the departments had to be quartered in Tanga. Dar es Salaam was too full of military headquarters for the civil authorities to find a place there. Even after January 21, 1918, when General van Deventer transferred the control of the rest of

German East Africa excluding the Songea and Lindi Districts to the civil administration, the township of Dar es Salaam was retained by the army because it was still full of troops. For a time the civil authorities thought of moving to Morogoro so as to be in closer touch with the area under their control and with the military commander, but on October 1, 1918, Dar es Salaam was at last handed over and the civil headquarters were transferred to the former German capital in February 1919.

One of the interesting features of the war had been the remarkable change which had taken place in the attitude of the British inhabitants of East Africa towards the German administration. At the outbreak of hostilities there had been little feeling of enmity towards the Germans who were looked upon as fellow-Europeans facing the task of introducing western civilization and economic prosperity into a new continent. Mainly as a result of events in Europe this feeling changed during the course of the war and the new attitude was reflected in the words of a resolution passed at a public meeting held in Kampala on September 28, 1918, which was attended by the leaders of all races in the Protectorate. It was none other than the Anglican Bishop of Uganda who proposed the resolution 'that it is the unanimous opinion of this public meeting of residents of Uganda that the territory hitherto known as German East Africa should not, under any circumstances, be returned to Germany.' This view was one which had been accepted in Europe some time earlier. In 1917 an unofficial approach had been made to Italy by the British Government suggesting that the Italians should take over the administration of the southern part of German East Africa which would have included the present Southern Province and parts of the Eastern and Southern Highlands Provinces. Britain's object was to avoid the reproach that she was anxious to profit from the war, but Italy regarded the offer as likely only to add an unnecessary burden to her own Government. In spite of further approaches she continued to reject the proposal, and when the same offer was made to the United States President Wilson also declined to accept since it was contrary to his political philosophy to add further territory to the American Empire.

It was General Smuts who finally urged that the administration of German East Africa should be taken over by Great Britain. Some, at least, of the motives underlying Smuts's proposal were revealed by the resolution he moved at Versailles in January 1919, to the effect that 'having regard to the record of German administration in the colonies formerly part of the German Empire, and to the menace which the possession by Germany of submarine bases in many parts of the world would necessarily constitute to the freedom and security of all nations, the Associated and Allied Powers are agreed that in no circumstances should any of the German colonies be restored to her'. After the long and bitter struggle which had been waged in Europe and other parts of the world, the victorious powers could scarcely be expected to regard Germany's defeat as a guarantee that she would never again create a problem. In the light of these fears the second part of Smuts's motion is wholly understandable, more especially since the German statesmen and officials had never hesitated to stress the military significance of overseas possessions. The criticism of German colonial administration contained in the first part of the resolution, however, was more the product of war-time feeling than an unbiased judgement as far as East Africa was concerned. It reflected the emotional temper of public opinion in Britain, the sort of attitude which led to the campaign to hang the Kaiser. As has already been shown in an earlier chapter,[1] it resulted in Charles Dundas being called upon to write a defamatory account of German administration in East Africa in order to satisfy the conscience of the British public in regard to the annexation of former German territory.

The European settlers in the British East Africa Protectorate felt no such pricks of conscience. The annexation of German East Africa would, in their view, be of the greatest importance in linking British East Africa with the British settlements to the south and would thereby promote the development of white leadership in the political and economic life of Eastern and Central Africa. A very high proportion of them had been engaged in the war and many of the Africans who would have worked on the European farms had been engaged in the carrier corps, so that agriculture had suffered heavily. This had meant a great sacrifice on the part of the settlers, many of whom had only just begun to prosper while many more had been interrupted by the war before they had got more than a foothold in the country. Even the Government's attempts to make some response to the settlers' demand for assistance in obtaining

[1] See page 177 above.

labour had produced poor results. An ordinance passed in May 1915, providing for the registration of all male Africans over the age of sixteen, could not be put into effect until the end of 1919 because of the lack of administrative staff. A second ordinance, introduced in October 1916, with the object of ensuring that any Africans living outside the reserves should have a regular contract to work with some European farmer, actually aroused a certain amount of criticism from the settlers who feared that it might limit their labour supply. Nevertheless, the settlers were prepared to undergo difficulties in what they believed to be a good cause and in the hope that their endeavours would meet with reasonable political recognition. The Convention of Associations went out of action during the war, to be revived only in 1918, but this did not mean that the settlers themselves were inactive in the political field. They continued their pressure for elective representation in the Legislative Council and were gratified to learn in October 1916 that the Colonial Office had accepted their claim in principle. In recognition of this concession the unofficial European community once again agreed to the nomination of members to the council in February 1917, and the nominated unofficials formed the majority on a committee appointed to consider the means to implement the elective principle.

The committee acted quickly. Its report was presented to the Legislative Council in May 1917, and was then forwarded to the Secretary of State. The European members of the committee had no intention of sharing the burden of responsibility for developing the country with the Asian population, nor did they consider that the African population was as yet in a position to take part in the work of the council. They recommended, therefore, that there should be ten European elected members and that Indian interests should be represented by two Indians to be nominated by the Governor, that Africans should be represented by the Chief Native Commissioner and that Arab interests should be represented by the Resident Magistrate in Mombasa. Only European adult males of unmixed descent would be allowed to vote, but upon them no further restrictions would be imposed save that of twelve months continuous residence in the territory. The question of votes for Indians and for women was not wholly ruled out but was left to be decided by the new legislature. The Secretary of State took some time to consider the committee's recommendations and in the meantime the settlers pressed for unofficial membership of the Executive Council. By the end of the war, however, no progress had been made towards either of the settlers' objectives. Although disappointed by the delay, the European unofficials were not discouraged from putting forward still further proposals for a more intimate participation in the political life of the country by European settlers. In 1918 they recommended that a finance committee should be appointed on which unofficials should sit so as to discuss the Protectorate's annual estimates as a step towards the control of finances by the Legislative Council and subsequently to the exertion of a more effective influence upon financial policy by non-civil servants.

In Uganda the wartime political climate was not so stormy as in Kenya, since the European unofficial community had never felt that its interests demanded such a prominent part in the country's political life as was called for by the European settlers in the neighbouring Protectorate. They were not as numerous as their neighbours, there was no serious clash either with the Asian population, which was mainly engaged in trade, or with the African population over rival claims for land, and at least until the end of the war the labour issue never reached boiling-point. Furthermore, although there were periods of crisis, and although the difficulty of exporting the country's produce created serious problems, Uganda's economy was not so badly hit by the war as that of the other two East African territories. This was mainly due to the fact that her wealth depended largely upon the crops grown by African peasants who were not so seriously affected by the war as were the European settlers upon whose efforts the East Africa Protectorate's economy was based. Unlike German East Africa, too, Uganda itself scarcely felt the effects of military conflict.

This is not to say that Uganda's problems were negligible. The British Cotton-Growing Association was gravely concerned lest the record cotton crop of 1914 should be followed by a period of discouragement due to export difficulties and the consequent unwillingness of traders to buy the cotton from the growers. The Association, therefore, evolved a scheme which aimed at obtaining the highest prices which the market offered for the cotton and this saved the situation for a time. In 1915, however, the prices offered were so low that many growers considered it a waste of time to carry their crop to the ginners. This crisis marked the lowest ebb in the cotton industry, however, and from 1916 there was a steady improvement. The planters also encountered difficulties caused by the demand for labour for the carrier corps, while other potential labourers were lost to them when they sought refuge from any obligation for military service by working for Baganda landowners. The labour shortage aroused some criticism of the Administration on the ground that little attention was paid to the legitimate problems of a planter population, and the view was strengthened in 1916 by the publication of a regulation requiring Africans with suitable land to grow at least a quarter of an acre of cotton. This meant that the incentive to work for planters for monetary reward would be greatly reduced. It was not, however, until the middle of 1918 that the situation became really serious. By that time many of the coffee trees planted some years earlier were at last beginning to bear and there was a danger that the best coffee crop so far achieved might be lost through lack of labourers to harvest it. On this occasion, however, the Governor and his administrative officers responded to the planters' appeal and everything possible was done to ensure an adequate labour force to gather the coffee.

In both the British Protectorates the war years witnessed important developments in the formulation of land policy, and in this connection the British Government intervened more directly in East African affairs than was its normal custom. The activities of the Carter Land Committee in Uganda and the demands of the European settlers in Kenya made it essential that some decision should be reached in both territories over the distribution of land between Africans and non-Africans. Experience in West Africa had clearly demonstrated that a policy of *laissez faire* might have serious repercussions. In the Gold Coast, chiefs holding land in trust for their tribes had made numerous concessions to Europeans looking for minerals, and in so doing had deprived the African population of land they urgently needed. In Southern Nigeria, where the quality of the soil was poor and had resulted in the practice of shifting cultivation by the African population, a complicated system of native land rights had been evolved with which the British Administration had been reluctant to interfere too actively. Northern Nigeria, however, was a less complicated field and thus provided an easier setting for the introduction of a policy of trusteeship which, after the experience of *laissez faire* in the Gold Coast, the British

Government was only too anxious to adopt elsewhere. In Northern Nigeria the fertile soil was capable of supporting a heavy population. Shifting cultivation was unnecessary. The Fulani Emirs who had conquered the land early in the nineteenth century had not seriously disturbed the customary system of land tenure. The Northern Nigeria Land Committee which reported in 1910 felt justified, therefore, in affirming that the ultimate ownership of the land, formerly vested in the chiefs, had been acquired by the British by right of conquest. The committee went on to recommend that rights so acquired should be used for the common benefit of the African population and in accordance with native custom. This declaration came to act as a pattern for British policy in the East African territories with suitable modifications where circumstances differed from those of Northern Nigeria. Even in the East Africa Protectorate, where the presence of a considerable number of European settlers introduced a new element, some attempt was made to assert the Nigerian principles. In 1915 the British Government succumbed to the demands of the settlers for greater security of tenure by extending leases of land from 99 years to 999 years. It is noteworthy, however, that the further transfer of land in freehold was simultaneously prohibited so that the Protectorate Government would be in a position to retain ultimate control. It was also stated that Crown Land would henceforward be held to include the native reserves. The object of the Imperial Government in adopting this interpretation was to protect the reserves against any encroachments by non-Africans. Unfortunately local circumstances made this policy unworkable. The boundaries of the reserves had never been gazetted and the Protectorate Administration found itself unable, for a number of reasons, to protect African lands against European expansion. Thus the good intentions of the Imperial Government appeared to the African population to be simply an attempt to deprive them of the last vestige of their right to the land they occupied.

The British Government's attempt to protect the land for the use of the African population had greater success in Uganda. The rejection by the Colonial Secretary of the Carter Committee's proposal to extend the Buganda system of private ownership to the rest of the Protectorate came as a shock to Europeans in Uganda, but much more startling was his proposal, made in 1916, that there should be a temporary suspension of all freehold transfer of land to non-Africans. It would seem that the Colonial Secretary's object was to try and formulate a scheme of leasehold, possibly similar to that introduced into the East Africa Protectorate, so as to put an end to the total alienation of land to non-Africans. His recommendation found little favour with either European officials or unofficials, however. It was argued that conditions in Northern Nigeria were utterly different from those existing in Uganda and that the British Government's caution was therefore unnecessary. There was no shortage of land in Uganda and the country badly needed the capital and experience of European planters to help its economy and to provide an example to African landowners of the most profitable ways in which to make use of their land. It was further pointed out that the Protectorate Administration, under existing legislation, was already able to exercise adequate control over the alienation both of Crown Land and of privately owned land, and that the main problem was not one of discouraging Europeans from taking up land but of providing an incentive to European planters which would rival the hitherto greater attractions of the neighbouring territory. During the war years, however, the issue was largely theoretical since no one was interested in acquiring land and it was only after the war that the problem was finally thrashed out.

The cessation of hostilities therefore found both the British Protectorates faced not only with the urgent problems attending the revival of their economy but also with a number of outstanding issues which involved not only the Protectorate authorities but also the British Government. The former German East Africa had virtually to begin all over again the task of constructing a territorial administration and an economic system, and it was to the British Government and to British enterprise that this task of re-creation fell.

CHAPTER EIGHT

POLITICS AND ADMINISTRATION, 1919–1939

WITH the return of peace a general reappraisal of the political and administrative problems of the East African territories was required. The territories were emerging from the pioneer stage into a new era in which more clearly defined policies would be required and in which, as a by-product of the recent struggle for survival and of the debate which followed upon the future of Germany's colonial possessions, the idea of responsibility for the well-being of the African peoples under their charge was being thrust upon the colonial powers. This did not mean that thoughts of African self-government were already abroad. In so far as the British Government thought in terms of self-government for the East African dependencies it did so only as a thing of the very remote future, and even then not necessarily as government entirely or even mainly by Africans. The theme of 1919 was the protection of the African population rather than the development of their potentialities. Indeed, in spite of the challenge offered by a new era of peace, there appeared to be no sense of urgency on the part of either the British Government or the East African Governments in regard to political or administrative innovations. The one call for urgent political action came from the European settlers in Kenya and their interest was confined to the desire that they themselves should play a more prominent part in the formation of policy in the Protectorate.

The part played by European settlers in the political life of Kenya during the war years had encouraged them to hope that self-government for the Protectorate, first called for by Lord Delamere in 1913, was now capable of realization. The new Governor, General Northey, who arrived in Nairobi in February 1919, had a distinguished war record in East Africa and was a popular appointment among the settlers. His first pronouncements, moreover, were reassuring to them and on February 24 an Electoral Representation Bill was introduced into the Legislative Council which envisaged a franchise limited to adult males of pure European descent. The bill reflected the settlers' own views on the development of a self-governing European colony, and an amendment moved during the second reading in April to extend the franchise so as to include every British subject possessing reasonable educational qualifications was defeated by thirteen votes to three. A further amendment aimed at securing for European women the same electoral rights as for European men was passed as a result of General Northey's casting vote after the Council had divided evenly on the issue. The bill received the Secretary of State's approval and in February 1920, the first elections were held to choose eleven Europeans to sit in the Council. Indian representation, meanwhile, was limited to one member nominated by the Governor.

The Europeans' success did not go unchallenged. The Indian community, already suffering from various economic disabilities arising from the country's land policy, were not prepared to suffer such an overwhelming political defeat without making any protest. Northey had discussed their position with the Secretary of State, Lord Milner, and on August 18, 1920, made the, to them, wholly inadequate offer that there should be two Indian elected representatives in the legislature. A mass meeting of protest was held in Nairobi on August 22 at which the Indians declined to take advantage of the concession. The one nominated member continued to sit until January 1921, when he resigned over yet another attack upon the position of Indians in Kenya society. This attack took the form of a Public Health Bill which had been given its first reading in November 1920 and which had originally contained proposals for racial segregation in the towns. A select committee, consisting of three elected members, three officials and one nominated member had subsequently recommended unanimously that the segregation clauses should be deleted but during the debate which followed in the Legislative Council the committee's recommendation was defeated by twenty votes to two. The decision of the Council was later reversed by the Secretary of State but there was no doubting the strength of feeling against the Indians which existed among the European settler community.

271

In an attempt to achieve some compromise General Northey himself presided over a conference between representatives of the Indians and the Convention of Associations in May 1921. The attempt proved to be unsuccessful and Lord Delamere founded his Reform Party with the intention of opposing the Indians' claims. Instead of the Indians' demand that there should be an adult franchise based on an educational qualification which would produce as many Indian as European elected members the Convention of Associations urged that there should be only two Indian members of the Council, both of whom should be nominated. The intensity of European settler feeling undoubtedly had its deepest roots in economic rivalry, but the Indians' persistence in claiming equal rights with the Europeans in the political field encouraged the conviction among European unofficials that to men of British descent alone should be entrusted the responsibility for protecting the interests of the African population. It is clear that, in the years which followed, this latter view was sincerely held by a large proportion of the European unofficial population in Kenya, although little attempt was made to define what were the true interests of the African population except in terms of the benefits they would derive from contact with Europeans and by their participation as labourers in European enterprises. Nevertheless, the manner in which European responsibility for the welfare of the African population was used as an instrument with which to attack Indian claims to political equality gave to the campaign an aroma of insincerity which brought little credit to its supporters. This very argument in favour of greater participation in the political affairs of the territory by European unofficials was itself to recoil upon the heads of its supporters and was to be used as the main justification for postponing the achievement of a self-governing colony dominated by Europeans. But in 1921 this fate was still two years ahead and in the meantime, although their views were not consulted, some of the African population were already learning lessons from the political tactics employed by the Europeans.

It was not until 1923 that the European settlers were firmly told that they could not look forward to the early achievement of responsible government, but in 1921 there were already signs that the departure of Lord Milner from the Colonial Office had removed from a position of authority one of the settlers' strongest supporters.

After consultations with Milner's successor, Winston Churchill, General Northey announced in October 1921 that he had arranged to appoint four Indians to the Legislative Council and one to the Executive Council. The new approach of Winston Churchill was reflected in an after-dinner speech which he made in January 1922, at an East Africa and Uganda dinner in London. It is not surprising that so proud a Briton as Churchill should have stressed his intention that Kenya should develop as a characteristically British colony with responsible self-government as the ultimate goal. At the same time he upheld the principle of equal rights for all civilized men and indicated that Africans and Indians who reached and conformed to British standards should not be denied the full exercise and enjoyment of civic and political rights.[1]

Encouraged by the views of the Colonial Secretary the Indian community agreed to accept the proposals announced by Northey in the previous October. It looked, too, as if further concessions would be made to Indian opinion when, after negotiations between the Colonial Office and the India Office, further proposals, later to be known as the Wood-Winterton Agreement, were transmitted to Kenya in the first week of September 1923. The main recommendation embodied in the agreement was that there should be a common electoral roll in Kenya for all British and British-protected subjects, male and female, of twenty-one years or over, who possessed certain qualifications which, it was hoped, would enable 10 per cent of the Indian population to vote. It was clearly stated that the qualifications should not be reduced to an unreasonably low level simply in order to achieve the desired percentage, while European voters already on the register would be admitted to the new roll even though they lacked the required qualifications. The official majority in the Legislative Council would be retained.

The Wood-Winterton proposals were never formally published, and their importance lay mainly in the evidence they supplied of the deep interest taken in East African affairs by an Indian Government which did not wish to add fuel to the fires of criticism already raging in India by watching in silence the unequal treatment of British Indians in other British dependencies. The non-publication of the proposals did not, however, prevent the European settlers from subjecting them to a heavy attack. These criticisms provided a

[1] *The Times*, January 28, 1922.

lively overture to the governorship of Sir Robert Coryndon who had moved to Kenya from Uganda to take over from General Northey who was recalled to Britain a few days before the Wood-Winterton proposals had become known in East Africa. They also gave the new Governor some indication of the relative political importance of the Convention of Associations and the Legislative Council for while the former was most active in its opposition to the new proposals the latter never even debated them. For the moment, therefore, the Indian campaign for greater political rights had received a sharp setback.

It was not long before the Convention of Associations in its turn suffered a serious blow to its political aspirations. The Indian question in Kenya in both its political and economic aspects reached such a stage in 1923 that it was thought necessary to send representatives from the different communities to discuss the matter with the United Kingdom Government. In the course of the discussions Lord Delamere, speaking on behalf of the European unofficials, overplayed the argument that it was important that African interests should be protected by Britishers alone. The progress of Southern Rhodesia towards responsible self-government had given Kenya's Europeans a greater feeling of confidence in their own cause but their hopes proved to be unfounded. British public opinion, recently disturbed by the labour policy adopted by the Kenya Government in response to unofficial pressure, was in no mood to surrender light-heartedly the control of African affairs to a handful of European settlers. In any case there were a number of factors which affected the decision over Southern Rhodesia but which could have no relevance in Kenya. In the first place the European population in Southern Rhodesia greatly exceeded that of Kenya. Secondly, the British South Africa Company had already, for a considerable period, exercised governmental authority in Southern Rhodesia so that the transfer of power to the unofficial European community was not so great a change as it would have been in Kenya where the European unofficial community had never exercised any political authority. The British Government, with the sympathetic Lord Milner at the Colonial Office, had been prepared in 1920 to recognize the importance of the European unofficial community to the extent of declaring Kenya to be a colony, but in the more critical temper of 1923 the settlers received nothing but a complete reverse. The Devonshire

White Paper of 1923[1] laid it down unequivocally that 'His Majesty's Government cannot but regard the grant of responsible self-government as out of the question within any period of time which need now be taken into consideration'. This was the greatest blow to the settlers' hopes but there was an added thrust in the further statement that 'In no responsible quarter is it suggested that the Indians in Kenya should not have elective representation upon the Legislative Council of the Colony.' Further, in a mood in which a sense of trusteeship and the desire for fair play joined to obscure practical issues, the White Paper also stated that African interests in Kenya must be paramount but that there would be no drastic reversal of the conditions under which Europeans and Indians had established themselves in the territory. The allocation of land alone made these hopes almost impossible of realization, while the more advanced state of the non-African communities placed the Africans at a serious disadvantage in every sphere. In the event, although the protection of the paramountcy of African interests was frequently quoted as Britain's policy in Kenya, the United Kingdom Government made no attempt to interfere in Kenya's policy.

If the settlers were temporarily stunned by the White Paper the Indian community was also dissatisfied. Their hopes of a common roll were dashed when they learned that the White Paper contained a suggestion for a communal franchise on a wide basis with provision for five elected Indian members and one elected Arab while the Europeans should continue to elect eleven members. In addition the Indians were offered elective representation on a communal basis on town councils. The communal franchise proved unacceptable to the Indians, however, and the Labour Government which briefly held office in Britain in 1924 agreed to the revival of the former practice of nominating Indian members to the Council.

The Devonshire White Paper, by its failure to satisfy the hopes of the Indian community, resulted in a decline in the political importance of Indian views in Kenya, a state of affairs which was accentuated by the fact that until 1926 Indians refused even to accept nomination to the Legislative Council. In 1927 one Indian contrived to get himself elected in accordance with the White Paper's proposals and took his place in the Council along with four other Indians who had been nominated. In the meantime the rival merits of common

[1] *Indians in Kenya.* Cmd. 1922, H.M.S.O., London, 1923.

roll elections with property and educational qualifications on the one hand and of a common roll with adult suffrage on the other were freely discussed. A White Paper issued by the United Kingdom Government in 1930[1] declared in favour of a common roll but before any action could be taken to implement this view a joint select committee of both Houses of Parliament, sitting in 1931, decided that the suggestion was impracticable at that time although it should not be lost sight of in the future. With these and other statements of opinion the issue of Indian participation in Kenya's politics faded steadily into the background, to be replaced by the increasingly important issue of the relations between the European and African populations to which the British Government's White Paper in 1923, with its insistence upon the paramountcy of African interests, had given a new and surprising point. From now on the main obstacle to the settlers' hope for responsible government was no longer the Indians' claim to equal representation in the legislature but the British Government's sense of trusteeship for the African population.

Another factor also caused the European settlers to view the future with some concern. This was the interest shown by the British Government in the later 1920s in the possibility of some form of closer union between the British East African dependencies. Although the primary object of such an association would be to strengthen East Africa's economic position, no very clear definition of what was intended was ever published and the European settlers saw themselves in danger of being swallowed up by the overwhelmingly African populations of Uganda and Tanganyika. This fear gave an edge to their argument for immediate constitutional changes in Kenya to protect and to strengthen their position. Meetings of European settlers from Kenya, Tanganyika, Nyasaland and Northern Rhodesia were held in 1925 and 1926 and called for some relaxation in imperial control. In the latter year the eleven European elected members of the Kenya Legislative Council were returned on a pledge to press for a European elected majority so as to defend their position against the possibility of Kenya's incorporation in an East African union.

The new Governor, Sir Edward Grigg, who took office in 1926, was well disposed towards the settlers' aspirations and indeed claimed a close friendship with the settler community. Grigg himself had

---

[1] *Statement of the Conclusions of His Majesty's Government as Regards Closer Union in East Africa; 1929–30.* Cmd. 3574, H.M.S.O., London, 1930.

been sent to Kenya with instructions from the Colonial Secretary, Mr. L. S. Amery, to try and bring about a closer association between the British East African territories. He did not consider that this need clash with the plans of the European unofficials in Kenya and when, in 1927, he submitted his first proposals for a federation to the Secretary of State he included a recommendation supporting the creation of an unofficial majority in the Kenya legislature which would consist of elected representatives of the European community together with other unofficials nominated to represent African interests. The British Government was not opposed to the idea of the immigrant communities in East Africa playing a part in the country's political development, but they made it clear when the Hilton Young Commission was appointed in 1927 to investigate the possibility of closer union that responsible government in Kenya was not contemplated. The Hilton Young Commission itself adopted a similar view. They recognized the right of the European community to effective representation in all matters affecting taxation and to protection against any measures which might fundamentally change the economic conditions on the basis of which they had settled in the country. They even went so far as to admit the Europeans' right of consultation on all questions of government. But they insisted that although the European community could claim partnership in the development of Kenya they could not assume the right to control its future. The report went on to say that until the African population was able to take part in a representative system, the Imperial Government as trustee must retain the right to intervene in all the business of government. Even looking still further ahead the task of protecting African interests appeared to the Commission to be the primary responsibility of the British Government, and the report frankly stated that in view of the differences in outlook which would continue to persist between Europeans and Africans the Imperial Government must permanently remain in a position to act as arbiter between the two communities.

If the hopes of the Europeans were disappointed it is clear that the Hilton Young Commission had certainly not begun to think ahead to the prospect of a self-governing Kenya dominated by Africans. Even the idea of full participation by the African people in the political affairs of the country appeared to be a matter of the remote future. The Imperial Government itself announced in 1930 that while recognizing that the goal of constitutional evolution in Kenya should be the achievement of responsible government with a ministry representing an electorate in which every section of the population had its rightful voice, there must be no important change for the time being. A measure of the absence of urgency felt in Britain regarding the need for African political activity was the Government's suggestion that the nominated representatives of African interests in the Kenya legislature should be increased from one to two, a proposal which was duly implemented in 1934.

The abandonment of the British Government's campaign for closer union in 1931 did not mean that all discussion of the topic in East Africa ceased immediately. Indeed, other considerations, more particularly the fear that Tanganyika might be handed back to Germany, resulted in a more friendly disposition towards the scheme becoming apparent in the 1930s. But with the absence of pressure from Britain Kenya politics began to lose their guerrilla character. Delamere's Reform Party had already declined in influence because it was seen to be dividing the European community. In the 1930s even the Convention of Associations, that symbol of European unofficial protest which had earned for itself the title of the Settlers' Parliament, also began to lose influence. In its hey-day it had considered legislation in the most minute detail before ever bills had been discussed by the legislature. It had claimed the right to summon government officials to its meetings to explain their policy. Its proceedings had been opened by the Governor who had used the occasion to make important statements of policy. These two latter privileges had ceased in 1927 and eleven years later the Convention itself met for the last time. European unofficial opinion began to find its outlet more regularly through the meetings of the Legislative Council. In 1935 there was a brief resurgence of the old resistance tactics when a vigilance committee was formed to oppose the introduction of an income tax. Even then, however, wiser counsels prevailed when it was recognized that unorthodox political action of that sort might set a bad example to the African population whose own political activities had begun to attract European attention. But the European unofficials did not readily lose an opportunity to promote their own political claims. Although rejecting unconstitutional action, the elected members of the Standing Finance Committee agreed in December 1936 to recommend the acceptance of a

278

small income tax on condition that consideration be given to the possibility of granting greater influence in the Executive Council to the European unofficial community. This proposal was accepted subject to the ultimate constitutional responsibility remaining with the Imperial Government.[1]

While the European political tactics undoubtedly acted as an example to the African population of Kenya it would be wrong to stress too heavily the importance of the form taken by European political activities in providing a pattern for African political expression. By the end of the First World War some of the African tribes of Kenya had already begun to recognize certain grievances, more particularly in connection with the European occupation of land, with European claims for African labour, with conditions of employment and with wages. The tribes most affected, the Kikuyu and the Kavirondo peoples, possessed no traditional form of central organization through which they could voice their discontent and it is not surprising that they did not turn to the chiefs and district officers, since both of these appeared to be instruments of the central government which was apparently responsible for the grievances which the people felt. That new associations should emerge to act as mouthpieces for the disgruntled tribesmen is not therefore surprising although the existence of the Convention of Associations might have acted as something of a prototype of the pressure group needed to influence Government policy. Nor is it surprising that the Africans' criticisms were directed immediately against the central government since there was nothing to act as a buffer between the peasants and that government. It is important, also, to note that in their early stages the African associations which grew up between the two wars were not political parties in the sense that they were striving to gain a place in the country's legislature. They were, more accurately, pressure groups which hoped to bring about a change in the Government's policy from outside.

The first African association, the Kikuyu Association, which was founded in 1920 did not, in the long run, fit into the pattern described. Its leading members were chiefs, trusted by the Government, moderate in outlook and loyal to the Government during the disturbed years which followed. Indeed, although the association was formed with the object of voicing some of the grievances of the

[1] Lord Hailey: *An African Survey.* O.U.P., 1938, p. 169.

Kikuyu, it came in time to act as something of an insulator between the central government and the more violent criticisms of the tribe. That it was the Kikuyu who took the lead in voicing the protests of the African population was only to be expected, since they were the tribe most closely affected by European contact with Kenya. The central government was at their doorstep. A certain amount of land formerly occupied by Kikuyu was now inhabited by European settlers. The Kikuyu supplied a considerable proportion of the labour force on European farms and they had seen the lively political activities which went on in Nairobi. Missionary societies had been active among them and education, if not of a very advanced character, was relatively widespread. It was among the Kikuyu, therefore, that the next pressure group also emerged.

The Young Kikuyu Association founded by a government telephone operator, Harry Thuku, in 1921, was very different in character from its predecessor. The immediate cause of its formation was the proposed reduction in Africans' wages moved by the settlers as a result of the currency changes which took place in 1921 and the fall in the world prices for primary commodities. Its failure to co-operate with the already existing Kikuyu Association was partly due to the lack of confidence in a group dominated by chiefs appointed by the Government but perhaps even more to the absence of any natural association in matters of importance between different age-sets in the tribe. As the name of the new association suggests, its membership consisted of young men, educated, for the greater part, in mission schools, while the chiefs were generally older men. The views of the association were published in an Indian-owned Nairobi newspaper[1] and a missionary, Mr. A. R. Barlow, who was an excellent Kikuyu scholar, assisted by translating the complaints of the association into English.[2] The association itself achieved prominence as a result of a public meeting summoned at Dagoretti on June 24, 1921, in response to its memorandum containing the grievances of the tribe which had been submitted to the Acting Chief Native Commissioner. For the first time a group of young men had stepped over the heads of the chiefs to put the case of the people before the Government. Thuku even went further and sent cables

[1] G. Bennet: 'The Development of Political Organisations in Kenya.' *Political Studies*, Vol. V, No. 2, June 1957, p. 119.

[2] W. McGregor Ross: *Kenya from Within*. Allen and Unwin, London, 1927, p. 224.

to the British Government. Not unnaturally these actions were resented by the elders of the tribe who disliked the interference of the young men in affairs traditionally held to be the responsibility of older men. The Kikuyu Association openly denounced Thuku's telegrams,[1] but Thuku himself only became more outspokenly critical of the Government. He toured the Fort Hall district and then attempted to extend the limits of his association beyond the confines of the Kikuyu tribe by addressing large gatherings of Africans in Kavirondo. He was arrested in March 1922 and deported to Kismayu, and his embryo movement collapsed.

In Kavirondo, however, the work begun by Thuku was taken up and directed into officially acceptable channels by Archdeacon Owen of the Church Missionary Society. Recognizing the dangers inherent in the sort of critical pressure group organized by Thuku, Owen tried to ensure that the views of the people of Kavirondo should be openly expressed in an orderly fashion. In 1923 he was successful in converting the Young Kavirondo Association, which had already begun to attract adverse criticisms from the Government, into the Kavirondo Taxpayers' Welfare Association and became the association's first president. By these means he was able to encourage an informed local interest in taxation, in the allocation of public funds, in child-welfare and in improved housing and simple hygiene. Government officials were impressed by the work of the association and on one occasion a meeting was attended by the local European elected member of the Legislative Council.

This promising beginning was soon to be marred by local divisions of loyalty. Tribal differences made it necessary to split the association into Luo and Bantu branches in 1923, while religious divisions resulted in the formation of a Native Catholic Union which demanded special Catholic representation on the local native council and a Luo paramount chief. Before long the Catholic Union itself split into Bantu and Luo sections. Owen's influence, however, was not wholly lost and although in time he came into conflict with the Government over the right of the K.T.W.A. to discuss political issues, the note of restraint which he was able to introduce into Kavirondo politics was in sharp contrast to the more heated developments among the Kikuyu.[2]

[1] *The Leader of British East Africa*, August 6, 1921.

[2] G. Bennett: op. cit., pp. 121–2.

281

After the arrest of Harry Thuku there was a short break in the activities of the Young Kikuyu Association, which then re-emerged as the Kikuyu Central Association, drawing attention to itself for the first time in 1925 when its members petitioned the Government on a number of issues. The first request was that Africans should be allowed to grow coffee, the second was for the institution of a Kikuyu paramount chief, and other requests included the publication of the colony's laws in Kikuyu and the release of Harry Thuku. Described by the Chief Native Commissioner as 'An indeterminate collection of malcontents with no constitution, no representative authority and no constructive programme of reform',[1] the K.C.A. undoubtedly won greater attention from the Kikuyu owing to the ferment among the tribe in 1925 arising out of the transfer of authority from one age-set to another. This traditional process, which took place about every twenty years, provided the K.C.A., consisting mainly of young men, with an opportunity to emerge into the forefront of local politics. While continuing to press for the reforms mentioned in their petition the members of the Association extended their field by asking for three African representative members in the Legislative Council. In making this claim they were not only many steps ahead of the Government of the colony but also in advance of their own people. When, however, they took up arms against a Church of Scotland mission pronouncement that its supporters should have nothing to do with female circumcision they were able to gain considerable support from Kikuyu of all ages. As an indication of their resentment at what they regarded as unwarranted interference in their tribal practices the Kikuyu began to organize more frequent dances of a traditional character in the reserves and among those taking part were a number of former Christians and Church members. The Government claimed that the dances were indecent in character and were being used for political propaganda and so prohibited them on December 17, 1929.[2]

Official concern at the activities of the K.C.A. had already been reflected in the Governor's speech at the opening of the Legislative Council in October, when he had warned agitators against any attempt to undermine constitutional authority. In January 1930 the Convention of Associations entered the field

[1] *Kenya Colony: Native Affairs Department Annual Report for 1925.* Government Printer, Nairobi, 1926, p. 2.

[2] *East African Standard*, January 9, 1930.

with three resolutions attacking compulsory female circumcision and urging the setting up of a committee to investigate the problem of African unrest.[1] The K.C.A. responded by firmly repudiating the suggestion that seditious tendencies existed anywhere in Kenya and declared that it would welcome any inquiry into the alleged unrest. It added that compulsory circumcision formed no part of the association's campaign.[2] In an endeavour to seize the initiative and to win support from outside Kenya the association sent its secretary, Mr. Johnstone (later Jomo) Kenyatta to England to present the case over African taxation. English interest in events in Kenya was indeed awakening. A Labour member of Parliament, Mr. A. McElwee, asked the Under-Secretary of State if steps could be taken to restrain the Governor of Kenya from preventing the Kikuyu from giving their allegiance to the Kikuyu Central Association and from collecting money without permission.[3] The United Kingdom Government was not prepared to intervene light-heartedly in the affairs of Kenya, however, and in reply to another question asked by another Labour member on April 3, 1930, about the prohibition of dances and songs in Kikuyu Dr. Drummond Shiels, Under-Secretary for the Colonies, announced that the Kenya Government would be supported in taking any proper steps, consistent with legitimate freedom of speech, to maintain public order and decency.[4] Nevertheless, it was mainly due to prolonged pressure from England that Harry Thuku was allowed to return from deportation in 1930. In 1932 he was elected President of the K.C.A., defeating the previous President, Mr. Joseph Kangethe. But the association was soon in the throes of internal disagreement and it split into two groups. In 1935 Thuku himself founded the Kikuyu Provincial Association as an indication of the division which was appearing between him and the younger, more extreme members of the K.C.A. with whom, as he grew older, he found it increasingly difficult to associate.

Although the Kikuyu Central Association was the most prominent and most active among the political pressure groups in Kenya, personal ambitions and local interests encouraged the development

[1] *East African Standard*, January 30, 1930.

[2] ibid., January 31, 1930.

[3] ibid., March 8, 1930.

[4] Parliamentary Debates.

of a number of other associations. Even the K.C.A. itself gained little support outside the Kikuyu tribe in spite of attempts to invite the co-operation of other tribes. Among the Kikuyu the former Kikuyu Association continued to flourish and in 1931 changed its name to the Kikuyu Loyal Patriots to emphasize its members' support for the Central Government. The main if not the sole interest of this association was the question of land for the tribe, and under the leadership of Chief Koinange and a number of other chiefs and headmen it resisted the more radical demands of the rival K.C.A. The Progressive Kikuyu Party, formed in 1928, was another association with a moderate outlook and supported the Church of Scotland views on female circumcision. Its supporters, few in number, were limited to the Nyeri District. In Kavirondo a North Kavirondo Central Association was founded in 1934, modelled on the K.C.A. Its demand for a paramount chief, however, emphasized its tribal character. Meanwhile, the Kavirondo Taxpayers' Welfare Association had become an increasingly Luo group and the non-Luo had been absorbed in the North Kavirondo Taxpayers' Association. All these societies claimed African representation in the Legislative Council and asked for better educational facilities and better treatment for Africans in regard to land.

One of the more significant aspects of the development of political parties in Kenya was their tendency to break away from the missions. This led to the formation of a number of independent churches. One particularly fanatical group, calling itself the *Watu wa Mungu* (the People of God) was known to have existed as early as 1931. Its members lived like ascetics and at times believed themselves to be possessed by spirits. Believing the Europeans to be out of sympathy with the needs of the African population they rejected all things of Western origin. They spread misconceptions to the effect that aeroplanes were the cause of drought and locust invasions and they may have been responsible for an epidemic of housebreaking and for an attack with bows and arrows against a force of police in the Ndarugu Forest in February, 1934.[1]

As a result of the break with the missions a number of independent schools were founded. Conscious of the power of education, yet resenting the discipline imposed by the missionary schools, the Kikuyu political leaders established the Kikuyu Independent Schools

[1] *Tanganyika Standard*, February 22, 1934.

Association and its offshoot in Kiambu, the Karinga Schools Association, to make provision for themselves. These schools inevitably became the breeding ground for the ideas upon which future political parties were to thrive.

In spite of the strength of the political movements among the Kikuyu and in Kavirondo the Kenya Government persisted in regarding most of these movements as being unrepresentative of general feeling. They looked to the local councils for a true reflection of public sentiment, loyally supporting the chiefs whom the Government itself had created. Any associations which tried to work outside the councils were dismissed as consisting solely of dissident elements. The Kikuyu chiefs made a genuine attempt to encourage the younger men to associate themselves with the native councils in spite of the difficulties involved in mixing age-sets. But the young men wanted to move more quickly than their elders so that accommodation appeared to be impossible. Throughout the inter-war years, therefore, political development among the Africans of Kenya was forced into channels of permanent opposition to established authority, whether that authority was the European Government or the elders who appeared to the younger men to be the tools of the European Government.

Compared with the political upheavals which accompanied the development of Kenya's Legislative Council between the wars, the Legislative Council in Uganda came into being relatively unobtrusively. This was mainly due to the fact that the handful of Europeans living in Uganda who were not civil servants took little interest in political affairs. They were not settlers and they did not feel any obligation to look too far into the future. They did not expect that their sons would inherit property in the Protectorate. There was no clash between them and the Asian population over the use of land since Asians only began to show an interest in obtaining land in the mid 1920s when the Europeans were, in many cases, anxious to sell their holdings. In trading circles Europeans and Asians worked side by side without having to indulge in severe competition for business. Both races were represented in the Uganda Chamber of Commerce. Yet even in these favourable circumstances some echoes of Kenya were heard in Uganda and for a time the Indians feared that the Government was trying to place them in an inferior position compared with the European community although this period of doubt did not result in any hostility developing between the Indian community and the European unofficial community.

The first public reference to the establishment of a Legislative Council in Uganda had an almost casual note. On July 18, 1919, the secretary to the Kampala Chamber of Commerce addressed a letter to the Chief Secretary asking if any proposals had been made for the creation of a Legislative or Advisory Council. Sir William Morris Carter, the Deputy Governor, was an enthusiastic supporter of the proposal. Ever anxious to encourage European settlement in Uganda he saw in the creation of a legislative council a further means of assisting relations between the Administration and the community of European unofficials. He believed, moreover, that the prestige of the Protectorate now demanded a constitutional advance of this sort. The Governor, Sir Robert Coryndon, shared his views, and when the Chief Secretary received a similar request from the Uganda Planters' Association in September he was able to reply with some satisfaction that the subject was already receiving consideration. Two months later, in November, the Secretary of State, Lord Milner, announced his acceptance of the idea in principle, for Milner, like Coryndon and Carter, was anxious to assist the Europeans in East Africa.

The Order in Council providing for the establishment of an Executive and a Legislative Council was received in June 1920. It contained no restrictions upon the number of official or unofficial members of either council and after toying with various proposals Coryndon concluded that it would be advisable to start with only a small membership in each council. As far as the Executive Council was concerned he thought the country too small to admit of unofficial membership. He decided, therefore, that it should consist of the Chief Secretary, the Attorney General, the Treasurer and the Principal Medical Officer. The same four officials would then represent the Government in the Legislative Council and, since an official majority was necessary at that stage of development, there would be only three unofficial members.

It was the question of who should sit as unofficials which aroused the first misgivings among the Indian population. Coryndon's original intention was to nominate a representative of the European planters and one European business man and to ask the Kampala Indian Association to put forward three names from which he would select one. In this way he sought to include representatives of the three groups chiefly involved in the country's economic life. The African population, who through their participation in cotton-growing contributed most to the country's wealth, were not yet deemed ready to take part in the Legislature. Coryndon's proposal failed owing to the difficulty of selecting a member to represent the planters. He therefore abandoned the original scheme and simply invited two Kampala business men, Dr. H. H. Hunter and Mr. H. E. Levis to accept nomination. Meanwhile, however, the Indian Association had protested against the allocation of only one seat to the Asian population. If planters and business men were to be represented, how much more necessary it was to represent the different branches of the Indian community, they argued. The Shia Ismailis, an important group, would scarcely regard themselves as being represented by a member of the Kampala Indian Association. These reasonable grounds for extending Indian representation were quickly lost sight of, however, in the dispute which soon sprang up over the broader issue as to whether or not the Indian community should have equal representation with the unofficial Europeans.

Undoubtedly, events in Kenya were casting their shadow over the affairs of Uganda. Many of the Indians in Uganda had relations in the neighbouring territory and the friendship existing between Europeans and Asians in Uganda scarcely seemed to them adequate protection against the apparently unlimited demands of the Europeans in Kenya. In September 1920 the Indian Association appealed to the Secretary of State. Sir Robert Coryndon, who had little sympathy with the Indian community, opposed their claims. Lord Milner, who usually acted on the advice of his senior officials in Uganda, supported Coryndon's view, authorizing the Governor to inaugurate the Council if necessary without any Indian representative. The Legislative Council therefore assembled for the first time on April 23, 1921, with only six members in addition to the Governor who took the chair.

Two days earlier, a section of the African population demonstrated their interest in the new Council for the first time when the Kabaka and ministers of Buganda inquired of the Governor as to whether the establishment of a Legislative Council would in any way affect the 1900 Agreement. They were assured that the Agreement would neither be prejudiced nor interfered with and there was no further question raised. Indeed, the leading figures in Buganda took no further interest in the legislature. Their attitude was clearly explained by the Treasurer of the Buganda Government, Mr. Serwano Kulubya, in his evidence before the Joint Select Committee on Closer Union ten years later. In reply to a question by Lord Ponsonby, Kulubya said, 'We would like to follow our own constitution ... If we get a representative on the Legislative Council, it is quite possible, say, with one representative or two representatives, that we will be outvoted there by the majority, and when we have been outvoted in that way, it will be very difficult for us to reopen the questions, because we have got our representative there; so if you leave it as it is, we have got every chance of complaining on anything which may be passed by the Legislative Council, and we can always approach the Secretary of State if nothing is allowed.'[1] Clearly, the leaders of the Baganda recognized the strong position in which they stood so long as they abided by the terms of the 1900 Agreement, and they had no desire to weaken that position by encouraging the absorption of Buganda in the political life of the Protectorate as a whole. The remainder of the Baganda, although probably unable to appreciate the motives which influenced their leaders' actions, continued to regard the Kabaka as their sovereign and the Lukiko as the focus of Buganda's political life. Outside Buganda the creation of a Legislative Council made no impact upon the African population who, for the most part, thought of the Protectorate Government only in terms of the local district officer.

In Uganda the grievances which aroused the African population of parts of Kenya were virtually non-existent. The only land issue of any importance affecting the Africans was that arising from the 1900 Buganda Agreement. Just as immediately after the First World War the Kikuyu had begun to recognize the permanent nature of the arrangements by which Europeans had occupied land in Kiambu so, too, in Buganda those who had not benefited from the *mailo* settlement were beginning to realize that a revolution had taken place in which others had emerged as the victors. Gradually it was borne in upon the rather better educated Baganda that land was no longer a temporary reward for the work done by the chiefs but instead belonged to individual families, to be handed down from father to son. Hence there was some criticism of the chiefs

[1] Joint Select Committee on Closer Union in East Africa, *Report and Minutes of Evidence: 1930–31*. Vol. 2, H.M.S.O., London, 1931. Minute 5935.

as landowners and of the Lukiko as the council in which the chiefs were able to exercise such great influence. But the criticism did not extend to the Protectorate Government. It was a division among the Baganda themselves and one which was to influence Kiganda political affairs for the next forty years. Those who had failed to benefit from the 1900 Agreement tried increasingly to seize power from those who had benefited from the Agreement. But the power they tried to seize was power in the Lukiko and in the hierarchy of chiefs at the head of which the Lukiko stood. It was not until after the Second World War that participation in Protectorate politics was recognized as a possible means to circumvent the power of the Kiganda hierarchy. The nearest approach to a political party in Uganda was, in fact, a group calling themselves the Young Baganda Association. These young men, less than a score in number and all of them sons of chiefs, adopted a policy of enlightened self-interest. Deploring the differences, religious and otherwise, which divided their elders and at the same time helped to justify their critics, they endeavoured to show how young men of intelligence could co-operate in spite of conflicting philosophies. Their hopes were not realized, however. Within a few months of the association's appearance on the Buganda scene the members split sharply into Protestant and Catholic factions because of a disagreement over the Catholic candidate for the post of Chief Justice in Buganda. The opponents of the association, the critics of the hereditary nature of land ownership, never organized themselves into a party although a newspaper, *Sekanyolya*, published in Nairobi in Luganda, frequently expressed their views. This preoccupation of the Baganda with their internal disputes was in marked contrast to the outlook of the Kikuyu and the fact that Uganda's largest tribe, and the one in the midst of which the Protectorate Government had its headquarters, caused relatively few difficulties for the British authorities, was an important factor in the contrasting development of relations between the African population and the territorial governments in Uganda and Kenya.

Meanwhile, however, the Indian communities remained dissatisfied with their political position. At the end of March 1921 their cause was taken up by the Viceroy of India who was disturbed lest racial disputes should spread from Kenya to her neighbour. The Secretary of State for the Colonies, Winston Churchill, supported the existing constitutional arrangements in Uganda, however, and in May the

Secretary of State for India decided to advise the Uganda Indians to co-operate in the work of the Legislative Council without prejudice to the further consideration of the number of Indian representatives. In June the Kampala Indian Association made a last gesture when they suggested the preparation of a common register of voters with a franchise based upon educational and property qualifications. The proposal was not accepted and for the time being the issue ceased to attract any considerable attention. Throughout the discussions the Kampala Indian Association had acted as the leading spokesman and the Ismaili community had refused to co-operate in the claim for increased Asian representation. In general, however, the division between different Indian factions was not so marked as over this particular problem, all the Indian communities working well together. Relations between European unofficials and Indians had also remained friendly and the only evidence of racial animosity came from a surprising quarter. On July 1, 1921, the newspaper *Sekanyolya* published an attack on the Indians in Uganda. The Secretary of the Kampala Indian Association appealed to the President of the Young Baganda Association and the latter group dissociated itself entirely from the critical sentiments expressed in the Press. A letter to the *Uganda Herald*, from a Muganda living in Nairobi, then accused the Indians of exploiting the African population, and a further letter from the Editor of *Sekanyolya* charged the Young Baganda with entertaining feelings of jealousy towards his newspaper and added that *Sekanyolya* was far more representative of Kiganda opinion than was the Young Baganda Association. This brief incident was quickly closed and was probably more indicative of the divisions among the Baganda than of any organized hostility towards the Indian population generally.

In recognition of the importance of agriculture and education in the Protectorate the heads of the Government departments dealing with those two branches of administration became members of the Legislative Council in July 1925. There was no addition to the unofficial membership of the Council to balance this increase on the official side. Soon after his arrival in the country in 1925, however, Mr. W. F. (later Sir William) Gowers set himself the task of settling the issue of Indian representation. His first plan was to revive the theory of the representation of interests in the Council, believing that the Indians' leader, Mr. C. J. Amin, would be more willing to co-operate on the basis of the representation of interests rather than of races. This approach was abandoned, however, in favour of the concept that unofficial members were selected for their individual qualities. No change had in fact been made since 1921, but Gowers's conciliatory attitude impressed the Indians who agreed to accept a seat in the Council and Amin himself was appointed in March 1926.

Still the Indians continued to press for equality with European unofficials, and in 1929 refused for a time to nominate any successor to Amin on the conclusion of the latter's period of office. Gowers argued that since there was, in any case, an official majority in the Council, equality of representation among the unofficial members was politically meaningless. But the Indians' pride was involved. They readily agreed that they had suffered no inconvenience from the existing constitutional arrangement but this did not satisfy their feelings. When Gowers was succeeded by Sir Bernard Bourdillon in 1933 the Indians immediately submitted a memorandum claiming equal representation. There seemed little point in resisting further and on the advice of his Executive Council Bourdillon agreed to increase the number of unofficial members by one. He insisted, however, that all the unofficial members were chosen to represent the whole Protectorate, but in practice it was tacitly acknowledged that the additional member should be an Indian. In June, therefore, Mr. S. H. Shah joined Amin on the unofficial side of the Council. Indian pride was assuaged and there was no further criticism of the constitution of the Legislative Council from that quarter.

The Council, however, remained remote from the life of the Protectorate. Sitting at Entebbe it was insulated from the vigour of Kampala's commercial life and the African population also continued to show little interest in its activities. The unofficial members themselves felt at times that the Government paid scant attention to their existence. In 1931, and again in 1932, Dr. H. H. Hunter complained that the country's estimates had been presented to the unofficial members on the very eve of the budget debate, leaving no time for careful consideration. Yet Hunter himself was opposed to the election of unofficial members lest such a scheme should disturb the delicate situation regarding racial representation. The Legislative Council, then, pursued its course until the mid 1940s without any further change.

In Tanganyika, the name adopted for the former German East African dependency, political and constitutional developments were delayed until the results of the deliberations of the victorious powers became known. In the meantime the administration of the territory remained in the hands of the British and Belgians, and on January 31, 1919, Sir Horace Byatt became Civil Administrator of the whole of the territory occupied by British troops. Byatt was a man of prudent disposition, not at all disturbed by the delay in determining Tanganyika's future. He considered it unwise to embark upon large-scale plans for the revival of administration or of the country's economy until the African population had had some little time in which to recover from the blows they had sustained during the war. Although the pattern of Tanganyika's future government began to emerge at a fairly early stage in the peace discussions, Byatt professed to be unable to take any decisive steps until he had received clear instructions as to Britain's status in regard to the territory.

The application of the mandatory system to Germany's former possessions in Africa was an extension of a plan originally drafted to deal with the problems of Europe and the Middle East. The annexation of conquered territory by the allied powers threatened to create new frontiers along which they would clash with the defeated countries of central Europe. The object of the mandatory system, therefore, was to set up buffer states which would, as soon as possible, become independent and where this would have to be delayed for some years the countries themselves would be placed under the general supervision only of one of the victorious nations. The transposition of the scheme to Africa was a not unnatural development in the light of the history of colonial activity in Africa during the preceding generation. The question of avoiding border clashes between the imperial powers had been a constant problem and one which both the Berlin and Brussels Conferences had attempted to overcome, and one, too, which the powers themselves had endeavoured to manage by means of bilateral treaties. In May 1917 the British Foreign Secretary, Mr. Balfour, had suggested to the American Ambassador that Germany's captured dependencies might be internationalized, and the Foreign Office took up and developed this theme eighteen months later, urging the establishment of a system of mandates for the more backward territories captured from Germany, including those in tropical Africa. President Wilson shortly afterwards recommended that the German colonies should become the property of the League of Nations so that the American draft of the League of Nations Covenant also came to contain a proposal for a system of mandates in Africa. When the Covenant itself was published it was seen to contain proposals to set up three types of mandate depending upon the stage of development reached by the countries concerned. Tanganyika was classed as a B mandate, that is as a territory in which some mandatory authority must be responsible for the administration. The actual task of drafting and allocating the mandates fell to the Supreme Council of the Great Powers since the League of Nations had not yet come into being. Nevertheless, the powers themselves intended to transfer responsibility for the supervision of the mandates to the League of Nations as soon as possible.

Although the League came into existence in January 1920, a series of delays resulted in the publication of the terms of the B mandates being held up until July 1922. In the meantime the first step towards the establishment of British administration in Tanganyika had been taken by the publication of the Tanganyika Order in Council of July 22, 1920.[1] Under the terms of the Order the title of Administrator was changed to that of Governor and Commander-in-Chief and the holder of the office, with the advice of an Executive Council, was empowered to make ordinances for the good government of the country. In addition, a High Court was established which possessed full criminal and civil jurisdiction over all persons in the territory. To all intents and purposes, therefore, British mandatory control in East Africa began in 1920 and the publication of the terms of the mandate had little effect on policy. The Great Powers had no intention of defining too rigidly the manner in which the mandatory authorities conducted the administration of the mandated territories, and even the machinery established to supervise the mandates was of a sort which could not interfere directly in the affairs of the dependent territories. The mandatory powers were simply required to submit to the Permanent Mandates Commission an annual report in the form of answers to a questionnaire. The Commission, which consisted of members acting in their personal capacity rather than as representatives of any governments, inevitably

[1] *Tanganyika Territory: Ordinances, Proclamations, etc.*, Vol. 1. Waterlow, London, 1921, p. 92 ff.

found itself examining reports of events which had taken place some considerable time earlier. The members themselves believed it to be their duty to assist the mandatory powers with their advice rather than to undermine their authority by their criticisms. In fact the Commission had power to do no more than to advise the League of Nations, and the League itself usually transmitted the Commission's views in the form of questions to the mandatory authority. It will be seen, therefore, that Byatt's policy of caution was one of his own choosing.

In one field, however, Byatt acted with a lack of prudence which was in startling contrast with the general pattern of his behaviour; that was in his method of promulgating legislation without consulting in advance the views of those most likely to be affected by his ordinances. The Tanganyika Order in Council authorized the Governor to act in this way since he would undoubtedly seek the advice of the members of his Executive Council which comprised the Chief Secretary, the Attorney General, the Treasurer, and the Principal Medical Officer. Nevertheless, the handful of European unofficials in the territory and the Asian business men, too, considered that much inconvenience could have been avoided if, on a number of occasions they had had an opportunity to express their views on the terms of proposed legislation. Discontent with Byatt's attitude in this respect led some of the European unofficials to suggest to the Ormsby-Gore Commission of 1924 that they would welcome the establishment of a Legislative Council. This view appears to have been rather more extreme than that generally held among the Europeans in the territory and with Byatt's departure the idea dropped into the background.

It was revived by Byatt's successor, Sir Donald Cameron, soon after his arrival in the territory. Cameron was a man of bold ideas and great energy. A West Indian of Irish parentage, he had had little formal education. This may have been in part responsible for the defensive attitude which he tended to adopt when dealing with members of the Colonial Service who had come to office through more traditional channels. It was an attitude, too, which frequently manifested itself in impatience and some intolerance. Yet there was no doubting the sincerity of Cameron's desire to promote the well-being of Tanganyika and the welfare of its people. Before leaving London he seized the opportunity to discuss a number of the country's problems with members of the Ormsby-Gore Commission, and it was in the course of these informal exchanges that he learned that the Commission proposed to recommend the introduction of an Advisory Council in Tanganyika. Arriving in the territory Cameron was quick to appreciate the strength of feeling against his predecessor's methods and he recognized the need to establish some more formal method of communication between the territorial government and the non-African population. Nevertheless, he did not approve of an Advisory Council. If unofficials were to be consulted in the formulation of policy they must be prepared to take responsibility for the decisions subsequently made. A Legislative Council, therefore, was clearly a better instrument for achieving this objective.

The Dar es Salaam Chamber of Commerce was the first body to receive the news of Cameron's decision to introduce a legislative body within a few months. The Chamber was startled by this proposal and indeed expressed some doubt as to whether the country was ready for such an advance.[1] But Cameron's enthusiasm and the prospect of fuller participation in the political life of the territory soon overcame their doubts, and when there was some delay in obtaining the approval of the Secretary of State numerous inquiries were made as to when the Council would come into being. Cameron's views on the membership of the Council were clear-cut. There must be a reasonable official majority but there must also be sufficient unofficial members to enable the Council to represent adequately the views of the non-African community. In adopting this view he displayed greater wisdom than Coryndon had done in Uganda, for the Tanganyika legislature made a greater impact upon the territory than did the Uganda Legislative Council in the northern Protectorate. On the composition of the unofficial membership of the Council Cameron also had clear ideas. Each individual should be chosen for his ability to render sound advice to the Governor and not for his membership of any particular group or community. This principle, however, proved more difficult to observe than Cameron might have wished. In practice he was forced to admit that of the seven original unofficial members it would be advisable to select men from the various commercial, banking, shipping and planting interests and also two from the Indian community. When this number was

[1] *Tanganyika Times*, January 18 and 20, 1926.

increased to ten in 1929, racial interests were further observed by the addition of two Europeans and one Indian.

The Council held its first meeting on December 7, 1926, with a membership comprising fourteen officials and seven unofficials. The Indians accepted their two seats readily enough with none of the discord which had been witnessed in Kenya and Uganda. This was due in part to the more amicable situation which had developed in the legislatures of both the other territories earlier in the year and in part, as in Uganda, to the absence of any grounds for rivalry in the economic sphere between Europeans and Asians. The open-door policy laid down by the mandate made it clear to the British that they could hope for no monopoly of trade or land. In any case, the number of European nations represented among the non-African population of Tanganyika was so great that any solidarity of European feeling against the Indians was virtually impossible. The only example of friction took place very early in the British period of administration. In March 1922 the Indians in Dar es Salaam closed their shops and attempted to organize a boycott of British goods as a protest against the arrest of Gandhi. The disapproval of the European community in this instance was marked, but it was based upon anti-racial rather than upon racial grounds since the Europeans considered that the Indians were attempting to introduce a racial and nationalist controversy into a country where none existed.[1] But the dispute was short-lived. Only eighteen months later, when the Indians again closed their shops, in protest on that occasion against a recently-published ordinance about which there had been no public consultation, their action had the support of the European unofficial community which was as critical as the Indians themselves of the Administration's policy.[2]

In contrast to Cameron's recognition of the place which Indians must hold in the Legislative Council he firmly refused to admit Germans to membership. The latter had been required by the terms of the peace treaty to quit Tanganyika completely, but in 1925 they were readmitted. Cameron had no objection to their return and even took steps to enable them once again to hold land. But when a number of Germans asked for representation in the legislature in 1929 the Governor stated categorically that aliens could not be admitted to the Legislative Council in a British mandate.

[1] *Dar es Salaam Times*, March 18 and 25, 1922.

[2] ibid., November 17, 1923.

Another important decision taken by Cameron was that the Council should not be required always to meet in the same place. This provision was of considerable political value in December 1929, when the legislature sat in Arusha and in so doing demonstrated to the European planters in the Kilimanjaro area that the Governor, with whom they had recently had a dispute, was far from being indifferent to their interests.

African membership of the Legislative Council, Cameron considered, was a thing of the distant future. Few Africans in the 1920s had sufficient command of the English language to enable them to participate fully in the work of the legislature, and many of those who had were young men who, in Cameron's opinion, would be unable to command allegiance among the different tribes of which Tanganyika's population was composed. Looking well ahead, therefore, he believed that political progress would best come by stages. Local African authorities in time might send chiefs to regional councils which in turn might send their representatives to a central native council, the final stage being reached when African and European delegates sat together to formulate the laws of the land.[1] Even at this remote stage it does not seem that Cameron envisaged Africans taking full control of the territory, for the protection of African interests against the claims of non-Africans was so much the theme of the inter-war years that administrators could scarcely look forward to a time when Africans might be capable of handling their own affairs. Until Africans could take a fuller part in the country's political life, Cameron maintained that it was better they should not be brought into conflict with the more experienced non-African population in the legislature. It was his view that during this period of waiting African interests would be fully protected by the Governor, the Chief Secretary and the Secretary for Native Affairs.[2]

If Tanganyika's Legislative Council came into being with little disturbance to the country's political life the administrative system introduced by Cameron involved both considerable discussion and considerable effort. In the field of local administration, as in the sphere of central government, Sir Horace Byatt had been reluctant

[1] Sir Donald Cameron: *My Tanganyika Service*. Allen and Unwin, London, 1939, p. 115.

[2] *Tanganyika Territory: Proceedings of the Legislative Council. First Session, 1926-27*. Government Printer, Dar es Salaam, 1927, pp. 5-7. Address by Sir Donald Cameron.

to take any precipitate action which might add still further to the disruption of African life brought about by the war. Even had he planned more boldly he would have been greatly hampered by the shortage of administrative officers. Some of those loaned by other East African Governments during the war were recalled soon after the restoration of peace while the settlers, planters and business men who had been temporarily employed as officials returned to their former occupations.[1] Administration, therefore, continued for some time on a provisional basis, German ordinances and regulations being retained where necessary, while political officers continued to exercise the judicial functions conferred upon them during the war until their powers were redefined by the Courts Ordinance of 1920. In other departments the shortage of experienced men was equally acute and as new departments were established they were forced to operate with a skeleton staff recruited from other territories. In 1920 the departments of Agriculture, Forest, Education and Land and Survey were created. It was some time, however, before the boundaries of the territory were finally settled. On March 22, 1921, the Belgians handed over Ujiji District and the parts of Ufipa and Biharamulo which were still in their hands but the boundary of the Belgian mandated territory of Ruanda-Urundi was not finally fixed until December 1923.

During this period of preparation Byatt hoped by his policy of caution to encourage the revival of tribal authority which he looked upon as offering the best prospect of peaceful development in the future. He was even prepared to retain, where possible, the services of the experienced akidas formerly employed by the Germans so as to assist in maintaining stability. Their status and privileges were to be reduced, however, so as not to conflict with the main process of restoring tribal authority. But Byatt's tactics could not infuse new life into a system which had undergone so serious a buffeting during the war years. The lack of a clear directive to the administrative officers, in fact, had the very opposite result to the one for which Byatt hoped. Wide divergencies in policy developed between one district and another and a new District Commissioner was free to reverse completely the plans of his predecessor. Even the Native Authority Ordinance of 1923, which gave limited powers to local

[1] G. F. Sayers, ed.: *The Handbook of Tanganyika*. Macmillan, London, 1930, p. 95.

chiefs and councils, and, it should be added, to the akidas also, was too limited in its objectives to effect any significant change. Byatt's departure in 1924, therefore, provided the opportunity for a reappraisal of the country's administrative needs. A conference of senior administrative officers recommended that the twenty-two districts organized by the Germans should be grouped into provinces so as to ensure greater administrative uniformity. They also proposed that in future native administration should be based upon the principles of indirect rule and that a Secretary for Native Affairs should be appointed to supervise the introduction of this policy.[1]

The arrival of Cameron made the implementation of these proposals not only possible but certain. Although he denied that he had gone to Tanganyika with the intention already formulated of introducing indirect rule, Cameron's experience as Chief Secretary in Northern Nigeria had made him a supporter of this technique of administration. Within a few days of his setting foot in Tanganyika the unsatisfactory arrangements for the payment of chiefs, which he had inherited from his predecessor, provided him with the opportunity he needed to investigate the whole system of native administration. The problem, as Cameron saw it, was to secure the future of the African population not simply as producers of wealth but rather as members of the state. He was opposed to the introduction of a system of European law to achieve this purpose since he believed this would inevitably lead to detribalization. The alternative was to build upon a type of organization which the African population had inherited and which they could understand. Traditional law and custom could then be gradually adapted to suit changing requirements and in the meantime Africans would be gaining experience in regulating their own affairs without any danger of a breakdown in discipline and authority. This policy, Cameron believed, would prove to be one of the strongest safeguards against unfriendly race relations. In addition the Government's economic and social policies would be more successfully promoted because traditional chiefs and councils would act as agents of change.

To make his plans effective it was necessary for Cameron to rediscover the indigenous rulers of African society and to endow them with the authority necessary to carry his policy forward. The

[1] Sir Charles Dundas: *African Crossroads*. Macmillan, London, 1955, pp. 132–3.

Native Authority Ordinance of 1926 provided the foundation for his scheme. Under the terms of the Ordinance recognized native authorities could be granted a threefold power which was the very essence of Cameron's ideal[1] In them would be embodied executive, judicial and financial powers adequate to enable them to control the affairs of their tribes. In their executive capacity, it is true, the only positive duty laid upon native authorities was the maintenance of peace and order. But as they grew in efficiency they were granted additional powers over a wide field which ranged from the encouragement of the cultivation of food crops to the control of the manufacture of intoxicating liquors.[2] In the financial powers of the native authorities lay one of the main grounds for hoping that they would develop as local governments in the English sense of the term. To them now fell the task of collecting Hut and Poll taxes formerly undertaken by the European district officers. This arrangement had the double advantage of being a cheaper method of collection, while at the same time underlining the status of the native authorities in the eyes of the African population. A portion of the revenue thus collected was then remitted to the native authorities by the Treasury and their income was further augmented by native court fines and fees. Out of this revenue officers and servants of the local authorities could be paid and the balance might then be spent on works and services for the benefit of the community.

Even more important, however, was the judicial power of the native authorities. The power to administer justice had formed an integral part of the authority of the traditional chiefs and councils and it was therefore essential in Cameron's view that the native authorities should also be granted judicial powers to enforce their decisions. In the first place this was done under the terms of the Courts Ordinance of 1920. In 1929, however, a more significant step was taken when a new Native Courts Ordinance was enacted which removed the native courts from the supervision of the High Court and placed them under the control of the Provincial Administration. This, in Cameron's view, constituted a vital link between administration and justice but his action was criticized by lawyers and laymen alike who disapproved of the exercise of executive and

[1] *Tanganyika Territory: Proceedings of the Legislative Council. First Session, 1926–27.* Government Printer, Dar es Salaam, 1927, pp. 5–7. Address by Sir Donald Cameron.

[2] Cameron: op. cit., p. 171.

judicial functions by the same persons. The Chief Justice, himself, addressed a number of protests to the Governor but Cameron insisted that the ordinance should be enacted in spite of the unanimous opposition of the European and Indian unofficial members of the Legislative Council.

The implementation of Cameron's policy was not always an easy task and along the coast it was virtual impossibility. In the late nineteenth century the Germans had imposed their rule in that region with ruthless strength while for generations before that the coastal tribes had been dominated by Arab traders and slavers so that Islamic Law rather than indigenous tribal institutions formed the basis of life for the African population. In these circumstances it would have been advisable to make use of experienced akidas but Cameron preferred to make a clean sweep, only agreeing after considerable persuasion to retain the liwalis in the important towns.[1] An indication of the problems likely to arise from this unbending policy was to be seen in Tanga Province where the population found difficulty in grasping the difference between the old akidas and the new native authorities who were as much the appointees of the Central Government as their predecessors had been. In consequence a group of malcontents was able for a time to pose as the mouthpiece of a genuinely apprehensive population, and in so doing was able to create considerable trouble for the Administration.

Inland the problem was not so great. As has already been shown the period of German administration had not destroyed the memory of indigenous political systems and the war had even provided an opportunity for their revival. Spurred on by Cameron's enthusiasm, therefore, district officers sought out indigenous tribal authorities which in due course became formally recognized as native authorities. The administrative officers, however, were not always able to recognize the true nature of the authorities they had discovered and some of these latter proved unsuited to the demands put upon them under the new régime. For the time being, however, the main problem arose from the creation of authorities which were too small and consequently too poor to be wholly effective. Efforts were made wherever possible to induce these smaller units to join together voluntarily into larger federations on the basis of genuine tribal or

[1] Sir Philip Mitchell: *African Afterthoughts*. Hutchinson, London, 1954, p. 133.

clan affinities. In Bukoba this policy met with considerable success. The chiefs of that region possessed long traditions of independent authority but they ruled over very small groups of people. Before the end of Cameron's governorship they had come together in a satisfactory relationship which made possible far greater developments than any one of them could have achieved on his own. In 1929 two sections of the Ngoni tribe also agreed to co-operate although the establishment of a satisfactory judicial hierarchy which derogated from the authority and prestige of neither group was not accomplished without considerable thought. Similarly, the financial and judicial advantages offered by larger units were not lost upon the Wasukuma of Shinyanga and some of the Wanyamwezi chiefs who agreed in 1927 to form the Sukuma Federation and the Nyamwezi Federation respectively. But the issue proved to be more complicated than was at first apparent. The chiefs of Sukumaland had no intention of surrendering executive authority over their own particular groups of people, however ready they might be to enjoy the benefits to be derived from the increased revenue of the federation or to escape the odium resulting from the infliction of punishment upon erring members of their own tribes. The Wanyamwezi chiefs, meanwhile, agreed to accept the executive decisions of a majority of their number in the event of differences of opinion, a decision which was taken by the district officer to imply that they were prepared to surrender their individual authority to the council of the Federation. Within less than two years, however, this interpretation was shown to be wrong. In 1930 it was necessary to deprive the federal councils of both the Wasukuma and the Wanyamwezi of their status as superior authorities. They continued to act as courts of appeal from the courts of individual chiefs, however, and they continued to enjoy the benefits of a federal treasury.

The confusion in the minds of some administrative officers over the implementation of Cameron's policy was, in fact, only a pale reflection of the uncertainty felt by many of the African chiefs. It was Mwanza Province which provided yet another example of the unexpected lines along which indirect rule might develop. It had been Cameron's hope that the presidents of councils might in time develop into paramount chiefs. This, he believed, would give direction to policy and a unity of approach upon which efficient local government could thrive. In Mwanza Province paramount chiefs

302

were quickly recognized by the Government with the apparent approval of the local population. But it was soon seen that they were thought of and indeed acted as little more than the presidents of councils composed of their equals. This development was in marked contrast to events among the Chagga who were traditionally divided into more than twenty independent chiefdoms. After overcoming Chagga resistance the Germans had replaced the existing chiefs by others of a more compliant spirit but they had continued to recognize the independence of each chiefdom. Under Cameron's direction the British now tried to draw the Chagga into a closer association by means of a council of chiefs. The council did not find favour with the people for although the chiefs exercised recognized powers in their own areas there was no tradition of corporate action between them. Nor was the practice of permitting each chief to take his turn as chairman of the council likely to encourage continuity and efficiency. Recognizing its own shortcomings the council called a mass meeting at Moshi in 1934 at which a popular chief, Petro Itosi Marealle, was elected paramount chief. The Government refused to ratify the election, however, and insisted that the existing administrative system should be retained.

In general, nevertheless, the African population co-operated with Cameron's innovations, and the satisfactory foundations which had been laid for local government development in most areas were demonstrated during the economic depression of the early 1930s. For, in spite of the serious reduction in the revenues of the native authorities and in the salaries of the chiefs, they continued to carry out their duties and in most cases were able to maintain their schools, farms, dispensaries and clinics.[1] In view of the vast distances to be travelled in administering the country the development of some degree of local and tribal self-sufficiency was of the greatest importance. It was only in the more politically conscious times after the Second World War that criticisms were heard of this development on the ground that it divided the people and hindered the emergence of a sense of nationhood; or that it encouraged slow progress under conservative chiefs instead of a more rapid advance under younger and better educated leaders. And even these criticisms did not hold good for long.

[1] *Tanganyika Territory: Annual Report for the Year 1931.* Colonial No. 71, H.M.S.O., London 1932, p. 11.

There were, of course, areas in which progress was impossible. The stubborn Wagogo, as unchanging as the arid plains of central Tanganyika which were their home, had been noted by Henry Stanley in 1871 for the proliferation of their petty chiefs demanding *hongo*. By 1937 there had been little change of heart among the members of the tribe and when a provincial commissioner recommended that the numerous chiefs' courts should be federated in the interests of efficiency and to promote the greater dignity of the courts themselves the experiment proved a failure. In the estimation of the Wagogo chiefs efficiency and dignity were an inadequate substitute for unquestioned authority. The main weaknesses arising from Cameron's policy, however, were due to the hurried appointment of local authorities which sometimes led to an unsatisfactory choice being made. In the Masasi District of southern Tanganyika, where there had been an experiment in appointing clan heads as native authorities it was soon seen that the traditional social system could not easily be adapted to the demands of the 1930s. The authority of the clan leaders was exercised over individuals, not over districts. No matter where a man moved he remained subject to the rule of his clan. This arrangement scarcely suited the type of regional responsibility exercised by the native authorities instituted by Cameron, and a number of changes proved necessary. The Masai of northern Tanganyika were also difficult to turn from their old ways. As one government official remarked, 'We all reorganize the Masai when we first meet them but they continue to function as they please.' The appointment of the Masai Laibon as a superior authority with the title of chief of Masai, therefore, had its inevitable yet unexpected repercussions. In theory this was a sound move, for the Laibon was the only member of the tribe who could be said to exercise any general influence. But his traditional authority was of a religious character and he did not aspire to wield secular power. Nor did the Masai want him to do so. As a power behind the executive he was all-important and his advice was sought on any major issue. But he simply delegated the executive powers conferred upon him by the Government to a body of elders who from time to time reported their decisions to him and received his blessing.

Another source of weakness was the doctrinaire fervour with which some officials applied the policy of indirect rule. Indeed, local self-government, as Cameron's successor, Sir Stewart Symes,

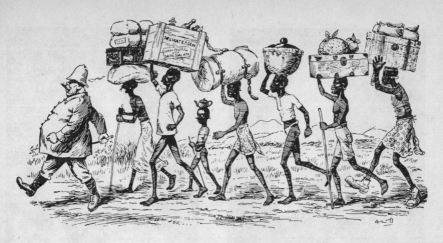

THE VANQUISHED.

THE VICTOR.

Cartoons depicting the outcome of the East African Campaign
during the First World War

Sir Donald Cameron

Sir Edward Grigg
(later Lord Altrincham)

Sir Philip Mitchell

Sir Charles Dundas

preferred to call it, became invested with an almost divine aura in the eyes of certain administrative officers. To the handful of European unofficials in Tanganyika it appeared to have a much more sinister character, however, and Symes had no little difficulty in convincing them of the merits of a policy which seemed to them unduly sensitive to the needs of the African population.[1]

No such uniformity of administration as Cameron tried to introduce into Tanganyika existed in Uganda between the two wars. Probably the greatest obstacle to any such development was the existence of Buganda with its numerous population, forming about a quarter of the population of the whole Protectorate, with its traditional form of bureaucratic administration and with its 1900 Agreement which placed it in a special position in its relations with the Protectorate Government. As has already been shown the Baganda looked upon their own government as a central government rather than as a local administration. In addition to Buganda there existed three other smaller and less populous units of district size possessing a hereditary ruler, two of which also had their own agreements with the British Government. These districts, however, did not pose such a difficult problem as did Buganda, since administration was mainly carried on along the same lines as in the remainder of the territory, with district officers giving orders to and supervising the work of the hereditary rulers as they did in respect of the chiefs in other areas. Three ordinances passed in 1919 formed the basis of local administration for the area outside Buganda. The Native Authority Ordinance defined the powers of the hierarchy of chiefs which the Protectorate Government was attempting to build up on the basis of the pattern already existing in Buganda. The Courts Ordinance laid down the powers of the native courts and, potentially the most important of all, the Native Laws Ordinance empowered the Governor to recognize or to constitute councils in each district although limiting the power of the councils virtually to the amendment of customary laws. This latter ordinance was only an enabling law and district councils came into being in different parts of Uganda over a period of years, the Lango Native Council, for example, being recognized only towards the end of 1935. Nevertheless, the Native Laws Ordinance provided a basis for the development of district councils and subsequently of local government along more

[1] Sir Stewart Symes: *Tour of Duty*. Collins, London, 1946, pp. 167–9.

western lines. In the meantime the district officers continued to exercise most of the authority in the districts.

Two other developments of considerable significance took place in the 1920s in the administration of the various districts of Uganda. These were the replacement of the Baganda agents by local men and the changing attitude of the district officers towards the older chiefs. The removal of the Baganda agents, frequently before there were local men fully capable of replacing them, at least gave a challenge to a tribe to accept some responsibility for the control of its own affairs. At the same time it encouraged the misconception, widely held by European administrative officers, that a system of indirect rule was being introduced into Uganda. In fact the locally appointed chiefs were just as much agents of the Central Government as the Baganda agents themselves had been. Even though every attempt was made to employ accepted leaders and there was a pretence that they were exercising traditional authority, in practice they owed both their appointments and their powers to the Protectorate Government. Their incomes were partly paid from a rebate on the poll tax they collected and partly from tribute which was gradually converted into a cash payment. The modern turn which local government was gradually taking also helped to emphasize the change in character of the office of chief. In the 1920s frequent criticisms were levelled by a new generation of district officers against the conservatism of the older chiefs who appeared unable, through lack of education, or unwilling, from personal reasons, to adapt themselves to the functions they were now required to fulfil. Men who as leaders in battle had won the respect of the people under their charge were not always the best suited to the bureaucratic administration which was being gradually introduced. The most striking example of this clash between the officers of the Protectorate Government and the local chiefs occurred in Buganda. There, after many years of almost undisputed authority Sir Apolo Kagwa greatly resented any interference from administrative officers of the Protectorate Government. Indeed, so strong had he become that even the Kabaka himself, still a young man and still labouring under the disadvantages he had inherited from a lengthy regency, felt his own authority challenged by that of his powerful Katikiro. In 1926 the crisis was reached when a trivial dispute over the issue of beer licences became a trial of strength between Kagwa and the Provincial Commissioner, Mr.

J. R. P. Postlethwaite. The Governor upheld the general principle of the superior authority of his administrative officers although conceding the minor issue of the licences and Kagwa resigned in August 1926.[1] He died in February of the following year nearly two years before his former rival Kakunguru who had also come into conflict with the Protectorate authorities. Kakunguru's dispute, in fact, had lasted for many years. Although holding a number of offices under the Protectorate Administration he was too proud a character to accept a subordinate role and he ended his days living as a private person and waging a sporadic war against the Veterinary Department's schemes for the inoculation of cattle.

Although the clash between Postlethwaite and Kagwa was to a large extent, at least as far as the latter was concerned, a clash of personalities, it was also a reflection of the Protectorate Government's increasing tendency to interfere in the affairs of Buganda. Like the chiefs in the other districts, although on a larger scale, the Buganda Lukiko was finding itself incapable of meeting the requirements of modern administrative methods. In 1916 the Protectorate Auditor had drawn attention to the inefficient handling of money by the Lukiko and during the next ten years criticisms of the misuse of Lukiko funds became so intense that the Kabaka himself agreed in 1926 to appoint a commission of inquiry. This opened the way for Protectorate intervention which had been previously rendered difficult by the fact that under the terms of the 1900 Agreement the Buganda Government had its own treasurer and was therefore, presumably, responsible for handling its own finances. In 1926, however, the Kabaka recognized that expert advice was needed to avoid the errors which had crept into the management of Buganda's finances, through inexperience it should be added and not through dishonesty. Not unnaturally the Lukiko was jealous of its privileges and resisted any attempt at undermining them. In 1920, for example, the Kabaka and his ministers made it clear in response to a demand from the Protectorate Administration that the Lukiko should repeal one of its laws, that orders of this sort carried no authority since only the Lukiko, of its own volition and with the consent of the Governor, could change Kiganda law. Nevertheless, as in the case of the Lukiko's finances some weakness had to be admitted, for the laws

[1] J. R. P. Postlethwaite: *I Look Back*, T. V. Boardman and Co., London, 1947, pp. 80–82, 106, 111.

of Buganda were frequently confused and needed amendment to suit more modern conditions. In the struggle between the authority of the Protectorate Government and that of Buganda, therefore, the former triumphed increasingly between the wars even if only because it was better adapted to the more specialized demands of a modern administration.

One area of Uganda developed far more slowly than the rest. In the extreme north-east civil administration was introduced for the first time into Karamoja in the early 1920s but little advance was made beyond the continued maintenance of peace and order and the restraint of the pastoral Karamojong from their established pastime of cattle raiding. In 1926 Rudolf Province, still farther east, was transferred to Kenya since its administration from Uganda was inconvenient if not completely impossible. This transfer, like the transfer of Uganda's old Eastern Province to Kenya in 1902, was later to become one of the grievances of some of Uganda's political leaders, but at the time the new arrangement was looked upon by the Protectorate Government with particular satisfaction since it removed an irksome and unprofitable responsibility from Uganda's shoulders.

If the development of a uniform administration in Uganda was complicated by the special position of Buganda the existence side by side of European settled areas and African reserves presented the Kenya Government with an equally difficult problem. Until 1929 two separate types of local administration existed side by side, the settled areas being administered as separate units outside the provincial organization. In 1924 there had been an important development in the administration of the reserves when an amendment to the Native Authority Ordinance authorized the Governor in Council to establish local native councils in the reserve areas. These councils would be presided over by the district commissioner and would consist of the other district officers in the area, together with a number of headmen and other Africans, the people of the district being given an opportunity to nominate suitable persons whose names would be submitted to the Governor together with the district commissioner's recommendations. The councils would perform definite duties and would administer funds raised by local contributions to provide services of common benefit. This was an important step forward from the native advisory councils which had

308

existed previously and in most districts the new councils were greeted with enthusiasm by the African population. By 1926 the Machakos District Council was employing two whole-time European officers, one a forest officer, the other a roads supervisor. The Council had also provided generous funds for afforestation, educational and medical buildings and road construction.[1] These councils were not directly linked with the native tribunals which administered customary law so that there was not the same degree of integration in African local government in Kenya as had been achieved in Tanganyika. There was, however, the same deliberate attempt to associate the councils with traditional tribal authority. But in Kenya this attempt came too late to be truly effective and frequently indigenous councils existed side by side with the authorities established by the Central Government although their existence was unknown to the Government. These traditional authorities regulated much of the day-to-day life of certain of the tribes whose members would refer their disputes to the jurisdiction of the recognized elders rather than to the councils or tribunals created by the Europeans.

In the rural areas occupied by European settlers the constitution of the district councils was provided for by the District Councils Ordinance of 1928 and by the middle of 1929 Councils had been set up in Nakuru, Nyanza, Uasin Gishu, Naivasha and Nairobi Districts. At first their main function was that of a district road authority and only later did they extend their activities to include public health. Practically the whole of their revenue was derived from Government grants. The introduction of this new system appeared to the Central Government to provide an opportunity to try and focus the interests of Africans and non-Africans by providing some means of local liaison between them. The method proposed was the creation of provinces consisting of groups of African and settled districts which possessed closely connected interests. In most areas this scheme met with some success although in other parts of the territory such links could not be created.

The District Councils Ordinance had been drafted as a result of a report submitted by a Local Government Commission which had been appointed in 1926. Another result of the Commission's work was the Local Government (Municipalities) Ordinance which was

[1] *Kenya Colony: Native Administration Department Annual Report for 1926.* Government Printer, Nairobi, 1927, p. 23.

also enacted in 1928. Previously all urban areas, with the exception of Nairobi, had been administered as townships and in the more important ones the district officers had been advised by Township Committees. Under the new ordinance the municipalities of Nairobi and Mombasa were constituted towards the end of 1928 and Municipal Boards were set up in Nakuru and Eldoret early in the following year. The four municipalities received financial assistance from the Central Government, Nairobi and Mombasa under the terms of the new ordinance and Nakuru and Eldoret on the basis of the cost to the Government of administering local services in the year 1928. The constitution of the municipal boards provided for elected European and Indian membership together with nominated government members. In all cases except Nairobi African interests were represented by the District Commissioner who presided at the meetings of the boards. Kenya, therefore, between the wars was attempting to adapt its system of local government more closely to the pattern of English local government than was deemed possible or advisable in either Tanganyika or Uganda.

If circumstances shaped a variety of approaches to the political and administrative problems of the three East African territories there was one political factor which disturbed them all. That was the idea of closer union, no less disturbing because it was never clearly defined. But closer union has another claim to attention besides the opposition it aroused in East Africa. For, unlike almost every other policy proposal before the Second World War it originated entirely in Britain and drew no strength from East Africa itself. There were other issues in which the British Government interfered to criticize or even to change policies formulated by East African Governments but closer union is probably unique in having been conceived in Britain without any prior consultation with the East African territories.

The leading author of closer union was Mr. L. S. Amery who, even before the end of the First World War, had allied himself with General Smuts to ensure that the terms of the Tanganyika mandate would make it possible to link German East Africa with the neighbouring British dependencies. Already Amery was beginning to formulate an imperial policy which could withstand the economic challenge of American mass production and of the cheap labour of western Europe and the Far East. Like Joseph Chamberlain before

310

him, he looked to closer co-operation within the Empire to solve his problem and above all he was anxious that small units should be organized into larger states which would be capable of contributing more fully to the needs of the Empire as a whole.

When rumours of closer union reached Kenya in 1920, however, they aroused serious misgivings among the European settlers who feared that the proposal might undermine their plans for a European self-governing colony. 'I feel very strongly,' wrote Lord Delamere, 'that for the next few years this country should stand alone if it is to realize its ideals of civilization and progress . . . until we are a self-governing colony and have digested the problems of this country first.'[1] European opinion in Uganda, in so far as it looked upon closer union as anything more than a vague theory at this early stage, was also hostile mainly because of the conviction that Uganda's financial interests, more particularly in regard to railway revenue and customs duties, were already too subordinate to those of Kenya. In September 1921 a meeting of European and Asian unofficials in Dar es Salaam agreed to send a resolution to the Secretary of State protesting against the assimilation of Tanganyika's finances and economy with those of Kenya.[2] Only recently the railway expert, Colonel Hammond, had suggested a redeployment of East Africa's railway system so as to make Kilindini the outlet for the produce of the Kilimanjaro area, Tanganyika's richest district,[3] and the territory's commercial population was no more willing than its counterpart in Uganda to surrender its profits to Kenya. African opinion at this stage was silent but events in Kenya made the Indian population of Uganda and Tanganyika extremely wary of any proposals to associate the territories more closely with Kenya.

In spite of these early doubts Amery remained confident of the rightness of his plan and took every opportunity to urge closer union in public speeches and in conversation. From a purely legalistic point of view the plan did not appear difficult to accomplish. Buganda, and to a lesser extent Toro and Ankole, had a special position because of their agreements with the United Kingdom

[1] E. Huxley: *White Man's Country*. Macmillan, London, 1953, Vol. 2, pp. 83-84.

[2] *Dar es Salaam Times*, December 10, 1931.

[3] *Report on the Railway System of Kenya, Uganda and Tanganyika, Pt. I.* By Lieut.-Colonel F. D. Hammond. Crown Agents for the Colonies, London, 1921, Appendix I, pp. 163-71.

Government. In their case separate arrangements would have had to be made, yet this might not have presented the same degree of difficulty as would have been involved at a later date when political consciousness had grown more acute among the African population. In all other respects the constitutions of the territories were defined by Orders in Council, Royal Instructions and Letters Patent which could be and which were varied at will by the British Government.[1] Lord Milner and his two successors at the Colonial Office, Mr. Winston Churchill and the Duke of Devonshire, were, however, too fully occupied with other issues to pursue the question of closer union with enthusiasm. It was not until 1924 that action was taken in response to a resolution moved in the House of Commons by a Conservative member, Sir Sidney Henn, urging the Colonial Secretary to dispatch a commission to East Africa to report on the practicability of co-ordinating policy and services throughout Kenya, Uganda, Tanganyika, Zanzibar, Nyasaland and Northern Rhodesia, and to advise on a programme of economic development.

From one point of view at least the moment seemed more auspicious than any that had gone before, for there was a brief rapprochement between European unofficials in Kenya and Tanganyika early in 1924. This was mainly due to the Europeans' disappointment with Byatt's policy in Tanganyika and in fact formed part of the Kenya Europeans' plan to strengthen the European unofficial community in Kenya rather than contributing towards a more general scheme of closer union. It took the form of a proposal to attach the Kilimanjaro region to Kenya and for a time it aroused some interest among the European planters in the area concerned. It was carefully fostered by Lord Delamere, and in March 1924 Kenya candidates for election to the Legislative Council pledged themselves to support a readjustment of the boundary between Kenya and Tanganyika. But the Kenya settlers overplayed their hand. Even before the Labour Colonial Secretary, Mr. J. H. Thomas, had appointed the commission for which Henn had asked, Tanganyika's Europeans were beginning to have second thoughts. Delamere's opposition to the extension of the Tanganyika Central Railway from Tabora to Mwanza on the ground that it would deprive Kenya of the profits from transporting the produce of the Lake Victoria region to the coast was well known. Less well known

[1] Sir Philip Mitchell: op. cit., p. 108.

but generally suspected was Delamere's hope that the southern boundary of Kenya should be extended so as to include most of the northern part of Tanganyika from the coast to the Belgian border. This arrangement would have deprived Tanganyika of both its most fertile regions and also of its labour supply and although this made little difference to the Europeans of Kilimanjaro it aroused considerable resentment in other parts of the territory.[1] What particularly incensed the Kilimanjaro planters was the argument pressed by Delamere and others that the Kilimanjaro area should be transferred to Kenya as a reward for the loss of the unproductive province of Jubaland to Italy. Apart from the unfavourable comparison between the two areas it was pointed out that no one in Kenya had previously objected to the loss of Jubaland so that to do so now appeared to have little justification. At a meeting of the Kilimanjaro Planters' Association on August 7, 1924, it was agreed that the approach to Kenya had been ill considered. Even this breach, however, appeared to offer some hope of closer union, for the Planters' Association accepted the view that in due course the whole of Tanganyika might be federated with the other East African territories provided there was no question of either amalgamation or of domination by Kenya.[2]

Somewhat surprisingly, when the terms of reference of the East Africa Commission were announced in July, 1924, they contained no reference either to political amalgamation or to federation. The Commission was required simply to consider and report on the measures to be taken to accelerate the general economic development of British East Africa and on means of securing closer co-ordination of policy over transport, cotton-growing and medical and agricultural matters. In addition it was required to investigate the steps to be introduced to improve the social conditions of the African population and their relations with non-Africans.[3] In spite of these limitations, however, the Commission heard a lot of views on closer union when, with its chairman, the Hon. W. Ormsby-Gore, it reached East Africa in the second half of 1924. The Kabaka and Lukiko of Buganda presented a memorandum setting out the

[1] *Dar es Salaam Times*, November 1, 1924.

[2] ibid.

[3] *Report of the East Africa Commission*, *1925*. Cmd. 2387. H.M.S.O., London, 1925, p. 3.

grounds of their opposition to closer union because it might adversely affect the position established for Buganda by the 1900 Agreement. Other communities, looking to their own interests, displayed similar hostility. The Commission therefore reported that in spite of the common needs of the East African dependencies the difficulties of communication and the expense involved in introducing any form of closer union for the time being presented an insuperable obstacle. It did suggest, however, that the territorial governors should meet periodically to discuss problems of mutual interest. In this way greater efficiency might be achieved in the over-all administration of East Africa while the rights and privileges by which the different territories and communities set great store would be protected.

The Commission's proposals did not satisfy Amery who had become Colonial Secretary on the fall of the Labour Government. He could not, however, act in direct opposition to the Commission's recommendations, so that he was unable to accept the demand of Lord Lloyd, whom he wished to appoint as Governor of Kenya, that he should become Governor-General of the three East African territories. Instead, he appointed Sir Edward Grigg as Governor in 1925 with instructions to prepare a scheme of closer union for further consideration. Characteristically Lord Delamere was quick to appreciate the degree of Amery's determination. Already in 1924 he had recommended the erection of an imposing new Government House in Nairobi so that in the event of closer union becoming a reality Kenya should be its centre. More than a year later, in October 1925, he summoned a meeting of representatives of the settler communities of East Africa, Nyasaland and Northern Rhodesia at Tukuyu in the southern highlands of Tanganyika. There by dint of exercising his personality and determination he convinced the others of the need to put forward a united settler policy to meet any proposals for a change in the political organization of East and Central Africa. A second unofficial conference held in Livingstone in September 1926 made it clear that Nyasaland and Northern Rhodesia had no intention of being linked with their northern neighbours. Delamere concluded, therefore, that British policy was likely to favour the federation of the two groups as separate units. In these circumstances he was even more anxious to ensure that the European elected members of Kenya's Legislative Council should be in the majority in order to face up to federation with some degree of confidence. In December 1926, he and the other European unofficial members of the Kenya legislature published an election programme for the following year with, as its main platform, favourable consideration for a scheme of co-ordination between Kenya, Tanganyika, Uganda and possibly Nyasaland conditional upon approval being given to an elected majority in the Kenya Legislative Council. To this extent the settlers of Kenya had become reconciled to federation and Amery was encouraged by the news to continue his efforts.

If Delamere had shown some readiness to bargain Sir Donald Cameron did not. Cameron in fact proved to be the most effective opponent of political and administrative association during the whole of this crucial period. His appointment as Governor of Tanganyika had preceded that of Grigg in Kenya and he knew nothing of the latter's instructions regarding closer union. Towards the end of 1925 the Governors of the three East African territories met to consider the agenda for the first Governors' Conference to be held in accordance with the Ormsby-Gore Commission's recommendations. At the meeting the question of extending Tanganyika's Central Railway from Tabora to Mwanza came under discussion. Subsequently the Governors of Kenya and Uganda sent a joint telegram to the Secretary of State urging that instructions should be sent to the Government of Tanganyika to cease work on the project. Cameron at once took up arms in defence of Tanganyika's interests and succeeded in obtaining the Colonial Secretary's approval for the railway's extension. From now on, he was on his guard against interference by Kenya and he was particularly anxious about the threat which closer union constituted to his native administration policy. In 1927 he was summoned to England to take part in a Colonial Office Conference. There he learned that Sir Edward Grigg had produced a scheme for closer union based upon the appointment of a federal council charged with the control of the main transport services, the customs system, communications, defence and research. Grigg had obtained support for this fairly innocuous arrangement from the European settlers in Kenya on the promise of an unofficial but not wholly elected majority in the Legislative Council. Cameron, however, would have none of the plan and threatened to resign if the theme were pursued further.[1]

[1] Cameron: op. cit., pp. 224–5.

315

Grigg's plan was then submitted to a sub-committee whose views and recommendations were published in a white paper in July 1927.[1] The economic importance of closer union in East Africa was stressed once more. Territories whose boundaries were in the main the result of historical accident could not, in the opinion of the sub-committee, be allowed to waste further energy and money in pursuing their separate ways when combined effort might produce impressive results. Thus summarily were dismissed the thirty years of individual development enjoyed by the three territories. An investigation was needed, the white paper went on, to show how closer union between the territories might be most effectively secured and to see if it was possible to provide for the increasing association of the immigrant communities in the responsibilities of government, while at the same time creating more effective machinery for African representation. The whole tone of the white paper echoed the voice of Amery but the Cabinet as a whole was not prepared to agree that closer union had been proved to be essential. A new commission there should be but among its terms of reference was the task of investigating once more whether federation was in fact desirable. Nor was that the only blow which Amery suffered. After appointing Sir Hilton Young as Chairman of the commission the Colonial Secretary himself set out on a Commonwealth tour to consolidate his policy of closer co-operation and left the appointment of the rest of the commission to others. Consequently, a number of men of the greatest ability but of an extremely varied outlook were appointed, with the result that when the commission took up its task a number of issues were investigated of which closer union was only one.

By this time opinion in East Africa was a little less united in its opposition to closer union. Europeans and Indians in Uganda were not wholly averse from some form of economic co-operation with the other territories. This change of view was mainly the result of a more equitable allocation of customs revenue between Uganda and Kenya and of the introduction of a Railway Council upon which Uganda was represented and which was able to ensure that the revenue from the railway was used for the upkeep and betterment of the railway system rather than for the general benefit of Kenya.

[1] *Future Policy in regard to Eastern Africa—1926–27.* Cmd. 2904. H.M.S.O., London, 1927.

But Uganda was still wary of political union, the Kabaka and Lukiko as surely as the Chamber of Commerce. In Tanganyika, too, Cameron maintained his role of chief opponent to closer union, while the Indian community was as suspicious of Kenya as ever. Yet in spite of this opposition the Commission agreed that federation of the three northern territories was desirable. The members were clearly influenced in their recommendation by their anxiety to introduce a uniform policy in dealing with all matters affecting the existing position and the future development of the African population and its relations with the immigrant communities.[1] This objective, they believed, could best be achieved by the appointment of a High Commissioner without any advisory council save the three Governors but possessing virtually autocratic powers in the framing of native policy in the three territories. Such an appointment would have amounted to a local projection of the Secretary of State and it won little approval in any quarter in East Africa. The European settlers in Kenya saw in it a final obstacle to their hopes of achieving responsible self-government. Uganda's Europeans preferred to deal with Whitehall rather than with Nairobi. African opinion in Uganda saw little to be gained from an over-all native policy formulated in Kenya. The Indian communities of all the East African territories, whose hopes had been stirred by the direction of the Commission's inquiries, were also disappointed by the absence of any recommendation in favour of equal representation for Indian and European unofficials in the territorial legislatures.

Anyone less determined than Amery would have abandoned his scheme two years earlier, but even now he was determined to try to salvage something from the wreckage of his plan. To Cameron's annoyance he was summoned to London, together with Sir Edward Grigg, towards the end of 1928 to discuss the Hilton Young Report. On his arrival he did not hesitate to canvass members of the House of Commons for support in his campaign against closer union, a proceeding which did not have Grigg's approval any more than did Cameron's further threat to resign.[2] But Cameron's opposition had some effect, for the only result of the discussions was that Sir Samuel Wilson, Permanent Under-Secretary of State, was sent to

[1] *Report of the Commission on Closer Union in the Dependencies in Eastern and Central Africa: 1928–29.* Cmd. 3234. H.M.S.O., London 1929, p. 7.

[2] Lord Altrincham: *Kenya's Opportunity.* Faber and Faber, London, 1955, p. 213.

East Africa in 1929 with the sober task of trying to ascertain on what lines a scheme for closer union would be administratively workable and at the same time acceptable to the population. It is to Wilson's credit that in the unsettled atmosphere created by the Hilton Young Report he was able to achieve any agreement whatsoever over the issue even of economic co-operation. In fact the East African Indian National Congress roundly opposed even economic co-operation since in its view this was the first step towards political federation which could only be prejudicial to the status of the Indian communities.[1] These fears were not wholly imaginary for there were rumours abroad that various distinguished public figures had already been invited to accept office as High Commissioner,[2] and the London *Times* maintained early in 1930 that a political settlement must accompany economic closer union if a sense of security was to be encouraged. The Africans of Uganda and Tanganyika also remained unshakeably opposed to any more intimate association with Kenya and objected to the establishment of any authority which would come between the Governor and the United Kingdom Government.

Wilson's final proposals were not very different from those eventually accepted in 1947[3] but they came at an unacceptable time. The Labour Government which came into office in time to receive Wilson's report still believed that some form of closer union was necessary in East Africa to promote African development but they wisely decided to submit the issue to a joint committee of both Houses of Parliament before taking any action. In the meantime they issued as a basis of discussion a white paper in which it was proposed that a High Commissioner should be appointed with the dual function of acting as chief adviser to the Secretary of State on native policy while at the same time administering and legislating in respect of certain services common to all three territories.[4] But the evidence presented to the Joint Committee could not be ignored. Although the European unofficials of Tanganyika were prepared to accept Wilson's proposals[5] the African witnesses impressed the

[1] *Uganda Herald*, December 28, 1929.

[2] *East African Standard*, February 28 and April 11, 1930.

[3] Report by Sir Samuel Wilson, G.C.M.G., on his visit to East Africa, 1929. Cmd. 3378. H.M.S.O., London, 1929.

[4] Statement of the Conclusions of His Majesty's Government as regards Closer Union in East Africa. Cmd. 3574. H.M.S.O., London, 1930.

[5] *Tanganyika Standard*, August 16, 1930.

committee with their view that since they were fully engaged in trying to develop their own institutions they wished to remain under the control of the Secretary of State and Parliament, acting through their own Governor, for as long as they could foresee.[1] The committee was even more moved by the lucidity with which Uganda's African representatives set out their case against closer union. The Labour Government's white paper had also aroused considerable opposition among the European communities in East Africa, the views of Kenya and Tanganyika unofficials being fairly well summed up in a letter to the *East African Standard* which asked, 'Where in history has a civilization been established in primitive and backward regions in which the whole or principal aim is to safeguard the interests of savagery and ignore the paramount pressure of progress and enlightenment?'[2] European commercial men in Uganda were not so critical of the ideals expressed in the white paper. But they did consider that the situation in Kenya had unduly influenced the British Government and had resulted in proposals which implied that European and African interests were in conflict throughout East Africa, a state of affairs which they firmly denied so far as Uganda was concerned.[3] The Indian communities alone appeared to be impressed by the Government's proposals, hoping that by some means or another they themselves would be able to play a greater part in the political life of the territory.[4]

The recommendation of the Joint Select Committee was that closer union of a political or constitutional character was out of the question for the time being although the Governors' Conference would be called upon to play an increasingly active role. With this declaration the matter was dropped so far as the British Government was concerned. The whole scheme had derived its impetus from outside East Africa and was based upon the assumption that the benefits of economic co-operation could override deeply felt local differences. Those benefits, although self-evident to Amery and his supporters, had proved unattractive to all races in East Africa. Moreover, the whole issue had caused grave concern in the Permanent Mandates Commission since the time of the Hilton

[1] Sir Philip Mitchell: op. cit., pp. 119-22.

[2] *East African Standard*, June 23, 1930.

[3] *Uganda Herald*, July 4, 1930.

[4] *East African Standard*, June 25, 1930 and *Uganda Herald*, August 8, 1930.

Young Report. Several members of the Commission doubted whether such proposals were acceptable in the light of Article 22 of the Covenant of the League of Nations even if administrative and fiscal union between Tanganyika and her neighbours was countenanced by Article 10 of the Mandate. Even the report of the Joint Select Committee did not entirely allay suspicion, for the use of the words 'political and constitutional union' suggested the possibility at some future date of an association which stepped beyond anything envisaged by the Mandate.

In East Africa itself the question of closer union lingered on in the 1930s, fostered mainly by the European unofficials of Kenya and Tanganyika. It was not that they had suddenly been converted to Amery's point of view. It was rather that they were overcome by the fear that Tanganyika might be handed back to Germany. The growing menace of Germany during the 1930s was in itself adequate ground for concern, and this, coupled with the indecisive attitude of the British Government, disturbed a number of the leading imperialists in Britain as well as the European inhabitants of East Africa. Amery himself and Sir Edward Grigg, now retired from his governorship, were extremely anxious about the Government's attitude towards the colonies and mandated territories. The attitude which had led to non-interference in Italy's conquest of Ethiopia was far from reassuring to Ethiopia's southern neighbours. Perhaps even more disturbing was the reaction of Lloyds who, when approached by some of those who had invested capital in Tanganyika, quoted a contingency rate of $36\frac{3}{4}$ per cent for insurance against the possible transfer of the territory to a foreign power.

Much of the uncertainty about Tanganyika emanated from Kenya rather than from Tanganyika itself, and when the Tanganyika League was founded in 1938 to press for the retention of the territory under the British flag its headquarters were set up in Nairobi while the chairman and organizer in chief was Major F. W. Cavendish-Bentinck, himself a Kenya resident. Even the telegraphic address of the Nairobi branch of the League, 'Tenacity', echoed the traditional defensive cry of European settlers oppressed by an inconsiderate government. By contrast the adoption by the Dar es Salaam branch of the address 'Probritman' sounded a more sturdy if somewhat naïve note. As early as 1936 the elected members of the Kenya Legislative Council had begun to press for an assurance concerning Tanganyika's future by means of questions asked by their friends in the House of Commons. With considerable force it was pointed out that there had been a marked change in the attitude of the British Government since 1920 when Amery and Lord Milner had stated categorically that 'Tanganyika Territory has now been permanently incorporated in the British Empire. It is an entire delusion that it is less British than any other colony.' Mr. Stanley Baldwin in 1936 and Mr. Neville Chamberlain in 1938 appeared to be far less confident about Tanganyika's status in refusing to commit themselves as to future policy in regard to the mandate. They did, in fact, state that neither in the past nor at the time at which they were speaking was there any intention on the part of the Government to transfer any mandate to another power, but their deliberate silence about the future brought little comfort to their interrogators. In these circumstances there were many Europeans in East Africa who saw in the closer union of Kenya and Tanganyika one of the only possible safeguards against the transfer of Tanganyika to Germany. Yet not all the members of the inter-racial Tanganyika League were agreed upon this solution, for the Indian Association of Dar es Salaam rejected in August 1939 a resolution in favour of the complete unification of the East African territories passed by a convention of European business and professional men which had met in Iringa during the previous month.[1]

Behind the backs of these anxious proponents of closer union, however, co-operation between the East African territories was developing unobtrusively and efficiently. From 1930 the Governors' Conferences met annually and although they possessed no executive or legislative powers a joint approach to such important issues as African taxation, elementary vernacular education, transport, communications and industrialization was discussed. In 1932 an amalgamation of the postal services of the three territories took place, to the annoyance of the German Colonial Association which made its protest heard through the Permanent Mandates Commission. Some members of the Commission had undoubtedly been worried by the prospect of the political union of Tanganyika with her East African neighbours throughout the discussions which Amery had instituted. In 1934 Sir John Simon gave the Commission a firm assurance that Britain would not infringe the terms of the League

[1] *Weekly Tanganyika Standard*, August 11, 1939.

321

Covenant, but the more frequent meetings of the Governors' Conference, together with the news of the unification of the postal services, resulted in a lengthy debate in the League Council itself. The Council expressed the view, although not unanimously, that by virtue of Article X of the mandate Britain was entitled to constitute Tanganyika into an administrative union with adjacent territories, but she could not include Tanganyika in any political union with her neighbours.

Prominent among the critics of Britain's policy in Tanganyika during 1933 was the German member of the Permanent Mandates Commission, Dr. J. Ruppel. Ruppel even went so far as to argue that anything which deprived Tanganyika of independence or placed any of Tanganyika's services under the executive control of an outside organ or of a common authority was contrary to the mandate and must be forbidden. Few other members were prepared to adopt such an extreme attitude but while the Belgian and Dutch members supported Britain whole-heartedly there were others who complained that they had been left in the dark about Britain's intentions regarding the Governor's Conferences and the postal union until action had been taken. Sir Stewart Symes, the Governor of Tanganyika, was able to give a complete assurance that no political or constitutional change was contemplated and this satisfied the majority of the Commission. Germany, however, continued to watch British policy in Tanganyika closely and through the numerous German settlers who had made their homes in Tanganyika began to lay the foundations of the restoration of Germany's rule there. This was not at first clearly appreciated by the British in East Africa. They disliked the German settlers' interest in National Socialism because it seemed as if they were looking to their homeland rather than to the land of their adoption for inspiration. Yet good farmers were badly needed and there was little opposition to willing workers on grounds of nationality. But the ominous events of 1938 forced upon all the East African Governments and the populations under their control the realization that war was imminent and that steps must be taken to deal with the German community as a first step towards the defence of British East Africa.

During the inter-war years Zanzibar's administrative and political progress was as unobtrusive as the affairs of Kenya and Tanganyika were lively. Between 1914, when the control of the Protectorate was transferred from the Foreign Office to the Colonial Office, and 1923 the liwalis who had previously administered Zanzibar as the Sultan's agents were gradually replaced by British district officers. In 1924 the Zanzibar Order in Council laid down the extent of the jurisdiction to be exercised by the Protectorate authority and in 1926, following the prevalent East African fashion, the Sultan established Executive and Legislative Councils. The former was presided over by the Sultan himself with the British Resident as Vice-President and its membership included the Heir Apparent and seven British officials. The Legislative Council was presided over by the Resident and comprised nine officials and eight unofficials nominated by the Sultan. The unofficial membership was remarkable in that it consisted of three Arabs, two Africans, two Asians, and one European, an inter-racial arrangement which might have provided a useful pattern for the disputing communities on the mainland.

CHAPTER NINE

THE ECONOMIC PENDULUM

ECONOMICALLY as well as administratively German East Africa had suffered more seriously during the war of 1914–18 than had her northern neighbours, yet it was the last to take active steps towards recovery. Here, as in other fields, the cautious influence of Sir Horace Byatt played its part. By contrast Uganda in the months immediately after the war had ended was in a ferment of activity. Following upon his intervention to ensure an adequate supply of labour to harvest the coffee crop of 1918 the Governor, Sir Robert Coryndon, appointed a Development Commission to consider the problem of establishing Uganda's economy upon an active peacetime footing once again. The Commission, which consisted of both government officials and unofficials, held its first meeting on December 2, 1919, and heard evidence from government departments, planters, commercial men, missionary societies, Indians and various groups of Africans. Its report, published early in 1920, was evidence of enthusiasm rather than of any profound grasp of the problems which the country faced. This was probably due to a large extent to the fact that the members of the committee were unsympathetic towards the encouragement of cotton growing by Africans upon which the country had now come to depend so heavily. It was cotton which made it possible for the Africans to pay their poll tax, and poll tax constituted a large part of the country's revenue. It was cotton, too, which enabled the African population to buy the foreign manufactured goods on which the Government collected considerable import duties. Yet it was towards a planter-based economy that the Commission directed most of its attention. Mr. S. Simpson, the Director of Agriculture, was criticized for allegedly encouraging cotton-growing to the detriment of the European-owned plantations. The prohibition of the sale of land to non-Africans was roundly condemned, and the railways, indeed the transport system in general, came under heavy fire. The 1900 Agreement was declared to be in need of review and the Buganda Lukiko was criticized for its conservatism. The educational system was also stated to be in need of attention, which was true enough, but the main object of improvement suggested by the report was to provide Africans with a more practical form of education which would not make them discontented. But the report proved to be the last gesture of those who believed that Uganda's future would depend upon a plantation economy. Not even the period of prosperity which the Protectorate experienced immediately after the war could justify the planters' claims. For the great increase in the country's revenue during the nine months from April 1 to December 31, 1920, as compared with the previous fifteen months, was almost entirely due to the high price paid for cotton. The slump of the early 1920s and the difficulty of obtaining land and labour contributed to the planters' downfall, but above all the success of cotton was responsible for laying down the lines of Uganda's economic development.

In Kenya, too, there was a great revival in the immediate post-war years. In spite of the derelict condition in which many settlers found their farms after the years of neglect imposed by the war there was no lack of a will to work and there was considerable confidence in the future. The banks were ready to lend money at reasonable rates and the Discharged Soldiers Settlement Scheme, first mooted in 1915, was adopted with enthusiasm. The scheme provided an opportunity for ex-servicemen to buy land on easy terms and was greatly welcome in Britain where it appeared as a useful means of lightening the burden of unemployment with which the country was faced as a result of the demobilization of its armies. It was welcomed in Kenya, too, because the settlers believed it would help to consolidate their position in the country and would give further support to their conviction that Kenya's future prosperity must be based upon European enterprise. Although selection boards were set up in London and Nairobi, however, there appears to have been little attempt to distinguish between the ex-soldiers who had and those who had not sufficient capital or experience of farming. When the first settlers arrived this did not seem to be a matter of great importance. Loans were readily obtainable and the prices offered for flax and sisal were so high that it seemed impossible not to make a success of farming in Kenya. Land was rapidly allocated and heavy equipment was purchased and then there followed the problem of obtaining labour which was to arouse such strong feelings in Britain and which was to colour British opinion about Kenya during the vital 1920s. Before the labour issue was settled, however, the demand was suddenly reduced by the disaster which struck so many of the settlers in 1921.

Post-war enthusiasm was still at its height when the slump of 1920–21 struck a sickening blow at East Africa's economy. To countries which relied entirely upon the export of primary produce for their revenue the fall in world prices was shattering in its effects. Of the three East African mainland territories Tanganyika suffered least, since it had taken few steps towards the rehabilitation of the country's economy when the first effects of the slump were felt. In any case, it was not expected that Tanganyika should pay its way for some time. Kenya, on the other hand, needed several years of stability to ensure that the lively if temporarily precarious economic structure which was being created by settler enterprise was to survive. The soldier settlers who had wagered their keenness and will to work against bankers' loans were particularly hard hit. Flax which was fetching £500 a ton in August 1920, dropped to £100 a ton and other primary products followed suit. In 1922 a continuous drought ruined the coffee crop. Many settlers were forced into bankruptcy while others struggled on under a burden of debt. To add to the confusion a decision had been taken to convert the currency of East Africa from rupees to East African florins. The origin of the scheme lay in the sudden post-war rise in value of the Indian rupee from 1s. 4d. to 2s. 8d. This meant that East Africa, trading simultaneously with India and Britain, was placed in an awkward position. The banks were particularly anxious to cover themselves against possible loss as a result of these violent fluctuations so that it was decided that the introduction of an East African coinage with a fixed value in terms of sterling and Indian rupees was essential. The announcement of the florin currency was particularly disastrous to the settlers whose loans had been raised at the earlier money values and were thus, suddenly, increased by 50 per cent while interest rates rose accordingly. Protests were of no avail and new cases of bankruptcy and still heavier burdens of debt were the outcome. The African population suffered too, for as a first step to the currency change the paper Indian rupee notes circulating in the country were declared, without any warning, to be no longer legal tender. Hundreds of former members of the Carrier Corps had been paid off in paper currency which they had accepted reluctantly and only after an assurance that it would be honoured at all times. Now their earnings were swept away in a few hours. An opportunity was offered to exchange silver rupees for the new coins within a limited period but even this involved some hardship since it was difficult to make an already suspicious people appreciate what was intended. Equally serious to the labouring population was a concerted attempt by the Convention of Associations in 1921 to induce all employers, the Government as well as private individuals, to reduce labourers' wages by $33\frac{1}{3}$ per cent on the ground that the florin was one and a half times the value of the rupee. This argument was indefensible. Labourers still paid as many florins in tax as they had formerly paid rupees. Their purchases, too, cost them as many florins as they had cost rupees. But the settlers, ruinously hit by the slump and living, as many of them were, in the most reduced circumstances, had little time for logic. They were strengthened, too, by General Northey's assurance that government wages would not exceed current wages for similar work in any area. Before this plan could be implemented, however, the value of the Indian rupee had slumped as rapidly as it had risen and it was decided that florins should be replaced by shillings. Nevertheless, the proposal regarding African wages had fired the resentment of many of the better educated Africans and had resulted in the founding of the Young Kikuyu Association.

Not surprisingly the settlers' sense of frustration at the effects of the slump found some outlet in criticism of the Government and not least of the recent rapid increase in the civil service. In an attempt to meet the rising cost of administration Sir Edward Northey proposed an increase in customs duties which had been made possible by the recent treaty of St. Germain-en-Laye, by the terms of which the 10 per cent ceiling on customs duties imposed at the Brussels Conference was rescinded. But settler opinion demanded economies, not higher taxation. In response to the strong demand the Governor appointed an Economic and Finance Committee under the chairmanship of the Colonial Secretary, Sir Charles Bowring. The committee had wide terms of reference and with a membership which included Lord Delamere and Major Grogan it set to work with a will to draft a new economic policy for Kenya. The Governor co-operated whole-heartedly and the committee's resolutions were immediately put into effect. The remaining export duties were abolished. Heavy import duties were imposed on wheat and flour in an attempt to reduce the unfavourable balance of trade and to encourage wheat growing in Kenya. An income tax which had been introduced in 1920 as an emergency measure was abolished as having proved impracticable. Above all, severe cuts were made in the working costs of Government departments. This did not effect the Government's policy of railway extension which was regarded as being too important to curtail even to meet the more straitened circumstances of the depression.

The success of the Bowring Committee's proposals was remarkable. But it was the improvement in world economic conditions, beginning in 1923, which saved Kenya. The improvement, moreover, came not a moment too soon. In addition to its other burdens the Kenya Government, determined to maintain the impetus of its railway and harbour development schemes had borrowed £5 million in 1921 and within two years was preparing to raise a further loan of £3 million. The payment of the interest on these loans in itself necessitated the starkest economy in Government expenditure.

The effects of the slump were not felt so swiftly in Uganda as they were in Kenya. Indeed, for the sixth year in succession, the Protectorate's revenue for 1921 showed a surplus over expenditure which brought the total surplus funds of the territory to about £300,000. Some coffee estates were forced to close down but those which carried on were able for a time to get a fair price for their crop. The record cotton crop gathered early in 1921, however, encountered disaster. World prices were low and the crisis resulting from the change in currency meant that there was a temporary shortage of available cash at buying time. In spite of the Government's attempts to introduce a buying scheme which would protect the growers as much as possible, the African peasants were gravely discouraged by the reward for their efforts. Ill equipped as they were to understand the vagaries of a world economic system which appeared to repay their response to the Government's exhortation to grow more cotton with ridiculously low prices, they were reluctant to plant large quantities of seed later in the year. Unseasonable rainfall reduced the crop still further so that the output in 1922 dropped to 25,000 bales (about 4,500 tons), compared with 81,000 bales in the previous year. As a result the Government saw its estimated surplus of income over expenditure in 1922 reduced from £100,000 to a deficit of a similar amount. Nevertheless, because the vast majority of Uganda's producers were African peasants who relied upon cotton for their luxuries rather than for their subsistence, there was not the wholesale bankruptcy that was experienced in Kenya and once world prices showed signs of improvement cotton-growing could start again untroubled by any backlog of debt. Uganda, therefore, was able to ride the storm with less genuine suffering than could Kenya.

Zanzibar was even less troubled by the depression. Its economy was firmly based upon the Arab-owned clove plantations which had a virtual monopoly of the crop in the world market. This fortunate situation, however, was in danger of being threatened by a variety of dishonest practices in which the growers, traders and exporters were all involved. Watering of the cloves to increase their weight and therefore their sale price was becoming increasingly common and although this practice benefited those responsible in the first place, retribution quickly followed. All sales of cloves were subject to arbitration clauses which permitted the ultimate buyers to obtain redress if crops were unsatisfactory. This had its repercussions on the merchants who soon lost heavily as a result of the dishonest transactions and ultimately the whole process threatened to bring Zanzibar's main crop into disrepute. The Government was seriously perturbed by this unhealthy development, not least since its revenue was based almost entirely upon a 10 per cent *ad valorem* duty on articles imported into the country and upon the income from the sale of the 25 per cent of the clove crop which it claimed in lieu of other tax. If one of the pillars of the country's wealth were to be undermined by malpractices the clove growers would not be the only sufferers. Strict measures of supervision were therefore introduced by the Government wherever possible and met with a certain amount of success.

In East Africa, generally, the shortage of money in 1921 and 1922 had a serious effect upon the import trade. The bulk of the imports consisted of cotton piece goods and petroleum products, a high proportion of which was bought by Africans. It was here, then, that the main effect of the fall in cotton prices was felt, for the African demand for imported wares dropped rapidly. By 1923, however, the situation had improved as a result of the rise in cotton prices and Africans were once more looking for things to buy. This improved state of affairs brought with it its own problems for there was a danger that importers, gambling on a new wave of prosperity might import an excessive amount of goods into the territories. Most of the wholesale and retail trade was in the hands of Indians who had relatively little capital and whose hopes of quick returns tended to cloud their judgement regarding the state of the market. They were encouraged in this rash policy by offers of long-term credit, particularly from German firms who, however, were soon to learn a sharp lesson when a number of their transactions failed in the mid 1920s. British business men benefited little from the improved conditions which followed the depression. They were slow to recognize East Africa as a potential market and they did not appreciate the fact that the main buyers, the African population, could only afford to buy the cheapest products. By the 1930s, however, when money was circulating more freely, Africans began to realize the importance of quality as opposed to price, but this was a somewhat later development. In the meantime printed textiles from Holland challenged the product of British factories not only because they were cheaper but also because of their attractive designs.

In general the recovery after the slump was reassuring. In Kenya a series of excellent coffee and maize crops began once more to build up the country's prosperity so that by 1928 the confidence of the settlers was fully restored. In Uganda, largely as a result of the work of administrative officers, the African peasants were induced to plant cotton once more and in 1923 there was a record crop which was rewarded by good prices. Nevertheless, the depression had taught the Government and Uganda's business population a sharp lesson. In 1923 a Cotton Control Board was formed consisting of members of the Government, the Ginners' Association, the Chamber of Commerce and the Middlemen's Association. Although it had only an advisory role its creation bore witness to Uganda's recognition of the need to keep a closer watch upon price fluctuations. More important from a long-term point of view was the Government's decision to encourage Africans to grow coffee so as to reduce the country's dependence upon cotton. Previously only European planters had grown coffee as an economic crop although some had been grown by Bugisu peasants on the lower slopes of Mount Elgon since 1912. In 1921 the Government bought all the Bugisu crop and in 1922 and 1923 erected two pulping stations in the district. As a result of this encouragement the acreage of coffee grown by Africans exceeded that of plantation coffee by 1930. Marketing arrangements were unsatisfactory, however, and at first little attention was paid to quality. The Government, therefore, made it compulsory for all hulled coffee to pass through a licensed curing works. At the same time the Bugisu native administration began to assist in marketing the crop. It was not until the 1950s that coffee seriously challenged cotton as Uganda's chief producer of revenue but the Government's decision to encourage African-grown coffee in the 1920s was to prove a source of great wealth to large numbers of Africans and at the same time it underlined the fact that the Government had abandoned its hopes of an economy resting heavily on planter production. The Acting Governor, Mr. E. B. Jarvis, made this plain in a speech delivered at the annual conference of the Uganda Planters' Association in January 1922. 'The more I turn over the matter in my mind,' he said, 'the more convinced I become that Uganda's future lies in the cultivation of the soil and the growing of the crops by the natives under scientific supervision by the Agricultural Department, and the purchasing and marketing of these crops by Europeans.' Yet one new plantation crop made its appearance in the 1920s and achieved considerable success. In 1923 an Indian business man, Mr. Nanji Kalidas Mehta, found himself in a sound financial position through having bought cotton during the slump and selling it when prices improved. With the proceeds he erected a sugar refinery between Kampala and Jinja and developed a large sugar estate. Shortly afterwards a second estate was started farther east, beyond the Nile, in Busoga. Sugar never approached cotton and coffee as one of the outstanding contributors to Uganda's income but it none the less provided a valuable addition to the variety of the Protectorate's crops.

If the experiment with African-grown coffee in Uganda was to have long-term results far exceeding the expectations of its originators, a similar experiment in Tanganyika which started about the same time was to produce even more rapid results. While searching through captured German records in 1916 Mr. (later Sir Charles) Dundas had noticed a reference to coffee-growing by a handful of

Chagga on the slopes of Kilimanjaro. The experiment had been abandoned owing to the difficulty of marketing the crop, but when Dundas became an administrative officer in the Kilimanjaro region after the war the idea recurred in his mind and he determined to see how practical it might be. Crowded upon the mountain slopes the Chagga had scarcely room enough to grow the plantains which formed their staple diet. If, however, the plantains were to be used as shade trees to protect coffee bushes an economic crop could share the land with the vital food crop. On investigation Dundas discovered that the soil on the higher slopes occupied by the Chagga was more suited to coffee-growing than that on the lower slopes which the Germans had occupied. He therefore encouraged the former growers to prune and tend their bushes so that before long a good quality crop could be obtained. In order to achieve the next stage of successfully marketing the coffee it was necessary to induce larger numbers to grow the crop. At Dundas's instigation a union of Chagga coffee-growers was founded with the title of the Kilimanjaro Native Planters' Association. Crops were pooled and it was soon possible for the Association to sell reasonably large quantities of good quality coffee to the Indian merchants who handled the commercial side of the industry.

The European coffee-growers on the mountain were seriously perturbed by this African competition and were genuinely afraid that coffee disease might result from encouraging unskilled Africans to grow *Arabica* coffee. It was, in fact, their disapproval of the part played by the Government in promoting the African coffee-growing scheme which led them to toy briefly with the idea of a transfer of the Kilimanjaro region to Kenya to which reference has already been made. The arrival of Cameron, it was hoped, would result in a sounder policy in respect of coffee-growing as well as in many other fields. Although Cameron was fully alive to the value of European assistance in the development of Tanganyika, he was, however, unwilling to check the enterprise shown by the Chagga growers. On the Governor's first visit to Moshi the Chagga demonstrated the extent of their development as business men by approaching Cameron for permission to market their own coffee since the prices offered by Indian traders were, in their view, much too low. In the face of such enthusiasm the Governor felt he could do no more than take steps to ensure that the European growers' fear of coffee disease should be allayed as a result of adequate precautions. These limited measures did not satisfy the European planters and their suspicions of Cameron continued until they reached a climax during 1928. Towards the end of that year the situation became strained in the Kilimanjaro area owing to the spread of rumours among the Chagga that the Government intended to reduce the size of landholdings and to absorb the K.N.P.A. in the local authority. Although neither of these rumours was correct the Chagga were not surprisingly disturbed by what appeared to them to be a threat of unwarranted interference in tribal custom and of an attack upon an institution of which they had become extremely proud. This discontent was interpreted by European planters as being an indication of hostility to the Government and possibly of the existence of an anti-European plot. Dundas, now Secretary for Native Affairs, was sent to Kilimanjaro where his reputation among the Chagga was such that he was soon able to give them the reassurance they needed. To the planters, however, the dispatch of Dundas, the virtual founder of the K.N.P.A., appeared as a weak attempt by the Government to conciliate the Chagga without any concern for the safety of the territory as a whole. They pressed for an inquiry into the discontent which had recently existed but Cameron wisely refused their request on the ground that it was more likely to excite ill feeling than to allay any fears. In fact the problem had already been solved by Dundas's intervention and the opening of the new railway extension from Moshi to Arusha, coupled with Cameron's decision to hold the budget session of the Legislative Council in Arusha in 1929, did something at least to assure the planters that the Government was not wholly indifferent to their interests. Gradually better relations were established between the two races and coffee-growing on Kilimanjaro proved to be one of the most successful fields of co-operation between Africans and Europeans.

Kilimanjaro was not the only region in which Africans were able to grow coffee successfully. In the Bukoba District *Robusta* coffee was being grown most successfully, again in conjunction with plantains as a food crop. This coarser type of coffee was exported mainly to Egypt and the Red Sea Coast until its value as a basis for coffee essences was recognized and exploited commercially. Nevertheless, coffee did not challenge sisal as Tanganyika's most valuable export and although the territory continued to produce a fairly wide variety of crops, sisal remained supreme as a producer of wealth.

Economic expansion in all three mainland territories called for an urgent extension of communications, and Kenya's insistence on pursuing its policy of rail development even during the slump of 1921–22 has already been remarked upon. One of the most important extensions of the railway in Kenya was the construction of a branch line from Nakuru to the Uasin Gishu Plateau. The alignment of this extension was heavily criticized because it was said by some to be wasteful of money and to have been planned to suit the interests of Lord Delamere. Nevertheless, the opening up of the Uasin Gishu and subsequently of the Trans Nzoia farmland farther north was a vital development as far as Kenya was concerned and paved the way for a direct rail link with Uganda. Uganda itself quickly recognized the importance of such a link when the revival of cotton-growing after the slump placed an excessively heavy demand upon the transport system and more particularly upon the section between Jinja and Kisumu where, owing to the dependence upon Lake transport, loading and off-loading created a heavy demand for labour. In 1924 surveys began for an extension of the line from Turbo, some seventy miles over the Kenya border, westward to Jinja. The line itself was opened in 1928 and the final link between Kampala and the coast was completed in 1931 when a railway bridge was opened over the Nile within sight of the Ripon Falls.

Tanganyika, even more than its northern neighbours, needed to improve its communications if the scattered centres of production were to be exploited satisfactorily. To make the construction of branch lines a feasible proposition, however, a prosperous main line was needed as a starting-point. To achieve this first objective negotiations were pursued with the Union Minière in the Katanga Province of the Belgian Congo, and from these discussions it became reasonably clear that when the Benguela and Matadi railway lines were in full working order there would still be heavy consignments of minerals to be transported along the Tanganyika Central Line. With this encouragement a variety of proposals for branch-line extensions were considered although most of them were either rejected or shelved owing to lack of money. The Tanga Line was extended from Moshi to Arusha to take fuller advantage of the important producing area around Kilimanjaro. The extension of the

Central Line northward from Tabora to Lake Victoria, however, proved to be a far more controversial issue. Byatt considered this development to be inevitable in view of the resources of the lake region and of their importance to Tanganyika's wealth. It was left to Cameron, however, to set the work in hand, and in doing so he encountered stiff opposition from Kenya. Cameron persisted in his plan, convinced that it was justified by the quantity of trade and in no spirit of unfriendly rivalry towards his northern neighbour. In fact competition was avoided by the introduction of similar tariffs for goods travelling along both the Kenya and Tanganyika sections of line, and Kenya's fears were thus proved to be groundless. Nevertheless, the dispute over the Tabora–Mwanza extension provided an illustration of the difficulties which could arise in an area which the Secretary of State, Mr. L. S. Amery, was so ready to regard as an economic unit while apparently ignoring the diversity of outlook which had developed in the three territories.

A sphere in which co-operation was fairly easily achieved was that of customs duties. A common customs tariff came into effect in the three mainland territories on January 1, 1923, and simultaneously a reciprocal arrangement was made enabling goods produced or manufactured in any of the territories to enter any other of the territories duty free. This was followed on May 1, 1927, by the introduction of a general Customs Management Ordinance which, although it did not establish a full customs union, none the less achieved considerable uniformity of practice. All these arrangements were accomplished without friction between the countries concerned although it was seen within a few years that they tended to benefit Kenya more than the other two territories. Zanzibar, meanwhile, found itself unable to take part in these joint measures. Although participating in the discussions which led to joint action Zanzibar was too dependent upon its revenue from customs duties to abandon its 10 per cent *ad valorem* duty on imported goods and indeed found it necessary to increase this scale to 15 per cent in October 1927.

Minerals contributed little to the economic development of East Africa between the wars although for the first time hopes of mineral wealth were raised. The early explorers in speaking of East Africa as a potentially wealthy country had thought only in terms of agricultural development, and the Europeans who had been attracted to East Africa had gone there in the hope of developing farms or

335

plantations. A little mica in German East Africa had been the only mineral product before the 1920s. In that decade, however, undue hopes were aroused by the discovery of gold in the Mwanza and Musoma districts of Tanganyika and along the Lupa River in the extreme south-west of the territory. In 1925 small deposits of tin were found in Ankole, in Uganda, and there were rumours of coal on the Uganda side of Mount Elgon. Traces of copper in the eastern foothills of the Ruwenzori Mountains of western Uganda seemed for the time being to hold out little hope of economic return, but the discoveries in the other areas resulted in a ready demand for prospectors' licences. There was even some hope of interesting the Anglo-Persian Oil Company in investigating for oil in the vicinity of Lake Albert but this proposal came to nothing and, indeed, minerals in general continued to be unrewarding.

Just when East Africa's economic position seemed to have been securely established further and still greater difficulties were encountered. Their arrival was foreshadowed by natural omens in the shape of a plague of locusts which swept across the territory in the latter half of 1928, while in Tanganyika in the early months of 1929 floods interfered with rail transport and put the roads out of action. In Tanganyika, too, a promising cotton crop was ruined by a plague of rats.[1] Soon the rumblings of disaster were heard in New York where the stock market collapsed in 1929. Once again, as had happened ten years earlier, countries depending on primary produce were quickly affected. Throughout East Africa there was a call for greater economies in the administration of the territories and in Kenya the new Governor, Sir Joseph Byrne, was subjected to particularly heavy criticism by the European settlers. Demands for cuts in expenditure were accompanied by protests against any increase in taxation and there was a suggestion that an independent expert should be invited to review the situation.[2] The Kenya Government was far from idle in the face of these criticisms and civil service salaries were cut and leave regulations altered. In February 1932 it was announced that Lord Moyne, formerly Financial Secretary to the Treasury and Minister of Agriculture and Fisheries in the United Kingdom Government, had been appointed

[1] *Tanganyika Territory: Annual Report for the Year 1930.* Colonial No. 60. H.M.S.O., London, 1931, p. 34.

[2] *East African Standard*, January 9, 16 and 30, 1932.

Sir Edward Twining
(now Lord Twining)

Sir Andrew Cohen

Sir Evelyn Baring
(now Lord Howick)

Sir Richard Turnbull

Jomo Kenyatta

Milton Obote

Serwano Kulubya

Julius Nyerere

Financial Commissioner to investigate Kenya's problems. His report brought little comfort to the settlers, however.[1] The African population, he estimated, was contributing $37\frac{1}{2}$ per cent of the colony's total revenue in direct taxation in addition to their share of indirect taxation. The non-Africans, on the other hand, were paying less than their due. Furthermore, the Africans were getting very few services in return for their money. In these circumstances, whatever the settler contribution to the country's development, research was urgently needed into the best means of encouraging African agriculture while there must also be better provision for African education. For a time it seemed that the introduction of an income tax was inevitable if the costs of administration were to be met, but the Colonial Office was finally induced to agree to alternative proposals, including the introduction of a graduated non-native poll tax, which the settlers, led by Lord Francis Scott, had put forward. The decision of the Colonial Office was undoubtedly influenced by the great improvement in trade of which there was evidence early in 1933, and for a further four years at least the threat of an income tax was removed. The settlers were so encouraged by the improvement in the economic situation that after criticizing the graduated poll-tax bill in the Legislative Council they asked Lord Francis Scott to open immediate negotiations with the Secretary of State with a view to establishing a greater measure of control by unofficials over the country's finances.

If Lord Moyne's report could be so readily dismissed in Kenya, it left its mark upon opinion in Britain. The Secretary of State was taken to task my members of the Labour Party for his decision over the income tax and Labour members were far from satisfied that labour and land issues in Kenya had been dealt with in an equitable fashion. Moyne, for the first time, had virtually posed the question as to whether Kenya's reliance on a settler economy was justified by its economic results and defensible from the point of view of its social implications. These questions had hitherto been obscured, partly by the manner in which the settlers themselves had retained the initiative in argument, partly by the primitive character of African farming which held out little hope, it seemed, of the quick economic returns which the country needed, and partly, perhaps principally,

---

[1] *Certain Questions in Kenya*, Report by Financial Commissioner, Lord Moyne, May 1932. Cmd. 4093, 1932.

by the excellent pioneering qualities and unflagging industry of the settlers themselves. The settlers' defence that the rate of development could not be determined by the most backward people had been hard to answer on the assumption that the alternative method had brought prosperity to Kenya. But the shock of the slump had made it necessary not only to examine the very foundations of the country's economy but also to investigate its effects upon the social development of the people. The recovery in the world situation, however, came before the inquiry had been pursued very far and the later 1930s saw little change in Kenya's economic programme.

In 1930 Tanganyika stood in possibly greater danger even than Kenya. The country's economy was only just beginning to emerge from its foundations while at the same time Cameron had undertaken a modest, but by the standards of Tanganyika an expensive programme of educational, medical and other forms of social development. Expenditure on all government projects had now to be seriously curtailed. Most important, however, was the effect of the slump upon the African population. On the whole the Africans suffered no real hardship for they still relied to a large extent upon what they could produce themselves and could easily forgo the few items of foreign manufacture which they had begun to buy in the 1920s. But peasants who had responded with no great enthusiasm to Government demands that they should grow economic crops were quickly discouraged when the prices offered became impossibly low. Native authorities, too, were faced with a severe test when their income was drastically cut at the very moment when they were hoping to expand their activities. In addition there was a background of recriminations, the European unofficials criticizing the Government for its ineptitude and the Africans for their sloth, and the Africans condemning the Indian traders for their sharp practice.

Something of the problem which the Government faced is to be seen in the figures for African hut and poll tax which in 1929–30 amounted to £750,000 and which dropped to £450,000 in 1931–32. This tax was both the main source of government revenue and also the main source of income for the native authorities. In March 1931 a Retrenchment Commission was appointed and its report was submitted in May. Sir Stewart Symes, who became Governor of Tanganyika just as the depression was getting a firm hold upon the country, adopted many of its proposals and looked around for still further ways of dealing with the economic problem. New and more effective methods of collecting the hut and poll tax were instituted, including payment in instalments and by deduction from wages. More fundamental, however, was the 'grow more crops' campaign, with food crops as the highest priority, instituted by the Director of Agriculture, Mr. E. Harrison. Although informed that the Government had no control over world prices the chiefs were told to impress upon their people the vital need to increase their output of crops, and their response to this far from stimulating line of argument was remarkably good. Following up his success in this direction Harrison introduced greater control over the marketing of crops so as to ensure the best possible prices for the growers. This was vitally necessary not only to combat the country's poverty but also to check the rare outburst of racial feeling against the Asian traders to which the effects of the slump had given rise. In calmer circumstances both Europeans and Africans were ready to admit the debt the country owed, not only to the wealthier Asian financiers and merchants at the coast but more particularly to the small-scale traders who had set up their stores in remote parts of the territory. By their efforts they had not only supplied the African population with many articles they could not otherwise have obtained but also, by displaying their goods, had encouraged Africans to grow economic crops so as to have the cash to buy the goods. Under the stress of the slump the friendly relations which the traders had established deteriorated rapidly. They could not offer good prices for produce and there were undoubtedly cases of fraud. Fortunately the situation did not last long owing to the personal intervention of the Governor, and the harsher demands for discriminatory legislation against the Asians were soon dropped. The Asian leaders also played their part by using their influence to improve the behaviour of the traders.[1]

As in Kenya the suggestion that non-Africans should be subject to direct taxation met with lively opposition. Symes argued that it was unfair that the relatively wealthy non-Africans should be exempt from a form of taxation which the Africans had paid for ten years and he called for some sacrifice to meet the country's needs. His appeal met with little response but he was able, with the aid of the official majority in the Legislative Council, to pass an ordinance

[1] Sir Stewart Symes: *Tour of Duty*. Collins, London, 1946, pp. 172–74.

introducing a graduated poll tax for non-Africans. Within twelve months the threat of an income tax had transformed the loudest critics of the poll tax into its warmest supporters.

Sir Sydney Armitage-Smith performed a similar task for Tanganyika to that which Lord Moyne had carried out in Kenya. Seconded by the Lords Commissioners of the Treasury in February 1932, he made a careful investigation of Tanganyika's revenue and expenditure. And just as in Kenya Lord Moyne's report had met with little enthusiasm so, too, Armitage-Smith's report had a lukewarm reception in Tanganyika. Rightly he stressed the fact that since the economy of the country was based predominantly upon African production, the Government's machinery should be adapted to meet the needs of the African population and should recognize the limited resources available for expansion. With less justification he criticized some of the social services introduced during the more prosperous period of Cameron's governorship as being expensive and beyond the means of the country. Since Cameron had had the approval of the Permanent Mandates Commission for his policy and since the steady increase in Tanganyika's resources in the 1920s had appeared adequate to meet the Government's modest innovations, Symes believed he was on firm ground in rejecting these criticisms when the report was considered by the Mandates Commission. It was Armitage-Smith, too, who suggested the introduction of an income tax but this measure was thought to be premature and was not adopted. In the event, by 1933 Tanganyika was able once again to balance its budget without any further measures of economy. Recovery, however, was a slow process and was still further retarded by the fear that Tanganyika might be handed back to Germany, a factor which discouraged investment in the territory throughout the later 1930s.

Uganda suffered least among the mainland territories as a result of the slump and ironically a considerable proportion of the hardship the Protectorate was called upon to endure was due to the fact that the Secretary of State had given instructions in 1929 that the Government must take a less cautious view of its estimated revenue and must plan more boldly for the territory's development. After the excellent coffee crop of 1929 this advice appeared to be fully justified and the estimates for 1930 were framed with a view to a considerable extension of the country's social services and with the deliberate intention of drawing upon surplus balances to meet the increased expenditure. In spite of the slump, expenditure in 1930 did not seriously exceed income but the new schemes which had been introduced during the course of the year meant that the Protectorate would be liable to increased recurrent expenditure in the future when retrenchment would have appeared more appropriate. In 1931, therefore, the Governor, Sir William Gowers, called for a sharp revision of the country's development programme and at the same time appointed a committee to recommend economies and to suggest new sources of income. Inevitably the committee recommended a reduction in Government expenditure, but, more surprisingly in view of public opinion in Kenya and Tanganyika, it suggested that the non-African poll tax should be increased and that if possible an income tax should be introduced. Public opinion in Uganda, however, was not enthusiastic about the latter recommendation and the Indians were particularly disturbed by the proposal to increase the poll tax since many of them were in the lower income groups which would suffer most from any increase in direct taxation. The increase was never in fact introduced, and after the cuts in expenditure which were applied in 1932 the Government came to the conclusion that the country's economy was sufficiently buoyant to make further economies unnecessary. Indeed, so confident had the Government become that Uganda could weather the storm that it rejected the proposal that Lord Moyne should be invited to visit Uganda after completing his Kenya survey. It came as a shock, therefore, when the Secretary of State announced in July 1932 that as a result of Moyne's visit to Kenya he had decided that there should be an income tax in all three East African territories. Uganda was indignant, both on the ground that the measure was by that time unnecessary and also that it was a further example of the Protectorate's being treated as an appendage to Kenya. It was felt, too, that an income tax would be impracticable in the relatively undeveloped state of Uganda's administration.

Uganda's criticism was only a pale reflection of the outburst in Kenya but the new Governor, Sir Bernard Bourdillom, was unable to pacify the objectors by arguing that the income tax was neither a response to slump conditions nor an indication of Uganda's subordination to Kenya but was rather a forward step in the process of modernizing the Protectorate's fiscal system. There was even

some disappointment among Uganda's European unofficial population when the income tax proposal was later abandoned since once
again the decision appeared to have been taken in Kenya's interests
rather than for the benefit of Uganda. Bourdillon continued to argue
that the non-African population was inadequately taxed in comparison with the Africans and in this he had the support of the
European unofficials at least. The introduction of a graduated non-
African poll tax in 1934, therefore, was criticized only by the Indian
population and even they argued that a genuine income tax would
be more acceptable since it would weigh less heavily upon the lower
income groups. Uganda's recovery had indeed begun as early as
1932 when there was once again a satisfactory balance of income
over expenditure. As in Tanganyika Uganda's main producers, the
African peasants, because of the little capital involved in their work,
were able to ride out of the slump with less hardship than Kenya's
European settlers with their more highly capitalized farms. Uganda,
too, had had many more years of economic development than had
Tanganyika, so that her Government services were more firmly
rooted that were those of her southern neighbour when the storm
struck them.

Throughout the disappointments and difficulties of the early
1930s Zanzibar remained largely undisturbed. It was, indeed, the
world's economic anomaly. In spite of a sharp fall in the income
from customs duties in 1931, which pointed to the folly of Zanzibar's
remaining aloof from the customs arrangements of the mainland
territories, cloves saved the day. While other countries suffered
from an overproduction of necessities, the demand for Zanzibar's
semi-luxury commodity, cloves, increased, while prices were maintained as a result of the opening of a new market in the Dutch East
Indies where cloves were now used in the manufacture of cigarettes.
Throughout the period of the depression Zanzibar's revenue and
expenditure remained stable as it continued to do throughout the
rest of the decade. While, therefore, Kenya emerged from its sufferings with a new-found confidence in 1934 and Tanganyika faced new
problems of a political origin, Zanzibar remained untroubled and
unambitious.

In the inter-war years and more particularly in the 1920s two
issues affected both the economy and the political and social life of
East Africa to such an extent that they deserve special mention. These

were the problem of labour supply and the distribution of land. Inevitably Kenya, with its larger European settler population, was more seriously affected by both issues than was either of its neighbours. Indeed, Kenya's labour question achieved notoriety at the very moment when the European settlers were hoping to win support for their political aims. In the post-war campaign to develop the country's economy, once again the demand for labour became an immediate issue, and one which was enhanced by the influx of soldier settlers. The Chief Native Commissioner, John Ainsworth, a man of considerable experience who had played a vital part in the recruitment and organization of the labour corps during the war, was anxious to protect the African population from a prolongation of the hardships they had undergone in the struggle against the Germans. While recognizing the legitimate needs of the settlers he was opposed to any policy which aimed simply at getting the Africans out of their reserves so as to make them permanently dependent upon paid employment.[1] His views were strongly criticized by European farmers who, in their desperate search for labourers had looked to Tanganyika, to the annoyance of the unofficial European population of that territory who believed that their country would need all the labourers it could muster for its own development.[2] There was considerable irony, therefore, in the fact that it was a circular drafted by Ainsworth, although amended by the Governor, Sir Edward Northey, which aroused such violent criticism in England.

The sections of the circular to which exception was taken stated that the Governor hoped administrative officers in charge of what were termed labour-supplying districts would do all in their power to increase the supply of labour for the farms and plantations in the territory. The circular went on to say that the Governor considered that a large and continuous flow of labour from the reserves would improve the relations between the African population and the settlers and between the settlers and the Government. It would also have the advantage of enabling the young men to become wage-earners instead of remaining idle in the reserves for the greater part of the year. This statement of policy did not introduce any fundamental change in the existing instructions to district officers. The important difference was that Northey, unlike his predecessors,

[1] *The Leader of British East Africa*, August 9, 1919.

[2] *Dar es Salaam Times*, September 11, 1920.

expected his suggestions to be treated as orders.[1] The Governor had no doubt that his policy was in the interests of the country as a whole and of the African population in particular. There was no note of hypocrisy in his letter to the Convention of Associations dated October 21, 1919, in which he wrote: 'Our ideal must be to combine the progress and prosperity of the Protectorate with the welfare of the natives. The white man must be paramount. The best possible relations must exist between the paramount and subject races. We must make the native a useful and contented citizen, playing a part in the economic development of the country. This he will not do if left to his own resources. We must give the native reasonable education, especially technical, industrial and agricultural. The workshops on the farms should be the schools for education; Government should encourage the assistance of the well-conducted missions. . . . With regard to native labour there are two points to consider, firstly, that native labour is required for the proper development of the country, and secondly that we must educate the native to come out of the reserve and work, for his own sake, because nothing can be worse for the young native than to remain, according to his inclinations, in the reserve. Those that do so are likely to become vicious and effete.'[2] As an earnest of the Governor's good intentions steps were taken to amend the Masters' and Servants' Ordinance so as to give added protection to labourers by the appointment of labour inspectors at the same time as the Labour Circular was published.

The first to challenge Northey's views were the Protestant missionary societies of Kenya, their views being laid before the Governor by their spokesman, Dr. J. W. Arthur at a meeting held in Thika in January 1920. Their approach was practical rather than emotional, and they were able to lay bare some of the ill-founded suppositions upon which Northey had based his policy. In particular they challenged the charge of idleness which had been indiscriminately levelled against the inhabitants of the reserves, and they also questioned the accuracy of the Government's opinion as to the number of potential labourers in the country. At the same time, while protesting vigorously against the principle of forced labour,

[1] M. F. Hill: *Permanent Way*, East African Railways and Harbours, Nairobi. 1950, p. 391.

[2] *The Leader of East Africa*, November 1, 1919.

they recognized the needs of both Government and settlers alike. Their objective, therefore, was to improve the conditions under which labourers would be employed rather than to condemn the employment of labourers out of hand. Their most valuable suggestion was that a labour bureau be created to handle the specialized problems likely to arise. At the same time this would release administrative officers to carry out their proper duties.[1]

The missionaries were not alone in their criticisms of the Government's labour policy but they were far better informed and considerably more level-headed than many of those who took up the cry of condemnation in England itself. In the British Parliament and in the Press the campaign was soon raging furiously, and in such a charged atmosphere it was not surprising that accuracy tended to disappear. The Labour Circular which had been the initial cause of the outburst became confused with the Native Authority Ordinance of 1912 which, among other things, had empowered the Government, in accordance with tribal custom, to require the menfolk of a tribe to work on communal projects for six days in each quarter. Legislation of a similar character existed in Uganda, but aroused little comment since there was no serious demand for labour for European plantations to confuse the issue there. The Secretary of State, Lord Milner, however, remained unperturbed by the emotional outburst. In August 1920 he endorsed the view that the use of lawful means to improve the labour supply for settlers engaged in work of importance to the country and to the Empire as a whole was a direct responsibility of the Protectorate Government.[2] But, while Milner's attitude was reassuring both to the Government and to the settlers, it did not mean that public criticism in Britain was silenced.

It was the depression of the early 1920s which eased the situation to some extent. With prices falling the settlers were not so anxious to obtain labour as they had been immediately after the war. The Government, on the other hand, could not entirely abandon its development programme and labour was in heavy demand for extensions to the railway. Confident in the support of Lord Milner the Native Authority Ordinance was amended in 1920 to meet the Government's requirements by extending to sixty days a year the

[1] *The Leader of East Africa*, January 10, 1920.

[2] Dispatch to the Governor of the East Africa Protectorate relating to Native Labour and Papers connected therewith. Cmd 873, 1920.

period for which tribal labour could be called upon for public works. The amendment did no more than bring the powers of the Kenya Government into line with those recently adopted in Uganda, but in 1921 Mr. Winston Churchill, who had succeeded Lord Milner as Colonial Secretary, sent a dispatch urging that although his predecessor had approved the terms of the amendment British public opinion must not be ignored. He insisted that recourse should not be had to compulsory labour for Government purposes unless it was absolutely necessary. To ensure that this policy was adopted he laid it down that there should be a further amendment to the Native Authority Ordinance making it compulsory for the Government to obtain permission from the Secretary of State before employing forced labour.[1] The provision was embodied in a new ordinance passed in 1922 and its rigid enforcement is illustrated by the lengthy correspondence between successive governors and Colonial Secretaries in the early 1920s over the provision of labour for railway extensions.[2] Thus, arising out of the question of labour for European-owned farms the whole question of compulsory labour in Kenya was subjected to the closest scrutiny.

Churchill's intervention had not been directed against the demands of the settlers, but his dispatch had shown clearly enough that what the Government might not do the settlers also could not hope to undertake. While approving of the inculcation of habits of industry both inside and outside the reserves, the Secretary of State firmly restricted the part to be played by district officers to the indication of areas where labourers were needed or where they were available. The position of neutrality which was imposed upon the Government was heavily criticized by the settlers so that the labour issue continued to disturb the Kenya scene throughout the inter-war period. But the firm directive given by Churchill enabled the Government to adopt a more consistent attitude. There began to emerge a policy in which the legitimate demands of the Government and of European farmers were balanced against the importance of encouraging Africans to cultivate the land in the reserves to the best of their ability.

[1] Dispatch to the Officer Administering the Government of Kenya Colony and Protectorate relating to Native Labour, September 5, 1921. Cmd. 1509, 1921.

[2] *Compulsory Labour for Government Purposes*. Cmd. 2464. H.M.S.O. London, 1925.

In Uganda the labour problem never assumed the proportions that it did in Kenya, and with the decline in the number of European-owned plantations during the depression of the early 1920s it became an issue affecting only the Administration. None the less, for a brief period after the war Uganda, too, had its labour question. In September 1918 the Chief Secretary summoned a meeting of representatives of the Uganda Planters' Association, the Chamber of Commerce and the Cotton Ginners' Association, together with a number of prominent Government officials, in order to discuss the labour supply for non-Government as well as for Government projects. With the Governor's approval representatives of the missions and of the Indian Association were also invited to attend preliminary talks. From these discussions arose a proposal to appoint a labour officer whose first task would be to complete statistics of both the demand and supply of labour and who would subsequently be responsible for supplying the needs of both the planters and the Government. The planters had hoped for a more striking outcome to their talks but were satisfied that the Government was genuinely anxious to meet their difficulties. Mr. H. C. Rayne, who was appointed to the post of Labour Officer, died of influenza in August 1919, before any decisive steps had been taken. His draft report resulted in the Government's urging district commissioners to assist in any way possible to increase the labour supply. But, as in Kenya, before anything further was done the onset of the depression struck its blow at the planters, while the departure of Sir Robert Coryndon to Kenya removed their main supporter from the scene.

There remained the problem of compulsory labour for Government purposes, known as *kasanvu*. In Uganda as in Kenya the Government's need for labour for the construction of roads and buildings made it imperative that Africans should work on these projects and in view of the low wages which were current and of the profit to be derived from cotton-growing some form of compulsion was inevitable. In 1919 the Native Authority Ordinance extended the period of compulsory work on official projects from thirty to sixty days a year, a change which Lord Milner approved as he was to approve a similar move in Kenya a year later. But Churchill's dispatch of 1921 applied to Uganda as much as it did to Kenya and in 1923 an amendment was made to the Native Authority Ordinance

347

restricting the use of compulsory labour. In fact, after the early 1920s demands for compulsory labour for Government purposes became extremely rare and with the increase in African incomes from cotton even the traditional and less objectionable labour for local purposes, known as *luwalo*, was gradually commuted into a money payment until it was finally replaced entirely by a money tax in 1938.

The demand for labour in Tanganyika did not follow so closely after the war as it did in the other two mainland territories. Yet even the postponement of the problem was brought as a charge against the Government by some of its critics who claimed that the absence of any acute labour shortage was mainly due to the lack of initiative displayed by the Governor, Sir Horace Byatt, in encouraging the economic revival of the territory. By 1924, however, and in spite of the widely-held conviction that Tanganyika was still recovering too slowly, the Government's development programme, coupled with the revival of European-owned estates and the growing interest displayed by Africans in the production of economic crops had together produced a labour problem which demanded urgent attention. As the Government itself admitted, the view that Tanganyika contained a large reservoir of unemployed labourers, available even for export to adjacent territories, was very far from the truth.[1] Now the demand exceeded the supply, and labourers were becoming increasingly discriminating in their choice of employers. A planter's reputation could generally be assessed from the relative ease with which he obtained labour, although in some cases there were less justifiable grounds for the unpopularity of certain employers, such as the outbreak of an epidemic on a plantation which might arouse superstitious fears against the plantation owner.

The emergence of the labour problem showed up the British Administration in Tanganyika in an extremely good light. Article V of the Mandate under which Tanganyika was administered by Britain had made specific provision for the protection of labourers in the territory and the Tanganyika Government carried out its obligations conscientiously. In 1922 slavery was finally abolished without any undue disturbance. The Germans, probably overestimating the number of slaves in the territory and their importance to the country's social and economic life, had hesitated to take the bold action of

[1] *Tanganyika Territory: Annual Report for the Year 1924.* Colonial No. 11, H.M.S.O., 1925, p. 17.

making slavery illegal although they had insisted that all slaves born after 1905 should be free. The task of the British Administration, therefore, was easier than had been anticipated, yet their determination to stamp out slavery redounds wholly to their credit. In the same year in which the ordinance to abolish slavery was promulgated, fixed rates of pay for unskilled employees of the Government were also laid down. These were later raised in order to meet competition from planters and private contractors. Next, in 1923, a Masters' and Servants' Ordinance was passed which required contracts involving labourers travelling far from their homes to be put into writing and attested by either a magistrate or an administrative officer. It also emphasized that no contract should involve a man in absence from his home district for more than six months. The expense of recruitment and the time taken in travelling to the place of employment made it necessary for the period of absence to be extended to one year, but the Government took the opportunity offered by this amendment to insist that employers should provide adequate housing, food and health services for their labour forces.

The Government's concern for the welfare of labourers resulted in the appointment in 1924 of a Provincial Commissioner, Major G. St. J. Orde Browne, to act as temporary Labour Commissioner with the task of investigating the country's labour problems. On Orde Browne's recommendation Tanganyika took a step which placed the territory well in the vanguard of all the British dependencies in regard to the control of labour. In 1926 a Labour Department was created with Orde Browne himself as the first Labour Commissioner. The Department's responsibilities enabled it to investigate almost every aspect of labour on public and private undertakings. One particularly important facet of its work consisted in supervising the erection of labour camps on the routes to the employment areas. The privations of the journey, covering in many cases several hundreds of miles, from a man's home to his employment, took a heavy toll of the labour force. Ill health was accentuated by the shortage of food and by the strain of walking great distances with no provision for shelter at the end of a day's march. One of the first measures taken by the Labour Department, therefore, was the construction of a labour camp, manned by a labour officer, at Kilosa, one of the main junctions along the routes taken by the labourers.

The activities of the Labour Department came at a critical moment and they enjoyed the full support of Sir Donald Cameron who was anxious to see that Africans obtained profitable employment and that their working conditions were good. But he needed all the determination for which he was well known to counter the demands of European planters. In 1925 and again in 1926 the planting of coffee was held up owing to the shortage of labourers and this led to demands in certain sections of the Press that the Government should employ compulsion, whether by taxation or by other means, to force the African population to meet the growing demand for labour. Cameron resisted this pressure, but he recognized the genuine needs of the planters. He did not hesitate, therefore, to advise the tribesmen, through their administrative officers, to undertake work of some kind, whether on their own plantations or on behalf of the Government or for private employers. He was well aware that advice of this sort might be construed by the African population as an order from the Government, but he considered that employment of some sort was of such importance that the risk of misinterpretation might safely be taken.[1]

Forced labour was not entirely unknown in Tanganyika and it was recognized by the terms of the mandate, subject to the payment of adequate wages. Unpaid labour for projects initiated by native authorities on behalf of the community was also permitted, and in addition Africans might work for the Government without payment if they were unable to raise the money for their taxes. Compulsory labour on other essential projects was always paid, and it declined steadily throughout the inter-war period. In spite of an increasing demand for labour in the 1920s, therefore, the question of coercion scarcely troubled the territory save for a brief period in the middle of the decade. This happy situation was due in part to the firm line taken by Cameron and in part also to various improvements in the handling of labour. The wider use of motor transport to carry labourers to their employment reduced the wastage of time and of energy hitherto involved in the long and arduous journeys on foot. Better medical supervision cut down illness among employees and the provision of reasonable housing and food maintained their health and energy at a higher level. The labour camps also served a

[1] Sir Donald Cameron: *My Tanganyika Service*. Allen and Unwin, London, 1939, pp. 132-3.

useful purpose. In 1929, 72,055 labourers in transit were given free accommodation, while the dispensaries provided in the camps treated 11,358 cases of minor ailments in the same year.[1]

The native authorities also began to encourage their menfolk to seek paid employment as they came to appreciate the importance of increasing the spending power of the people in their administrative areas. At first there had been conservative elements who had opposed the idea of men travelling far from their homes lest they should be lost to their tribes. These fears were soon proved to be groundless, for unskilled labourers tended to return to their homes as soon as they had obtained the money they needed to pay their taxes or to purchase articles which attracted them. Moreover, outside the towns, which were still small, there were few forms of employment other than those of clerk, craftsman or overseer, which called for anything more than seasonal employment, and the biggest demand for labour arose in the coffee-picking season. It was over the harvesting of coffee that the issue of female and child labour attracted attention, although the problem was never a very serious one. For work in the coffee plantations women and children were usually engaged locally and were not given any particularly arduous tasks. The situation was in fact likened to the employment of families for hop-picking in Britain.

Under these various influences Tanganyika's labour force increased steadily, and representatives of several tribes which had not previously been engaged in wage labour were soon to be found passing through the steadily increasing number of labour camps. Above all, the system of seasonal employment ensured that men were not torn away permanently from their families, but retained an interest in the villages which they regarded as their true homes, bringing back to them more enlightened ideas as a result of their excursions in search of employment. Even during the slump of the early 1930s with its resulting wage cuts it was found possible to keep the labour force surprisingly intact, although some of the labourers who became unemployed took to cultivating their own land more actively and thus reduced the supply of labour when development began once again. In 1931, however, the Government decided to abolish the Labour Department and its functions were

---

[1] *Tanganyika Territory: Annual Report for the Year 1929.* Colonial No. 46. H.M.S.O., London, 1930, p. 48.

taken over by the Provincial Administration. This was partly an economy measure, but it was also believed to be in accordance with the pattern of administrative development laid down by Cameron who had stressed the importance of giving wide powers to administrative officers and native authorities. Cameron, in fact, was opposed to the change although, having left the country before the decision was taken, he could exercise no influence over the Government's policy. The Permanent Mandates Commission also inquired about the possibility of adverse effects upon the labouring population arising from the change but was assured that the inspection of labour conditions and the application of measures to safeguard the interests of the labourers would not be prejudiced.

The discovery of gold in southern Tanganyika introduced a number of new factors into the labour issue which the Administration found some difficulty in handling. This situation was aggravated when the slump of the early 1930s increased the value of gold and thus encouraged still more extensive mining in Tanganyika. Several thousands of Africans offered their services to small-scale employers engaged in alluvial mining and possessing very little capital to support their efforts. This resulted in working conditions which were very far from satisfactory. Many of the labourers came from Nyasaland and the Nyasaland Government sent the Rev. W. P. Young to the Lupa gold-fields to investigate working conditions and to report back. Young's findings were far from reassuring, and the Permanent Mandates Commission urged the Tanganyika Government to take action to improve the situation. Special labour officers were posted in the Lupa gold-fields and in 1937 a committee was appointed to advise on the supply and welfare of labour. Arising out of its recommendations a Standing Labour Advisory Board was set up in the following year. Once again Tanganyika had met its labour difficulties in a bold and enterprising fashion. Throughout the 1920s and 1930s, therefore, the Government's enlightened attitude towards labour issues reaped its reward in a satisfactory supply of labourers working under reasonably favourable conditions. The country was fortunate, too, in having virtually no problem of landless labourers dependent entirely upon their wage earnings. This was mainly a result of the Government's policy on land and non-African settlement.

The development of Tanganyika's land policy proved to be almost as satisfactory as its experiments in labour control. This was largely due to the absence of any serious competition between Africans and non-Africans or between different sections of the African population for the available land, and partly to the experience which had been gained by the British Government in dealing with land issues in other parts of the Empire. In the years immediately following the war there was considerable criticism from a handful of European unofficials of the way in which Sir Horace Byatt handled the problem of establishing a soundly-based land policy. In this case Byatt's position was undoubtedly made more difficult by the delay in publishing the Order in Council setting out Britain's position in relation to Tanganyika and by the decision that the German settlers must leave their estates. There could be no redistribution of the former German properties until the promulgation of the Order in Council, which did not take place until September 1920, so that the firms which were prepared to buy the deserted sisal plantations in 1919 in the hope of profiting from the post-war boom in sisal prices were disappointed, and their disappointment, not unnaturally, was directed against Byatt rather than against the United Kingdom Government. The *Dar es Salaam Times* repeatedly advocated the introduction of a soldier settlement scheme similar to the one in Kenya,[1] but met with opposition from the Governor, who did not consider the situation in Tanganyika merited such an experiment. The promulgation of the Tanganyika Order in Council freed Byatt from some of the restrictions which had previously encumbered him but the slump of 1921, together with his own cautious disposition, induced him to take no precipitate action until the terms of the mandate were known. Nevertheless he did arrange for the sale of leases of the former German estates which hitherto had been leased only on an annual basis. During that period of annual leases a number of Greeks had taken advantage of the reluctance shown by other planters and had laid the foundations of a very profitable participation in the country's economy. In the meantime the campaign to make land available to Europeans in Tanganyika continued unabated, and when the *East African Standard* announced in June 1922 that Byatt on leave in London had informed the East African section of the London Chamber of Commerce that the future of

---

[1] *Dar es Salaam Times*, December 10, 1919, and July 10, 1920.

Tanganyika rested upon the development of African agriculture the outcry redoubled in strength. For the Europeans in Tanganyika and Kenya were convinced that whatever the merits of encouraging Africans to grow crops suitable to small-holdings—and even this had its dangers in reducing the labour supply for European-owned farms—real wealth could only be obtained from large-scale farming and European enterprise.

When the terms of the mandate became known Byatt's caution proved to have been exaggerated. Under Article VI it was laid down that in framing laws relating to the holding or transfer of land the mandatory should take into consideration native laws and customs and should respect the rights and safeguard the interests of the native population. Nor could any native land be transferred to non-natives without the previous consent of the Government. But there was no further restriction either upon the transfer of land or upon the Government's land policy in general. In Byatt's defence it should, however, be added that he was not averse from properly organized and adequately financed settlement. Moreover, the interval before the promulgation of the Lands Ordinance of 1923 was not wasted. Conscious of the difficult task before him Byatt saw to it that German records were carefully investigated and that all relevant information was collected so that when legislation was drafted it was based on a real understanding of the situation in Tanganyika.

The Ordinance of 1923 bore the imprint of experience gained in Northern Nigeria although it did not follow the Nigerian regulations exactly. It was, furthermore, a surprisingly confused document. In the first place all land was declared to be public land, whether occupied or not, and was put under the control of the Governor to be used for the common benefit of the natives of the territory. This did not invalidate existing titles and interests and the Governor was required to have regard to native laws and customs in the exercise of his powers. With the inconsistency which was apparent throughout the whole ordinance it was then stated that no title was valid without the Governor's consent, although this was not in practice insisted upon so far as African-occupied land was concerned. Similarly, Africans as well as non-Africans were entitled, and indeed appeared to be required, to obtain rights of occupancy, but once again the rule was not insisted upon. Nor was it clear whether an African who did obtain a right of occupancy automatically ceased to hold his land according to customary law. More specifically then the Ordinance laid it down that leases were only for ninety-nine years' duration and that a non-African could only lease areas of more than 5,000 acres with the approval of the Secretary of State. Yet, in spite of the obscurity surrounding many of its provisions the ordinance proved effective for, however incapable the Government might be of expressing its intentions in clear, legal terms, it was in no doubt as to its objectives. Where the terms of the ordinance might cause confusion to the African population, therefore, they were tacitly ignored.

Sir Donald Cameron's views on European settlement were not basically dissimilar from those of Byatt but he believed that the advantages of introducing European capital and experience would be likely to outweigh some at least of the risks involved. From the earliest days of his governorship, therefore, he adopted a more positive approach towards settlement than Byatt had done. Soon after his arrival in Tanganyika he met a number of Europeans who were anxious to take up leases of land in the southern highlands in the vicinity of the farm which Lord Delamere had bought from the Custodian of Enemy Property. To these prospective settlers Cameron gave every encouragement, even offering to discuss the availability of land with the district officer when he himself visited the southern highlands in the near future. He was further influenced in favour of this project by the knowledge that in June 1925 the Ex-Enemies Restriction Ordinance of 1922 would lapse and that Germans would be anxious to return to Tanganyika and take up land there. Although not averse from this—indeed a new ordinance was enacted in November 1925 to make it legal—Cameron was anxious that the major role in the development of Tanganyika should be played by men of British descent. He was therefore disturbed to receive instructions from the Colonial Office to discourage applications for land in the southern highlands until adequate railway communications were available. For he was convinced that there was adequate land in the region for settlers without affecting the current or future needs of the African inhabitants and it appeared to him a wasted opportunity if the requests of the would-be settlers were rejected. Similar views were held by many European unofficials in East and Central Africa as was demonstrated at the conference of settlers summoned by Delamere at Tukuyu in October 1925, while the Governors of the East African territories lent the weight of their support at their first conference early in 1926.

In spite of this consensus of opinion there had, in fact, been no scientific study of the amount of land available for European settlement in Tanganyika. The Hilton Young Commission on closer union suggested therefore that a survey should be carried out in East and Central Africa to determine what land was available and suitable for alienation, and Cameron, who had promised both the Dar es Salaam Chamber of Commerce and the Legislative Council that he would readily admit settlers, seized upon the proposal with alacrity. A survey team was sent to the southern highlands and then to the Eastern Province and their work, which was completed in 1932, provided a sound basis upon which to base the Government's policy. The need for the survey had been underlined by the fact that Cameron had found it necessary to close further areas to non-Africans in 1930 in addition to those closed by Byatt in 1923. But, in accordance with his positive approach to the land problem, Cameron had also appointed a committee in December 1929 to investigate the various aspects of European settlement in Tanganyika so that he would be in a position to take advantage of the findings of the Land Development Survey. The Committee, which consisted of European and Indian unofficial members of the Legislative Council, reported in May 1930 in favour of a settlement scheme for non-Africans. It supported the recommendation of the Colonial Development Fund Committee that the Tanganyika Government should establish a fund to provide assistance for settlers and it also recommended the creation of a Land Settlement Board.

Unfortunately for Cameron's hopes the economic depression which began to be felt in Tanganyika towards the end of 1930 discouraged further settlement, and when three years later the country appeared to be on the road to recovery, fears that the territory might be returned to Germany proved so great that until the outbreak of the Second World War there was little hope of any large-scale immigration of Europeans into Tanganyika. As a result of these various factors, therefore, Tanganyika avoided a clash between Europeans and Africans struggling for the same pieces of land. At the same time, because the Indian population was almost entirely involved in trade and commerce, Tanganyika, unlike its northern neighbour, did not become involved in racial disputes of either an economic or of a political character.

In Kenya, too, however, the inter-war years witnessed a very serious attempt to introduce a more satisfactory system of land holding, but land issues in the colony had already engendered such intense feeling between the different races that they were now bedevilled by political and ideological elements. Among the Kikuyu, in particular, the early 1920s was a period of awakening to the realization of permanent loss. The fact that Europeans had occupied land formerly occupied by the Kikuyu, although probably empty at the time the Europeans arrived, had not appeared to be a matter of profound importance at the time. The Kikuyu practice of allowing people to use their land subject to the understanding that it could at any time be reclaimed, together with their ignorance of European ideas of individual ownership, had blinded them to the fact that in the eyes of the European settlers the land had been permanently forfeited. The renewed expansion of the Kikuyu tribe after the ravages of smallpox had died down in the 1890s began to make itself felt as far as the pressure upon land was concerned only towards the end of the war and it was then that the realization of their losses struck home. This situation, coupled with the declaration in 1915 that all reserves were henceforward to be regarded as Crown Land, deepened the feeling of insecurity among the Kikuyu, a feeling which was to be shared by the peoples of the Kakamega area when the discovery of gold led to the alienation of their land. The East Africa Commission of 1924–25 recognized the discontent which the Government's land policy had stirred up and arising out of their recommendations it was decided in 1926 that the reserves should be gazetted so as to give more formal recognition to the boundaries of African-occupied territory. Following upon the Hilton Young Commission's report the Government took a further step in 1930 by issuing an ordinance declaring all reserves to be set aside for the benefit of the African tribes in perpetuity. A Native Lands Trust Board was also appointed which consisted of a number of Government officers and two unofficial members of the Legislative Council, one of them the member representing African interests.

The security of the reserves was now fairly established, but there still remained the question of their adequacy. Attention was drawn to the need for an inquiry into this aspect of Kenya land policy by the Joint Select Committee on Closer Union in 1931. Two years later a commission was appointed under the chairmanship of Sir William Morris Carter who had already had experience of investigating land issues in Uganda. The Commission was charged with the task of estimating the land requirements of the African population and of making recommendations for the extension of the reserves where this was deemed to be necessary. It was also required to define the boundaries of the European highlands and to investigate cases where European settlement was said to have encroached upon African land rights. As a result of the Commission's inquiries the reserves were extended by more than 2,600 square miles. The boundaries of the white highlands were demarcated so as to embrace an area of 16,700 square miles of which nearly 4,000 would be forest reserve while a considerable proportion of the remainder would require extensive watering to make it profitable. At the time of the investigation some 10,345 square miles of land were actually held by Europeans. The investigation showed that only $106\frac{3}{4}$ square miles of tribal land could be fairly said to have been affected by European settlement, but in the atmosphere of insecurity existing among the African population it was upon this latter item that attention was focused, instead of upon the more fundamental issue of the place of European farming in Kenya's economy and its relationship to African peasant agriculture. The Commission further recommended that the reserves should no longer be regarded as Crown Land but should be declared to be native land. They should then be vested in a Native Lands Trust Board, consisting entirely of unofficials, who would be responsible for the protection of the reserves but would have no administrative duties. The enactment of the regulations necessary to make the commission's proposals effective could best be achieved, it was thought, by an Order in Council which would offer a greater sense of permanence than would an ordinance of the Kenga legislature. In the event the committee's recommendations were embodied in a series of Orders in Council during 1938 and 1939, and the Native Lands Trust Board, consisting of unofficials, was brought into being under the chairmanship of the Chief Native Commissioner.

There still remained the problem of the squatters, the several thousands of Africans, mostly Kikuyu, living on European-owned farms, of whom only a small proportion had occupied their present homes before the coming of the settlers. To them, the Commission recommended, should be offered alternative plots of land in the reserves, but where they elected to stay on European farms it was laid down in a series of ordinances in 1937, 1939 and 1941 that employers should pay a stipulated wage and should provide land for the cultivation of food crops and grazing for a specified number of cattle.

In these many ways what might be termed a reasonable settlement of the Kenya land issue was reached. But to describe the arrangement as reasonable would be to overlook the refusal of the Kenya Africans and particularly of the Kikuyu to accept a situation in which their only contribution to the country's economy, other than as producers of subsistence crops, was as labourers on other men's farms or as employees in other men's industries. The reserves might be adequate to satisfy the subsistence requirements of the African population. They might be overgrazed solely as a result of the indiscriminate stocking of cattle. They could not provide the basis for sound, progressive farming without a revolution in social life and in agricultural methods which could only be achieved as a result of outside stimulus and probably even then only by autocratic methods such as it was possible to adopt after the Mau Mau rising in the 1950s. For the contribution of the Kenya African population to the country's exports was limited by the degree of stimulus which the Government was prepared to give and little assistance was provided by the Department of Agriculture in the years between the wars.

In Uganda during the same period an old problem declined in importance while a new one made its first appearance. The old problem centred around the activities of Sir William Morris Carter and his land committee which, in spite of the rebuff their earlier proposals had received from the United Kingdom, were still wholeheartedly pursuing their campaign to secure land for European farming in the years immediately after the war. Carter's committee had been asked by the Governor, Sir Frederick Jackson, to review the land question once more in the light of the Secretary of State's criticisms. But Carter persisted in his proposal to allot a limited area for African reserves without demarcating where that land should be. His object was to ensure that European farmers should not at some future time be prevented by arbitrary boundaries from using good land not yet occupied by Africans. Now, however, the Provincial Commissioners began to show more concern than they had done when Carter's scheme had been first discussed. In 1918 they suggested that larger areas should be set aside for the use of Africans than those which Carter had proposed and they recommended that the reserves should be demarcated at once in the interests of the African population. In Lord Milner, however, England had a Secretary of State of a different temper from Bonar Law, and in Sir Robert Coryndon, Uganda's post-war Governor, the Protectorate had an administrator who was anxious to encourage European enterprise. When, therefore, Milner received Carter's latest proposals, which contained virtually no changes from the original plan, he reacted as he did over so many issues by supporting the view of the senior officials on the spot. In 1919 he had already submitted to the argument from Uganda that, whatever he might do as regards the rest of the country, he could have no power to forbid African *mailo* owners from selling their land to whomsoever they wished. Now, in 1920, he accepted Carter's recommendations and asked that they should be embodied in specific regulations. When a more detailed scheme was put forward Milner had been succeeded by Winston Churchill but there appeared to have been no change in the attitude of the Colonial Office. The Provincial Commissioners, therefore, took up their case more actively and with European plantations suffering from the effects of the slump this change in attitude of some of Uganda's leading administrative officers resulted in the submission of a new scheme which embodied the request for the immediate demarcation of adequate lands for African use. The Duke of Devonshire, who received the request, had already agreed to a proposal from the Buganda Lukiko that he should once again ban the alienation of *mailo* land to non-Africans. Now, in response to the Uganda Government's recommendations he agreed that the Provincial Commissioners' plan should be adopted and embodied in legislation. In practice there was little need to create reserves and after a number of attempts at plotting them had proved unsuccessful the idea of legislation was tacitly dropped. Consequently, with the exception of *mailo* and a few pieces of freehold, all land in Uganda came to be regarded as Crown Land under the Crown Lands (Declaration) Ordinance of 1922. Owing to the difficulty of producing regulations applicable throughout the territory the land then continued to be administered according to customary tribal law.

Potentially more serious in its political as well as in its social implications was a new problem arising from the belated realization by some of the better educated Africans in Buganda that the 1900 Agreement had achieved a revolution in land tenure which had deprived the majority of the population of their customary rights. During the twenty years immediately following the Agreement the change in the nature of land ownership had not been appreciated since few people had been disturbed in the occupation of their plots. The realization that a new era had begun first seems to have struck not the more educated people but the leaders of sub-clans. Traditionally, clan leaders had held certain land, and particularly burial places, in trust for the members of their clans. This form of tenure had not interfered with the administrative rights exercised by the chiefs prior to 1900 and even the share-out occasioned by the Agreement had not affected some of the more important clan leaders who had themselves received grants of *mailo*. Many of the lesser clan leaders, however, had not shared in these benefits but they did not recognize their loss until the new landowners began to forbid burials on their land. Then, however, the Bataka, or clan leaders, began to complain bitterly. To their complaints were added the criticisms of a more educated section of society who, simultaneously, were beginning to gain a faint appreciation of economic issues and to recognize that certain families, by the good fortune of having held office in 1900, had acquired a valuable capital asset which was denied to everyone else. An attempt by the Kabaka to provide some means of redress for the dispossessed Bataka was rejected in 1922 by the Lukiko which housed the most powerful landed interests in Buganda. It was, too, this same Lukiko whose refusal to permit the alienation of *mailo* land to foreigners had led to the reversal of Lord Milner's policy. Their triumph in the Bataka issue only served to confirm the power now resting in the hands of the chiefs, power which had formerly been exercised by the Kabaka alone. This position was partly due to the independence which the ownership of land had given to some of the Kabaka's subjects. But there is no doubt that the lengthy regency to which Daudi Chwa had been subjected had also weakened the Kabaka's authority, more particularly in relation to the three chiefs who had ruled during his minority. At the same time it must be recognized that the Bataka question had been raised too late. In most cases land had already been in

361

the hands of its new owners for some years and any reversal of this situation would have caused confusion if not a serious upheaval. At the request of the Bataka, however, an investigation of their claims was carried out by the protectorate Government, but in 1926, the Governor, Sir William Gowers, felt constrained to recommend to the Secretary of State that nothing could be done to remedy past events.[1]

The system of *mailo* ownership brought with it other evils. Before 1900 chiefs had collected tribute in labour and in kind from their subordinates to whom, in return, they gave their protection. This tribute was known as *busulu*. They had also received gifts of produce, usually beer and bananas, as a form of tithe, known as *nvujjo*. In 1900, however, it was agreed that chiefs should receive salaries so that tribute was no longer necessary. As landlords they were, at the same time, free to collect rent from their tenants provided this was not confused with the tribute formerly due to them as chiefs. That this arrangement should cause confusion is understandable, and with the increase in the value of cotton produced by the peasants some of the chiefs did not hesitate to make heavy demands for tribute which could not by any stretch of imagination be regarded as a fair, economic rent. The matter was taken up by the Protectorate Government and after negotiations with the Lukiko the *Busulu* and *Envujo* Law came into effect on January 1, 1928. This law protected the peasant in the enjoyment of the fruits of his industry while at the same time guaranteeing to the landlord a reasonable rent. The death of Apolo Kagwa, the strongest of all the chiefs, and the opportunity it gave to the Kabaka to assert his authority over the Lukiko may well have made this reform possible.

The failure of the Protectorate Government to produce satisfactory land legislation had unfortunate effects in Toro where the Mukama and the handful of chiefs who had been granted land under the terms of the 1900 Toro Agreement had made such inflated claims that the peasantry were in constant doubt over their own rights. An attempt in 1921 to define the areas to which the chiefs could lay a reasonable claim aroused considerable opposition among the landowners, and even after the Mukama himself had been reprimanded for his criticisms of the Government's proposals the peasants

---

[1] H. B. Thomas and A. E. Spencer: *A History of Uganda Land and Surveys*. Government Press, Entebbe, 1938, pp. 70–72.

were little better off. Early in the 1930s, therefore, a system of certificates of occupancy was introduced for a time into the Western Province in the hope of giving the peasants security of tenure, but the experiment was not a success. Meanwhile, an offer by the Protectorate Government which would have enabled the chiefs of Busoga to mark out freehold plots of land amounting to eighty-five square miles in all was withdrawn in 1935 when the chiefs failed to show any interest in the proposal. In fact the chiefs had no complaint against the existing tribal system of land tenure so that they were not attracted to unoccupied and uncultivated land even with the prospect of freehold possession. Between the wars, therefore, grievances over land in Uganda centred upon the relations between chiefs and people rather than upon the fear of European domination such as troubled Kenya.

Another problem which exercised the East African Governments for the first time in the 1920s was that of African education. The first report published by the Tanganyika Government in 1921 commented with admiration on the results of the German educational system at least in so far as it had made administration easier through the relatively widespread knowledge of reading and writing which it had inculcated. Not content with attempting to emulate this achievement the British authorities appointed a Director of Education in September 1920, to whom was given the task of preparing a scheme which, it was hoped, would produce boys with the sort of elementary education which would fit them to take an active part in the economic development of the country. This may have appeared a modest proposal but it is clear that the Tanganyika Government had a genuine desire to improve the lives of the African population in addition to making them simple contributors to the country's economic revival. In order to achieve their object provision was made for the training of teachers, elementary schools were started in district headquarters and in the larger villages, and primary schools were opened in Dar es Salaam and Tanga in 1921. The British missionary societies which had taken over the work of their German predecessors were also beginning to develop their own educational system so that Tanganyika was able to make a good start upon its educational programme.[1]

[1] *Tanganyika Territory: Annual Report from the Armistice to the end of 1920.* H.M.S.O., London, 1921, p. 40.

By contrast, the Kenya Government had a more practical view of the purpose of African education. The report of the Department of Education for the year 1920–21 stated, 'It will be readily admitted by most educationists that literary education *per se* is harmful to the ordinary native of Africa.' To this remarkable dictum the *Leader of British East Africa* added piously, 'We need hardly elaborate this well tried and proved opinion.'[1] The Education Department's statement served as a preamble to the enunciation of an educational policy heavily weighted in favour of technical instruction. It involved grants in aid to certain approved mission schools for the teaching of technical subjects and also the provision of technical schools in each administrative district where carpentry, bricklaying and allied subjects would be taught. The plan had the whole-hearted support of the Convention of Associations which, a year earlier had urged the self-same policy upon the Government and had itself appointed a sub-committee to interview prospective employers and to make recommendations as to the best means of providing apprentice training and other forms of technical instruction.[2] Unfortunately, even the limited plans thus proposed by the Government were not put into effect.

The views of the Convention of Associations did not differ greatly from those of Uganda's Development Committee of 1919–20 and, indeed, from those of a committee appointed by the Governor in 1919 to report upon a Native Civil Service. This latter group stated, 'We are opposed to any extensive literary education for the general native population, and we consider that it should not proceed beyond a standard which will enable a native to learn a trade by which he can earn a living. Unless literary education is complete, or is accompanied by technical training, the native is apt to regard himself as a superior being for whom the ordinary duties and responsibilities of life have no significance.' The Uganda Government, however, was not so ready as the Kenya Government had been to respond to recommendations which were put before it. In 1922 Makerere College was established on the outskirts of Kampala to provide instruction in certain skilled trades, but it was not until the end of 1923 that the Governor, Sir Geoffrey Archer, invited Mr. Eric Hussey, Chief Inspector of Schools in the Sudan, to visit

[1] *The Leader of British East Africa*, September 24, 1921.

[2] *The Leader of British East Africa*, February 14, 1920.

Uganda and to make recommendations for the development of a sound educational system. It is significant that in announcing this step the Governor stressed Hussey's experience and his understanding of and sympathy with African aspirations. Arising out of Hussey's report the Government at last abandoned its policy of simply offering meagre grants-in-aid to missionary societies and, while continuing to subsidize these valuable contributors to educational development, itself undertook a comprehensive educational programme. Makerere College was converted into an African Training College affording both literary and technical education to 170 pupils, a number which, it was hoped, would in time rise to 340. In order to make this development at a higher level effective it was also proposed to endow and where necessary to establish an adequate number of elementary and intermediate schools. An Education Department was created in 1924 to put the programme into effect and Hussey himself was invited to become the first Director.

In 1925 there was published a white paper on Education Policy in British Tropical Africa,[1] which was to have a stimulating effect on the Governments of both Uganda and Tanganyika. While not ignoring the importance of technical and vocational training the white paper stated in broader terms, 'Material prosperity without a corresponding growth in the moral capacity to turn it to good use constitutes a danger. The well-being of a country must depend in the last resort on the character of its people, on their increasing intellectual and technical ability, and on their social progress.' One factor in particular was stressed, namely the importance of the contribution made by voluntary agencies and the white paper went on to emphasize the obligation of governments to assist these agencies financially. Indeed, the importance of those agencies cannot be over-emphasized. In all three East African territories they had provided the backbone of the educational system. In Uganda they had provided the only education of a western character in the territory while the same might almost equally be said of their work in Kenya. Moreover, while recognizing the need for training in crafts, they had refused to be turned aside from their belief in the value of a more literary education. On this latter issue they were not blind romantics. They were well aware that many Africans

[1] Cmd. 2374.

365

learned to read and write simply to enable them to obtain employment as clerks and so to avoid manual labour. They were conscious, too, that others put the knowledge they had acquired to wrong uses. But they persevered in their conviction that whatever bad resulted from their work was outweighed by the good that was also achieved. In Uganda, therefore, the British Government's white paper gave further support to the missionaries' activities while in Tanganyika, under the enthusiastic impulse of Cameron, an Education Conference was held in Dar es Salaam in 1925. As a result of its deliberations the Government agreed for the first time to give grants-in-aid to approved mission schools and to constitute a Central Advisory Council, supported by provincial and district committees, on each of which missionary societies, native authorities and plantation owners, as well as government departments were represented. In 1929, also, Tanganyika introduced a scheme of grants-in-aid for Indian schools, a policy which had been adopted in Uganda some years earlier.

These developments in the later 1920s did not go wholly unchallenged. At a dinner arranged by the Uganda Planters' Association in January 1927, the Chairman said, 'There are many of us who look upon the money which is being spent in this country upon education with considerable alarm. The country is not yet ready for such methods of education.'[1] As has already been seen, Sir Sydney Armitage-Smith in the course of his review of Tanganyika's revenue and expenditure in 1932 similarly criticized the unduly large sums of money spent on education and other social services in that territory. The Tanganyika Government took these comments to heart and even after the depression adopted a cautious policy aimed, it was said, at ensuring that the output of pupils with different levels of educational training did not exceed employers' demands. The previous, indiscriminate policy was thought to have led to disillusionment and discontent among Africans who were unable to obtain the sort of employment to which they believed their education had entitled them.[2] Although retrenchment in Uganda was not so severe as in Tanganyika in the early 1930s the impetus which had been given to education in the later 1920s was also lost under the governorship of Sir Bernard Bourdillon who was unfavourably

[1] *Uganda Herald,* January 28, 1927.

[2] *Tanganyika Territory: Annual Report for the Year 1934.* Colonial No. 105. H.M.S.O., London, 1935, pp. 158-61.

disposed towards advanced or literary education for Africans. His successor, Sir Philip Mitchell, who took office in 1935, turned the scale firmly in the opposite direction. Mitchell was convinced of the overriding importance of education at all levels and perhaps his greatest contribution to East Africa during a long and distinguished public career was to urge the appointment of a commission to investigate the territories' need for higher education. Such a commission was duly appointed by the United Kingdom Government in 1936 under the chairmanship of Earl de la Warr and its report[1] laid down a bold pattern of development which included the transformation of Makerere College into a university institution as soon as possible. This had been Hussey's dream thirteen years earlier but it had been forgotten in the intervening period of scepticism and financial crisis. To create a university institution, however, involved the strengthening of the whole educational system and in particular rendered necessary a sound policy for secondary education. Mitchell did not shrink from these implications, and it was mainly due to his energy that Makerere College received substantial sums of money from the United Kingdom Government as well as from the three East African Governments to launch it upon its programme of expansion. Although this advance was held up by the war a secure foundation had been laid as a result of Mitchell's efforts and only twelve years later university status was achieved. In spite of many vicissitudes, therefore, and in spite, above all, of an acute shortage of funds, educational development in Uganda and Tanganyika made satisfactory if unspectacular progress during the inter-war years. Kenya, however, as Lord Moyne's Report demonstrated, lagged far behind the other territories except in so far as the efforts of the missionary societies bore fruit.

---

[1] *Higher Education in East Africa.* Colonial No. 142. H.M.S.O., London, 1937.

CHAPTER TEN

THE SECOND WORLD WAR
AND THE YEARS OF PLENTY

By 1938 the threat of war hung heavily over the world. Neville Chamberlain's visit to Hitler in Munich held off hostilities for a time, but although everyone hoped for peace the nations were steeling themselves for the struggle. East Africa, no less than the rest of the world, employed the brief period of respite after Munich to prepare itself for the coming conflict. Early in 1939 there began the voluntary registration of men of all races for national service, and this was followed by measures to improve the territories' food supplies. It was difficult, however, to know exactly what should be done until war was actually declared, so that East Africa was fortunate in having a breathing space during the 'phoney war' of late 1939 and 1940 in which to adjust itself to the new world struggle.

Because war had been in the air so long it came to East Africa with less of a shock than in 1914. Nor, on this occasion, were there any scruples about dealing firmly with enemy aliens even though they might be Europeans. The Germans in Tanganyika, who at the outbreak of war numbered 3,205, of whom 1,858 were males, were quickly interned without a struggle. This easy success was partly due to the efficiency with which the undertaking was organized but partly, too, to the fact that, expecting an early German victory, the German leaders had issued instructions forbidding their followers to resist arrest. None the less, the internment of the Germans was an important step since Nazi groups had been organized in centres as far apart as Dar es Salaam and Bukoba and they might have caused serious trouble had they been so inclined.

The next potential military threat came from the Italians in Ethiopia. Anxious to encourage Italian neutrality, however, the British Government had sent a telegram to East Africa on August 30 forbidding any military movements of a provocative nature in the Northern Frontier District of Kenya, so that it seemed after the first few days of uncertainty that East Africa's role was not to be a dramatic one. At the meeting of the Governors' Conference in November 1939 it was possible to draw up the first statement of general policy and in the circumstances this laid stress upon increased productivity so as to reduce East Africa's dependence upon imports and so to lighten the burden of the merchant shipping fleets of the western allies. This decision was whole-heartedly endorsed by the Secretary of State in June 1940, but in the meantime the peoples of East Africa were anxious to make a greater contribution to the allies' war effort. In spite of its limited financial resources the Tanganyika Government readily exhausted its reserve funds in order to contribute £200,000 to Britain.[1] In Uganda and Kenya various methods were adopted to raise public subscriptions and all met with a generous response. Income tax, which had been resisted so fervently during the 1930s, was also now accepted with equal fervour in Tanganyika and Uganda, thus bringing the two territories into line with the policy adopted in Kenya three years earlier in 1937.

But East Africa was not to escape military activity for long. The likelihood that Italy would join the war on the side of the axis steadily increased although it was considered that if she did so her main thrust would be in the vicinity of the Mediterranean since Ethiopia was too far away to act as a base for large-scale operations. In February 1940, therefore, East Africa's forces became part of Middle East Command and they were assigned the task of harassing the Italians along the Kenya border. Meanwhile, the King's African Rifles were rapidly expanded and the defensive positions at Moyale, Marsabit and Wajir were strengthened against a possible Italian advance southward. An armoured thrust towards the coast was not inconceivable, and the East African ports would be of considerable strategic value if traffic through the Mediterranean should be halted and all shipping from Britain to the Middle East had to be diverted round the Cape.

When Italy did declare war on June 10, 1940, the news came as no surprise and East African patrols were raiding over the Ethiopian border before midnight on the same day. Inevitably, however, in

---

[1] *Tanganyika Territory: Proceedings of the Legislative Council, Fifteenth Session, 1940–41, Pt. I.* Government Printer, Dar es Salaam, 1941, p. 4.

view of the larger forces of men at their disposal and of their ample equipment, it was the Italians who, supported by artillery, began the first full scale advance at dawn on July 1. After a fortnight's fighting Moyale was occupied and then the Italian advance came to a surprising halt. This, however, offered little consolation to East Africa, for the news of the fall of its own insignificant border outpost was received against the graver background of the evacuation of the allied forces from Dunkirk and the fall of Belgium and France. East Africa's position appeared to be extremely insecure. For a time, even, it seemed possible that the Government of the Belgian Congo might surrender to Germany, thus presenting a hostile front to the west. But the Governor-General, M. Ryckmans, refused to follow the example of his home Government and the danger from the Congo was removed.

In the meantime, reinforcements began to arrive from Nigeria, the Gold Coast and South Africa, and towards the end of 1940 the East African Commander, Lieut-General (later Sir Alan) Cunningham, began to contemplate an attack upon the Italians. Encouraged by General Wavell's astonishing successes in the Western Desert in December 1940, the British advance in East Africa began in January 1941. At first it met with strong resistance, but, after some determined fighting on the way, Kismayu was occupied without opposition. Cunningham then decided upon still more vigorous action and by the end of February Italian Somaliland had been occupied by the forces from East Africa. The Italian threat to Kenya was at an end and Cunningham's troops took up the pursuit of the retreating enemy until the Italian empire in East Africa was finally overthrown.

At the end of 1941 a new situation arose with the entry of Japan into the war. This at once changed the strategic significance of East Africa, and its defenders had to look eastward instead of northward. After the fall of Singapore and the transfer of the main British far-eastern naval base to Ceylon the importance of Mombasa as a reserve base for naval patrols operating in the Indian Ocean was greatly increased. Even the possibility of a Japanese landing in East Africa could not be ruled out in 1942, the year of their triumph. Madagascar, too, presented a threat to East Africa and an even greater threat to allied shipping if it should fall into Japanese hands. The Vichy French who controlled it could not be induced by negotiations with Britain to agree to resist the Japanese, so the British decided to seize the island. The main campaign, which took place in the latter part of 1942, provided a further opportunity for East African forces to show their qualities and at the end of 1943 there were still 12,000 African troops on the island. American naval victories in the Pacific and the checks given to the Japanese land forces in south-east Asia now began to reduce the threat to the African continent and in 1944 East African troops fulfilled a new role when they took part in the campaign against the Japanese in Burma. Within four years East Africa had been freed from all danger of attack while East African troops had played a worthy part in the defeat of both Italy and Japan.

If the possibility of East Africa's becoming a battlefield was short-lived the British dependencies did not pass through the war years entirely free of hardship and strain. A particularly heavy burden fell upon the chiefs because many district officers joined the fighting forces while others were so fully engaged in tasks peculiar to wartime that they could devote but little time to their normal duties. In all three territories this situation had important repercussions upon local governments. In Tanganyika the main problem arose from the fact that the native authorities, particularly where those authorities were individual chiefs rather than councils, had already shown some inclination to arrogate to themselves even greater powers than the Government had intended. When district officers were able to give less attention to the control of this tendency it became more pronounced and the gap between the native authorities and the people widened. In Uganda similar difficulties were experienced. Even before the war the authority of the chiefs had been questioned in a number of areas and now that they were required to enforce rigid and often unpopular wartime restrictions their position became still less stable.

This situation was particularly marked in Buganda. In November 1939 the Kabaka, Daudi Chwa II, died and was succeeded by his fifteen-year-old son, Edward Mutesa. This meant a further period of regency which encouraged rivalries and jealousies among the leading chiefs. The new Governor, Sir Charles Dundas, who had achieved such success as Secretary for Native Affairs in Tanganyika, did not consider that the war, or indeed local problems of a temporary character, should hold up the natural development of African authorities towards assuming greater responsibility for the control of their own affairs. Furthermore, unlike his predecessors, he did not believe responsibility could be acquired while the Protectorate Government continued to interfere at every point. As an indication of his anxiety that the Baganda should set their own house in order he acquiesced in 1941 in the desire of the Lukiko that the Katikiro, Martin Luther Nsibirwa, should resign. The reason quoted for this demand was that Nsibirwa had agreed to and had actually assisted in the remarriage of the Namasole, Daudi Chwa's widow, contrary to Kiganda custom. In fact, the whole affair was primarily a trial of strength between different factions among the chiefs, so that the Protectorate Government's apparent unwillingness to support those in authority gave added licence to the critics. When the young Kabaka took over his duties on his eighteenth birthday in 1942 he found himself in the unenviable position of being unable to support his own ministers without being attacked by their rivals.

It was, then, at a particularly precarious moment in 1944 that the Governor, with a bold stroke, removed the district officers from Buganda, leaving only a Resident and a small staff whose role was not to administer the kingdom but simply to give advice to the Kabaka. Judged by Dundas's own principles this move was a sound one, but in practice so great were the divisions between the various leading families in Buganda that it was difficult for any group to maintain order without the active support of the Protectorate authorities. Since the passing of the resolute Apolo Kagwa, the Baganda chiefs had perforce regarded themselves as subject to the intimate control of the Protectorate Government upon which, since they were required to carry out its directives, they had not unnaturally come to rely heavily for support. Dundas's action, therefore, appeared as a betrayal of those who had given the Protectorate their most loyal co-operation. Nor, in view of the unpopular character of some of the policies which they had helped to promote, could the Kabaka's ministers hope for public approval in the face of what were often purely selfish and irresponsible attacks. At the same time the rivalries between the chiefs became confused with and were often heightened by the growing discontent at European over-rule which now, for the first time in recent years, could be criticized openly. Land, that familiar source of discord, also contributed to the turmoil and succeeded in bringing the Kabaka himself more intimately into the struggle. For Mutesa supported a proposal to amend the 1900 Agreement so as to empower the Protectorate Government to acquire land compulsorily, in return for compensation, for the extension of Makerere College. This plan, reasonable in itself, was inflated by certain sections of the Baganda into an accusation that the Government intended to seize land wholesale and to give it to Europeans.

Dundas was not unaware of the dangers which his policy entailed but again he took the liberal view that the best method of averting trouble was to widen the field of political responsibility in Buganda so that more people could take either a direct or an indirect share in the management of affairs and in this way gain a better understanding of what was going on. To achieve this end he advised the Kabaka to change the composition of the Lukiko so as to make it a more representative institution. Before steps could be taken to augment this proposal Dundas left the country and early in 1945 riots broke out in different parts of Buganda. These disturbances were fundamentally a part of the struggle for power in Buganda but the rival factions of chiefs were able to win support from the peasants and wage-earning classes as a result of the economic discontent occasioned by the high cost of living due to the war. A shortage of essential commodities such as sugar and the inevitable growth of a black market had also added to the general feeling of frustration. There was, too, another group which achieved some prominence during the riots but it is unlikely that its members played an important part in fomenting trouble. These were the young, fairly well educated Baganda who felt themselves excluded from political life by the entrenched position of the chiefs. They took the opportunity of what was essentially a domestic crisis in Buganda to publicize themselves, but it was upon the national stage that they were to perform most actively in the future. For they saw in a protectorate-wide approach to Uganda's problems a way of overcoming the restrictive powers of the established families in Buganda. In 1945, however, the activities of this new group had scarcely begun.

As a reaction to the riots the new Governor, Sir John Hall, reversed certain of the steps taken by his predecessor. In particular, he restored assistant residents to the district headquarters in Buganda on the assumption that the difficulties of the previous months had arisen as a result of a lack of supervision by Protectorate officers.

This, however, was an over-simplification of the issue for the riots had been primarily a foretaste of the problem as to who could command enough popular support to direct the affairs of the country when British protection was withdrawn. That the problem would arise again was presaged in July by the assassination of the restored Katikiro, Nsibirwa, the day after he had introduced a motion in the Lukiko to enable the Kabaka to acquire land for public purposes.

Outside Buganda the war years did not bring such serious problems although there was a growing demand in some areas for greater popular representation in local government affairs. The belief still held by certain district officers that indirect administration simply meant ruling through African officials tended to blind them to the fact that chiefs appointed by the Government were not necessarily popular among the general public just because they were Africans. The pattern of local government in Buganda also added its quota of confusion to African thinking on local government matters in other parts of the Protectorate. Far from underlining the importance of developing other provinces to equal Buganda in size and wealth, the fact that Buganda was mainly occupied by one tribe tended to emphasize the importance of tribal units. These, in most cases, coincided with district boundaries and it was such inadequate units that tried to mould themselves to the Uganda pattern.

In Kenya the main administrative difficulties arose from the restrictions imposed by wartime conditions upon the working of the Native Authority Ordinance of 1937. Local government finances were particularly affected and assistance from the Central Government usually took the form of whatever expedient happened to be handy rather than being based upon any standard principles. This meant that while the wealthier native councils were able to fulfil their responsibilities fairly satisfactorily, the poorer councils became proportionately poorer still. In the circumstances, the appointment in 1942 of a standing committee on local native council estimates could have only limited benefits, in spite of its unofficial African majority and of its advisory role in helping the Governor to decide upon the wisdom of the financial planning of the native councils. Consequently, among those tribes where traditional authorities still exercised a deep influence or where a younger generation was already to some extent hostile to European rule, the councils created by the colonial Government could not hope to make the desired progress.

374

One of the most important results of the war in so far as the internal administration of East Africa as a whole was concerned, was the revival of the idea of closer co-operation between the three territories. Towards the middle of 1940 demands began to be heard in Kenya for the appointment of a Joint East African War Council or at least for a common policy under unified direction. Opinion in Tanganyika remained cautious and the claim that the measures proposed would result in greater efficiency was felt to need more substantiation in view of the fact that an over-all military organization already existed.[1] Uganda, too, remained suspicious of Kenya. Although the Governor, Sir Philip Mitchell, was a strong supporter of closer union, opinion in the Protectorate was still divided over the principle of association with Kenya so that the whole-hearted acceptance of a Joint War Council was still a thing of the future. Mitchell, however, was prepared to make a bold stand in support of his convictions and was even willing to meet the constitutional and legal objections of the Governor of Tanganyika to his proposal that the Governor of Kenya should be appointed High Commissioner for all the territories north of the Zambezi with the argument of expediency, *inter arma silent leges*.[2] Mitchell's scheme, however, did not bear fruit but an important step was taken at a meeting of delegates from all six Governors' Conference territories in Nairobi on August 1, 1940, when it was decided that a joint economic council should be set up, with a small secretariat, to enable East Africa to act as an economic and commercial unit. This was a purely wartime measure and the council did not intend to trespass upon the work of existing organizations. Each territory participating in its work would have one vote and the main function of the council would be to provide a small directing and planning staff which would work through existing bodies and which, where possible, would resolve inter-territorial differences of opinion.

The council began its work, the first meeting being held on August 28 and 29, 1940. It cannot, however, be said to have been wholly successful in reconciling divergent interests. Indeed, its activities were described in a leader in the *Uganda Herald* on October 13, 1943, as amounting to nothing more than Kenya rule. In 1944 the Uganda

[1] *Tanganyika Standard*, June 3, 1940.

[2] Sir Philip Mitchell: *African Afterthoughts*. Hutchinson, London, 1954 p. 188.

and Eastern Province Chambers of Commerce and the Cotton Association issued a joint paper in which they described their painful experience of wartime economic controls 'operated, supposedly impartially, from Nairobi, but in actual practice resulting in a distinct brake on Uganda's commerce'. Reverting to the question of political or administrative union they went on to reiterate the difference between the native policies of Uganda and Kenya which, they argued, rendered co-operation extremely difficult.[1] In raising once again the question of political union Uganda's business men were not tilting at imaginary devils. Although the appointment of Sir Philip Mitchell as deputy chairman of the Governors' Conference in 1940 had so far produced closer co-operation without any indication of the political subordination of Uganda and Tanganyika, there were certainly those who felt that political union was still desirable. In October 1943 the Association of Chambers of Commerce and Industry of Eastern Africa, in which Uganda was not represented, had once again resolved to urge this policy upon the territorial governments. Moreover, the Europeans of Uganda were conscious, as the Kenya settlers had been in the mid 1920s, that the tide of opinion in England was running in favour of grouping the colonies into larger units. This attitude was illustrated by a statement made by the Duke of Devonshire in the House of Lords towards the end of 1944 when he stressed that the British Government were thinking in terms of stronger units rather than of greater fragmentation. In these circumstances the unofficial European community in Uganda considered it to be imperative that constructive proposals should be put forward if Uganda's views were not to be overlooked in the rapid flow of events. At a meeting held in Kampala in November 1944, it was freely admitted that a properly organized federal system might prove to be satisfactory as regards the organization of certain services common to all the three territories.[2] In the event, however, no formal steps were taken to legalize any form of closer union until the war was over.

Against this background of administrative strain the maintenance of productivity throughout the war years proved to be no easy task. The absence of many able-bodied men on military duties seriously affected the labour force of the East African territories. In Kenya,

[1] *Uganda Herald*, March 15, 1944.
[2] ibid., November 29, 1944.

in particular, where so much depended upon the direction given by a relatively small number of European farmers, many of whom were now in the armed forces, a heavy burden was imposed upon the womenfolk, and these latter fulfilled the tasks created by the demands of war in noble fashion. In Uganda the difficulty of exporting the country's main crop, cotton, also caused suffering to the growers who could not sell their produce for a reasonable price. From 1941 onwards, however, the Government was able to intervene to ensure that prices did not fall too low. Tanganyika's economy, meanwhile, fluctuated in a startling fashion. Sisal, the country's most valuable crop, could not be freely exported in the early years of the war because of the lack of shipping for so bulky an item. When, however, Japanese military successes deprived the western allies of alternative sources of supply Tanganyika's sisal suddenly became an essential commodity. By contrast, gold, which during the first part of the war was in heavy demand, steadily lost its importance after the introduction of lend-lease. In Uganda as well as in Tanganyika rubber, too, became a vital commodity on the fall of Malaya, and every possible source of latex was tapped. Food crops, however, were the main concern of all the East African territories, but in 1943, owing to drought and a wave of locusts, one of the staple crops, maize, fell into short supply and famine measures had to be introduced. Indeed, Tanganyika found itself in the position of having to import maize throughout the greater part of the war.

A false impression of prosperity was given by the astounding increase in the revenues of all the territories, for this was due not so much to any marked improvement in output as to the rocketing prices offered for essential produce. During the war years at least, however, the people of East Africa did appear to be financially better off than they had been previously because the shortage of goods available for purchase meant that more money remained in the hands of the producers. Although a black market developed in some essential foodstuffs the variety of goods for sale was too small to make serious inroads into the people's savings. The problem, therefore, was one for the future when, with the return of trade goods in large quantities, it would be seen to what extent the war years had undermined the purchasing power of cash.

All three territories made early preparations for the return of peace and they were encouraged in their planning by the Colonial

Development and Welfare Act passed by the United Kingdom Government in 1940. This law, which made available the sum of £5 million a year for a ten-year period to encourage development in British overseas dependencies, had seemed an unusual piece of legislation at the time of its enactment. In the opening year of a world war it had demonstrated Britain's conviction that the struggle with Germany must not blind her to her responsibility for the trusteeship of her dependencies. Some of the inhabitants of Tanganyika had been awed by this gesture to the extent of fearing that the offer of money from Britain might encourage idleness at a time when an all-out effort was called for in the territory. Less generous commentators pointed out that £5 million a year would not go far towards assisting the many schemes so badly needed in different parts of the Empire. Yet these ignored the fact that the shortage of manpower and other equally cogent reasons would have rendered a large-scale development programme in wartime wholly nugatory. On the other hand, when the tide of war began slowly to turn in Britain's favour and when the East African territories could begin to plan for peace, Britain's offer of financial aid provided a vital foundation for schemes of recovery.

Until war had ceased it was only possible to draft in broadest outline the various proposals for reconstruction and expansion. On August 1, 1945, however, a Development and Reconstruction Authority was appointed in Kenya to enable the Government to deal more effectively with post-war planning. A Development and Reconstruction fund was also created in 1946 into which all funds set aside for capital development were paid. Each territory, too, soon had a ten-year development programme as a basis for recovery since one and all felt the need to make up for lost time. This was a twofold task which involved repairing so much that had been left to crumble during the war years in addition to planning for the expansion which would normally have fallen due in the late 1940s. All three territories, too, found themselves faced with unexpected delays in the fulfilment of their programmes owing to the shortage of the materials which everywhere were needed for reconstruction. The rapid rise in prices also meant that the development programmes had to be recast in the light of new estimates of expenditure. Fortunately, since East Africa was producing the primary commodities which were in heavy demand all over the world, revenue too was rising and the territories were able to face the rising cost of reconstruction with relative equanimity. The total volume of Tanganyika's trade, for example, rose from about £17½ million in 1946 to nearly £52½ million in 1949.[1]

One problem did not prove to be so overwhelming as had been feared; that was the rehabilitation of the askaris who had fought on many distant battlefields and whose experiences, it was thought, might make it difficult for them to return to the relatively uneventful lives which had satisfied them before the war. In the event, the resettlement of the askaris was carried out both swiftly and competently. Like amateur soldiers the world over the men of the King's African Rifles were only too glad, for a time at least, to let their wartime experiences become transformed into colourful memories to be recalled in the calm setting of their own homes but not to be relived. The Tanganyika Government, indeed, was disappointed by the apparent lack of interest shown by returned askaris in the new plans for administrative reform. None the less, the Governments' concern had not been wholly misplaced even if it had to some extent been mistimed. For when the first satisfaction of homecoming had worn off some, at least, of the soldiers became restless at the restrictions of civilian life and some, certainly, were to play a prominent part in the disturbances which took place in Kenya in the 1950s.

Two of the most striking schemes set on foot during the period of expansion in the later 1940s were the Tanganyika groundnut scheme and the Owen Falls electricity project in Uganda. Each plan in its own way illustrated the ambition of the East African territories to increase their wealth. In the one case agricultural output was to be stepped up by the use of large-scale mechanization and in the other industry was to be encouraged by making available an adequate supply of power. Both schemes had their weaknesses but whereas one ended in disaster the other went on to provide an important service and a valuable amenity for both Kenya and Uganda.

The failure of the groundnut scheme was mainly due to over-enthusiasm resulting in a grave lack of preliminary planning and experiment. Thus a large-scale undertaking was set on foot without any prior knowledge of the problems to which it might give rise.

[1] J. P. Moffett, ed.: *Handbook of Tanganyika*. Government Printer, Dar es Salaam, 1958, p. 126.

The idea was taken up in the first place by the Colonial Office and as a result of very cursory inquiries a proposal was put forward envisaging the cultivation of no less than three million acres of land divided into large units of 30,000 acres each. The execution of the project fell to the Ministry of Food and after April 1948 to the recently created Overseas Food Corporation. It was then intended that in due course, when the scheme was satisfactorily launched, it should be handed over to the Tanganyika Government and thence to the people of Tanganyika on a co-operative basis or under some other suitable arrangement. The estimated cost of the undertaking was £25,000,000, and even before the Overseas Food Corporation had taken charge the lavish expenditure of money on equipment which was frequently unsuitable had already set the tone of extravagance and even of fantasy which was later to characterize the whole scheme. To develop a project of this magnitude it was also considered necessary to build a new port in southern Tanganyika and to connect this with the centre of operations by a railway. The estimated cost of this additional scheme was £4,550,000, and it was believed that by 1952 the amount of groundnuts exported would be such as to justify the outlay of capital.

But the vivid red soil of the Kongwa-Mpwapwa region of Tanganyika, baked into the finest powder by the harsh sun of the dry season and supporting at that time of the year only sun-blackened thorn bushes, soon proved unsuitable for the mechanized programme contemplated by the originators of the groundnut scheme. By 1949 signs of failure were already visible and the expenditure incurred was so heavy that the capital resources of the Overseas Food Corporation were in danger of being exhausted. In 1950 His Majesty's Government decided to abandon the undertaking in favour of a much more limited project which aimed at investigating some of the problems of land clearance and mechanized agriculture under tropical conditions. So, within five years of its inception, the great groundnut scheme had collapsed. Had the more modest project now envisaged preceded instead of replacing it a vast saving might well have been made. The new scheme was to last for six and a half years and was expected to cost no more than £6,000,000. The railway and port had not been completed, however, and although they were now expected to cost all of £6,000,000 the probable traffic no longer appeared to justify this outlay. In order to avoid still further waste, therefore, it was decided that while the railway should be completed the British Government would not ask for repayment of the capital invested by the Overseas Food Corporation, which amounted to £3,691,403. It was then considered that the balance of about £2,500,000 would not be an excessive sum for the East African Railways and Harbours Administration to invest so long as the Tanganyika Government assumed responsibility for any deficits on the cost of operation. Under these revised arrangements the scheme worked satisfactorily but it was only a pale shadow of the original, grandiose groundnut project.[1]

The fortunes of the Owen Falls electricity scheme proved to be much more satisfactory although far more money was involved than had been originally intended while many of the hoped-for consumers failed to make the demands expected of them. The first survey was carried out in 1946 and in the following year the Protectorate Government agreed to the construction of a hydro-electric scheme at an estimated cost of £4,803,700. The decision was an act of faith, for the immediate needs of Uganda could not justify such a large undertaking. Indeed, doubting that capital on the scale needed would be forthcoming from private investors without a Government guarantee, a public corporation, the Uganda Electricity Board, was created to take charge of the scheme. Even then it was necessary to negotiate a bulk supply agreement with Kenya so as to ensure an adequate demand for electricity and, although the terms of the agreement appeared reasonable, after a few years of inflation they proved to be less satisfactory than had been hoped. Furthermore, it was soon found that to carry electricity from the Owen Falls dam over great distances was uneconomic, so that except where a considerable demand could be anticipated the prospect of electricity for household use was often delayed. None the less, the availability of this vast source of power had an encouraging effect upon industrial development and offered a reasonable incentive for further industrial expansion.

Yet the high hopes of industrialization held in Uganda in the post-war era were never fulfilled. Encouraged by the rapidly increasing revenue accruing from the high prices offered for Uganda's primary produce the Protectorate Government created the Uganda

[1] J. P. Moffett, ed.: *Handbook of Tanganyika.* Government Printer, Dar es Salaam, 1958, pp. 133-4, 141-3.

Development Corporation with an initial capital of £5,000,000 and with the object of assisting in the establishment, financing and management of industrial and mining schemes. It was hoped that the existence of the Corporation would encourage companies from outside Uganda to invest their capital in joint enterprises. One example of the success of this policy was the agreement reached towards the end of 1953 between the Canadian firm of Frobisher Limited, the Colonial Development Corporation, and the Uganda Development Corporation to provide the capital needed to develop the copper resources of the Kilembe mines in the Ruwenzori Mountains. Other enterprises encouraged by the U.D.C. included a cement-producing scheme on the eastern borders of the Protectorate, a textile factory, an enamelware factory and a chain of hotels in those parts of the country most attractive to tourists.

Carried on by the high tide of enthusiasm the Uganda Government also decided as a result of a report on the resources of the western region of the Protectorate, published in 1951,[1] to set on foot the first important extension of Uganda's railroad system for twenty years. The plan was to build a railway westward from Kampala almost to the foothills of the Ruwenzori Mountains so as to encourage the development not only of the Kilembe Mines but also of the agricultural resources of western Uganda. When the work was completed in 1956 the demand for transport from the coppermines fell well below expectation but in little more than two years general traffic had made the line into an economic project. But the schemes for industrial expansion were faced with a variety of obstacles. Uganda's natural resources were limited and to import machinery or raw materials to encourage the growth of industries would have unduly inflated the cost of the finished product. Exports, too, were bedevilled by the high cost of carrying goods many hundreds of miles by rail to the coast even before they could be shipped onward to the markets of the world, while the internal market was limited and unlikely to expand at any great speed. At the same time there was no very stable labour supply to support large-scale industrial development. Gradually, therefore, it came to be recognized in the later 1950s that Uganda must, after all, continue to rely heavily for its wealth upon its agricultural produce and that industry, to be profitable, could only be of the type needed to supply

[1] *The Way to the West*. Government Printer, Entebbe, 1951.

the small internal demand. Even the prospect of selling goods to the other East African territories was weakened because each territory was anxious to meet its own internal requirements by developing its own industries. The plea of the Royal Commission of 1953–55[1] that East Africa should think of itself in terms of an economic unit could make little headway. During the prosperous years of the early 1950s co-operation seemed unnecessary, and in the years of recession which followed each territory was anxious only to obtain revenue by any means which came to hand, irrespective of any wider economic concepts.

One field of industry in which major changes took place in Uganda, however, was in the processing of the Protectorate's old-established agricultural products. Not only cotton but coffee, too, was being grown more extensively by Africans, and in the boom year of 1955 the value of the coffee exported exceeded that of cotton. Indeed, the value of the coffee crop to African growers in that year, even after the deduction of sums to support the price assistance funds, amounted to £15,000,000, while the value of cotton after a similar deduction was still £11,500,000. The change in the cotton- and coffee-processing industries which took place after the war, however, was one of management rather than of technique or expansion. Under the governorship of Sir John Hall, immediately after the war, proposals were made, with the approval of the Labour Government in Britain, to enable African co-operative societies to purchase ginneries, if necessary after the Government had compulsorily acquired them from their present owners. Any African co-operative society which could put up one third of the price could then buy a ginnery, assisted by a loan from the Protectorate Government of the remaining two thirds which must be repaid over a period not exceeding thirty years. In spite of criticisms from the ginners themselves the scheme was adopted in 1952 under Hall's successor, Sir Andrew Cohen, and it had the approval of the Conservative Government which had replaced the Labour Government in Britain. The first ginnery was transferred to African ownership in January 1953. African participation in coffee-processing was also assisted by Government intervention, in this case by the control which was exercised over the number of coffee-curing works in the

---

[1] *East Africa Royal Commission 1953–55 Report.* Cmd. 9475, H.M.S.O., London, 1955.

Protectorate. By maintaining a watch on the development of competition the Government was able to ensure that curing works newly acquired by Africans should not be squeezed out before they had begun to pay their way. In 1956, also, smaller African coffee-growers were authorized to set up their own coffee-pulping and curing factories, either as individuals or in associations, subject to the maintenance of satisfactory standards.[1]

In 1955 Uganda took a further important step towards associating Africans with more varied aspects of the country's economic life, when the report of a committee set up to assist Africans in trade was adopted by the Legislative Council. The main recommendations of the committee were that a fund of £400,000 should be established to be used over a five-year period for building shops to be rented to Africans in towns and trading centres, that training should be provided in trading techniques and that wholesale showrooms should be established in areas remote from the main wholesale supply centres.[2] One of the chief problems facing Africans in Uganda as well as in the other East African territories, was to obtain enough capital to enable them to start new enterprises with a reasonable hope of competing on equal terms with already established concerns. Indeed, in Kenya and Tanganyika legal restrictions controlled the amount of money which could be lent to Africans, the object of the legislation being to prevent Africans being oppressed by debt. In Uganda where controls were less rigid the absence of any adequate security itself imposed a serious restriction upon the majority of Africans hoping to enter business. Only the landowners of Buganda, together with a few co-operative societies owning permanent property, could offer the sort of security normally required in commercial transactions and it was they, therefore, alone who could benefit from the operation of the Credit and Savings Bank established by the Protectorate Government in 1950. To meet this difficulty an African Loans Fund was created in 1953 from which Africans might obtain loans without a normally recognized security if their application was supported by a committee on which local residents who knew the applicant were sitting.

[1] *Report of an Ad Hoc Committee set up to consider the position of the licensed scheduled hulleries in the coffee industry, and a memorandum by the Government on the Report.* Government Printer, Entebbe, 1956.

[2] *Report of the Committee on the Advancement of Africans in Trade.* Government Printer, Entebbe, 1955.

Neither Kenya nor Tanganyika contemplated any large-scale industrial undertakings upon the lines planned in Uganda. In Kenya much of the expenditure envisaged by the development programme was on soil conservation and the improvement of agriculture. Nevertheless, since the early days of Delamere the colony had made an attempt to process its agricultural produce and it was in the development of such secondary industries that progress was made. There was a reassuring willingness on the part of external investors to put their capital into industrial expansion of this sort and confidence in Kenya appeared very high when the Municipal Council of Nairobi raised a loan of £1,500,000 at 3¼ per cent in London and Nairobi simultaneously in 1949 and found it over-subscribed several times over.[1] In Tanganyika the biggest feature of the development programme was the extension and development of communications. Three important railway extensions were set in hand, including the one already referred to in connection with the groundnuts scheme, but when the amalgamation of the East African railways took place in 1948 the provision for capital expenditure on railway development was cut out of the territory's programme. Roads still needed to be developed, however, and the rapid rise in cost for a mile of bitumenized road from an estimated £2,500 in 1946 to £10,000 in 1950 made a revision of the development programme essential. Indeed, all three territories found in the 1950s that rising prices were making the sums estimated in the early stages of post-war reconstruction seem utterly inadequate. Some indication of the change that was taking place is to be seen from the rise in the value of Tanganyika's trade to £85,000,000 in 1952. This was mainly the result of the high prices offered for sisal but although the value of trade dropped to £69,500,000 in 1954 the country could feel justifiably confident of its financial position.

Along with high prices, however, went a startling increase in the cost of living. As early as 1950 ominous signs were noted in Kenya where the African cost of living index rose fourteen points during the year and the European index also rose eleven points. This was only a foretaste of worse to come, for between January and October of 1951 the African index rose fifty-two points. Wage increases were urgently necessary and in the buoyant circumstances of trade

[1] *Kenya Colony: Annual Report for the Year 1949*. H.M.S.O., London, 1949, p. 5.

at the time they could be met with some confidence. So prosperous did the territories think themselves in the early 1950s that all were encouraged to produce important schemes for the development of social services and in particular of education. Kenya had included a sum of nearly £2,500,000 in its original development programme for educational purposes, laying the main emphasis upon the provision of secondary education for African children and on the training of teachers for African and Indian schools. At the same time the problem of adult education was to be met by increasing the provision of community centres in African areas. Some indication of the rate of expansion of Kenya's educational programme is reflected in the increase in annual expenditure from £750,000 in 1948 to over £1,000,000 in 1949. But even this was not enough, and in 1949 a comprehensive examination of the education provided for the African population was carried out by a committee sitting under the chairmanship of Archdeacon Beecher. The committee's report contained recommendations aimed at improving the standard of education at all levels, starting with closer supervision of primary schools by Government inspectors and going on to the rapid expansion of schools providing courses which led to the School Certificate examination and to the raising of the standards of admission to teacher training courses and the lengthening of the courses themselves. The acceptance of this programme, the Government believed, would involve a capital expenditure of £1,500,000 over a five-year period and an increase in the recurrent cost to the Government from £401,000 in 1950 to £719,000 in 1955.

Tanganyika was faced with an even greater task. Alongside its general development programme, therefore, the territory had adopted a ten year plan for educational development which was expected to cost £4,750,000. The main object was to provide schools for 36 per cent of the children of school age, but the census of 1948 revealed that the population was much greater than had been thought, so that the programme had to be recast in 1950. The revised plan envisaged the creation of middle schools for pupils who had passed the primary level but were not of secondary standard. Indeed, the main emphasis of Tanganyika's planning had to be upon the provision of primary education for as many children as possible with secondary and higher education only for the few who showed particular ability. None the less, the prosperity of the early 1950s made it possible to expand the provision of secondary education considerably, while at the same time achieving considerable improvements in the standard of the pupils' attainment, so that the original caution could be somewhat modified.

In Uganda there had been talk of mass education even before the end of the war with, among its aims, the improvement of the standard of living of the African population. In the immediate post-war years, however, there had been much greater emphasis upon the development of the country's resources than upon the provision of social services. It was the years of prosperity of the early 1950s, coupled with the dynamic influence of Sir Andrew Cohen, who became Governor in 1952, which changed this. Soon after his arrival Cohen appointed a committee under the chairmanship of Mr. B. de Bunsen, Principal of Makerere College, to survey the country's educational needs. The committee's report stressed the need to reorganize the system of teacher training in the Protectorate so as to raise the standard of the teachers and it also recommended a revision of the organization of senior secondary schools. It was proposed that these changes should take place over a five-year period at an estimated cost of £7,000,000.[1] But the Government modified the suggestion so as to increase the period of development to eight years while at the same time raising the money involved to £8,000,000. So rapid were the changes which took place when the committee's programme had been adopted, however, that in the event the five-year estimate proved to be more accurate than the longer period recommended by the Government.

Makerere College, too, made rapid advances in the post-war years. The vision of Hussey and the enthusiasm of Sir Philip Mitchell and the members of the de la Warr Commission at last bore fruit in 1949 when the College was accepted into special relationship with the University of London. From 1950 onwards courses leading to the B.A. and B.Sc. degrees of London University were commenced in what now became the University College of East Africa. This advance was followed some years later by the introduction of degree courses in agriculture, while the medical school, the oldest faculty of the College, gained the recognition of the General Medical Council for its licentiateship in medicine and surgery. Meanwhile, in 1953, the Royal Technical College was founded in Nairobi with the initial

[1] *African Education in Uganda.* Government Printer, Entebbe, 1953.

intention of providing technological training for students from all the East African territories in the same way that Makerere College was providing university education. This object was modified a few years later by the suggestion that the College should be absorbed into another university college similar in its basic structure to Makerere but providing a different range of professional courses. Simultaneously, the number of students receiving higher education in both institutions was increasing at a rapid rate while the standard required at entrance was raised appreciably as a result of the improvement in secondary education.

Underlying this improvement was the deeply felt desire of large sections of the African population for formal education in accordance with the western pattern, a desire which induced parents to pay a high proportion of their incomes in school fees so as to ensure that their children might have equal opportunities with other children. The motives behind this enthusiasm comprised a mixture of uncomprehending faith in the moral and material value of western education and the more specific hope that success in school would enable a child to find better paid employment. While, therefore, the support of the African population greatly assisted the territorial governments in their campaign to extend educational provision, the craving for education created a number of difficulties. Not least among them was the problem of countering the belief that every child should be educated to the highest level irrespective of his attainments or interest. Although this difficulty could be handled at a practical level by examinations and by the sheer lack of money for more secondary schools, it continued to be a cause of deep dissatisfaction and one which was not improved by the fact that many able children were also excluded from senior schools because of the shortage of places. Another, perhaps more serious, problem arose from the unwillingness of children with even a minimum education to return to agricultural work. This was partly a question of pride but it was also the result, in part, of the small incomes derived by the majority of peasants from their agricultural labours as compared with even the lowest-paid and under-employed messengers and office workers in the towns.

The problem of obtaining satisfactory employment outside the realm of agriculture was becoming increasingly difficult. Yet more and more young men tended to gravitate towards the larger towns as much for the excitement offered by urban life as for the economic reward they were likely to gain. Save, perhaps, in Nairobi and Mombasa, this movement did not create an urban unemployment problem in the generally accepted sense. The problem to which it did give rise was that of a shifting labour force. The number of openings for skilled workers was limited and many of these posts were already occupied by Indians. Opportunities for semi-skilled or unskilled labourers, on the other hand, were numerous, and Africans generally took up this type of employment. Wages, how-ever, although attractive when viewed from the remote perspective of the villages, were not high by comparison with the cost of living in the towns, so that while it was possible to subsist at a low level for a limited period, there was a strong desire among the labourers to return to their villages with the savings achieved after several months of meagre living. At home the money had greater value and, in any case, the attachment felt by most Africans to their land was so strong that even the regular employee in a town tended to regard himself as being fundamentally a farmer whom circumstances had attracted away from his land for a limited period. This attitude had unfortunate reactions for, since there was no shortage of unskilled labour, if a man was prepared to accept a low wage because he knew his employment would last only a limited period, there was no incentive to employers to raise the level of wages for this type of work. Furthermore, although legislation was passed in all three territories to make possible the enactment of minimum wages, the minimum was based upon the requirements of a single man, it being assumed that his wife and children would be maintained by the produce of their own land.

In Kenya, where the land available for Africans was not so plentiful as in Uganda and Tanganyika this arrangement was recognized as being unsatisfactory. In Kenya, too, the wider variety of industrial employment created a stronger demand for a stable labour force. In Nairobi, and to a less extent in Mombasa, there were labourers who could not rely on their own farms to provide the basic needs of their families while they themselves simply earned enough for their own keep, to pay for their children's education, to meet their taxes and to supply any small luxuries which they might hope to acquire. It was in these circumstances that the Kenya Government in 1955 accepted the recommendation of a committee on African wages that minimum wages in the larger towns should in future be based on the requirements of a family unit. The committee also proposed that in order to avoid too great an upheaval the implementation of their suggestions should be gradual and should cover a ten-year period.[1] Neither Uganda nor Tanganyika followed Kenya's example, however, and Kenya itself soon experienced serious difficulties in financing the proposed increases.

The reluctance of Uganda and Tanganyika to change their policy was partly due to the fact that their need for a stable labour force was less acute than was the case in Kenya but partly also because it was thought undesirable to make urban employment so attractive financially that agriculture might be in danger of total neglect. There was a great need in all three territories to make the rewards of agriculture more attractive. A further difference also existed between Kenya and the other two territories in that in the former country European-owned farms could supply the demand for food created by a large urban population whereas in the other two territories, with the exception of the plantains supplied to some of the larger towns by the surrounding countryside, food production was limited to a family's own requirements. This difficulty of supplying food for large urban populations might in time have been overcome if the financial return appeared sufficiently attractive to the growers, but it would have involved an important revolution in the outlook of African farmers.

It was not always an easy task to make agricultural work more attractive. The peasants themselves were often disinclined to produce more than was necessary to meet their own immediate requirements, while the type of incentive which might stimulate the enthusiasm of a more sophisticated population often failed miserably to impress men whose wants were limited to a bicycle or to school fees for their families. This problem was not hidden from the territorial Governments and in 1955 the Uganda Government adopted the report of an agricultural productivity committee which had been investigating means of increasing the output of the land.[2] Yet even then the Protectorate's main crops showed no significant increase. The poor return for peasant crops such as cotton must not be overlooked in

[1] *Report of the Committee on African Wages.* Government Printer, Nairobi, 1954.

[2] *Agricultural Productivity Committee, Report.* Government Printer, Entebbe, 1955.

assessing the reasons for the low level of output. Even after the years of inflation of the 1950s a peasant with a tiny patch of land might make no more than £15 a year from cotton-growing. This led to criticism of the policy of price stabilization adopted by the territorial governments, criticism echoed by the Royal Commission on Land and Population which visited East Africa in 1953 and 1954.[1] The basis of the criticisms were that guaranteed prices deprived the producers of the benefits to be obtained in good years while shielding them from economic realities in bad years. This meant that a guaranteed price would reduce the incentive to produce more in bad years as well as in good. In other words, sound economic development was being sacrificed in order to guarantee security at a very low level. It was argued that this approach was the product of wartime shortages when a fair distribution of limited resources was more important than a viable economy. In peacetime this attitude could only be stultifying both to the growers and to others concerned in marketing the produce.

The territorial Governments could not agree with these conclusions. Depending for a high proportion of their revenue upon the income derived either directly or indirectly from one or two important crops they were in no position to jeopardize the security of East Africa, even if only for a few years until a new situation might develop. Nor were the controls exercised over marketing simply the result of an innate delight in paternalism which feared to witness the emergence of normal commercial practices. The enactment in 1949 of an ordinance to permit the establishment of a Lint Marketing Board in Uganda was the Protectorate Government's reaction to heavy criticism of the cotton industry, not only by a commission of inquiry set up the previous year from within the Protectorate itself, but also from the chairman of the Council and Executive of the Empire Cotton-Growing Corporation who visited Uganda in 1949. The Coffee Industry Board had a similar function of guaranteeing prices and quality, both of which were necessary if growers were not to be discouraged in lean years, as they had been in the past, and if Uganda's products were to maintain their attraction in the world market. For the same reasons a Kenya committee on the development of agricultural marketing was prepared to go as far as to recommend the abandonment of the idea of exporting certain cereals

[1] Cmd. 9475, pp. 66–70.

391

so as to guarantee a reasonable price for the growers since the internal market would be more predictable than the external market. After the boom years of the early 1950s when huge reserves were built up in the price assistance funds the Uganda Government did, however, agree to allow greater freedom of marketing to African coffee growers but it continued to guarantee prices to all who opted in advance to sell their produce through the agency of the Coffee Industry Board.

The question of security was not one which affected only the policies of Governments. It was one of the underlying motives behind the attitude of Africans towards their land. With a background of subsistence farming stretching far beyond the limits of human memory and with, as yet, no alternative source of security, the African population fiercely resisted any suggestion of altering traditional systems of land tenure lest in the process their own rights to the area needed to maintain their families should be lost. Once again the Royal Commission pointed unerringly to this impediment to economic expansion, stressing the need to abandon subsistence farming in favour of greater specialization in all economic activities. But the territorial Governments counselled caution. It was enough for the Uganda Government to publish a white paper recommending that Africans should have the opportunity to acquire a freehold title to their land to arouse the greatest fears in many parts of the Protectorate, even though the Government made it clear that there was no intention of introducing this policy against the wishes of the people. Some of the suspicions aroused by the white paper were undoubtedly encouraged by political leaders to suit their own ends. Yet the ease with which concern could be stirred up was in itself an indication of the delicate nature of the issue. In any case, the system of individual freehold had existed in Buganda for more than half a century but there was no sign that the Baganda were any less worried than were any other tribe by the prospect of losing their land.

The Tanganyika Government, while accepting the need to provide for individual tenure of land, took care to emphasize the importance of controlling excessive fragmentation of holdings and also of supervising the transfer of land between Africans and non-Africans. And even with these conditions the Government went on to stress that the change proposed by the Royal Commission must be of a gradual nature. In Kenya the situation was oddly complicated. On the one hand the idea of freehold was already accepted by a section of the African population, not least in Kiambu, where the Kikuyu had settled relatively recently and professed to have bought their land from the Dorobo who had lived there before them. At the same time the impossibility of providing subsistence farming for the whole African population with the limited amount of land available in the reserves was already creating a group which was virtually dependent upon its wage earnings. Consequently the policy of creating African reserves on a tribal basis, and what might be regarded as a European reserve in the highlands, tended to perpetuate the view that tribal ownership of land gave greater security than individual ownership. Within the tribal system, it was thought, an individual could hope to retain some traditional rights to the land, reduced though they might be by the increasing pressure of a growing population. A freeholder, by contrast, would have to fight his own battles and in any event would lose his grazing rights on the common land. The loss of these rights could be disastrous to the average African peasant and it was no easy matter to demonstrate the dangers of unrestricted grazing on inadequate communal land. So, one more obstacle to economic progress had to be overcome.

The publication in 1954 of the Swynnerton plan for the intensification of African agriculture,[1] with the adoption of a programme of land consolidation, went a long way towards illustrating the economics of farming in Kenya, more particularly in the heavily populated and fertile lands of Central Province and Nyanza Province. Since the war Africans had taken an increasing interest in cash crops. *Arabica* coffee, formerly grown only by Europeans, had proved particularly successful as an African-grown crop and was being processed and marketed by a number of co-operative societies. Sisal, too, was producing a valuable cash income for a number of African growers while small quantities of pyrethrum were being cultivated by Africans at higher altitudes. In 1952 the amount of wattle bark sold by Africans was three times as great as the quantity produced by Europeans. The Swynnerton plan, therefore, sought to take hold of this new trend and to develop it. Some £6,745,000 was to be spent over a five-year period between 1954 and 1958, towards

[1] *A Plan to Intensify the Development of African Agriculture in Kenya.* Government Printer, Nairobi, 1954.

which amount a grant of £5,500,000 was made by the United Kingdom Government. Under the stimulus given by this new programme the number of African coffee-growers increased from 10,609 in the middle of 1952 to nearly 75,500 by the end of 1958, when some 20,300 acres were under crops. Two-thirds of this area was in the Central Province and most of the remainder in Nyanza Province and the success of the land consolidation scheme is illustrated by the fact that by the end of 1958 it had embraced 779,547 acres in the Central Province, including the whole of Kiambu District, and over 909,000 acres in Nyanza Province.

Important psychologically was the publication of the Government's white paper on land policy in 1959 which held out a promise that the highlands would be opened to suitable African farmers. The report submitted by a special commissioner, Mr. L. G. Troup, in 1953, on farming in the highlands,[1] had shown that a much more intensive use could be made of the land in the European zone. But the Government white paper, not surprisingly, produced violent opposition from some of the European landowners who regarded it as a breach of past pledges and who would have preferred to see an increase in the number of white settlers. At the same time many Africans professed to regard the Government's proposals as a simple deception. Yet the possibility that a breach might be made in the 'tribal' ownership of land could not but be a stimulus to those whom political and racial issues had not blinded to the importance of a sound economy in Kenya based upon the productivity of all races.

The importance of the tribe in an African's life could not, however, be easily ignored even in the interests of economic advancement, for his social, even more than his economic, stability depended heavily upon tribal customs and sanctions. This state of affairs was clearly recognized in Tanganyika. In spite of the criticisms of some educated Africans, who claimed that the insistence upon tribal loyalties had a retarding effect upon political growth, the Government's policy, in fact, provided a stable and realistic background against which the educationally more advanced sections of the African community could carry on their political activities. For the relatively low level of education achieved by most Africans provided no moral substitute for tribal sanctions and even the spread

---

[1] *Inquiry into the General Economy of Farming in the Highlands.* Government Printer, Nairobi, 1953.

of Christianity and Islam could not provide an entirely new set of acceptable values for the whole population of East Africa. In these circumstances it was fortunate that the impact of new ideas did not result in the wholesale detribalization of the African people which many Europeans had feared. Even those Africans who went into the larger towns for the most part joined colonies of their own tribes already established there, and although many tribal restraints were cast aside in urban surroundings they were accepted once again when a man returned to his home.

A different problem arose over the appearance of slum dwellings on the outskirts of the larger towns. This situation was often due to the temporary nature of the employment of the people housed in the slums so that the attempts of municipal authorities to enforce high building standards simply resulted in the transfer of the shanty towns outside the municipal boundaries. Evil though these housing conditions were, it was an evil which was usually of a temporary character as far as the majority of their occupants were concerned. Nevertheless, the slum areas undoubtedly became centres of crime; but even more important was the unnatural lives which so many employees were forced to live for many months of the year, separated from their families and with few of the amenities of village life. Attempts were made by some of the municipalities to overcome this difficulty by building or assisting in the building of housing estates with some sort of communal life and in this attempt some degree of success was achieved. Unfortunately, however, even the low rents charged on these estates were often far beyond the resources of the vast body of unskilled labourers.

The opportunity of benefiting from the years of high prices was to a large extent lost to Kenya owing to the waste of manpower and money as a result of the state of emergency which lasted from 1952 until 1959. The Colony had emerged from the Second World War with good financial reserves and a healthy future. There was considerable interest shown in immigration by prospective European settlers possessing a variety of skills and capital which they were prepared to invest in the territory. Then came the emergency and with it a reorientation of the Government's scale of priorities for expenditure. A high proportion of the country's income had to be spent on the maintenance of law and order. Unlike older countries Kenya could not expect to see its social services expanding upon foundations laid long before. In many cases the foundations themselves were still to be laid, but the Government had to avoid a level of taxation which would discourage internal effort on the one hand and the investment of external capital on the other. Moreover, at a time when it was no longer possible to make contributions towards capital expenditure from recurrent revenue Kenya's unsettled condition tended to reduce the country's ability to raise loans on a limited London money market. By its determination to maintain the country's development programme and with the aid of generous grants and loans from the United Kingdom the Kenya Government was able to carry on its work and the inflow of capital into the country remained at a not unsatisfactory level. Yet, in spite of the benefits of land consolidation and improved farming methods, political uncertainty and unrest continued to undermine the country's economic development throughout the later 1950s, and stability could not have been achieved without financial aid from Britain.

Uganda, which of all the three East African territories was able to take the fullest advantage of the favourable markets in the early 1950s, faced a different problem in the latter half of the decade. The period of recession which followed the boom years found the Protectorate with rapidly expanding social services involving a steadily increasing annual expenditure. The first reaction to this difficulty was not dissimilar from that of Armitage-Smith in Tanganyika during the slump of the early 1930s, namely, to condemn the Government's earlier extravagance. Yet Sir Andrew Cohen in Uganda, like Sir Donald Cameron before him in Tanganyika, had recognized that the time had come to make use of the resources of the good years and of the reserves so carefully accumulated by his predecessor to set on foot some of the urgent developments without which Uganda could not hope to prosper and which could only be undertaken at the crest of a wave of prosperity. The boldness of this policy bore fruit in spite of Cohen's critics for, although careful budgeting had to replace the comfortable spending of the early 1950s, the momentum of development was not wholly lost.

Tanganyika, with its greater population and with its greatly extended communications, illustrated better than either of her two northern neighbours the basic problems of East Africa's poverty. In spite of the high prices offered for Tanganyika's produce the territory, generally, could never rise far above a basic level of subsistence. There were exceptions to this state of affairs. The Chagga coffee-growers of Kilimanjaro prospered and so, too, did the coffee-producers of the Bukoba District and to a less extent the labourers in the diamond-fields around Shinyanga. These diamonds had been discovered during the war and had rapidly superseded gold as Tanganyika's most valuable mineral asset. Yet the standard of living of the majority of the African population remained low and the supply of public services was limited. The apparent increase in the country's wealth in the early 1950s created a spirit of optimism which was fostered by the determination and confidence of the Governor, Sir Edward Twining. But it was an optimism which always looked to the future instead of being based upon a bountiful present. For, so vast was the task of building up Tanganyika's material prosperity that large sums of money and a great deal of effort could be swallowed up with little noticeable result. The undoubted expansion of the educational services had always to be seen against the background of an overwhelming demand for still more schools even if the aim was no more than universal literacy. When, therefore, the recession struck Tanganyika its effects were more serious than in Uganda and only the promise of financial aid from the United Kingdom Government could restore a basis of genuine security. Yet public reaction in Tanganyika was far more restrained than in Uganda for Tanganyikans of all races had become inured to the struggle which was needed to make a livelihood in a harsh yet attractive country.

One remarkable achievement in the field of economic development in the post-war period was the creation of the East Africa High Commission. The Labour Party which came to power in Britain in 1945 was of the opinion that some of the British dependencies were unsatisfactory units in regard to both size and frontiers and was convinced that many of their problems could be solved only by closer co-operation.[1] So far as East Africa was concerned the outcome of this view was the publication, in December 1945, of Colonial Office Paper Number 191 which contained proposals for the establishment of a form of inter-territorial organization for Kenya, Uganda and Tanganyika. These three territories, the paper

---

[1] *African Affairs*, Vol. 44, No. 176, July, 1945, p. 114. Address by A. Creech Jones, M.P., delivered at a combined meeting of the Royal African and Royal Empire Societies on April 25, 1945.

maintained, comprised a solid geographical unit. There was already in existence a common system of customs and excise tariffs, and other inter-territorial organizations had been created during the war. In the less complicated days before 1939 the Governors' Conference had served a useful purpose in co-ordinating certain of the activities common to all three territories, but with the inevitable expansion of these services some better means of control appeared to be called for. Furthermore, the constitutional position of the Governors' Conference was unsatisfactory. Set up without any constitutional authority it was frequently called upon to make decisions without adequate public consultation and without the prior consent of the territorial legislatures. This state of affairs was undesirable, but at the same time public opinion was clearly opposed to the other extreme of political union between the territories. As a basis for discussion, therefore, it was proposed that an East Africa High Commission should be created, consisting of the Governors of the three territories under the chairmanship of the Governor of Kenya. In addition there would be an executive organization together with a central legislature competent to make laws regulating subjects placed under its control. It was felt by the British Government that equality of representation of the three main races among the unofficial members of the Legislature was the only practical basis to work upon in view of the impossibility of devising any other formula which would be universally acceptable. Accordingly it was proposed that two Europeans and two Indians should be elected by the European and Indian unofficial members of each territorial legislature, making a total of twelve. A further six members, as many as possible being Africans, should be nominated, two from each territory, by the High Commission to act as trustees for African interests while six more members would be nominated by the High Commission of whom two would represent Arab interests. The assembly should have a life of four years and would normally meet in Nairobi where the central secretariat would be located, but it might occasionally sit in Uganda or Tanganyika. The financing of common services would remain unchanged, the share of their cost to be borne by each territory being decided from time to time after inter-territorial discussions.

The *Uganda Herald* of January 30, 1946, described the white paper as a statesmanlike attempt to solve a pressing problem, while the president of the Uganda Chamber of Commerce, speaking at the annual general meeting of the Chamber on February 20, welcomed the white paper as a genuine attempt to move with the times. The Indian populations of all three territories were inclined to agree with him. Since most of them were engaged to a greater or less extent in commerce or trade the economic benefits offered by the white paper were clearly attractive. They were also pleased by the attempt at racial parity on the unofficial side of the Legislative Assembly, a state of affairs which they had not achieved in the legislatures of Kenya and Tanganyika. In Kenya, however, the reaction of European unofficials was one of violent opposition. Once again they regarded themselves as being on the defensive. They had received a sharp blow to their sense of security as a result of the success of the Labour Party, the known critics of the settlers, in the recent elections in Britain, and they had been watching with some trepidation for signs of revolutionary action regarding the white highlands. The publication of the white paper therefore let loose a flood of feeling. If the proposals contained in it were to be the basis of discussions why, it was asked, had there been no attempt to sound unofficial opinion before they were drafted? The desirability of coordinating common services was acknowledged, but what justification could there be for such an expensive method of achieving this objective? In any case, was not this simply a covert attempt to encompass the design for a joint East African legislature in which the Kenya European community would be reduced to parity with, say, the Arabs? The principle of racial equality in the Assembly was wholly illogical. Communal representation should depend upon the value of a community's contribution to the wealth and progress of the state. Again, how could Arabs be granted an equal share with Europeans in the trusteeship of the African people? There were other criticisms, too, that the political influence so arduously achieved by Europeans through forty years of endeavour might be destroyed at the stroke of a pen. The interests of Kenya might be endangered since the Governor of Kenya could be outvoted by his two colleagues. The power of the Secretary of State to add without consultation to the list of subjects reserved to the Central Assembly was a threat to the power and prestige of the territorial legislatures. In these circumstances Kenya's Europeans could do no other than reject the white paper completely. Their dismay at the Labour Government's policy was strengthened still further, when it was announced that it had been decided that Tanganyika should be placed under the supervision of the United Nations Trusteeship Council. This, it was thought, displayed a complete disregard for imperial strategy.[1]

African opinion was difficult to assess. In Buganda there were many, particularly among the wealthier landowning families, who regarded the proposals as comprising yet another attempt to subject Uganda to the will of the Kenya settlers and to deprive the Baganda of the benefits of the 1900 Agreement. There is some evidence, however, that among the more radical politicians the offer of equality of representation in the Central Assembly proved tempting. This was certainly the case in Kenya. The Kenya African Union welcomed the white paper but asked that the six members representing African interests should all be Africans as well as one of the four other unspecified members. Two representatives of the Union toured Uganda and Tanganyika to try to estimate African reaction in those territories and these men were quick to recognize the division of opinion in Uganda already referred to. In Tanganyika the Africans they consulted were so strongly opposed to anything which threatened to subject them to Kenya that they could not look with favour upon the proposals contained in the white paper. In their view the best prospects for future development in Tanganyika lay in the policy already initiated by the territorial Government.[2] To complete the story it is necessary to add that a meeting of Arabs in Mombasa early in 1946 accepted the proposals but asked for Arab representation equal to that of the other communities.

Mr. A. Creech-Jones, Under-Secretary of State for the Colonies, visited East Africa to hear the views of different sections of the population and as a result modified proposals were published early in 1947.[3] There was no change in the over-all objective of the new white paper and it was implicitly recognized that political union was not intended. The main change, and the one which attracted most

[1] *African Affairs*, Vol. 45, No. 180, July, 1946, pp. 136–9. The East African Political Scene: the European Point of View, by Major R. E. K. Ward, Secretary of the Kenya European Electors Union.

[2] *African Affairs*, Vol. 45, No. 180, July, 1946, pp. 139–41. The East African Political Scene: the African Viewpoint, by F. J. Khamisi, Secretary of the Kenya African Union.

[3] *Inter-Territorial Organization in East Africa, Revised Proposals.* Colonial No. 120, H.M.S.O., London, 1947.

attention, was in the composition of the Legislative Assembly. There, the unofficial representation was to be reduced to thirteen although there would still be an unofficial majority. The Governors of Uganda and Tanganyika, it was proposed, would each appoint one European, one African and one Asian while the Governor of Kenya would appoint one African member and the European and Asian unofficial members of the Legislative Council would each elect one member of their own community. In addition, the unofficial members of each of the three territorial legislatures would elect one member and there would be a further member of the Arab community appointed by the High Commission. The United Kingdom Government did not consider that the new proposals in any way affected the original recommendaticn of equal racial representation in the Assembly, but this view was not taken in East Africa. On the one hand the leaders of the Kenya Europeans assured their followers that a European majority among the unofficial members was now guaranteed. The Uganda Chamber of Commerce, meanwhile, together with the Central Council of Indian Associations in Uganda, reaffirmed their support for the original proposals and rejected the revised version on the ground that equality of representation had been jettisoned. Educated Africans in Kenya and Uganda also disliked the new plan while opposition to the whole proposal in Tanganyika remained unchanged. With the aid of the official majorities in the three territorial legislatures, however, the new proposals were adopted and the East Africa High Commission came into being on January 1, 1948. Its activities in the years which followed gave little support to any of the criticisms which had been levelled against it in advance. In general, however, it achieved the greatest disfavour among African politicians who maintained that it threatened political union. This argument was abandoned by the Uganda political leaders in 1959, however, in favour of the original Kenya settler protest that the central legislature deprived the territorial legislatures of some of their independence. In 1951 and again in 1955 the life of the assembly was extended for further periods of four years although not without criticism from African members of the territorial legislatures. By 1959, however, when the subject came up for consideration once again, the world economic situation had tended to undermine the desire for co-operation at least as far as Tanganyika was concerned, so that although Kenya and Uganda again agreed to a four-year extension of the Central Assembly Tanganyika voted for only a two-year extension. In these circumstances the Secretary of State recommended a compromise of three years during which period the functions of the Central Assembly were to be subjected to review.

The prospect that Tanganyika would achieve independence in December 1961 called for a still more fundamental reassessment of the structure and functions of the High Commission. In February 1961 an economic and fiscal commission urged that the East African common market area should be retained and to meet this recommendation it was decided in June that the High Commission should be replaced at the end of the year by an East African Common Services Organization. The principal ministers of the three territories thus became responsible for the working of the Organization which carried on the activities of its predecessor.

With independence Julius Nyerere, the Tanganyika prime minister. began at once to work for a closer political union between the East African territories. Such an amalgamation had to wait upon the constitutional advance of Uganda, Kenya and Zanzibar, but in 1963 there were high hopes that a federation of East Africa would come into being at the beginning of the next year.

CHAPTER ELEVEN

CONSTITUTIONAL DEVELOPMENT AND THE EMERGENCE OF AFRICAN NATIONALISM

IF the East African Governments were primarily concerned with economic reconstruction in the immediately post-war years the African population, or at least the more educated sections of it, was more interested in politics and constitutional advances. It was, moreover, in these latter fields that the most startling developments took place. Kenya, having gained an important lead over the other two territories in the development of its Legislative Council, took immediate steps to consolidate its position. Yet it was the other two territories in which the most striking changes were soon to take place. African political parties, hitherto virtually non-existent in Uganda and Tanganyika, now began to exert an influence upon affairs which more than equalled that exercised by the Kenya African political leaders. The unofficial membership of all three Legislative Councils was expanded, but in Uganda and Tanganyika the expansion was greater than in Kenya and the most important aspect of this change was the increasing number of African members. Africans, too, began to find their place in the Executive Councils of the East African territories until in December 1961 Tanganyika became the first East African territory to achieve independence. Uganda followed in October 1962. Simultaneously African participation in local government affairs took great steps forward and in 1959 an African became Mayor of Kampala. In 1950, meanwhile, Nairobi became East Africa's first city.

Kenya it was which took the lead in introducing Africans into its Legislative Council when Mr. Eliud Mathu was nominated as the first African member in 1944. Tanganyika followed suit in December 1945, with the nomination of two African members, both of them chiefs. In the same month three nominated African members took their seats in the Uganda Legislative Council each representing one of the provinces of the Protectorate. The representation of Buganda had aroused some debate, however, since many of the Baganda feared that such a step might threaten the 1900 Agreement while others feared that since the member must be one of the ministers of the Kabaka's government his decisions in the Legislative Council might prejudice the freedom of action of the Buganda Lukiko. The Protectorate Government, however, gave an assurance that the vote of the Buganda member would not commit the Lukiko in any way. Not to be outdone after having itself pointed the way, Kenya added a further African member to its legislature, first as a temporary measure in 1946 and subsequently on a permanent basis a year later.

In other directions, too, Kenya took the initiative. In 1945 the Government was reorganized so as to group the main departments under the control of Members of the Executive Council. The final responsibility formerly taken by the Chief Secretary for the activities of the various departments was now shared by six others. Initially, although there were three European unofficial members and one Indian member of the Executive Council, all the Members in the ministerial sense were officials, but this situation changed at a later stage. Another indication of the development of Kenya's legislature towards the form of a representative parliament followed in 1947 when a member was appointed to preside over the Legislative Council in place of the Governor. In the following year he took the title of Speaker. Following upon the elections of the European and Indian unofficial members of the legislature in 1948 Kenya, for the first time, had an unofficial majority in the Legislative Council. This consisted of eleven European elected members, five Indian elected members, one Arab elected member, four African nominated members and one nominated Arab member. Against this total of twenty-two there were sixteen official members only.

There were no parallel developments in Uganda and Tanganyika although political activity among the African population of Buganda was becoming steadily more pronounced. This activity, however, was still mainly centred upon the affairs of the Buganda Lukiko rather than upon the ultimate object of exerting influence upon the Protectorate as a whole. To this extent the riots which broke out in Buganda in 1949 belonged rather to the sphere of local government than to that of national politics. Again, although the disturbances were undoubtedly stimulated by political leaders, the claims of the rioters were of such a varied character that it must be assumed that the leaders had simply taken hold of every type of discontent in order to stir up trouble so as to attract attention to themselves. Their demands ranged from the dismissal of the Kabaka's ministers and of the Saza chiefs because they had acted unconstitutionally to the acceptance of a policy which would give Africans greater control of the cotton and coffee industries. Again the widespread nature of the riots, which resulted in the whole of Buganda being declared a disturbed area, was mainly due to the conviction of the peasant population that they were not getting a fair return for their crops. In its results, too, the disturbance was limited to Buganda, for the main outcome was a recommendation that a new election law should be prepared to encourage a more democratic approach to membership of the Buganda Lukiko.

In the constitutional affairs of Tanganyika probably the most important development in the later 1940s was the decision of the British Government to place the territory under the trusteeship system inaugurated as a branch of the United Nations Organization. In announcing this decision the British Foreign Secretary, Mr. Ernest Bevin, made it clear that Britain had no desire to cast off the responsibilities which she had borne for a quarter of a century. In the interests of the population of Tanganyika he emphasized that there would be no break in the continuity of administration until the territory achieved either self-government or independence. This move on the part of the British Government had a valuable effect upon the state of mind of the African population of Tanganyika. For the Trusteeship Council was no remote body such as the Permanent Mandates Commission had been. Visiting missions were sent to Tanganyika at intervals of three years, starting in 1948, and the presence of these visitors gave to the people of the territory the sense of being in the eye of the world rather than being shut off by an alien if generally benevolent administration. Again, the Trusteeship Council, unlike the Permanent Mandates Commission, did not hesitate to make recommendations on political matters, and although the United Kingdom Government might reject those recommendations it would do so publicly and with the full knowledge that its actions might well arouse widespread criticism. This impression of being a ward of the United Nations rather than a British colony did much to create confidence. Although the irresponsible recommendations of the visiting mission in 1954 created some embarrassment for the British Government there is no question that on the whole British relations with Tanganyika benefited greatly from international supervision through the Trusteeship Council.

The general satisfaction of the people of Tanganyika with the existing state of affairs was reflected in the subdued reaction to the appointment of a committee on constitutional development in 1949. This committee, which consisted of the Attorney-General and the Member for Local Government, together with all the unofficial members of the Legislative Council, travelled extensively about the territory and were not a little surprised to note the apparent absence of any widespread demand for reforms. Even the political leaders seemed to be engrossed in local rather than in national problems. In these circumstances the committee recommended on submitting its report in 1951 that the membership of the Legislative Council should be enlarged so as to extend its influence more widely. At the same time it suggested that before elections were introduced there should be an inquiry by an expert to discover whether such a step was practicable and if so how it should be put into effect.

This steady rate of progress in Tanganyika was in marked contrast to the rapid changes which were taking place in Uganda and Kenya in the early 1950s. Increasing political activity on the part of Africans in Kenya suggested that the time had come for elected African representatives to play a part in the Legislative Council. The Europeans, however, were anxious that any increase in the African membership of the Council should not affect their own numerical superiority while the Indians were also concerned about their position in the light of the emergence of African political influence. In an attempt to meet these various points of view temporary adjustments were made to the constitution to take effect in 1952. The unofficial membership of the Council was increased to twenty-eight, comprising fourteen Europeans, six Asians and one Arab, all of whom were elected, together with six Africans who were appointed by the Governor, from a list of names submitted by electoral colleges which were set up in six different parts of the colony. The number was completed by one Arab representative member.

The official side was increased from sixteen to twenty-six members and the twelve members of the Executive Council now included one African among their numbers.

Scarcely had these changes been considered when Kenya awoke with a shock to the presence of Mau Mau. The origins of the movement are not clear. One elderly Kikuyu stated that he had taken a Mau Mau oath in 1913 but he was probably referring to some earlier version of the society which was considerably less harmful than it was later to become. Its revival in its more modern form dated from 1947 when the Kikuyu Central Association was proscribed and one section went underground to form Mau Mau. Its supporters took oaths binding them to obedience and secrecy and their object was to drive the Europeans out of Kenya. Warnings of the existence of a dangerous secret society were passed on to government officers but appeared to create little concern in official quarters. In 1950, there was an outbreak of violence on the part of a religious sect calling itself the *Dini ya Masambwa* in the Baringo area, but this was put down with comparative ease and the success of the forces of law and order may well have lulled the suspicions of the Government. Even an outbreak of arson in the Nyeri district early in 1952 aroused no serious disquiet in Nairobi although it was clearly the work of Mau Mau.

In the succeeding months there were a number of acts of violence and robbery, and the missionaries in particular were conscious that trouble was threatening. In May 1952 the Vicar Apostolic in Nyeri issued a pastoral letter denouncing Mau Mau and threatening to excommunicate anyone who took the oath. His example was followed in August by the Roman Catholic Bishop of Zanzibar while in July the Legislative Council discussed the increase in crime in Kenya. Although the Council recognized the need for the general public to co-operate with the police in maintaining order no immediate action was taken. Later in the same month, at a mass meeting of 30,000 Kikuyu organized by the Kenya African Union in Nyeri, Chief Nderi was jeered by members of the crowd when he denounced acts of violence. At a later date he was hacked to pieces for his opposition to Mau Mau. In August the K.A.U. organized another mass meeting of Kikuyu in Kiambu, and Chief Waruhiu spoke vigorously against Mau Mau. He, too, was later to die for his opposition to the movement. The president of the K.A.U., Jomo

Kenyatta, also addressed the assembly and declared that the union had no link with Mau Mau. Indeed, the K.A.U. was regarded by many people in England as being the most responsible organ of African opinion in Kenya, so that there was considerable confusion as to the nature of the terrorist movement which was developing. Even the Kenya Government seemed uncertain as to its general policy, for in spite of imposing curfews in the Kikuyu districts of Fort Hall, Nyeri and Nanyuki in the month of August there appeared to be an unwillingness to recognize a genuine emergency. The European unofficials were not so sceptical, and they pressed the Government to take firmer action. But when the Chief Native Commissioner travelled to England in September to obtain the British Government's approval for sterner legislation to check crime in Kenya he declared that the newspaper accounts of secret societies were exaggerated. Mr. Eliud Mathu, a member of the Legislative Council, and Mr. Mbiyu Koinange, a delegate of the Kenya African Union, who were both in England about the same time agreed with this view, and even went so far as to express doubts about the very existence of Mau Mau. Towards the end of September, however, sterner laws were passed by the Legislative Council to control crimes of violence and the need for them was becoming increasingly obvious. An ordinance permitting evidence in Mau Mau cases to be taken on affidavit was in itself an indication of the Government's inability to protect witnesses.

The long awaited arrival of Sir Evelyn Baring, the new Governor, on September 29, 1952, was followed by official assurances of the Government's intention to check further disorders. In October a state of emergency was declared and a British battalion was flown in from the canal zone. Reinforcements of K.A.R. were also deployed to deal with the growing terrorism. Several of the leaders of the K.A.U. were arrested and after trial were sentenced to several years' imprisonment. Although the K.A.U. itself was not proscribed until the middle of the following year its president, Jomo Kenyatta, was found guilty of managing Mau Mau and sentenced to seven years' imprisonment. Late in 1952 thousands of Kikuyu were transfered from European farms to the reserves in the interests of security, although the loss of labour was a serious blow to the farmers and the influx of people into the reserves caused serious overcrowding and food shortages. In these emergency conditions there was a danger, too, that Kikuyu who had not yet been in contact with Mau Mau would fall under the influence of the terrorists.

Meanwhile, the sporadic acts of violence which had marked the outbreak of the movement were giving place to planned, large-scale attacks in which firearms were used. European settlers were raided on their isolated farms while Kikuyu who refused to co-operate with the terrorists were murdered in increasing numbers. This phase of the campaign culminated in a night of terror in March 1953 when the inhabitants of a number of villages in Lari were surrounded by a huge gang which set fire to the houses, spearing or cutting down with knives the people who tried to escape or throwing them back into the flames. In this one attack over a hundred perished, yet their very success recoiled upon the Mau Mau gangsters. Their object had been to demonstrate their invincibility and to strike terror into the hearts of the waverers. But so great was the horror aroused by the Lari massacre that some Kikuyu at least began to wonder if such unrestrained cruelty could be justified under any circumstances. Christians in particular, although not necessarily approving of the policy of the Government, could see little to be admired in such unbridled acts of horror against fellow-Kikuyu. Others, too, who had been alienated by Mau Mau excesses, rallied to form a home guard force to protect the settlements against surprise attack.

The trickle of young Kikuyu to the forests of the Aberdares and the slopes of Mount Kenya swelled into a steady stream under increasing military pressure. In their hide-outs they formed gangs which launched their attacks wherever they could strike terror or steal arms and ammunition. They relied for food upon the much larger group of passive supporters of the movement who remained in the reserves and in Nairobi. Some of these latter gave their support under duress, yet many believed that they were right to act as they did. Such was the binding force of the oaths they took that few dared betray their fellows, and the oaths appeared to be necessary to achieve the unity which the Kikuyu desired. Much has been written about the bestial character of the oaths and of the deliberate intention of the administrators of degrading the Kikuyu to such an extent that they would be ashamed to mix with decent people. It has been pointed out that many of the European victims of the gangs were chosen from among those who had done the greatest service to the tribe with, once more, the hope of destroying former loyalties. It has been said, too, that Mau Mau supporters sang blasphemous hymns to well-known tunes in which the name of Jomo Kenyatta was substituted for that of Jesus Christ.

While there is much truth in these assertions there must, too, be other interpretations or at least other emphases, for without them the many Christians who regarded the oaths as not incompatible with their religious loyalty could never have reconciled their outlook with their actions. Fundamentally, Mau Mau was a Kikuyu movement of resistance against alien forces which appeared to treat men as being less than human beings and which deprived them of their land and made them labourers on other men's farms. Against these forces it seemed that only tribal loyalty could act as a unifying factor and thus prevail. Mau Mau was not simply a reversion to barbarism. It was also a turning back to the unified concept of the Kikuyu tribe. Great emphasis was placed upon a show of reverence for the common ancestors of the tribes, Gikuyu and Mumbi, and for their god, Ngai. Frequently, the so-called blasphemous hymns were simply patriotic songs set to the tunes that everyone knew best, the hymn tunes taught in the mission schools. The first impression that the supporters of Mau Mau were mainly drawn from the independent schools seems, also, on more detailed investigation to be questionable. It is true that attempts were made to enlist the support of members of other tribes to withstand the pressure of the military forces at the disposal of the Government. But these were never successful, for a variety of reasons, not least among them being the fact that the tribal loyalty which bound the Kikuyu together could have no attractions for men of other tribes. That hatred was stirred up in the hearts of many who were no more than depressed by circumstances goes without saying, and for this the leaders who themselves hated foreign control were responsible. But the fact that the movement embraced to a greater or less degree almost the whole of the Kikuyu tribe and that it was the Kikuyu who had come more closely than any other people into contact with the white man and his Government suggests a deeply felt frustration at the lack of understanding which had existed for half a century. The paternalism which characterized the attitude of so many Europeans towards the African population of Kenya was no more palatable because its intention was benevolent nor yet because between certain individuals it might be justified. It was not so much that individuals might be treated as children but that in this attitude a whole people was being dismissed as irresponsible.

Since the Mau Mau movement had such ramifications it was not easy to root out, and the movement of the gangs to the forests and mountains made it difficult for the security forces to maintain contact with them. A disquieting situation arose in Nairobi also where Mau Mau still festered and murders became increasingly numerous in spite of attempts to clear away the slums on the outskirts of the city. The cost of meeting the emergency was also weighing heavily upon the country, and it came as a relief when the United Kingdom Government agreed to make funds available to enable the general revenue balance to be restored.

Gradually, however, military action and the activities of the Kikuyu Home Guard began to have an effect. It became increasingly difficult for terrorists to obtain food, and patrols and pseudo gangs penetrated deep into the forest in search of the Mau Mau hide-outs. By the end of 1955 the situation was much brighter and guerrilla warfare was virtually at an end. Between October 1952, when the emergency was declared, and September 1955, when it was announced that the campaign had entered a new and less strenuous phase the total emergency expenditure exceeded £30,000,000. And even by 1955 the difficult period was not over, for there remained the enormous task of rehabilitating the thousands of Mau Mau supporters who had been taken prisoner. It was not until early 1960 that the new Governor, Sir Patrick Renison, was able to declare the emergency to be at an end.

A remarkable feature of the emergency period was the determination of the United Kingdom Government to persist in maintaining the impetus of constitutional development in the Colony. In March 1954 the Secretary of State, Mr. Oliver Lyttelton, visited Kenya and announced that he intended to press forward with the constitutional changes envisaged by his predecessor but postponed because of the Mau Mau outbreak. After holding discussions with the leaders of the various sections of the community he announced a new constitution which was intended to associate the inhabitants of the Colony more closely with their Government and in particular to encourage a multi-racial approach to governmental responsibility. Under the terms of the new constitution Asians and Africans as well as Europeans would become ministers.

The Lyttelton constitution, as the new proposals came to be generally designated, took effect in April 1954, and at once produced some lively reactions. The European community, in particular, held divided views over the importance of the new arrangements, and from 1954 onwards a number of political parties began to emerge, the motivating force of each being the extent to which its founders supported or opposed multi-racial government. Few of these parties lasted for very long and their composition tended to vary, non-European membership being encouraged or discouraged in accordance with the parties' basic aims.

The Lyttelton constitution contained no suggestions for any change in the composition of the Legislative Council, but in 1956 it was agreed that the unofficial African members should henceforward be elected and that their number should be increased from six to eight. Elections on a qualitative franchise took place in March 1957, when there were thirty-seven candidates for the eight electoral areas. Out of a total of 126,811 registered voters 101,266 went to the polls. Even then further changes were in the air. In October 1957, the new Secretary of State for the Colonies, Mr. Alan Lennox-Boyd, visited Kenya for constitutional discussions and in the following month he announced important constitutional changes which would become effective during 1958. These would provide for further African representation, and in addition the Legislative Council would have twelve special seats for members elected by the Council sitting as an electoral college. Yet another important innovation would be the establishment of a Council of State, whose main function would be to scrutinize legislation to ensure that it did not include any discriminatory measures.

The steady increase in the number of African representative members in the legislature was an indication of the growing activity of African political leaders. The focus of their endeavours was mainly in Nairobi although the introduction of the electoral system encouraged politicians to travel more extensively in their constituencies. None the less, it was among the Kikuyu and the Luo that the greatest political interest was manifested and it was these tribes which produced the most able and outspoken leaders. Rifts there were between them, even though they were drawn together by the common desire for self-government and African leadership in the territory. Yet to say this is only to indicate that strong personalities

412

must, inevitably, clash. Again, the unremitting insistence upon an African-dominated government which was characteristic of the more successful leaders was only to be expected when to demand anything less was to open the way to popularity for more extreme rivals. Inevitably, the main political problem was not so much one of rivalries between Africans as of establishing some working relationship between Africans, Asians and Europeans.

As a step towards better relations the seven-year-old emergency was brought to an end on January 12, 1960. This was followed by a constitutional conference in London, but agreement was hard to reach. Finally the Secretary of State for the Colonies, Iain Macleod, proposed that at the next Legislative Council elections 33 members should be elected on a common roll with a fairly wide franchise: 10 further seats should be reserved for Europeans, 8 for Asians and 2 for Arabs, while 12 more members, 4 Africans, 4 Asians and 4 Europeans, should be elected by the other members of the Legislature. The governor should still retain the right to nominate additional members. Finally, the council of ministers should consist of 4 civil servants and 8 unofficials, 4 Africans, 3 Europeans and 1 Asian. Macleod's scheme was accepted by the African leaders taking part in the conference and by some Europeans. The more conservative Europeans believed it could only lead to disaster.

Two new African political parties now emerged which were to dominate the future scene. The Kenya African National Union represented for the most part the views of the Kikuyu, Luo and Kamba tribes. The Kenya African Democratic Union gained most of its support from the smaller tribes of the colony. Both wanted early independence, but, while KANU hoped for a strongly centralized government, KADU, fearing domination by the Kikuyu and Luo, preferred a federal form of constitution.

Elections under the new regulations were held between January and March 1961 and KANU won the largest number of seats without gaining an overall majority. The leaders of the party, however, refused to join any government until Jomo Kenyatta was released from captivity. After some hesitation KADU proved more amenable and Ronald Ngala, the party's leader, became leader of government business and later chief minister.

In August 1961, Kenyatta was allowed to return to his home and in January 1962 he was elected unopposed to the legislative council. Yet he failed to become the national leader of Kenya Africans and when a further conference opened in London in February agreement between KANU and KADU seemed only a remote possibility. After five weeks of discussion in which no progress was made the new Secretary of State, Reginald Maudling, attempted to formulate a compromise solution, including the proposal that there should be a strong central government in Kenya, together with six regional governments, each possessing extensive local powers. The proposal was accepted and Kenyatta, was now leader of KANU, and Ngala, leader of KADU; a further election in 1963 once more resulted in victory for KANU, Kenyatta became Kenya's first prime minister, and the country achieved independence on 12 December.

Kenyatta at once set himself the task of establishing confidence in the government. To anxious European settlers he gave assurances that their place in Kenya would be secure so long as they continued to contribute to the country's wealth and stability. Such was the conviction his statements carried that in spite of a less friendly attitude on the part of some of his subordinates the concern previously felt by the settlers was noticeably diminished. In any case, most of those who had felt they could not fit in with an African government had already left. The African opposition party, KADU, was less satisfied with Kenyatta's policy. Although some of its members defected to the rival party the stauncher KADU supporters firmly opposed the measures Kenyatta's government was taking to amend the constitution so as to strengthen the powers of the central government at the expense of the regional authorities.

In January 1964 Kenyatta was faced with an unexpected problem when a mutiny took place among the askaris of the Kenya Rifles. Without hesitation the Prime Minister appealed to Britain for assistance and the rising was quickly put down with a loss of only a few lives. Similar risings in Tanganyika and Uganda in the same month, coupled with the overthrow by force of the Zanzibar Government, induced Kenyatta to tread warily. The desire of several powers, including China, to exert influence in Kenya was only lightly disguised. But Kenyatta had no desire to submit his country to the domination of any other state although it remained an active member of the Commonwealth. The reputation which Kenyatta enjoyed as leader for so many years of Kenya Africans' campaign for independence enabled him to survive the divisions in his own country while his dominating personality made him a prominent figure in the affairs of the whole continent. His characteristic hat, his beard, his heavy figure and his fly whisk combined to create an image of authority confidently, even a little jauntily wielded and it was by using his personality that he was able to hold Kenya on a stable course.

Even in those two territories the hope of achieving early responsible government was one which flared up only after some years of political outcry by the predominantly African population. For the 1950s in Uganda was not a period of untroubled constitutional advance. The violence of the emergency in Kenya was lacking because the motivating force of racial rivalry was also lacking. But political feelings were intense and a precarious situation arose in 1953 with the deportation of the Kabaka of Buganda. This action was, in a sense, the culmination of the long struggle to establish Buganda's position in the Protectorate. It had been preceded in August of the same year by the announcement of further changes in the composition of the Legislative Council as a result of which the number of African representative members would be increased to fourteen. Eleven of them would be elected by district councils while the remaining three from Buganda would be elected by the Lukiko if that body were willing and if not would be nominated as before. The Lukiko's reluctance to support the Legislative Council had already been demonstrated in 1950 when the number of African representatives had been increased to eight, one of whom would have been nominated by the Lukiko if it had been prepared to co-operate. Nor, by 1953, had there been any change of heart.

How far the constitutional proposals were responsible for arousing a feeling of intransigence among the Lukiko members it is difficult to say. But it was a remark made by the Colonial Secretary, Oliver Lyttelton, in the course of an after-dinner speech in June which was seized upon and used as the basis for a demand that Buganda's affairs should be placed under Foreign Office control and that the Government should prepare plans for Buganda's independence. The remark in question had referred to the possibility of the federation of the East African territories at some future date and it had undoubtedly aroused the old fears of the Baganda that they might be subjected to domination by Kenya. Yet, sincere though these fears might in many cases have been, Lyttelton's comment could not of itself have spurred the Lukiko to take such drastic action.

The development of the Legislative Council into a stronger and more representative body constituted a much more relevant threat to Buganda's position. Representation on a district basis, which virtually amounted to tribal representation, was in some sense a retrograde step from the provincial representation which had previously existed. None the less, the association of African members with particular tribes gave a new vigour to the representative side of the Council. There was, too, every likelihood that under the enthusiastic guidance of its president, Sir Andrew Cohen, the Council might for the first time become both the forum in which African views were aired and the centre from which political ideas would permeate throughout the country. This, then, was scarcely a body in which the traditional Baganda leaders would wish to see themselves swallowed up. Not surprisingly, thoughts of breaking the link with the rest of the Protectorate which had been forged by the 1900 Agreement took hold of many prominent Baganda.

Although assurances were given that there would be no federation of the East African territories without the full consent of the people concerned, the Baganda leaders were unimpressed. The Lukiko persisted in pressing its demand for Foreign Office control and ultimate independence and the Kabaka supported its claims. In March the Kabaka had produced a joint memorandum with the Governor relating to the reorganization of the responsibilities of the Buganda Government, and Buganda's place as part of a united Uganda had been once again reaffirmed. The attitude adopted by the Kabaka later in the year was shown therefore to be in contradiction to his earlier announcement. But he was in a difficult position. If he accepted the Government's policy he would be opposing the views of his leading subjects and at the same time he could see the possibility that his own position might be undermined by the development of a more representative legislature. If he were to oppose the Government, however, he would be in danger of infringing the 1900 Agreement which at one time had seemed to be the main defence against the invasion of Buganda's privileges but which now appeared more in the light of an irksome curb upon Buganda's freedom of action. The Kabaka, then, had little choice, and on his continued refusal to support the Government's policy he was deported to Britain and Her Majesty's Government withdrew their recognition.

The Baganda were stunned. The criticisms which had been levelled against Mutesa II during the struggle for power of the 1940s were forgotten. The heavy-handed intervention of the Protectorate Government in Buganda's affairs rallied all sections of the people and made the Kabaka once more the focus of Baganda loyalties as he had not been so completely for over fifty years. There were few acts of violence and no threat of a general rising but it was clear that the British Government must produce some new policy if confidence in the Protectorate was ever to be restored.

Early in 1954 Sir Keith Hancock, Director of the Institute of Commonwealth Studies, was sent to discuss Buganda's constitutional problems with representatives of the Lukiko. After some hesitation the Lukiko appointed a committee to meet Hancock and as a result of several months of deliberations proposals for a settlement were agreed upon. Parallel with these negotiations the Governor was also attempting to formulate further suggestions for the development of the Legislative Council in such a way as to win the support of the Baganda as well as to take the legislature still further along the road to responsible government. The whole scheme was made public in November 1954, when it was seen that the British Government had recommended the introduction of a ministerial system with five ministers to be drawn from the general public, of whom three would be Africans. Simultaneously the membership of the legislature would be increased to sixty and although an official majority would be retained thirty of the members would be Africans. Faced with this important advance, together with a pledge that East African federation would not be imposed without the consent of the people of Uganda, the Lukiko committee agreed for the first time to recommend that Baganda representatives should sit in the Legislative Council. With regard to the issues affecting Buganda more specifically it had also been agreed that the 1900 Agreement should be amended in order to establish something resembling a constitutional monarchy with the Kabaka acting, henceforward, on the advice of his ministers. Buganda would then continue to be an integral part of the Protectorate and suggestions for the independence of Buganda alone would be dropped.

417

It had been suggested that the Baganda should have the option of electing a new kabaka or of agreeing to the return of Mutesa II after a nine-month period had elapsed from the signing of the new agreement. Mutesa, however, had become the hero of the whole tribe by his support of the Lukiko which had led to his deportation, and there was no question of any alternative ruler being acceptable. The Baganda also opposed a nine-months' delay before the Kabaka's return and the British Government did not press this point. Mutesa II, therefore, returned to Uganda in October 1955, and a new agreement was signed. The Legislative Council adopted its new organization and Baganda members took their seats after elections carried out by an electoral college. It was agreed, moreover, that no further major changes would take place in the Protectorate's constitution until 1961, although Buganda would have the option of holding direct elections to the new Legislative Council which would take office in 1957.

In every way the settlement appeared to be a happy one. The Kabaka himself was removed from an invidious position now that he was no longer responsible for the actions of the Lukiko. The Baganda rejoiced that their Kabaka had been restored to them, and from the point of view of the Protectorate Government the presence of elected Baganda members in the Legislative Council suggested that the basic problem of Buganda's relations with the rest of the territory was well on the way to a solution. But events were soon to show that this view was too optimistic. Few of the ruling families of Buganda were prepared to see their authority over-shadowed by the Legislative Council and it was not difficult for them to stir up the traditional pride of the Baganda as a whole in opposition to any arrangement which suggested that other tribes might be in a position to dictate policy to Buganda. In these circumstances the decision to have a Speaker in the Legislative Council instead of the Governor acting as chairman was seized upon by the Lukiko as being a breach of the agreement that no major constitutional change should take place until 1961. As a result, Buganda not only decided against direct elections for the legislature in 1957 but even refused to elect members by any means. But direct elections were held in most of the other districts of the Protectorate in 1958 at the insistence of African representative members of the Legislative Council although this had not previously been contemplated by the Protectorate Government.

Uganda's constitutional struggles at least had the effect of stimulating the development of African political parties. The only African political party of any importance which had existed before the deportation of the Kabaka was the Uganda National Congress, founded in 1952 ostensibly as a nation-wide organization open to membership from all races. In fact Europeans and Asians took no part in its activities although a few became members in the early days of the party's development. For some time the Congress was mainly a Kiganda organization, and this position was strengthened by the whole-hearted fashion in which it took up the cause of the deported Kabaka. Its primary object was to achieve self-government for the united peoples of Uganda and this, it was believed, would solve most of the country's political problems including that of the Baganda and the other tribes of the Protectorate. In 1954 a number of other parties made their appearance, again calling for self-government and denouncing the British Government's action with regard to the Kabaka. For some years, however, these parties failed to present a serious challenge to the popularity of the Congress but even this latter group displayed a regular tendency to split over a variety of issues. All were caught up in a vicious circle. The absence of any constructive policy beyond the reiterated demand for self-government failed to impress the Protectorate authorities. Consequently, the parties were offered no opportunity to shoulder any responsibility. Throughout the Buganda crisis the British Government insisted upon negotiating with the Lukiko in spite of the attempts of the National Congress to insinuate itself into the discussions. In their turn the parties showed their resentment of the way in which they were ignored by still more violent and unconstructive criticisms while the absence of any prospect of having to assume responsibility encouraged the less stable politicians to form still further parties with still more urgent demands for self-government.

In the Legislative Council itself African representative members experienced a similar sense of frustration. In spite of their numbers, and in spite of the fact that the Government was not unresponsive to their views on many topics, they were all too aware that they could be outvoted by the official majority and that over certain of the issues which they regarded as being of the greatest importance the official majority would undoubtedly be used against them. These issues included a timed programme for self-government and the more rapid Africanization of the civil service. It was not, therefore, until 1959 that an opportunity was given to the political leaders to accept the challenge of responsibility. This challenge resulted from the recommendations of a committee composed almost entirely of unofficial members of the Legislative Council which was appointed to make recommendations on the next stage of constitutional development to be introduced in 1961. The committee recommended that there should be an overwhelming majority of African representative members in the Legislative Council directly elected on the basis of adult suffrage, and that the political party obtaining a majority should be called upon to form the basis of the government side of the house.

The report was received with enthusiasm in most parts of Uganda and with gloom in Buganda. The British government responded only slowly, and this delay, coupled with the modifications they proposed, gave a breathing space to the traditional Baganda leaders and encouraged a revival of their fighting spirit. Thus the Democratic Party, founded in 1956 and drawing much of its support from among the more educated Baganda, found itself faced with considerable opposition when it began campaigning in favour of the new constitution. Yet the opposition of Buganda's traditional leaders proved to be of assistance to the Democratic Party, though only for a time. For the party's chief opponent on a protectorate-wide basis was the Uganda Peoples Congress, an amalgum of certain elements formerly belonging to the Uganda National Congress, now very weak, and various other political parties, and the U.P.C. drew its support almost entirely from the districts outside Buganda. Thus events in the kingdom could not affect the number of legislative council seats which the U.P.C. could gain since they had little hope of success in Buganda

Elections took place in March 1961 but were boycotted by the majority of potential voters in Buganda who feared that the kingdom's interests would not be safeguarded under the new constitution. As a result of their attitude the Democratic Party, led by Benedicto Kiwanuka, gained a majority of seats since the party won twenty of the twenty-one seats in Buganda where voting was very light. Since the issue of Buganda's future relationship with the rest of the country was clearly unsettled a three-man commission was appointed to make recommendations. Their report was one of the subjects discussed at a conference which met in London in September 1961, and which resulted in a decision that Uganda should achieve self-government on March 1, 1962. This would be followed by further elections to the legislative council in April and independence in October. After independence the Central Government would have wide powers, but although Buganda would send representatives to the country's legislature the kingdom would be in a federal relation with the rest of the country. Subsequently it was agreed that a semi-federal status should also be accorded Bunyoro, Toro, Ankole and Busoga.

Immediately before the conference an alliance had been cemented between two apparently opposing parties, the Uganda People's Congress, led by Milton Obote from Lango, and the supporters of the Kabaka, the Kabaka Yekka group. This rapprochement enabled the U.P.C. to obtain a majority of seats in the Legislature since Kabaka Yekka won all the Buganda seats from the Democratic Party. In association with Kabaka Yekka Obote then formed the government which led Uganda to independence on October 9.

The alliance of U.P.C. and Kabaka Yekka had been foreshadowed by Obote's consistent refusal to attack the views of the Baganda even when they had appeared to constitute the greatest obstacle to constitutional advance. The survival of the alliance in these circumstances was due more to a continued refusal to clash than to any fundamental unity of outlook between the two groups. In an attempt to strengthen this association and to draw the Baganda more closely together with the other peoples of Uganda the post of Governor-General was abolished and Kabaka Mutesa was elected President of Uganda by the National Assembly in October 1963. Even this action had its dangers since the western kingdoms were not wholly satisfied to see Buganda exalted while the Baganda themselves, although delighted at first, began to doubt after a time the feasibility of combining the functions of President and Kabaka without detriment to Buganda's interests.

The critical attitude of the Baganda became more pronounced in 1964 when the issue of the Lost Counties loomed up once again. At the independence conference this problem had been shelved in order to reach overall agreement on the constitution. While the bulk of the counties were left with Buganda the two most disputed areas in which the majority of the burial places of the former rulers of Bunyoro were located were to be administered by the central government for a period of not more than two years. Within that time there was to be a referendum to decide their future. In 1964 Prime Minister Obote made it clear that he intended to proceed with the referendum, a decision which Buganda's pride could not swallow. The Kabaka's dual role became even more invidious. Several Kabaka Yekka members of the National Assembly, including the Minister of Finance, Mr. A. K. Sempa, crossed the floor and abandoned their alliance with the U.P.C. The former Prime Minister and Democratic Party leader, Benedicto Kiwanuka, looked hopefully for a rapprochement between these elements of Kabaka Yekka and the strong Buganda faction in his own Democratic Party. A solution of this sort was remote, for whatever the difference between Buganda and the rest of the territory it was still easier for the Kabaka to cooperate with a Prime Minister from outside Buganda than to work on equal terms with a minister chosen from among his own subjects.

In January, 1964, Uganda, like Kenya, was faced with a mutiny in its army. The object of the mutineers seemed to be limited to obtaining higher pay and better promotion prospects for African troops, but Obote was taking no chances. At his request British troops arrived from Kenya within a few hours and the troubles quickly spent themselves without bloodshed. But the rising, even if not fomented for political reasons, underlined the precarious position of the government and emphasized its heavy reliance upon the decisive personality of the Prime Minister himself. In these circumstances it was to Obote's advantage that, in spite of the dominant role he was playing in his country's affairs, he was able to avoid the widespread adulation of his own people and the central position in the eyes of the world which were accorded to Kenyatta in Kenya and Nyerere in Tanganyika. For, as a result of this he was less beset by the criticism and jealousy of his rivals than were many other African leaders.

Uganda could not entirely escape external pressures. A evelopment programme involving the outlay of £90 million between 1961 and 1966 could not be undertaken without aid, and aid was likely to involve interference. Obote, however, strove to preserve a satisfactory balance in his relations with the powers. Uganda's way might be unobtrusive but in general it proved effective.

The year 1959 was an important one for Tanganyika as well as for Uganda in that in Tanganyika also a constitutional committee recommended a large elected African majority in the legislature, although in this case elections would be carried out on a qualitative franchise and some seats were to be reserved for non-Africans. But here the similarity with Uganda ended, for, whereas in the northern Protectorate the new constitutional proposals threw down the gauntlet to the political parties, the Tanganyika recommendations marked the triumph of Tanganyika's one African political party whose endeavours had been largely responsible for the constitutional progress which was being made.

After the modest advances of the early 1950s the tempo had increased in 1955 after Professor W. J. M. Mackenzie, Professor of Government in Manchester University, had made his expert comments upon the problems raised by the committee on constitutional development in 1951. In spite of the apparent lack of interest in national policies encountered by its members the committee had recommended a considerable increase in the membership of the representative side of the Legislative Council and had also proposed that the African, European and Asian communities should, for the first time, have equal representation. Thus, instead of the seven Europeans, four Africans and three Asians then sitting on the representative side there should be seven members from each race. Professor Mackenzie suggested a modification of this scheme. While accepting parity of representation for the three races he proposed that the members should represent constituencies based upon the eight existing administrative provinces together with the municipality of Dar es Salaam. He added that if the elective principle were introduced it should be based upon a common roll.

The enlargement of the Council took effect in 1955 when thirty representative members were nominated, three from each province, three from Dar es Salaam and a further three members to represent special interests. A Government majority was retained although a number of the members on the Government side were unofficials. Unofficial members were also associated more closely with the work of the Government with the introduction of a ministerial system to replace the member system which had existed before. The eight *ex officio* Members became Ministers while six unofficials, four Africans, one European and one Asian, were created Assistant Ministers endowed with executive powers and having specific responsibility for adjusting the direction of policy to the needs of the people. Elections were not introduced at this stage but a bill providing for elections was passed in June, 1956. This measure established a common roll with a qualitative franchise which gave the African electorate a considerable majority over the electors of the two other main races. Three members were to be elected from each constituency, one from each race, and each voter would have three votes which he must cast for three candidates, one of each race. The elections themselves were held in two parts beginning in 1958 owing to the huge problem of preparing electoral registers for the first time and of making the many other arrangements for holding elections in a democratic fashion.

One potential difficulty was overcome in a surprising fashion. It had been feared that the proposal that each elector should vote for a candidate of each race would provide an unrealistic result because in many cases few of the candidates would be known to electors of other races. In the event, however, every successful candidate owed his election to the support of the Tanganyika African National Union. The emergence of this party was a tribute to the leadership of Mr. Julius Nyerere, a former schoolmaster, who demonstrated that the tribal nature of Tanganyika's local government organization need not stand as a barrier to political parties organized on a national scale. The Tanganyika African National Union, or TANU as it came to be called, had been founded in 1954 in succession to the Tanganyika African Association. Its policy was to prepare the people of Tanganyika for self-government and to work for the establishment of democratic rule in the territory. In the first instance it was an African nationalist movement and inevitably, in its public utterances, adopted an extreme tone so as to capture popular support. Nevertheless, as the party grew in strength Nyerere's leadership enabled it to adopt a much more friendly attitude towards the idea of co-operation with other races. The importance of this change in outlook and the extent of its triumph was illustrated by the collapse of the United Tanganyika Party This latter group was formed in 1955 with, among its leaders, most of the representative members of the Legislative Council. It deliberately emphasized a policy of multi-racialism in contrast to the African nationalism advocated by TANU and it supported the idea of parity of racial representation in the legislature. But TANU's approach was more realistic. In a territory with such an overwhelming majority of African inhabitants a predominantly African legislature and government was an inevitable development. It was, however, the maturity of Nyerere's attitude towards members of other races which reconciled the European and Asian communities to the idea of co-operating voluntarily in the direction of the affairs of a Tanganyika in which the majority of the members of the Legislature and of the Government would, within a very short time, be Africans. The success of this co-operation found its outlet in the report of the constitutional committee appointed in 1959 under the chairmanship of a former civil servant, Sir Richard Ramage. The unanimous recommendation of the committee that there should be a large African elected majority in the next Legislative Council has already been referred to. But the spirit of co-operation and compromise present among the committee's members was still more clearly demonstrated by their recommendation that a certain proportion of the seats should be reserved for non-African members.

On December 15, the Governor, Sir Richard Turnbull, announced the Colonial Secretary's approval for the committee's report. Acting on the committee's recommendations elections were held in August 1960. The 50 constituencies returned 71 members, 50 of whom could be candidates of any race, while 11 must be Asians and 10 Europeans. Candidates supported by TANU were elected to 70 seats and Julius Nyerere was asked to form a government. Further constitutional discussions in March 1961 led to the achievement of self-government in May and independence on December 9. A year later Tanganyika became a republic with Nyerere as its first president.

Even before independence Tanganyika began to play a significant role in international affairs and one which reflected the idealism and sense of moral responsibility which had moved Nyerere in his earlier campaigns. If such a renunciation could have made possible the speedy achievement of an East African federation Nyerere would have been prepared to delay Tanganyika's independence. Moreover although fully conscious of the loss to his country, he was equally willing to forego membership of the Commonwealth rather than sit side by side with the Republic of South Africa. After independence Nyerere visited both Britain and the United States in an attempt to persuade them to exert pressure upon Portugal to change its policy in Africa, while the Tanganyika National Assembly passed a motion in April 1963 condemning Southern Rhodesia's bid for independence under a white majority. Dar es Salaam also offered hospitality to the headquarters of the African Liberation Committee.

Nyerere was not motivated by blind anti-colonialism. He recognized wholeheartedly Tanganyika's debt to Britain, and British civil servants were encouraged to stay in Tanganyika wherever they were needed. In December 1961 the Prime Minister himself threatened to resign if there should be unfair discrimination against non-Africans in Tanganyika's citizenship law. Nyerere's aim was to ensure that an independent Tanganyika should be free from any absolute commitment to an external power or group of powers. He wanted his country to be at liberty to seek friendship where it wished, a policy which he believed to be as important in world affairs as it was for Tanganyika itself.

Nyerere's idealism received a sharp setback in January 1964 when a mutiny in the Tanganyika army was suppressed only with the aid of British troops. Although, as in Uganda and Kenya, the disturbances were thought to be non-political in origin, the President's recourse to Britain for assistance weakened his claim to be uncommitted to either East or West and laid him open to criticism from other African states which had a more doctrinaire anti-colonialist attitude. For a period, too, the fact that Nyerere had hesitated to act decisively as soon as trouble broke out suggested that he feared to rely upon the support of his own people, while the very fact that the army, the ultimate sanction of the Government's authority, had proved insubordinate left the President in a dangerously weak position. Yet Nyerere rode out the storm in characteristic fashion. Summoning a meeting in Dar es Salaam of the Organization for African Unity he completely vindicated himself while striking a blow for African co-operation by inducing Nigeria to send a military force to replace the British marines who had restored order. In April he took a further step towards strengthening East Africa against undue foreign intervention when, together with President Karume of Zanzibar, he brought about a union between the two Republics and himself became head of the new state of Tanzania.

The policy of non-alignment had its problems. China in particular was attempting to extend its influence in Africa and, with a foothold in Zanzibar, was an ever present problem to Tanganyika. While Nyerere might earnestly seek friendship on every hand he faced the problem common to any country needing aid that assistance might entail intervention. Tanganyika, like every other emergent African territory, was being wooed by influential nations which sought to involve the country on one side or the other in the struggle between East and West.

The nationwide success of TANU had given the lie to those who had argued that Tanganyika's system of local government would act as an obstacle to political progress. Now, alongside the developments in the political sphere local government itself began to display a more modern pattern though at a steadier rate. In 1949 the system of local government was still based upon the policy laid down by Sir Donald Cameron. There were 435 native authorities in the territory, together with twenty-eight township authorities and the municipality of Dar es Salaam. A review of the existing structure of local government had been one of the tasks of the first committee on constitutional development and its recommendations had envisaged the introduction of a new system of county and urban councils more closely resembling the British pattern. Again Professor Mackenzie suggested modifications, and in 1953 a Local Government Bill incorporating the suggestions both of the committee and of Professor Mackenzie received the assent of the Legislative Council. The bill gave rise to some concern among the chiefs and in order to remove their fears a further ordinance, the Chiefs' Ordinance, was passed which gave an assurance that the Government did not intend to abolish the office of chief. The Local Government Ordinance, also, was accompanied by an assurance that no reforms would be imposed upon any section of the population which resisted the new pattern.

The main modification suggested by Professor Mackenzie had been that in addition to the county and town councils there should be local councils which would take the form of a more democratic version of the native authorities. It was hoped that these councils, like the county and town councils, would include European as well as African members. In the event these local councils proved to be more workable than the county councils. Since no council could be instituted without an instrument defining its powers and functions

427

and approved by the Legislative Council, it was clear that the changes would be slow to take effect. This meant that there was an opportunity for some experiment to ensure that the best methods were adopted. The first two local councils were set up in the Mafia and Newala Districts and were in each case a development of the existing native authority. The main work of the councils was done by standing committees while the councils themselves, under the chairmanship of the district commissioner, consisted of a considerable number of members who were nominated by the Provincial Commissioner and who were not office holders, together with a number of local liwalis. The activities of these local councils met with a considerable degree of success. This was in marked contrast with the very limited achievements of the first county council which was set up in Lake Province with the addition of a number of adjacent areas. The executive work of this council was largely carried out by district committees which served to emphasize the view already suggested by the success of the local councils that in fact the District rather than the Province was still the most suitable unit of local government. A bill was consequently prepared with the object of amending the Local Government Ordinance so as to make it possible to establish District Councils to serve whole districts. These new councils would have greater responsibilities than had been intended for the local councils and with the aid of funds from the central government would take over certain of the services previously performed by that government.

Every extension of the responsibilities of the local authorities called for greater numbers of executive and clerical officers and the training of suitable staff was one of the chief problems to be faced. A local government school was established in 1953 and chiefs and others recommended by the native authorities attended courses of instruction to prepare them for their widening functions. Again, the development of a more characteristically British form of local government posed the question of what was to become of the judicial activities which Cameron had deemed to be so vital a part of the work of the native authorities. Inevitably the chiefs sought to hold on to their judicial powers and it was no easy matter to convince the people generally of the need for a change or to provide acceptable officers to take the place of the chiefs. If, however, the introduction of changes into the local government structure of Tanganyika was a slow process, at least there was no disturbing demand for reform from the population as a whole. Thus, while changes were taking place at a national level at a surprising rate the vast majority of the people could watch these developments with equanimity because that branch of administration which most intimately affected their daily existence remained firmly based upon a pattern which had by this time become accepted as traditional. Nevertheless, one important change in the structure of urban councils was foreshadowed by the decision to elect on a common roll an African Mayor for Dar es Salaam in 1960.

In Uganda local government could not remain so passively divorced from the turmoil of national politics. Again, the reason for this was the status of Buganda which, although a province, was still regarded as the pattern for local government development by all the other tribes in the Protectorate. Had the other provinces developed into strong administrative units as Sir Philip Mitchell had hoped the problem of Buganda might have been smaller. During the 1950s, however, there was noticeable a growing tendency to stress the importance of the districts because of the tribal loyalties they could command. The African Local Governments Ordinance of 1949 had begun to prepare the way for this development, for under its terms district councils consisting of chiefs and both nominated and elected members provided a forum in which the views of the people could be heard and in which by-laws could be passed to regulate certain matters of local importance. There were, it is true, provincial councils as well which included members elected by the district councils in addition to others officially nominated, but these councils had no law-making powers.

The next stage in the development of district councils was reached as a result of an inquiry into local government problems in Uganda which was made by Mr. C. A. G. Wallis in 1953.[1] Wallis recognized that one of the big problems which would trouble any attempt to formulate a satisfactory policy for the progress of local government lay in the desire of other tribes to emulate Buganda by building up a hierarchy of authority more in keeping with the character of a central government than of a local administration. He urged, nevertheless, that the next advance in local government outside Buganda

[1] *Report of an Inquiry into Local Government in the Uganda Protectorate* Government Printer, Entebbe, 1953.

should consist of the devolution of responsibility for certain services from the central government, not to the provincial councils but to the district councils. This would involve the local authorities in the task of raising more money to meet their share of the increased expenditure on public services. It was recognized, however, that the central government would have to provide financial assistance for some time to come.

Since the potential rate of progress of the different districts varied considerably the Legislative Council, in adopting Wallis's proposals, also accepted the view that the new District Administration (District Councils) Ordinance of January 1955 should be an enabling ordinance and that districts would introduce the new proposals when they were ready for them. Some fears were expressed that under the new ordinance the position of chiefs would become an anomalous one since they would be serving two masters. Appointed by the central government and responsible through the district commissioners to that government they would also be the executive officers of the district councils in respect of certain of their activities. The proposal to introduce appointments boards to select the councils' officials also aroused criticism and this was one of the factors which delayed the acceptance of the new ordinance by a number of district councils throughout the Protectorate.

Wallis recognized that Buganda could not be dealt with in the same way as the remainder of the Protectorate since the existing administrative organization there carried far more authority than would normally be exercised by a local government. But there was no point in insisting upon a district organization in Bugnada when the relationship between the Lukiko and the *Sazas* or counties already operated satisfactorily. In March 1953, therefore, the Governor, Sir Andrew Cohen, and the Kabaka issued a joint memorandum in which it was stated that greater responsibility would devolve upon the Buganda Government which, among other duties, would henceforward take charge of education in the provinces up to junior secondary level. The implementation of these proposals was delayed by the deportation of the Kabaka but with Buganda once more in a settled condition the reforms were introduced and three new ministers were created in addition to the three recognized by the 1900 Agreement. The use of the term minister, however, only served still further to emphasize the national character of the Buganda organization, and the other districts of the Protectorate were not slow to ask for the transfer to their local governments of the same degree of responsibility as was accorded to the Buganda Government. It was the desire to be like Buganda which, strengthened by tribal pride, encouraged some districts to hope that Uganda would develop as a federal state. By contrast, the fear of Buganda hegemony or alternatively the envy of Buganda's special position encouraged other tribes to hope that by establishing a unitary state Buganda would be brought to the level of the rest of the Protectorate.

The development of urban local government in Uganda in the post-war period showed little progress. Kampala became a municipality with a nominated council in 1948 and in 1950 the first Mayor was appointed. Jinja followed suit with the appointment of a municipal council a decade later but the other towns of the Protectorate continued to be governed by township authorities. Even in Kampala there was no development such as the ordinance passed in Tanganyika in 1956 to make provision for the election of town councils.

In Kenya the main development in local government in the post-war years was the attempt to bring the councils in the African areas more into line with British local government practice. The most important step in this direction was the enactment in 1950 of the African District Councils Ordinance. Previously the twenty-six local native councils created under the terms of the Native Authority Ordinance of 1937 had laboured under a disadvantage because their duties and field of responsibility had never been very clearly defined. Until 1944 they had received no regular grants from the central government and had had to rely on the proceeds of local rates, land rents, forest dues, court fees, and fines and other sources of income of a necessarily limited character. In 1949 there was a further advance when the Government agreed to contribute two shillings in respect of every person who paid his local rate. At about the same time the functions of local councils were more clearly defined, the local authorities taking responsibility for the upkeep of minor roads, of primary education, of dispensaries, of markets and of cattle dips.

Under the terms of the ordinance of 1950 the local native councils were to be designated African District Councils with powers and legal status similar to those of the municipalities and of the district councils in European areas. With the authority of the Member for

Education, Health and Local Government the new councils might provide a wide variety of public services and also could enact by-laws of which some, for the first time, would be binding on persons of all races residing within the jurisdiction of the council concerned. The district commissioner was chairman of each of these councils but there was considerable flexibility regarding the composition of the remainder of the council. The ordinance laid it down that the members should be appointed as determined by the provincial commissioner although the intention was that where possible they should all be elected. Furthermore, as the councils gained in experience the presence of the district commissioner became increasingly a formality, most of the discussions being conducted by an African vice-president.

The revenues of the councils had been increasing steadily and in 1950 had reached £750,000 in comparison with £400,000 three years earlier. In addition, a number of the councils had agricultural betterment funds for which revenue was obtained by imposing cesses on produce. The object of the fund, as its name suggests, was to encourage soil conservation, to improving its fertility and generally to promote better standards of agriculture. Just as in the other territories, one of the problems faced by the councils was the dearth of Africans qualified to carry out the various duties appertaining to the services under local government control. None the less the councils were playing an increasingly responsible part in the lives of the African population. They lacked, however, the basis o tradition which in many parts of Tanganyika had strengthened the growth of local authorities. Over questions such as land tenure elected members or members nominated by some officer of the central government could scarcely be expected to have the same knowledge as the tribal elders. In Kenya, too, unlike Uganda and Tanganyika, the administration of justice had always been regarded as separate from local administration. Whenever possible native tribunals had been based upon the traditional councils of elders of the various tribes and this, also, had taken away a proportion of the authority of the councils. More recently, however, even the tribunals had lost something of their traditional character since they had been empowered to administer a number of ordinances passed by the central legislature. The increasing work imposed upon them had called for a higher standard of education among those who administered justice and this in turn had widened the breach between the tribunals and the traditions of the tribes. Consequently there was a tendency for the older members of the tribes to refer their disputes not to the tribunals but to private courts of elders who were thought to be better acquainted with the traditions and customs of the people.

Another development affecting the working of the African district councils was the growth of locational councils. These councils were originally established with the task of advising the chiefs of locations, but so successful were they that in 1955 the Minister for Local Government was empowered to grant them a formal constitution as bodies corporate with powers and duties appropriate to local authorities at their level. The widening scope of the district councils' activities, however, is reflected in the general fund revenue of all the councils which in 1957 had risen to £2,250,000 and in 1958 to an estimated £3,572,138. In the latter year the largest council had a turnover of more than £450,000 while there were one or two councils with less than £5,000.[1]

The most important change in the organization of the councils in the European areas was brought about by the Local Government (County Councils) Ordinance of 1952. Previously the district councils had had very limited functions. Practically the whole of their revenue had derived from grants from the Road Authority so that their duties had amounted to little more than the supervision of road construction and maintenance. The new ordinance, which was an enabling law, provided for a system of local government modelled on that prevailing in Britain with certain modifications to adapt it to local requirements. Whereas previously district councils, with the exception of the Nairobi district council, had neglected to exercise their power to levy rates the new councils were to be encouraged to raise money by rates to be collected by one or more of some half a dozen methods. A county council might now elect to become a public health authority, a town and country planning authority and an educational authority. By 1958 seven county councils had been established in Nairobi, Nakuru, Naivasha, Aberdare, Trans Nzoia and Uasin Gishu Districts and in the Nyanza area.

In this lively post-war period even Zanzibar was stirred by the spirit of change. The most striking reforms took place, however,

[1] *Kenya Colony: Annual Report for the Year 1957*, p. 150 and for the Year 1958, p. 126. H.M.S.O., London, 1958 and 1959.

not in the field of local government so much as in that of central government. In 1957 provision was made for the creation of local councils with nominated members and with the power to raise rates and to make by-laws. The power to impose taxation by means of rates was vital to the functioning of the councils and had the added significance of being the only provision for direct taxation in the Protectorate. The Zanzibar Township Council came into existence in 1950 after the amalgamation of the two town councils which since 1944 had been responsible for administering the business area and the residential area of the town. All the members of the new council were nominated by the British Resident and comprised four Africans, four Arabs, four Asians, one European, one Goan, one Comorian and four officials.

The almost automatic developments in the field of local government were not so readily acceptable to certain elements in Zanzibar society when applied to central government affairs. Among the Arab community there was a lively movement in favour of self-government. This view was not equally shared by the larger African population of the Protectorate which was not anxious to find itself under Arab domination. Nor, indeed, was it clear what the Arab nationalists intended, more particularly since so much of the wealth of the island was in the hands of Indians. The British Government, however, was not averse from accepting for Zanzibar the same ultimate goal of self-government as had been the declared policy for the other East African territories. In the light of the differing views as to the form which self-government should take, however, the Protectorate authorities proposed to advance towards their goal by carefully planned stages. The first of these steps, which was announced early in 1956, envisaged the creation of a Privy Council with purely advisory functions and, more important, the enlargement of the Executive and Legislative Councils. The former would then consist of the British Resident as President, four *ex officio* members, three officials to be nominated by the Sultan on the advice of the Resident, and three nominated unofficials, one Arab, one Indian and one African. The main feature of the new Legislative Council, which would have twenty-six members of whom twelve would be unofficials, was that six of the latter seats would be filled by elections on a common roll. The remaining six would be nominated by the Sultan on the advice of the Resident with the object

434

of ensuring a reasonable representation for all the communities. Perhaps the most startling result of these changes was the outcome of the elections to the Legislative Council. Hitherto the only political organizations were among the Arabs. Numerically, however, they were in a minority when compared with the African population and it was this latter group which suddenly organized itself sufficiently to win a surprise victory at the polls. So in Zanzibar as in Tanganyika the African population emerged with unexpected rapidity into the forefront of political affairs.

In 1960 further constitutional changes produced a legislature of thirty in which twenty-two members were elected while five of the nine members of the Executive Council were to be unofficials. The death in the same year of Sultan Seyyid Sir Khalifa bin Harub at the age of eighty-one removed from the scene a man who had guided the affairs of his country for well nigh half a century. His eldest son, Seyyid Abdullah, succeeded him but died less than three years later in 1963 when Seyyid Jamshid, his son, became Sultan just in time to head a self-governing state. Constitutional developments had been rapid. The first elections under the terms of the 1960 constitution were held in January 1961 but no party won a majority sufficient to form the basis of a government. Further elections in June were accompanied by rioting and again there was a threat of deadlock when both the African-dominated Afro-Shirazi Party and the Arab-led Zanzibar Nationalist Party each won ten seats. The balance was held by the Zanzibar and Pemba People's Party with three seats and this group agreed to combine with the Nationalists to form a government. New elections were held in July 1963 with newly defined constituencies and on the basis of universal adult suffrage. The ruling coalition was again victorious, obtaining eighteen seats to the Afro-Shirazi Party's thirteen. At once the Government called upon Britain to grant independence and after a conference in September independence day was fixed for 10 December. Simultaneously with the achievement of independence it was agreed that the Sultan's authority over the Kenya coast would cease and the region would be transferred to Kenya.

Although the December celebrations took place in an atmosphere of apparently general satisfaction a shock greeted the country in the new year. On 12 January there was a revolt against the Government. Within twenty-four hours the Sultan had fled and a new Government

435

had been announced under the Presidency of Abeid Amani Karume, leader of the Afro-Shirazi Party. The leader of the armed force which had seized power was, however, a Uganda African, John Okello, who had been working in Zanzibar. For a time Okello rather than Karume dominated the scene. But Karume's popularity and the concern of the other ministers lest Okello's power should become too great enabled the Government to rid itself of its dangerous ally. In March Okello found himself refused readmission to the island after a visit to the mainland and power now seemed to be shared between the President and Abdul Rahman Muhammad Babu, Minister of External Affairs. For a time relations with Britain and the United States were strained and East Germany and China began to exert a considerable influence in the island. At the end of April, however, Karume agreed to unite the new Republic of Zanzibar with Tanganyika under the Presidency of Julius Nyerere. This seemed to betoken an attempt to achieve a more widespread relationship with foreign powers but Nyerere did not press his authority in Zanzibar. In October 1964 the united republic was named Tanzania.

No one in 1945 would have predicted that during the next twenty years such changes could have taken place in East Africa. During the war there was evidence of a quickening tempo in the political life of the East African territories and both the British Governments in East Africa and the United Kingdom Government were prepared to assist in the advance of the East African territories towards political maturity. Indeed, the United Kingdom Government took the initiative by abandoning the creed of trusteeship in favour of one of partnership which, although never very clearly defined, implied that the peoples of East Africa should be encouraged to share with the people of Britain the responsibility for the development of the East African dependencies. But it was not long before the initiative was taken out of Britain's hands. The demand for self-government which had been on the lips of the European population of Kenya for more than a generation was now taken up by the African peoples in an atmosphere of world opinion which made it difficult for Britain to withhold its approval even though, in the interests of the African peoples themselves, the demand appeared premature. In an attempt to ensure that the experience of the non-African communities should not be wholly jettisoned the theme of multi-racial government was brought forward and was illustrated in Tanganyika by the idea of equal representation of the main races among the representative members of the legislature. In Kenya the European population carried this further by insisting upon the number of European representative members being equal to that of all other races on the ground that the European contribution to the Colony's economic, political and social development was of such paramount importance. Even in Uganda the British Government sought to maintain adequate and effective representation for the minority communities in the legislature. But the racing tide of African political enthusiasm rejected the idea of a multi-racial government imposed by an external authority. Tanganyika Africans were not unwilling to admit non-Africans to the country's law-making body but they must be in the minority and there was no question of their having an equal share in the government of the territory. As has been seen, the non-Africans were prepared to accept this position. In Uganda, too, the non-Africans for the most part rejected any claim to special representation in the legislature and the constitutional committee of 1959, the majority of whose members were Africans, unanimously proposed that the next elections to the Legislative Council should be on a common roll without any safeguards for minority representation. In Kenya a very different situation existed owing to the entrenched position of the European population in the economic as well as the political sphere, yet the demands of the African political leaders differed little from those of their fellows in Uganda and Tanganyika.

East Africa's African political leaders appear to have been little influenced by events in India, Ceylon or Burma but they were greatly affected by developments in other parts of the African continent. The grant of self-government to the Sudan aroused strong feelings since it was considered that the southern Sudan at least was in a less advanced state of political development than its southern neighbours. Above all, however, the pattern of events in Ghana coloured the thinking of African leaders, and the achievements of Dr. Nkrumah stirred up the spirit of emulation on the east coast. Nkrumah's success, against a background of *apartheid* in South Africa, seemed like a triumph for all Africans against white oppression. For events in South Africa tended to cast their shadow over East Africa, so that some African politicians talked as if they themselves were faced with similar problems to the African population in the Union. In this way the British Government's genuine desire to promote self-government was frequently ignored, so that instead of co-operating the African leaders have in some cases thought of themselves as fighting a campaign against what they regarded as a reactionary British policy. This view received some support from Britain's persistence in wishing to promote self-government by stages but without presenting any time-table for advance. The refusal to plan far ahead could easily be interpreted by the earnest seekers after immediate self-government as a clear indication of Britain's perfidy. Again, the introduction of the Central African Federation caused profound concern for the future of closer union in East Africa, in spite of frequent assurances by Britain that no steps would be taken to impose federation upon East Africa against the wishes of the people. In the later 1950s, however, it was not unusual for African political leaders to suggest that federation might not be unwelcome once the territorial governments were in African hands. The significance for the future of this apparent readiness to co-operate even in the closest fashion with other African-governed territories is not easy to assess. The pan-Africanism theme which gained some strength in the later 1950s undoubtedly owed much to the idea of the African struggle against white supremacy. But while East Africans as individuals might draw together readily enough, the attitude of African governments towards each other is an issue for the future.

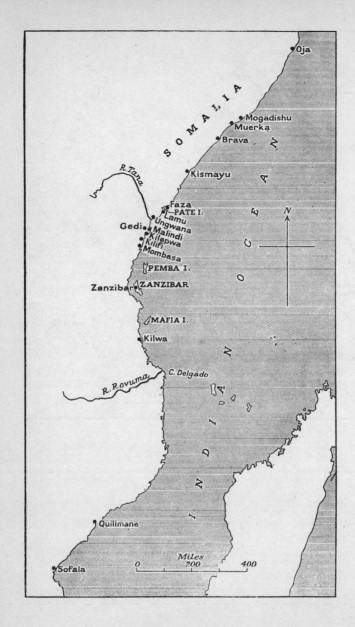

EARLY SETTLEMENTS ON THE COAST OF
EAST AFRICA

439

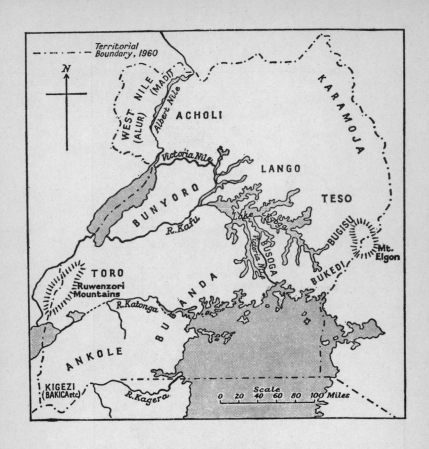

THE PEOPLES OF UGANDA

440

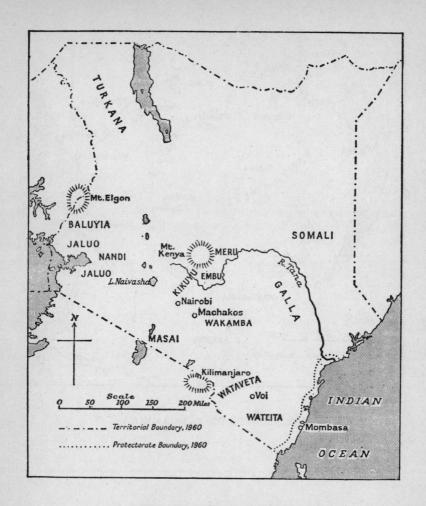

THE PEOPLES OF KENYA

441

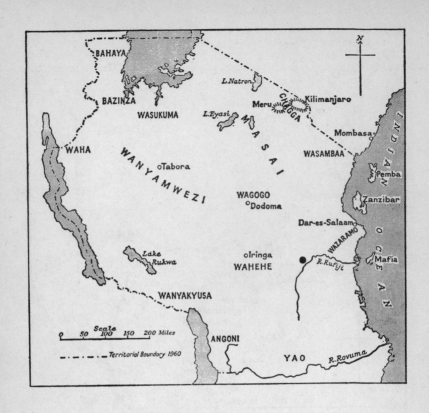

THE PEOPLES OF TANGANYIKA

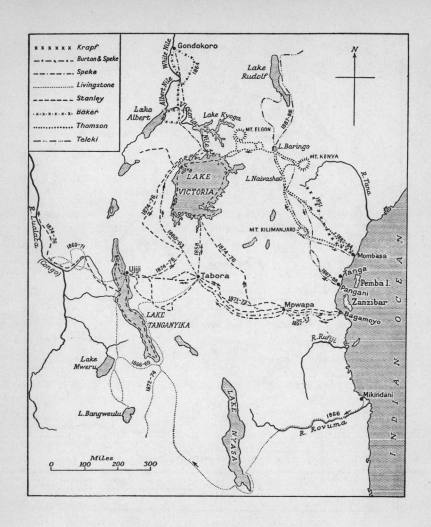

N

Gondokoro

White Nile

Albert Nile

1864

Lake
Rudolf

1887-88

Lake
Albert

Lake Kyoga

MT. ELGON

L.Baringo

MT. KENYA

R.Tana

LAKE
VICTORIA

L.Naivasha

1883

1874-76

1860-62

1862

1874-76

MT. KILIMANJARO

1882-84

1867-88

Mombasa

R.Lualaba

1874-76

(Congo)

1869-71

Ujiji

1874-76

Tabora

Tanga

1867-89

Pemba I.

Pangani

Zanzibar

LAKE
TANGANYIKA

1871-72

Mpwapa

Bagamoyo

1857-57

R.Rufiji

Lake
Mweru

1866-69

1872-74

L.Bangweulu

LAKE
NYASA

Mikindani

1866

R. Rovuma

INDIAN OCEAN

Miles

0   100   200   300

EXPLORATION OF EAST AFRICA

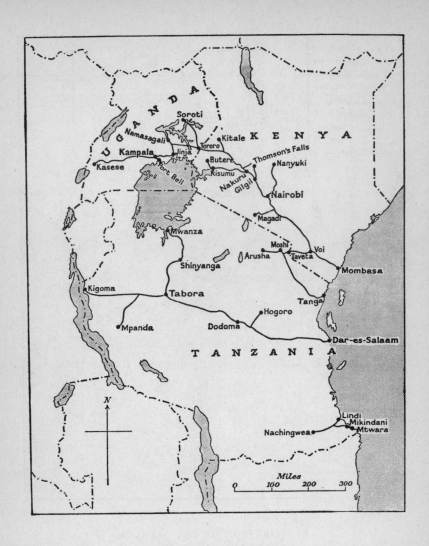

RAILWAYS OF EAST AFRICA

444

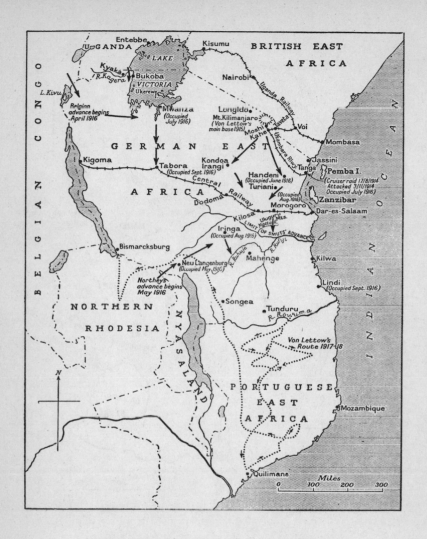

THE EAST AFRICAN CAMPAIGN, 1914–18

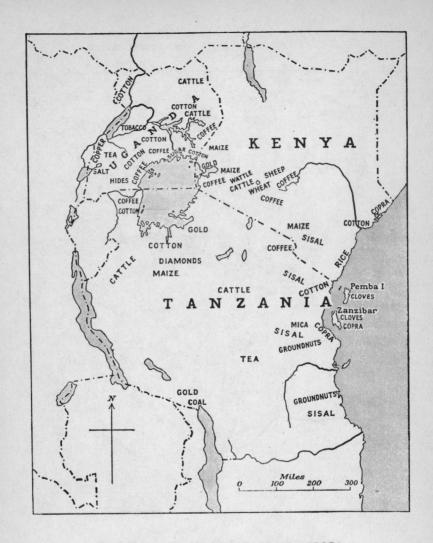

NATURAL RESOURCES OF EAST AFRICA

446

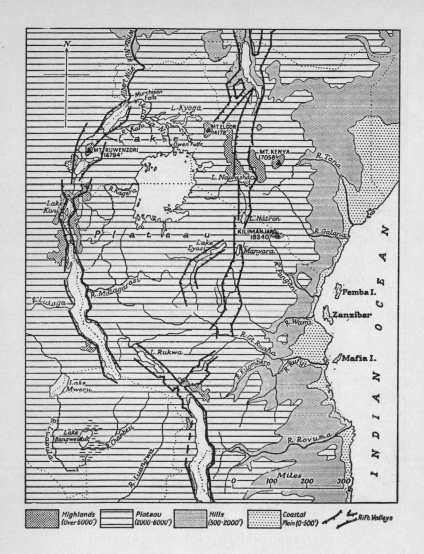

N

Albert Nile
Murchison
Falls
L. Kyoga
R. Kafu
L a k e
Owen Falls
MT. ELGON
14178'
MT. RUWENZORI
16794'
MT. KENYA
17058'
R. Tana
L. Naivasha
R. Kagera
Lake
Kivu
P l a t e a u
L. Natron
L. Eyasi
KILIMANJARO
19340'
L.
Manyara
R. Galana
R. Pangani
R. Malagarasi
R. Lukuga
Pemba I.
Zanzibar
R. Wami
R. Gt. Ruaha
L. Rukwa
R. Kilombero
Mafia I.
R. Rufiji
Lake
Mweru
Lake
Bangweulu
R. Chambezi
R. Rovuma
R. Luapula
R. Luangwa

Miles
0   100   200   300

I N D I A N   O C E A N

| Highlands (Over 6000') | Plateau (2000-6000') | Hills (500-2000') | Coastal Plain (0-500') | Rift Valleys |

PHYSICAL MAP OF EAST AFRICA

447

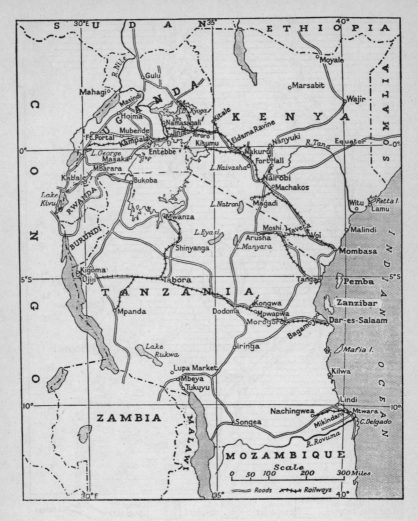

POLITICAL MAP OF EAST AFRICA, 1964

448

SELECT BIBLIOGRAPHY

Altrincham, Lord. *Kenya's Opportunity.* Faber & Faber, London, 1955.

Amery, L. S. *The Empire in the New Era.* Arnold, London, 1928.

Ansorge, W. J. *Under the African Sun.* Heinemann, London, 1899.

Ashe, R. P. *Chronicles of Uganda.* Hodder, London, 1894.

Ashe, R. P. *Two Kings of Uganda.* Sampson Low, London, 1890.

Austin, H. H. *With Macdonald in Uganda.* Arnold, London, 1903.

Baker, Sir S. W. *Albert Nyanza.* Macmillan, London, 1866.

Baker, Sir S. W. *Ismailia.* Macmillan, London, 1874.

Bell, Sir H. *Glimpses of a Governor's Life.* Sampson Low, London, 1946.

Bösch, P. F. *Les Banyamwezi; peuple de l'Afrique Orientale.* Aschendorffsche Verlagsbuchhandlung, Münster, 1930.

Boyes, J. *John Boyes, King of the Wa-Kikuyu.* Methuen, London, 1912.

Brode, H. *British and German East Africa.* Arnold, London, 1911.

Brode, H. *Tippoo Tib.* Arnold, London, 1907.

Brown, G. G. and Hutt, A. McD. B. *Anthropology in Action.* Oxford University Press, London, 1935.

Buell, R. L. *The Native Problem in Africa.* Shoe String, Hamden, Conn., 1965.

Burton, Sir R. *The Lake Regions of Central Africa.* Horizon, New York, 1961.

Burton, Sir R. *The Nile Basin.* Tinsley, London, 1864.

Cagnolo, Fr. C. *The Akikuyu.* Catholic Mission of the Consolata Fathers, Nyeri, Kenya, 1933.

Cameron, Sir D. *My Tanganyika Service and Some Nigeria.* Allen and Unwin, London, 1939.

Carey Jones, N. S. *The Anatomy of Uhuru: Dynamics and Problems of African Independence in an Age of Conflict.* Praeger, New York, 1967.

Casati, G. *Ten Years in Equatoria and the Return with Emin Pasha.* Warne, London, 1891.

Chaillé-Long, C. *Central Africa.* Sampson Low, London, 1876.

Chaillé-Long, C. *My Life in Four Continents.* Hutchinson, London, 1912.

Cohen, Sir A. B. *British Policy in Changing Africa.* Routledge and Kegan Paul, London, 1959.

Colvile, H. *The Land of the Nile Springs.* Arnold, London, 1895.

Cook, Sir A. R. *Uganda Memories, 1897–1940.* Uganda Society, Kampala, 1945.

Coupland, Sir R. *East Africa and its Invaders.* Clarendon Press, Oxford, 1938.

Coupland, Sir R. *Livingstone's Last Journey.* Collins, London, 1947.

Coupland, Sir R. *The Exploitation of East Africa.* Faber and Faber, London, 1939.

Cox, Richard. *Kenyatta's Country.* Praeger, New York, 1966.

Crazzolara, Fr. J. P. *The Lwoo.* Museum Combonianum, Verona, Pt. I, 1950, Pt. II, 1951, Pt. III, 1954.

Crowe, S. E. *The Berlin West Africa Conference, 1884–1885.* Longmans, Green, London, 1942.

Dawson, E. C. *James Hannington, first Bishop of Eastern Equatorial Africa.* Seeley, London, 1889.

Dilley, M. R. *British Policy in Kenya Colony.* Nelson, New York, 1937.

Driberg, J. H. *The Lango.* Unwin, London, 1923.

Dundas, Sir C. *African Crossroads.* Macmillan, London, 1955.

Dundas, Sir C. *Kilimanjaro and its People.* Witherby, London, 1924.

Duyvendak, J. J. L. *China's Discovery of Africa.* Probsthain, London, 1949.

Eliot, Sir C. *The British East Africa Protectorate.* Arnold, London, 1905.

Evans, I. L. *The British in Tropical Africa.* The University Press, Cambridge, 1929.

Fendall, C. P. *The East African Force, 1915–19.* Witherby, London, 1921.

Fisher, R. B. *On the Borders of Pigmyland.* Marshall, London, 1904 (?).

Gorju, Fr. J. *Entre le Victoria, l'Albert et l'Edouard.* Imprimeries Oberthür, Rennes, 1920.

Grant, J. A. *A Walk across Africa.* Blackwood, London, 1864.

Gray, Sir J. M. *The British in Mombasa, 1824–1826.* Macmillan, London, 1957.

Gregory, J. W. *The Foundation of British East Africa.* Marshall, London, 1901.

Grottanelli, V. L. *Prescatori dell'Oceano Indiano.* Cremonese, Rome, 1955.

Hailey, Lord. *An African Survey: Revised 1966.* Oxford University Press, New York, 1957.

Hailey, Lord. *Native Administration in the British African Territories.* Vol. I. H.M.S.O., London, 1950.

Hardinge, Sir A. H. *A Diplomatist in the East.* Cape, London, 1928.

Harlow, V. and Chilver, E. M. (eds.). *History of East Africa.* Vol. II. Oxford University Press, New York, 1965.

Hattersley, C. W. *The Baganda at Home.* Religious Tract Society. London, 1908.

Hemedi bin Abdallah bin Said el Buhriy. *Utenzi wa Vita vya Wadachi Kutamalaki Mrima.* (Trans. J. W. T. Allen.) East African Swahili Committee, Kampala, 1955.

Hill, M. F. *Permanent Way.* East African Railways and Harbours, Nairobi, 1950.

Hobley, C. W. *Kenya from Chartered Company to Crown Colony.* Witherby, London, 1929.

Höhnel, L. *Discovery of Lakes Rudolf and Stefanie.* Hölder, Vienna, 1892.

Hollingsworth, L. W. *Zanzibar under the Foreign Office, 1890–1913.* Macmillan, London, 1953.

Hollis, Sir A. C. *The Masai.* Clarendon Press, Oxford, 1905.

Hollis, Sir A. C. *The Nandi.* Clarendon Press, Oxford, 1909.

Hordern, C. *Military Operations East Africa.* 1914–18 War, vol. i. H.M.S.O., London, 1941.

Hore, E. C. *Tanganyika.* Stanford, London, 1892.

Huxley, E. *White Man's Country.* Macmillan, London, 1935.

Ingham, K. *The Making of Modern Uganda.* Allen and Unwin, London, 1957.

Jackson, Sir F. *Early Days in East Africa.* Arnold, London, 1930.

Johnston, Alex. *The Life and Letters of Sir Harry Johnston.* Cape, London, 1929.

Johnston, Sir H. H. *The Uganda Protectorate.* Hutchinson, London, 1902.

Karim bin Jamaliddini, Abdul. *Utenzi wa Vita vya Maji Maji.* (Trans. W. H. Whiteley.) East African Swahili Committee, Kampala, 1957.

Keltie, Sir J. S. *The Partition of Africa.* Stanford, London, 1895.

Kirkman, J. S. 'Historical Archaeology in Kenya'. *The Antiquaries Journal.* Vol. XXXVII, Jan.–April, 1957.

Kirkman, J. S. *The Arab City of Gedi.* Oxford University Press, London, 1954.

Kirkman, J. S. 'The Culture of the Kenya Coast in the Later Middle Ages'. *South African Archaeological Bulletin.* Vol. XI, No. 44, Dec. 1956.

Kirkman, J. S. *Men and Monuments on the East African Coast.* Praeger, New York, 1966.

Krapf, J. L. *Travels, Researches and Missionary Labours.* Trubner, London, 1860.

SELECT BIBLIOGRAPHY

Lawrance, J. C. D. *The Iteso.* Oxford University Press, London, 1957.

Lettow-Vorbeck, P. E. von. *East African Campaigns.* Speller, New York, 1957.

Lettow-Vorbeck, P. E. von. *My Reminiscences of East Africa.* Hurst and Blackett, London, 1920.

Leubuscher, C. *Tanganyika Territory.* Oxford University Press, London, 1944.

Lewin, P. E. *The Germans and Africa.* Cassell, London, 1939.

Leys, N. *Kenya.* Hogarth Press, London, 1925.

Listowel, Judith. *The Making of Tanganyika.* London House, New York, 1965.

Livingstone, D. *The Last Journals of David Livingstone.* Murray, London, 1880.

Lloyd, A. B. *Uganda to Khartoum.* Fisher Unwin, London, 1911.

Low, D. A. *Religion and Society in Buganda, 1875-1900.* (East African Studies No. 8.) East African Institute of Social Research, Kampala, undated.

Low, D. A. and Pratt, C. *Buganda and British Overrule.* Oxford University Press, London, 1960.

Lugard, F. J. D. *Reports of Captain F. D. Lugard on his Expedition to Uganda.* Doher y, London, 1890.

Lugard, F. J. D. *The Dual Mandate in British Tropical Africa.* Blackwood, Edinburgh and London, 1926.

Lugard, F. J. D. *The Rise of our East African Empire.* Blackwood, Edinburgh and London, 1893.

Lyne, R. N. *An Apostle of Empire.* Allen and Unwin, London, 1936.

Macdonald, J. R. L. *Soldiering and Surveying in British East Africa, 1891-1894.* Arnold, London, 1897.

Mair, L. P. *An African People in the Twentieth Century.* Routledge, London, 1934.

McDermott, P. L. *British East Africa or Ibea.* Chapman and Hall, London, 1895.

Meek, C. K. *Land, Law and Custom in the Colonies.* Oxford University Press, London, 1946.

Meinertzhagen, R. *Kenya Diary, 1902-1906.* Oliver and Boyd, Edinburgh, 1957.

Melland, F. H. and Cholmeley, E. H. *Through the Heart of Africa.* Constable, London, 1912.

Mitchell, Sir P. *African Afterthoughts.* Hutchinson, London, 1954.

Moffett, J. P. (ed.). *Handbook of Tanganyika.* Government Printer, Dar es Salaam, 1958.

Moyse-Bartlett, H. *The King's African Rifles.* Gale and Polden, Aldershot, 1956.

New, C. *Life, Wanderings and Labours in Eastern Africa.* Hodder and Stoughton, London, 1874.

Oliver, R. A. *Sir Harry Johnston and the Scramble for Africa.* Chatto and Windus, London, 1957.

Oliver, R. A. *The Missionary Factor in East Africa.* Longmans, Green, London, 1952.

Oliver, R. A. and Mathew, G. (eds.). *History of East Africa.* Vol. I. Oxford University Press, New York, 1963.

Patterson, J. H. *The Man-eaters of Tsavo and other East African Adventures.* Macmillan, London, 1907.

Perham, M. *Lugard—the Years of Adventure, 1858-98.* Vol. I. Collins, London, 1956.

Perham, M. and Huxley, E. *Race and Politics in Kenya.* Faber, London, 1956.

Peters, C. *New Light on Dark Africa.* Ward Lock, London, 1891.

Philp, H. R. *A New Day in Kenya.* World Dominion Press, London, 1936.

Portal, Sir G. *The British Mission to Uganda in 1893.* Arnold, London, 1894.

Postlethwaite, J. R. P. *I Look Back.* Boardman, London, 1947.

Prins, A. H. J. *The Coastal Tribes of the North-Eastern Bantu.* International African Institute, London, 1952.

Purvis, J. B. *Through Uganda to Mount Elgon.* Unwin, London, 1909.

Reusch, R. *History of East Africa.* Ungar, New York, 1961.

Roscoe, J. *The Baganda.* Barnes & Noble, New York, 1966.

Roscoe, J. *The Bagesu.* The University Press, Cambridge, 1924.

Roscoe, J. *The Bakitara or Banyoro.* The University Press, Cambridge, 1923.

Roscoe, J. *The Banyankole.* The University Press, Cambridge, 1923.

Ross, W. McGregor. *Kenya from Within.* Allen and Unwin, London, 1927.

Routledge, W. S. and K. *With a Prehistoric People, the Akikuyu of British East Africa.* Arnold, London, 1911.

Russell, L. M. (ed.). *General Rigby, Zanzibar and the Slave Trade.* Allen and Unwin, London, 1935.

Sayers, G. F. (ed.). *The Handbook of Tanganyika.* Macmillan, London, 1930.

Schnee, H. *Deutsch-Ostafrika in Weltkriege.* Quelle and Meyer, Leipzig, 1919.

Schweitzer, G. *Emin Pasha, his Life and Work.* Constable, London, 1898.

Smith, Mackenzie and Company Limited. *The History of Smith, Mackenzie and Company, Limited.* East Africa Ltd., London, 1938.

Southall, A. W. *The Alur.* Heffer, Cambridge, 1956.

453

Speke, J. H. *Journal of the Discovery of the Source of the Nile.* Blackwood, Edinburgh and London, 1863.

Stanley, Sir H. M. *How I found Livingstone.* Sampson Low, London, 1872.

Stanley, Sir H. M. *In Darkest Africa.* Sampson Low, London, 1890.

Stanley, Sir H. M. *The Autobiography of Sir Henry Morton Stanley.* Sampson Low, London, 1909.

Stanley, Sir H. M. *Through the Dark Continent.* Sampson Low, London, 1878.

Stanley, R. and Neame, Alan (eds.). *Exploration Diaries of H. M. Stanley.* Vanguard, New York, 1962.

Strandes, J. *Die Portugiesenzeit von Deutsch—und Englisch—Ostafrika.* Reimel, Berlin, 1899.

Swann, A. J. *Fighting the Slave-Hunters in Central Africa.* Seeley, London, 1910.

Symes, Sir S. *Tour of Duty.* Collins, London, 1946.

Tanganyika Notes and Records. Journal of the Tanganyika Society. Dar es Salaam, 1936–60.

Taylor, J. Clagett. *The Political Development of Tanganyika.* Stanford University Press, Stanford, Calif., 1963.

Taylor, Rev. J. *The Growth of the Church in Buganda.* S.C.M. Press, London, 1958.

Tew, M. *Peoples of the Lake Nyasa Region.* Oxford University Press, London, 1950.

Thomas, H. B. and Spencer, A. E. *History of Uganda Land and Surveys.* Government Printer, Entebbe, 1938.

Thomas, H. B. and Scott, R. *Uganda.* Oxford University Press, London, 1935.

Thoonen, Fr. J. P. *Black Martyrs.* Sheed and Ward, London, 1942.

Thruston, A. B. *African Incidents.* Murray, London, 1900.

Tippu Tip. *Maisha ya Hamed bin Muhammed el Murjebi yaani Tippu Tip.* (Trans. W. H. Whiteley.) East African Swahili Committee, Kampala, 1958–59.

Tucker, A. R. *Eighteen Years in Uganda and East Africa.* Arnold, London, 1908.

Uganda Journal. Journal of the Uganda Society, Kampala, 1934–60.

Waller, H. *Heligoland for Zanzibar.* Stanford, London, 1893.

Waller, H. *The Last Journals of David Livingstone in Central Africa,* John Murray, London, 1880.

Wallis, H. R. (ed.). *Handbook of Uganda.* Crown Agents, London, 1913.

Wilson, C. T. and Felkin, R. W. *Uganda and the Egyptian Soudan.* Sampson Low, London, 1882.

INDEX